Interdisciplinary Approaches to Information Systems and Software Engineering

Alok Bhushan Mukherjee
North-Eastern Hill University Shillong, India

Akhouri Pramod Krishna
Birla Institute of Technology Mesra, India

A volume in the Advances in
Systems Analysis, Software
Engineering, and High Performance
Computing (ASASEHPC) Book Series

Published in the United States of America by
    IGI Global
    Engineering Science Reference (an imprint of IGI Global)
    701 E. Chocolate Avenue
    Hershey PA, USA 17033
    Tel: 717-533-8845
    Fax: 717-533-8661
    E-mail: cust@igi-global.com
    Web site: http://www.igi-global.com

Library of Congress Cataloging-in-Publication Data

Names: Mukherjee, Alok Bhushan, 1985- editor. | Krishna, Akhouri Pramod,
  1962- editor.
Title: Interdisciplinary approaches to information systems and software
  engineering / Alok Bhushan Mukherjee and Akhouri Pramod Krishna, editors.
Description: Hershey, PA : Engineering Science Reference, [2019] | Includes
  bibliographical references.
Identifiers: LCCN 2018036341| ISBN 9781522577843 (h/c) | ISBN 9781522577850
  (eISBN)
Subjects: LCSH: Information technology. | Software engineering.
Classification: LCC T58.5 .I56525 2019 | DDC 005.1--dc23 LC record available at https://lccn.loc.
gov/2018036341

This book is published in the IGI Global book series Advances in Systems Analysis, Software Engineering, and High Performance Computing (ASASEHPC) (ISSN: 2327-3453; eISSN: 2327-3461)

British Cataloguing in Publication Data
A Cataloguing in Publication record for this book is available from the British Library.

All work contributed to this book is new, previously-unpublished material.
The views expressed in this book are those of the authors, but not necessarily of the publisher.

For electronic access to this publication, please contact: eresources@igi-global.com.

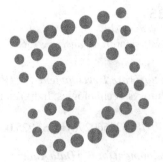

Advances in Systems Analysis, Software Engineering, and High Performance Computing (ASASEHPC) Book Series

ISSN:2327-3453
EISSN:2327-3461

Editor-in-Chief: Vijayan Sugumaran, Oakland University, USA

MISSION

The theory and practice of computing applications and distributed systems has emerged as one of the key areas of research driving innovations in business, engineering, and science. The fields of software engineering, systems analysis, and high performance computing offer a wide range of applications and solutions in solving computational problems for any modern organization.

The **Advances in Systems Analysis, Software Engineering, and High Performance Computing (ASASEHPC) Book Series** brings together research in the areas of distributed computing, systems and software engineering, high performance computing, and service science. This collection of publications is useful for academics, researchers, and practitioners seeking the latest practices and knowledge in this field.

COVERAGE

- Engineering Environments
- Network Management
- Parallel Architectures
- Software Engineering
- Computer System Analysis
- Computer Graphics
- Performance Modelling
- Distributed Cloud Computing
- Storage Systems
- Human-Computer Interaction

IGI Global is currently accepting manuscripts for publication within this series. To submit a proposal for a volume in this series, please contact our Acquisition Editors at Acquisitions@igi-global.com or visit: http://www.igi-global.com/publish/.

Titles in this Series

For a list of additional titles in this series, please visit:
https://www.igi-global.com/book-series/advances-systems-analysis-software-engineering/73689

Analyzing the Role of Risk Mitigation and Monitoring in Software Development
Rohit Kumar (Chandigarh University, India) Anjali Tayal (Infosys Technologies, India) and
Sargam Kapil (C-DAC, India)
Engineering Science Reference • ©2018 • 308pp • H/C (ISBN: 9781522560296) • US $225.00

Handbook of Research on Pattern Engineering System Development for Big Data Analytics
Vivek Tiwari (International Institute of Information Technology, India) Ramjeevan Singh
Thakur (Maulana Azad National Institute of Technology, India) Basant Tiwari (Hawassa
University, Ethiopia) and Shailendra Gupta (AISECT University, India)
Engineering Science Reference • ©2018 • 396pp • H/C (ISBN: 9781522538707) • US $320.00

Incorporating Nature-Inspired Paradigms in Computational Applications
Mehdi Khosrow-Pour, D.B.A. (Information Resources Management Association, USA)
Engineering Science Reference • ©2018 • 385pp • H/C (ISBN: 9781522550204) • US $195.00

Innovations in Software-Defined Networking and Network Functions Virtualization
Ankur Dumka (University of Petroleum and Energy Studies, India)
Engineering Science Reference • ©2018 • 364pp • H/C (ISBN: 9781522536406) • US $235.00

Advances in System Dynamics and Control
Ahmad Taher Azar (Benha University, Egypt) and Sundarapandian Vaidyanathan (Vel Tech
University, India)
Engineering Science Reference • ©2018 • 680pp • H/C (ISBN: 9781522540779) • US $235.00

Green Computing Strategies for Competitive Advantage and Business Sustainability
Mehdi Khosrow-Pour, D.B.A. (Information Resources Management Association, USA)
Business Science Reference • ©2018 • 324pp • H/C (ISBN: 9781522550174) • US $185.00

For an entire list of titles in this series, please visit:
https://www.igi-global.com/book-series/advances-systems-analysis-software-engineering/73689

701 East Chocolate Avenue, Hershey, PA 17033, USA
Tel: 717-533-8845 x100 • Fax: 717-533-8661
E-Mail: cust@igi-global.com • www.igi-global.com

I wish to dedicate this effort to maa & baba , my teachers, family & friends, my teachers & students of my first class (PGD(Geoinformatics)-II, (2017-2018), NEHU) who are very well natured, sincere, & good human beings.

Table of Contents

Detailed Table of Contents

Uttam Kumar, Indira Gandhi Krishi Vishwavidyalaya, India
Nirmal Kumar, National Bureau of Soil Survey and Land Use Planning,
India
V. N. Mishra, Indira Gandhi Krishi Vishwavidyalaya, India
R. K. Jena, National Bureau of Soil Survey and Land Use Planning,
India

Fields with rice-based cropping systems are unique from other wetland or upland soils because they are associated with frequent cycling between wetting and drying under anaerobic and aerobic conditions. This alters the C and N transformations, microbial activities and their diversity, and soil physical properties, depending on the other crop in rotation with rice. This chapter aims to compare the soil quality of vertisols of central plains of Chhattisgarh under rice-wheat and rice-chickpea cropping systems. Soil quality index was developed using analytical hierarchy process (AHP). Five soil quality indicators were selected under minimum datasets including soil organic carbon, mean weight diameter, available water content, available phosphorous and zinc. The results indicated that the rice-chickpea cropping system shows improved soil quality than that of rice-wheat cropping system.

Michael D. Dorsey, Texas Woman's University, USA
Mahesh S. Raisinghani, Texas Woman's University, USA

IT governance or IT outsourcing both have their own unique benefits but the decision to choose one over other is not always so clear. This chapter examines the impact of globalization of software development and localization of service delivery in the offshore software development and outsourcing services sector. A case study is used to illustrate the key ideas that helped contribute to a successful IT project that was outsourced by a US organization to a transnational IT outsourcing services provider based in India. The two key points illustrated by the case study discussed in this chapter are what are the issues facing a North American company that deals with an IT service supplier thousands of miles and many time zones away and what are the lessons learned from a successful outsourcing relationship.

Chapter 3

Soumen Mukherjee, RCC Institute of Information Technology, India
Arup Kumar Bhattacharjee, RCC Institute of Information Technology, India
Arpan Deyasi, RCC Institute of Information Technology, India

In this chapter, machine learning algorithms along with association rule analysis are applied to measure how the project teamwork success rate depends on various technical and soft skill factors of a software project. A real-life dataset is taken form UCI archive on project teamwork, which comprises of 84 features or attributes with 64 samples. The most effective feature set is therefore selected using meta-heuristic algorithms (i.e., particle swarm optimization [PSO] and simulated annealing [SA]) and then the data are given to support vector machine (SVM) and k-nearest neighbor (KNN) classifier for classification. Association rule mining is also used for rule generation among the different features of software project team to determine support and confidence. This chapter deals with how the project-based learning helps to manifest the students towards professionalism.

Chapter 4

Ramgopal Kashyap, Amity University Chhattisgarh, India

Decision makers require a versatile framework that responds and adjusts to the always changing business conditions. The personal information handling arrangement of an organization can offer the least help since it identified with exchanges. For this situation, the decision support system (DSS) joins human abilities with the abilities of PCs to give productive administration of information, announcing, investigation, displaying, and arranging issues. DSS provides a refinement between organized, semi-organized, and unstructured data. Specifically, a DSS lessens the amount of data to a ridiculous organized sum; because of this, choices are made to help the assembling procedure. The objective of these frameworks is to prevent issues inside the generation procedure. This chapter gives an outline of the state-of-the-art craftsmanship writing on DSS and portrays current methods of DSS-related applications inside assembling situations.

Chapter 5
    Arunima Nandy, North Eastern Hill University, India

Agartala, the capital of Tripura, is one of the most important and populated cities of North-East India. From the aspect of geomorphology, the whole area is characterized by highlands (tilla) and lowlands (lunga). Tectonically, Tripura falls under very active zone (Zone V). Assessment of tectonic activities of this region is very significant. For identification of tectonic activity, morphological or geomorphic signatures play very important role. The chapter identifies the presence of tectonic activity from morphological signatures in and around Agartala city. Landsat 8 OLI, maps from Geological Survey of India, Google Earth imageries have been used in this study. The presence of some lineaments and sag ponds has been identified on the basis of which fault mechanism of Agartala and Baramura hills has been delineated. This study contains a brief note on the conceptual demonstration of application of GIS and RS technologies and how morphological signatures and satellite images can help us to recognize tectonic activities over a region.

Chapter 6
    Amit Kumar, India Meteorological Department, India
    Anil Kumar Singh, India Meteorological Department, India
    Nitesh Awasthi, India Meteorological Department, India
    Virendra Singh, India Meteorological Department, India

Tropical cyclones are also known as typhoons or hurricanes. Also, special emphasis is given on the various aspects associated with cyclogenesis, like the six essential parameters required for cyclogenesis as given by W. M. Grey, and Dvorak technique is discussed in this chapter. INSAT-3D is an indigenous advanced dedicated meteorological satellite in geostationary orbit, which was launched on 26th July 2013. INSAT-3D was declared operational by IMD on 15th January 2014. INSAT-3D has four payloads, namely. IMAGER, SOUNDER, data relay transponder (DRT), and satellite aided search, aid and rescue (SAR). Three rainfall estimates are being generated from INSAT-3D, namely, hydro-estimator (HE), INSAT multispectral rainfall algorithm (IMSRA), and QPE (quantitative precipitation estimate). It has been found in this study that IMSRA performs better during initial stages of cyclogenesis (i.e., during T1.0, T1.5, and T2.0); during mature stages T2.5 to T3.0, HE performs better. During weakening stages IMSRA gives better results.

Chapter 7

In the most recent couple of decades, medical image processing stood out within picture preparing research fields because of its nonintrusive nature. Restorative imaging modalities, for example, MRI, CT filter, for the most part, rely upon computer imaging innovation to create or show advanced pictures of the inward organs of the human body, which causes the medicine professionals to envision the internal bits of the body. Here the proposed algorithm is thresholding different tissue type of brain MR image. Modes of the histogram represent different tissue types in brain MR image. So, this algorithm depends on the principle of finding maxima and minima using differentiation of the smoothed histogram. Using discrete differentiation, the author finds the multiple thresholds of brain MR image by selecting proper location of minima. The algorithm can be used as an initial segmentation of different tissue types of brain MR image for further accurate detection of the regions.

Chapter 8

Cognitive and somatic health is predominantly congruous. Happiness creates a propitious impact on a person's wellbeing. Likewise, stress can be detrimental to a person's overall health. Nevertheless, it is perplexing to truly understand an emotional state of a patient for an unerring diagnosis. Considering the old adage, necessity is the mother of invention, there is a need for a sentimental and emotional analysis tool for the accurate identification of the mental state of the patient. Thus, Sentilyser was created. It is a clinical decision support system. Using the recorded voice of a person, the mood is analyzed using support vector regression. Arousal and valence of the audio file is calculated, and thus, the corresponding mood is predicted. The objective of this chapter is to propose the use of Sentilyser as a part of a patient's diagnosis, which will not only help the physician reach a better conclusion but will also help them in cases where the patients themselves are unaware about their own psychological state.

Research and publication is considered an authenticated certificate of innovative work done by researchers in various fields. In research, new scientific results may be assessed, corrected, and further built up by the scientific neighborhood only if they are available in published form. Guidelines on accountable research and publication are currently set to encourage and promote high ethical standards in the conduct of research and in biomedical publications. They address various aspects of the research and publishing including duties of editors and authorship determination. The chapter presents research and publication system using big data analytics and research data management techniques with a background of information systems and need of information in research data management.

A major part of Indo-Gangetic plain is affected with soil salinity/alkalinity. Information on spatial distribution of soil salinity is important for planning management practices for its restoration. Remote sensing has proven to be a powerful tool in quantifying and monitoring the development of soil salinity. The chapter aims to develop logistic regression models, using Landsat 8 data, to identify salt affected soils in Indo-Gangetic plain. Logistic regression models based on Landsat 8 bands and several salinity indices were developed, individually and in combination. The bands capable of differentiating salt affected soils from other features were identified as green, red, and SWIR1. The logistic regression model developed in the study area was found to be 81% accurate in identifying salt-affected soils. A total area of 34558.49 ha accounting to ~10% of the total geographic area of the district was found affected with salinity/alkalinity. The spatial distribution of salt-affected soils in the district showed an association of shallow ground water depth with salinity.

Preface

With significant increase in data, there is now necessity of managing data systematically. Systematic presentation of data is absolutely necessary for containing data redundancy, and inconsistency. In addition, there are various aspects which are associated with an event, and therefore, it becomes necessary to assess relationship between these aspects. Effective relationship between them may be helpful in analyzing complexities which are associated with the event.

However, there should be a proper mechanism to analyze their relationship accurately. Furthermore, it is also required to have understanding that absence of proper interrelationship may lead to retrieval of inadequate information. It is also necessary to understand that extraction of accurate and consistent information depends upon the structure which is used to store data. Hence, role of information system is significant in terms of presenting data in a scientific manner, and extracting information from them. Consequently, various aspects of development of an information system is now being in research arena for analysis, and development such as research topics related to management information system, decision support system, spatial decision support system, geographic information system, expert system, and intelligent information system.

The proposed book aims to cover various aspects of information system, and approaches which are nowadays used to develop an information system. Especially, focus is on interdisciplinary approaches for development of information systems. In addition, various application areas of information system where it can be significant in characterizing and analyzing an event is also discussed and demonstrated. The event could be from any domain such as it could be of spatial nature or aspatial nature.

ORGANIZATION OF THE BOOK

Chapter 1: Chapter 1 is an attempt in the direction of assessment of soil quality. An index was also developed in the proposed study to assess soil quality. Fields with rice based cropping systems are unique from other wetland or upland soils, because they are associated with frequent cycling between wetting and drying under anaerobic and aerobic conditions. This alters the C and N transformations, microbial activities and their diversity, and soil physical properties, depending on the other crop in rotation with rice. This study aims to compare the soil quality of vertisols of central plains of Chhattisgarh under rice-wheat and rice-chickpea cropping systems. Soil quality index was developed using Analytical Hierarchy Process (AHP). Five soil quality indicators were selected under minimum datasets including soil organic carbon, mean weight diameter, available water content, available phosphorous and zinc. The results indicated that the rice-chickpea cropping system shows improved soil quality than that of rice-wheat cropping system.

Chapter 2: There exists a constant battle that all companies will be forced to confront irrespective of their size, service/s they provide, or industry of focus. They will be forced to decide if it is more beneficial to build upon current information technology (IT) infrastructure to meet the needs of their stakeholders such as decision makers/management, staff, and both current and expanding customer base, or to contract the service of those who specializes in the specific IT needs they are needing to have filled. IT governance or IT outsourcing both have their own unique benefits and challenges/risks, but the decision to choose one over other is not always so clear.

This chapter examines the impact of globalization of software development and localization of service delivery in the offshore software development and outsourcing services sector. A case study is used to illustrate the key ideas that helped contribute to a successful IT project that was outsourced by a US organization to a transnational IT outsourcing services provider based in India. The two key points illustrated by the case study discussed in this chapter are what are the issues facing a North American company that deals with an IT service supplier thousands of miles and many time zones away; and what are the lessons learned from a successful outsourcing relationship.

Chapter 3: In this chapter, machine learning algorithms along with association rule analysis are applied to measure how the project teamwork success rate depends on various technical and soft skill factors of a software project. Real life dataset is taken form UCI archive on project teamwork, which comprises of 84 features or attributes with 64 samples. Most effective feature set is therefore selected using meta-heuristic algorithms, i.e. Particle Swarm Optimization (PSO) and Simulated Annealing (SA) and then the data are given to Support Vector Machine (SVM) and k-Nearest Neighbor (KNN) classifier for classification. Association rule mining also used for rule generation among the different features of software project team to determine support and confidence. This chapter deals with how the project-based learning helps to manifest the students towards professionalism.

Chapter 4: Today decision makers require a versatile framework that responds and adjusts to the always showing signs of change business condition. The personal information handling arrangement of an organization can offer the least help since it identified with exchanges. For this situation, the Decision Support System (DSS) joins human abilities with the abilities of PCs to give productive administration of information, announcing, investigation, displaying and arranging issues. DSS provides a refinement between organized, semi-organized and unstructured data. Specifically, a DSS lessens the amount of data to a ridiculous organized sum; because of this, choices are made to help the assembling procedure. What's more, the objective of these frameworks is to stay away from issues inside the generation procedure even previously they develop. This chapter gives an outline of the state-of the-craftsmanship writing on DSS and portrays current methods of related DSS applications inside assembling situations.

Chapter 5: Agartala, the capital of Tripura, is one of the most important and populated cities of North-East India. From the aspect of geomorphology, the whole area is characterized by high lands (tilla) and low lands (lunga). Tectonically Tripura is falling under very active zone (Zone V). Assessment of tectonic activities of this region is very much significant. For identification of tectonic activity, morphological or geomorphic signatures play very important role. The present work is aimed at identifying the presence of tectonic activity from morphological signatures in and around Agartala city. Landsat 8 OLI, maps from Geological Survey of India, Google Earth imageries have been used in this study. Presence of some lineaments and sag ponds has been identified, on the basis of which, fault mechanism of Agartala and Baramura hills has been delineated. This study contains a brief note on the conceptual demonstration of application of GIS and RS technologies that how morphological signatures and satellite image can help to recognize tectonic activities over a region.

Chapter 6: Tropical cyclones are also known as Typhoons or Hurricanes. Also, special emphasis is given on the various aspects associated with cyclogenesis, like the six essential parameters required for cyclogenesis as given by W. M. Grey and Dvorak Technique are discussed in this chapter. INSAT-3D is an indigenous advanced dedicated meteorological satellite in geostationary orbit, which was launched on 26th July 2013. INSAT-3D was declared operational by IMD on 15th January 2014. INSAT-3D has four payloads namely: IMAGER, SOUNDER, Data Relay Transponder (DRT) and Satellite Aided Search, Aid and Rescue (SAR). Three rainfall estimates are being generated from INSAT-3D namely: Hydro-Estimator (HE), INSAT Multispectral Rainfall Algorithm

(IMSRA) and QPE (Quantitative Precipitation Estimate). It has been found in this study that IMSRA performs better during initial stages of cyclogenesis i.e. during T1.0, T1.5 and T2.0, during mature stages T2.5 to T3.0, HE performs better. Again, during weakening stages IMSRA gives better results.

Chapter 7: In a most recent couple of decades, Medical Image Processing wound up a standout amongst the most famous and testing picture preparing research fields because of its nonintrusive nature for review inner body organs. Restorative Imaging modalities, for example, MRI, CT filter, for the most part, rely upon computer imaging innovation to create or show advanced pictures of the inward organs of the human body which causes the medicinal professionals to envision the internal bits of the body. Here the proposed algorithm is thresholding different tissue type of Brain MR Image. Modes of the histogram represent different tissue types in Brain MR Image. So, this algorithm depends on the principle of finding maxima and minima using differentiation of the smoothed histogram. Using discrete Differentiation we find the multiple thresholds of Brain MR Image by selecting proper location of minima. The algorithm can be used as an initial segmentation of different tissue types of Brain MR Image for further accurate detection of the regions.

Chapter 8: Cognitive and somatic health is predominantly congruous. Happiness creates a propitious impact on a person's well-being. Likewise, stress can detrimental to a person's overall health. Nevertheless, it is perplexing to truly understand an emotional state of a patient for an unerring diagnosis. Considering the old adage, necessity is the mother of invention, there is a need for a sentimental and emotional analysis tool for the accurate identification of the mental state of the patient. Thus Sentilyser was created. It is a Clinical Decision Support System. Using the recorded voice of a person, the mood is analyzed using support vector regression. Arousal and valence of the audio file is calculated and thus the corresponding mood is predicted. The objective of this chapter is to propose the use of Sentilyser as a part of a patient's diagnosis, which will not only help the physician reach a better conclusion but will also help them in cases where the patients themselves are unaware about their own psychological state.

Chapter 9: Research and Publication is considered as an authenticated certificate of innovative work done by researchers in various fields. In research, new scientific results may be assessed, corrected and further built up by the scientific neighborhood only if they are available in published form. Guidelines on accountable research and publication are currently set, to encourage and promote high ethical standards in the conduct of research and in biomedical publications. They address various aspects of the research and publishing including duties of editors and authorship determination. The current article presents Research and Publication System Using Big Data Analytics and Research Data Management techniques with background of information systems and need of information in research data management.

Chapter 10: A major part of Indo-Gangetic plain is affected with soil salinity/ alkalinity. Information on spatial distribution of soil salinity is important for planning management practices for its restoration. Remote sensing has proven to be a powerful tool in quantifying and monitoring the development of soil salinity. The present study aims to develop Logistic Regression models, using Landsat 8 data, to identify salt affected soils in Indo-Gangetic plain. Logistic regression models based on Landsat 8 bands and several salinity indices were developed, individually and in combination. The bands capable of differentiating salt affected soils from other features were identified as green, red, and SWIR1. The logistic regression model developed in the study area was found to be 81% accurate in identifying salt affected soils. A total area of 34558.49 ha accounting to ~10% of the total geographic area of the district was found affected with salinity/ alkalinity. The spatial distribution of salt affected soils in the district showed an association of shallow ground water depth with salinity.

It is believed that this book would be significant in bridging gap between different application fields in the context of application of information system. There are chapters in this book which are from different disciplines. But, these works are an attempt to cover the scope of the book. Hence, they can provide good insights about different application fields and techniques as well.

Alok Bhushan Mukherjee
North-Eastern Hill University, India

Akhouri Pramod Krishna
Birla Institute of Technology Mesra, India

Acknowledgment

We wish to thank our advisory board members, Dr. Malay Mukul, Professor, Department of Earth Science, Indian Institute of Technology-Bombay, Powai, India, Dr. Prashant Kumar Champati Ray, Group Head, Geosciences and Disaster Management Studies group, Indian Institute of Remote Sensing (ISRO), India, Dr. Varun Joshi, Professor, University School of Environment Management (Block A), Guru Govind Singh Indraprastha University, New Delhi, India, Dr. Vandana Bhattacharjee, Professor & Head of the Department, Computer Science and Engineering, Birla Institute of Technology, Mesra, Ranchi, India, Dr. Sunil Kumar De, Professor, Department of Geography, School of Human and Environmental Sciences, North-Eastern Hill University, Umshing, Mawkynroh, Shillong, India, Dr. Bijay Singh Mipun, Professor, Department of Geography, School of Human and Environmental Sciences, North-Eastern Hill University, Umshing, Mawkynroh, Shillong, India, Dr. Bhaskar Karn, Associate Professor, Department of Computer Science and Engineering, Birla Institute of Technology, Mesra, Ranchi, India, and Mr. Nirmal Kumar, Scientist, Agricultural Physics, Remote Sensing Division, ICAR-National Bureau of Soil Survey and Land Use Planning, Nagpur, India for agreeing to become advisory members for this book, and providing their suggestions.

In addition, we also extend our thanks to the respected reviewers who supported us in our review process. Furthermore, thank you very much IGI Global team for their constant support, patience, and suggestions. We sincerely believe, without your support, this journey would have been very difficult.

Chapter 1
Soil Quality Assessment Using Analytic Hierarchy Process (AHP):
A Case Study

Uttam Kumar
*Indira Gandhi Krishi Vishwavidyalaya,
India*

V. N. Mishra
*Indira Gandhi Krishi Vishwavidyalaya,
India*

Nirmal Kumar
*National Bureau of Soil Survey and
Land Use Planning, India*

R. K. Jena
*National Bureau of Soil Survey and
Land Use Planning, India*

ABSTRACT

Fields with rice-based cropping systems are unique from other wetland or upland soils because they are associated with frequent cycling between wetting and drying under anaerobic and aerobic conditions. This alters the C and N transformations, microbial activities and their diversity, and soil physical properties, depending on the other crop in rotation with rice. This chapter aims to compare the soil quality of vertisols of central plains of Chhattisgarh under rice-wheat and rice-chickpea cropping systems. Soil quality index was developed using analytical hierarchy process (AHP). Five soil quality indicators were selected under minimum datasets including soil organic carbon, mean weight diameter, available water content, available phosphorous and zinc. The results indicated that the rice-chickpea cropping system shows improved soil quality than that of rice-wheat cropping system.

DOI: 10.4018/978-1-5225-7784-3.ch001

INTRODUCTION

Agricultural soil quality refers to the condition and capacity of soil for purposes of production, conservation, and environmental management and its assessment is essential for making decisions that will improve crop production and environmental sustainability. Soil quality assessment has been suggested as a tool for evaluating sustainability of soil and crop management practices. Several methods of soil quality assessment have been developed, such as soil health card and test kits, visual soil assessment, and soil quality index methods (Karthikeyan *et al.,* 2015). However, the most popular method for assessing soil quality is calculating soil quality index – a quantitative method – which needs identifying minimum soil properties as soil quality indicators and, scoring and integrating these indicators to get soil quality indices (SQI) (Karlen *et al.,* 2004 and Andrews *et al.,* 2002).

The methods for identifying a set of soil quality indicators from several soil properties, called minimum dataset (MDS), include Principal component analysis (PCA) and experts' opinion (EO). PCA is the most used method for identifying MDS as it is quantitative and objective method (Andrews *et al.,* 2002; Rezaei *et al.,* 2006; Govaerts *et al.,* 2006; Masto *et al.,* 2008; Sinha *et al.,* 2014; Cherubin *et al.,* 2016; Vasu *et al.,* 2016; Karthikeyan *et al.,* 2015). The other method i.e., EO, are equally effective and suitable (Cherubin *et al.,* 2016) and sometimes overweighs the results obtained by the PCA approach (Vasu *et al.,* 2016). The EO method for selecting MDS is also preferred, as the effects of some factors are not easily demonstrated by numeric equations (Richey *et al.,* 1985; Kangas *et al.,* 1998; Marggraf, 2003). Further, the PCA method will easily produce errors of inference in cases of small sample size (Kumar *et al.,* 2017). The EO method allows working with small sample size.

After identification of MDS, these indicators are then normalized and integrated using preferably a weighted additive method (Karlen and Stott, 1994). The variance explained by each indicator during PCA is used as weight of that indicator (Andrews *et al.,* 2002; Rezaei *et al.,* 2006; Govaerts *et al.,* 2006). In case of EO based MDS selection, the weighing scheme based on EO would be more pragmatic in practice. However, the EO method requires expert knowledge of the system and direct assignment of weights may be subject to disciplinary biases (Andrews *et al.,* 2002; Cherubin *et al.,* 2016). To check the biasness, Analytical Hierarchical Process (AHP), introduced by Saaty (1980), has been suggested to generate weight for each indicator in the MDS (Kumar *et al.,* 2017, 2018). AHP generates weights of each indicator in the MDS according to the expert's pair-wise comparisons of the indicators. In addition, the AHP checks the consistency of the decision maker's evaluations, thus reducing the bias in the decision making process. AHP can handle small to large samples with indicators of both quantitative and qualitative nature.

Analytical Hierarchical Process

AHP helps avoiding direct assignment of weights to the identified criteria or scores to the alternatives and checks the chance of biasness. AHP typically follows a three step procedure. Firstly, a multi-level hierarchical structure of objectives, criteria, and alternatives is made. Secondly, a matrix is developed by using pairwise comparisons between the identified criteria. The comparison matrix will be a square matrix $A_{m \times m}$, where m is the number of criteria (m) considered for decision. Each entry a_{jk} of the matrix A represents the importance of the j_{th} criterion relative to the k_{th} criterion. The entries a_{jk} and a_{kj} satisfy the following constraint:

$$a_{jk} \bullet a_{kj} = 1.$$

Importance of one criterion over another one in the pair is identified qualitatively between 1 and 9 based on the AHP preference scale (Table 1). The scale 1 indicates the equal importance, while 9 indicates that one factor is absolutely more important than other. The reciprocals of 1 to 9 (1/1 and 1/9) show that one is less important than other. The intensity of importance between two criteria in the matrix is filled based on experts' experience. Once the matrix **A** is built, it is possible to derive the weights by identifying the normalized principal eigenvector of the matrix (Saaty, 1980, 2001 and Ramanathan, 2001).

Table 1. Preference scale

AHP Scale of Importance for Comparison Pair	Numeric Rating	Reciprocal
Extremely Importance	9	1/9
Very strong to extremely	8	1/8
Very strong importance	7	1/7
Strongly to very strong	6	1/6
Strong Importance	5	1/5
Moderately to strong	4	1/4
Moderate importance	3	1/3
Equally to Moderately	2	1/2
Equal importance	1	1

(Source: Saaty, 2008)

3

The components of the eigenvector *w* sum to unity. Thus, a vector of weights is obtained, which reflects the relative importance of the various criteria from the matrix of paired comparisons.

The third step is to check the consistency of the judgment matrix. In AHP, an index of consistency, known as the consistency ratio (CR), is used to indicate the probability that the matrix judgment was randomly generated and is not biased (Saaty, 1987).

$$CR = CI/ RI \tag{4}$$

where RI is the average of the resulting consistency index depending on the order of the matrix given by Saaty (1980) (Table 2) and CI is the consistency index and can be expressed as

$$CI = (\lambda_{max} - m)/(m-1) \tag{5}$$

where λ_{max} is the largest or principal eigenvalue of the matrix and can be easily calculated from the matrix as the average of the elements of the vector whose j^{th} element is the ratio of the jth element of the vector A·*w* to the corresponding element of the vector *w*. *m* is the order of the matrix.

When the matrix has a complete consistency, CI = 0. The bigger CI means, worse consistency the matrix had (Saaty, 1980, 1987). When CR was less than 0.10, the matrix had a reasonable consistency. Otherwise the matrix should be changed. The calculated results of weight would be accepted when the consistency ratio was satisfactory (Saaty, 1980).

MATERIAL AND METHODS

Study Area

The area selected for this study is Balod district which lies between 20°24 to 21°03 N latitude and 80°47 to 81°31 E longitude at an elevation of 324 m above the mean

Table 2. Random inconsistency indices (RI) for N=10

N	1	2	3	4	5	6	7	8	9	10
RI	0.00	0.00	0.58	0.9	1.12	1.24	1.32	1.41	1.46	1.49

(Source: Saaty, 2003)

sea level (Figure 1). The study area falls under Chhattisgarh plain of Agro-climatic zone where 50% of the total geographical area (3527 sq. km) is under cultivation. The study area characterized by hot-humid tropical climate, with an average annual rainfall of 1027.9 mm, out of which maximum rainfall (88 per cent) received during rainy season (late June to October) and 12 per cent received during winter (December to February). The maximum temperature in summer may exceed up to 42°C and varies between 30 and 42°C whereas; the minimum temperature often falls below 10°C during winter season and varies between 0 to 25 °C. The hottest and coolest months are May and December, respectively. The soil moisture regime of the district is characterized by *ustic* whereas the soil temperature regime is *hyperthermic* (Soil Survey Staff 2014). Major soil types of study area are *Entisols* (Bhata-gravely), *Inceptisols* (Matasi- sandy loam), *Alfisols* (Dorasa – clay loam) and *Vertisols* (Kanhar – clayey).

Predominately rice based cropping systems are practiced under rainfed ecosystem of Chhattisgarh as well as in Balod such as rice – lathyrus, rice – chickpea, rice – wheat and rice – fallow. Irrigation sources include canal (maximum area – 67 t ha), tanks, open well and bore wells.

Soil Sampling

Stratified soil sampling was done from the 10% of the total village in the district from vertisol based on two cropping systems viz: rice-wheat and rice-legume (Figure 1). Composite surface (0- 15 cm) soil samples were collected from each site after the harvest of crop. From each site, five soil samples were collected and pooled as composite sample. A total 40 samples, 20 each from rice-wheat and rice-chickpea cropping system, were collected, air-dried, ground, sieved (< 2 mm) and analyzed for soil physical, chemical and biological properties. The average yields of the crops taken were recorded by farmers' interview.

Soil Physical, Chemical, and Biological Analysis

The collected soil samples were analysed for their physical, chemical, and biological properties by methods described in the Table 3.

Figure 1. Study area and location of soil sampling

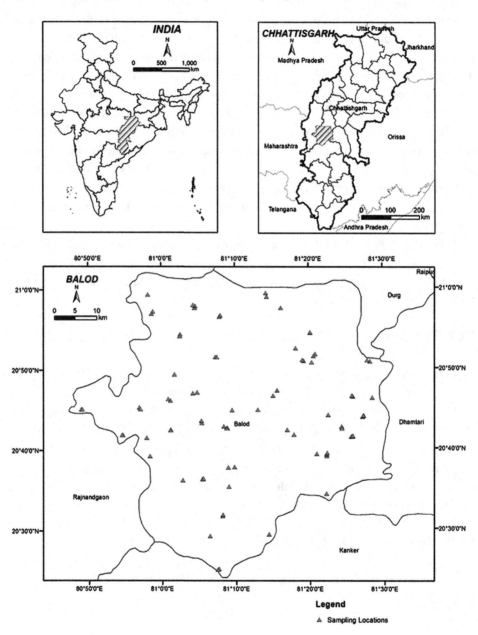

Table 3. Methodology adopted for soil physical, chemical, and biological properties

Sr. No.	Particular	Method	Reference
A.	**Physical Analysis**		
1.	Particle-size distribution (%)	International pipette method	Jackson, 1950
2.	Water retention (at 33 and 1500 kPa)	Pressure plate apparatus	Richards, 1954
3.	Bulk density (Mg m^{-3})	By clod coating	Black, 1965
4.	Hydraulic conductivity	Constant head method	Kulte, 1965
4.	Water stable aggregates	Wet sieving method	Richards, 1954
B.	**Chemical Analysis**		
5.	pH (1:2)	pH meter	Jackson, 1950
6.	EC (dSm^{-1})	Conductivity meter	Jackson, 1950
8.	Cation exchange capacity (CEC) (cmol(p+)kg^{-1})	NH$_4$OAc/NaOAc method	
10.	Available N (kg ha^{-1})	Alkaline potassium permanganate method	Subbiah and Asijia, 1965
11.	Available P (kg ha^{-1})	Olsen's modified method	Kumar *et al.*, 2018
12.	Available K (kg ha^{-1})	Extraction with neutral 1N NH$_4$OAc using Flame photometer	Kumar *et al.*, 2018
C.	**Biological Analysis**		
16.	Organic carbon (g kg^{-1})	Wet-oxidation method	Kumar *et al.*, 2018
17.	Microbial biomass carbon (MBC)	Fumigation extraction method	Kumar *et al.*, 2018

DEVELOPMENT OF SQI

Selection of MDS

The selection of MDS was done based on experts' opinion. Opinions were taken from the experts working in the area of soil science and agronomy. In the present study, productivity function is given prime importance among the soil functions though crop cultivation amidst adverse hot-humid regions is influenced by both edaphic and non-edaphic factors.

Normalizing the MDS

After determining the variables for the MDS, every observation of each MDS indicator was transformed for inclusion in the SQI. Selected indicators in MDS were scored into dimension less values to normalize all indicators ranging from 0 to 1 using linear scoring method (Liebig *et al.*, 2001). Indicators were ranked in ascending or descending order depending on whether a higher value was considered "good" or "bad" in terms of soil function. For 'more is better' indicators, each observation was divided by the highest observed value such that the highest observed value received a score of 1. For 'less is better' indicators, the lowest observed value (in the numerator) was divided by each observation (in the denominator) such that the lowest observed value receives a score of 1. For many indicators, a threshold or optimum value is better, observations were scored as 'higher is better' up to the threshold value (e.g. pH 7.0) then scored as 'lower is better' above the threshold (Liebig *et al.*, 2001 and Andrews *et al.*, 2002).

Integration of Indicators Into Index

After transformation using a linear scoring method, scores, thus obtained for each observation was multiplied with the weighted factor obtained from the AHP results. After performing these steps, to obtain SQI, the weighted MDS indicator scores for each observation were summed up using the following relationship:

$$SQI = \sum_{i=1}^{n} w_i s_i$$

where s_i is the score for the subscripted variable and w_i is the weighing factor obtained from the AHP analysis.

RESULTS AND DISCUSSION

Soil Properties

Data on soil properties studied under rice-wheat and rice-chickpea cropping systems are summarized in Table 4. All the forty sites chosen for study belongs to black soil as evidently indicated by high clay content, poor sand content and low infiltration rates. Extensive swelling and shrinking upon wetting and drying is the major characteristics of these soils. Because of their swell –shrink characters and development of deep, wide cracks and slickensides, these soils pose many tillage problems during cultivation. With irrigation, they can be cultivated for two crops in a year. Under rainfed conditions, these soils can support one crop in a year either during monsoon (*Kharif*) period or on stored moisture in *Rabi* (winter) season. Paddy is grown on *Vertisols* in lower topographic positions and where irrigation is available. Therefore, cropping systems of rice-wheat or rice-chickpea seems to be suitable for such type of soils.

Table 4. Descriptive statistics of soil properties under two cropping systems

Soil Properties	Rice-Wheat					Rice-Chickpea				
	Min	Max	Mean	SD	CV	Min	Max	Mean	SD	CV
MBC (ppm)	187.18	254.38	219.21	22.98	10.48	197.49	271.28	237.61	21.26	8.95
Soil organic Carbon (g kg^{-1})	3.70	6.10	4.68	0.64	13.70	4.70	6.70	5.81	0.53	9.16
pH	6.80	8.20	7.56	0.35	4.61	6.80	7.60	7.18	0.24	3.41
EC (dS m^{-1})	0.16	0.32	0.23	0.05	23.40	0.08	0.23	0.14	0.04	29.06
CEC (cmol (p$^+$) kg^{-1})	35.59	51.47	45.22	4.18	9.25	34.28	59.24	50.03	6.43	12.85
Available N (kg ha^{-1})	197.00	251.00	230.15	15.13	6.57	199.00	275.00	246.95	19.06	7.72
Available P (kg ha^{-1})	10.20	21.80	15.07	3.00	19.91	14.50	23.90	19.14	2.77	14.46
Available K (kg ha^{-1})	367.00	459.00	412.65	27.70	6.71	387.00	501.00	439.90	31.65	7.19
Sand (%)	9.40	25.40	15.70	4.19	26.68	9.40	19.20	15.55	3.06	19.67
Silt (%)	18.30	28.80	24.32	2.87	11.80	18.50	29.40	25.09	3.30	13.14
Clay (%)	50.10	69.10	59.99	5.27	8.78	52.30	68.90	59.37	4.01	6.76
Bulk density (Mg m^{-3})	1.29	1.49	1.40	0.05	3.83	1.27	1.44	1.34	0.05	3.44
Water retention at -1/3 bar	22.40	32.50	27.74	3.26	11.77	26.70	38.20	32.43	3.56	10.98
Water retention at -15 bar	12.60	21.60	16.54	2.53	15.28	15.10	27.80	21.45	3.21	14.98
Hydraulic conductivity (cm hr^{-1})	0.68	0.87	0.77	0.06	8.16	0.67	0.96	0.86	0.08	9.70
Mean weight diameter (mm)	0.58	0.82	0.71	0.06	9.15	0.76	0.98	0.87	0.07	8.34
Rice Yield (q ha^{-1})	39.00	51.00	45.55	2.91	6.39	45.00	57.00	51.25	2.44	4.78
Available water content	5.00	19.90	11.20	4.02	35.90	6.50	22.50	10.98	4.50	40.98
Available Fe (ppm)	18.50	30.50	25.42	3.60	14.16	18.30	39.40	30.69	5.83	19.01
Available Mn (ppm)	9.50	16.40	13.56	1.78	13.09	11.70	23.70	16.78	3.22	19.20
Available Cu (ppm)	0.30	1.50	0.89	0.35	39.53	0.70	1.80	1.26	0.34	26.80
Available Zn (ppm)	0.20	0.70	0.46	0.15	32.27	0.30	0.90	0.62	0.19	29.88
Available B (ppm)	0.20	0.70	0.46	0.15	33.04	0.30	1.20	0.71	0.20	27.79

The vertisols under rice chickpea cropping system were found to be better than rice-wheat cropping system in microbial biomass carbon (MBC), salinity, soil organic carbon, available nutrients, bulk density, and water retention characteristics. Inclusion of pulses in the rice based cropping sequence has been found more beneficial than rice-wheat sequence (Kumpawat, 2001; Raskar and Bhoi 2001). Legume crops fix atmospheric N, enrich soil fertility, and improve soil structure, reduce disease incidence and promote mycorrhizal colonization (Wani *et al.,* 1995). It has been well documented that the rice-wheat cropping system can be diversified using grain/fodder legume for green manure as a substitute crop (Raskar and Bhoi 2001). The yield of rice crop was also found higher in case of rice-chickpea cropping system. Inclusion of legumes in the rotation hastened the N and P transformation (Wani *et al.,* 1995; Kannaiyan 2000) and also increased root growth and N use efficiency of cereal crops, resulting in greater productivity of cereal-based production system (Yadav *et al.,* 2000).

Development of SQI

MDS were selected from different soil properties/indicators analyzed, based on the experts' opinion and the values were then normalized by linear scoring. The weights were obtained by AHP method for weighted summation of the MDS scores into a SQI. The results are discussed in the following sections.

Selection of Indicators

The concept of soil quality is centered on the ability of the soil to perform specific functions like sustaining biological activity, regulating water flow, buffering, storing, and cycling of nutrients, etc. (Karlen *et al.,* 1997). The MDS was selected taking into account the indicator's ability to detect soil function changes as well as the ease, practicality and cost-effectiveness for sampling, analysis and interpretation. The expert opinion method identified 5 soil properties under the MDS (Zn, P, SOC, MWD, and AWC), with the first two being fertility parameters important for rice and legumes. The SOC ensures long-term sustainability and overall productivity of cropping systems (Swarup *et al.,* 2000). As recommended by Doran and Parkin (1994), these indicators are desirable for SQ assessments because they are: easy to sample for, readily available in commercial laboratories at a low cost, and the results can be easily interpreted using pre-defined thresholds. The fourth indicator, MWD, provides an integrative assessment of soil structural/physical quality related to size, strength and porosity of aggregates. The fifth indicator, AWC, is important for the second crop and if rain-fed, to the rice crop too.

The selected MDS was consistent with Andrews *et al.* (2002) and Karlen *et al.* (1997), who recommend that SQ assessments could be made using a minimum of five indicators- one at least from soil chemical, physical and biological properties and processes. However, Andrews *et al.* (2003) did warn that the expert opinion method does truly require expert knowledge of the entire production system and may be subject to disciplinary bias.

Calculation of Weights

AHP was used to identify the weights for the MDS selected to avoid the biasness. The comparison matrix was established based on the expert opinions. The weight for factor AWC was highest (38.2%) followed by SOC (32.5%), MWD (17.8%), P (7.6%) and organic carbon (3.9%). The consistency of the comparison matrix was 0.075 (Table 5), which suggests that the matrix for the factors was consistent.

SCORING AND INTEGRATION

A linear scoring method was used to score the values of each attribute (Table 6). A weighted additive method was adopted to calculate the SQI for all the soils (Table 6). The SQI values for R-C and R-W cropping systems were 0.71 and 0.61, respectively. The ANOVA (Table 7) shows that the SQI differs significantly between the cropping systems. Thus, the SQI of rice-chickpea cropping system was found significantly better than that of rice-wheat. Seasonal cycles of puddling (wet tillage) and drying, over the long term intensive cropping, lead to the formation of hardpans or plow pans in rice fields (Thompson *et al.*, 1992; Bruneau *et al.*, 2004 and Glab 2007). Therefore improvement in total porosity of soils, under rice-based system is mandatory. The rotation of rice with legume crops have been found to increase microbial activities resulting in enhanced N and P availability, root growth, and

Table 5. Comparison matrix and calculated weights

	Zn	P	SOC	MWD	AWC	Weight	CI	CR
Zn	1	1/3	1/7	1/5	1/7	0.039	0.084	0.075
P	3	1	1/3	1/5	1/8	0.076		
SOC	7	3	1	3	1	0.325		
MWD	5	5	1/3	1	1/3	0.178		
AWC	7	8	1	3	1	0.382		

Table 6. Linear scores and SQI for the soils of the study area

Rice-Chickpea

Weight → Cropping System	SOC (0.325)	Av. P (0.076)	MWD (0.178)	Av. Zn (0.039)	AWC (0.382)	SQI
	0.94	0.74	0.83	0.67	0.29	0.65
	0.87	1.00	0.79	0.56	0.31	0.64
	0.88	0.61	0.89	0.33	0.31	0.62
	0.87	0.72	0.93	0.44	0.32	0.64
	0.81	0.74	0.94	1.00	0.35	0.66
	0.84	0.62	0.84	0.56	0.36	0.62
	0.85	0.87	0.95	0.78	0.36	0.68
	1.00	0.95	0.99	0.78	0.37	0.75
	0.85	0.67	0.96	0.89	0.37	0.67
	0.70	0.79	0.89	0.33	0.40	0.61
	0.93	0.85	0.89	0.56	0.44	0.71
	0.93	0.98	0.97	0.67	0.47	0.75
	0.93	0.79	1.00	0.44	0.48	0.74
	0.88	0.95	0.86	0.67	0.49	0.72
	0.72	0.81	0.84	0.89	0.52	0.68
	0.81	0.77	0.81	0.78	0.66	0.75
	0.90	0.90	0.79	0.67	0.67	0.78
	0.78	0.69	0.84	1.00	0.74	0.77
	0.88	0.74	0.98	0.89	0.87	0.88
	1.00	0.83	0.78	0.89	1.00	0.94

Rice- Wheat

Cropping System	SOC	Av. P	MWD	Av. Zn	AWC	SQI
	0.70	0.70	0.71	0.67	0.22	0.52
	0.79	0.43	0.84	0.33	0.27	0.55
	0.79	0.64	0.84	0.67	0.28	0.59
	0.76	0.71	0.74	0.56	0.28	0.56
	0.85	0.74	0.65	0.78	0.29	0.59
	0.67	0.52	0.72	0.56	0.39	0.56
	0.67	0.91	0.66	0.67	0.39	0.58
	0.61	0.64	0.69	0.33	0.41	0.54
	0.69	0.80	0.73	0.33	0.48	0.61
	0.58	0.68	0.68	0.56	0.51	0.58
	0.63	0.62	0.73	0.44	0.52	0.60
	0.70	0.58	0.79	0.67	0.55	0.65
	0.69	0.53	0.76	0.33	0.58	0.63
	0.78	0.49	0.62	0.44	0.58	0.64
	0.63	0.54	0.74	0.44	0.61	0.63
	0.64	0.74	0.59	0.44	0.66	0.64
	0.91	0.78	0.77	0.56	0.67	0.77
	0.55	0.49	0.79	0.22	0.68	0.62
	0.76	0.56	0.70	0.33	0.71	0.70
	0.57	0.52	0.64	0.78	0.88	0.71

Table 7. Comparison of means between SQI of two cropping systems

		Sum of Squares	df	Mean Square	F
Between Groups	.101	1	.101	17.779	.000
Within Groups	.215	38	.006		
Total	.316	39			

soil organic carbon and improved soil structure (Wani *et al.,* 1995; Kumpawat, 2001; Raskar and Bhoi 2001). The improvements in soil quality lead to enhanced productivity of rice. A significantly positive correlation was observed between SQI and yield of rice (Figure 2) indicating that the soil properties selected from the comparative data set had biological significance, and are capable to evaluate effectively d the status of soil quality of rice based cropping system (Li *et al.*, 2013; Mukherjee and Lal 2014 and Vasu *et al.,* 2016).

Figure 2. Positive correlation observed between SQI and rice yield

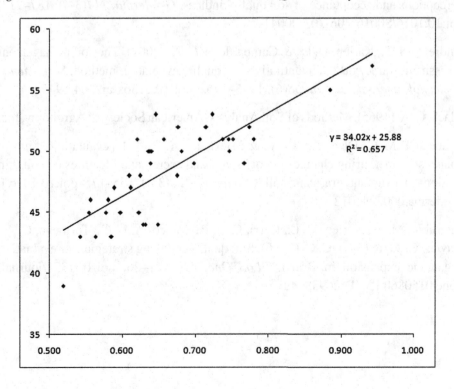

CONCLUSION

Rice based cropping systems are unavoidable cropping system for India to meet the increasing demand for food. Such rotations affect the soil C and N cycles, make the chemical speciation and biological effectiveness of soil nutrient elements varied with seasons, increase the diversity of soil organisms, and alter the soil physical properties, depending on the second crop in rotation. Consequently, selecting the right crop in rotation for maintaining or improving soil quality at a desirable level is needed. The present study develops and compares SQI for soils (vertisols) under rice-wheat and rice- chickpea cropping systems. For calculating the SQI, expert opinions were used for selecting MDS and identifying their weights. To avoid the biasness in direct assigning of weights, AHP method was deployed. The indicators identified in the MDS were SOC, AWC, MDW, Available Zn and P. The quality of soils under rice-chickpea was found to be significantly better than that of soils under rice-wheat. This resulted in higher yield of rice in case of rice-chickpea rotation.

REFERENCES

Andrews, S. S., Flora, C. B., Mitchell, J. P., & Karlen, D. L. (2003). Growers perceptions and acceptance of soil quality indices. *Geoderma, 114*(3-4), 187–213. doi:10.1016/S0016-7061(03)00041-7

Andrews, S. S., Karlen, D. L., & Cambardella, C. A. (2002). The soil management assessment framework: A quantitative soil quality evaluation method. *Soil Science Society of America Journal, 68*(6), 1945–1962. doi:10.2136ssaj2004.1945

Black, C. A. (1965). Methods of Soil Analysis. American Society of Agronomy, Inc.

Bruneau, P. M. C., Davidson, D. A., & Grieve, I. C. (2004). An evaluation of image analysis for measuring changes in void space and excremental features on soil thin sections in an upland grassland soil. *Geoderma, 120*(3-4), 165–175. doi:10.1016/j.geoderma.2003.08.012

Cherubin, M. R., Karlen, D. L., Cerri, C. E. P., Franco, A. L. C., Tormena, C. A., Davies, C. A., & Cerri, C. C. (2016). Soil quality indexing strategies for evaluating sugarcane expansion in Brazil. *PLoS One, 11*(3), 1–26. doi:10.1371/journal. pone.0150860 PMID:26938642

Doran, J. W., & Parkin, B. T. (1994). Defying and assessing soil quality. In J. W. Doran, D. C. Coleman, D. F. Bezdicek, & B. A. Stewart (Eds.), *Defying Soil Quality for a Sustainable Environment* (pp. 3–21). Madison, WI: Soil Science Society of America, Inc. doi:10.2136ssaspecpub35.c1

Glab, T. (2007). Application of image analysis for soil macropore characterization according to pore diameter. *International Agrophysics, 21*, 61–66.

Govaerts, B., Sayre, K. D., & Deckers, J. (2006). A minimum data set for soil quality assessment of wheat and maize cropping in the highlands of Mexico. *Soil & Tillage Research, 87*(2), 163–174. doi:10.1016/j.still.2005.03.005

Jackson, M. L. (1950). *Soil Chemical Analysis* (Indian Edition). Delhi: Prentice Hall of India Ltd.

Kangas, J., Alho, J. M., Kolehmainen, O., & Mononen, A. (1998). Analyzing consistency of experts' judgments- case of assessing forest biodiversity. *Forest Science, 44*, 610–617.

Karlen, D., Mausbach, M., Doran, J., Cline, R., Harris, R., & Schuman, G. (1997). Soil quality: A concept, definition, and framework for evaluation (a guest editorial). *Soil Science Society of America Journal, 61*(1), 4–10. doi:10.2136ssaj1997.03615 995006100010001x

Karlen, D. L., & Andrews, S. S. (2004). Soil quality, fertility, and health Historical context, status and perspectives. In P. Schjonning (Ed.), *Managing soil quality: Challenges in modern agriculture* (pp. 17–33). Oxon, UK: CABI International Publication. doi:10.1079/9780851996714.0017

Karlen, D. L., & Stott, D. E. (1994). A framework for evaluating physical and chemical indicators of soil quality. In J. W. Doran, D. C. Coleman, D. F. Bezdicek, & B. A. Stewart (Eds.), *Defining Soil Quality for a Sustainable Environment. SSSA Special Pub. 35* (pp. 53–72). Madison, WI: Soil Science Society of America.

Karthikeyan, K., Kumar, N., Prasad, J., & Srivastava, R. (2015). Soil Quality and Its Assessment: A Review. *Journal of Soil and Water Conservation, 14*(2), 100–108.

Kulte, A. (1965). Method of soil analysis part-I. Academic Press.

Kumar, N., Singh, S. K., Mishra, V. N., Obi Reddy, G. P., & Bajpai, R. K. (2017). Soil quality ranking of a small sample size using AHP. *Journal of Soil and Water Conservation, 16*(4), 339–346. doi:10.5958/2455-7145.2017.00050.9

Kumar, N., Singh, S.K., Mishra, V.N., Obi Reddy, G.P., Bajpai, R.K., & Saxena, R.R. (2018). Soil suitability evaluation for cotton using analytical hierarchic process. *International Journal of Chemical Studies, 6*(4), 1570-1576.

Kumar, U., Mishra, V. N., Kumar, N., & Rathiya, G. R. (2018). *Methods of Soil Analysis*. Ludhiana: Kalyani Publishers.

Kumpawat, B. S. (2001). Production potential and economics of different crop sequence. *Indian Journal of Agronomy, 46*(3), 421–424.

Li, P., Zhang, T., Wang, X., & Yu, D. (2013). Development of biological soil quality indicator system for subtropical China. *Soil & Tillage Research, 126*, 112–118. doi:10.1016/j.still.2012.07.011

Liebig, M. A., Varvel, G., & Doran, J. W. (2001). A simple performance-based index for assessing multiple agro ecosystem functions. *Agronomy Journal, 93*(2), 313. doi:10.2134/agronj2001.932313x

Marggraf, R. (2003). Comparative assessment of agrienvironment programmes in the federal state of Germany. *Agriculture, Ecosystems & Environment, 98*(1-3), 507–516. doi:10.1016/S0167-8809(03)00109-9

Masto, R. E., Chhonkar, P. K., Singh, D., & Patra, A. K. (2008). Alternative soil quality indices for evaluating the effect of intensive cropping, fertilisation and manuring for 31 years in the semi-arid soils of India. *Environmental Monitoring and Assessment, 136*(1-3), 419–435. doi:10.100710661-007-9697-z PMID:17457684

Mukherjee, A., & Lal, R. (2014). Comparison of Soil Quality Index Using Three Methods. *PLoS One, 9*(8). doi:1 0.1371/journal.pone.0105981

Ramanathan, R. (2001). A note on the use of the analytic hierarchy process for environmental impact assessment. *Journal of Environmental Management, 63*(1), 27–35. doi:10.1006/jema.2001.0455 PMID:11591027

Raskar, B. S., & Bho, P. G. (2001). Producing and economics of winter surghum Sorghwn bicolor summer egetables cropping s stems under irrigated conditions of western Maharastra. *Indian Journal of Agronomy, 46*(1), 17–22.

Rezaei, S. A., Gilkes, R. J., & Andrews, S. S. (2006). A minimum data set for assessing soil quality in rangelands. *Geoderma, 136*(1-2), 229–234. doi:10.1016/j. geoderma.2006.03.021

Richards, L. A. (1954). *Diagnosis and improvement of saline-alkali soils. USDA Handbook No. 60*. Washington, DC: U.S. Department of Agriculture.

Richey, J. S., Mar, B. W., & Horth, R. R. (1985). The Delphi technique in environmental assessment. *Technological Forecasting and Social Change, 23*, 89–94.

Saaty, T. L. (1980). *The Analytic Hierarchy Process: Planning, Priority Setting and Resource Allocation*. New York: McGraw-Hill.

Saaty, T. L. (1987). Rank generation, preservation and reversal in the analytic hierarchy process. *Decision Sciences, 18*(2), 157–177. doi:10.1111/j.1540-5915.1987. tb01514.x

Saaty, T. L. (2001). Decision Making for Leaders: The Analytic Hierarchy Process for Decisions in a Complex World, New Edition 2001. Pittsburgh, PA: RWS Publications.

Saaty, T. L. (2003). Decision-making with the AHP: Why is the principal eigenvector necessary? *European Journal of Operational Research, 145*(1), 85–91. doi:10.1016/ S0377-2217(02)00227-8

Sinha, N. K., Chopra, U. K., & Singh, A. K. (2013). Cropping system effects on soil quality for three agro-ecosystems in India. *Experimental Agriculture, 50*(3), 321–342. doi:10.1017/S001447971300046X

Subbiah, B. V., & Asija, G. L. (1956). A rapid procedure for the determination of available nitrogen in soils. *Current Science, 25*, 259–260.

Swarup, A. (2002). Lessions from long –term fertilizer experiments in improving fertilizer use efficiency and crop yield. *Fertilizer News, 47*(12), 59–66.

Thompson, M. L., Singh, P., Corak, S., & Straszheim, W. E. (1992). Cautionary notes for the automated analysis of soil pore-space images. *Geoderma, 53*(3-4), 399–415. doi:10.1016/0016-7061(92)90067-H

Vasu, D., Singh, S. K., Ray, S. K., Duraisami, V. P., Tiwary, P., Chandra, P., ... Anantwar, S. G. (2016). Soil quality index (SQI) as a tool to evaluate crop productivity in semi-arid Deccan plateau, India. *Geoderma, 282*, 70–79. doi:10.1016/j. geoderma.2016.07.010

Wani, S. P., Rego, T. J., Rajeswari, S., & Lee, K. K. (1995). Effect of legume-based cropping systems on nitrogen mineralization potential of *Vertisol*. *Plant and Soil, 175*(2), 265–274. doi:10.1007/BF00011363

Yadav, D.S., Singh, R.M., Alok, K., & Ram, A. (2000). Diversification of traditional cropping system for sustainable production. *Indian Journal of Agronomy, 45*(1), 37-40.

Chapter 2
IT Governance or IT Outsourcing:
Is There a Clear Winner?

Michael D. Dorsey
Texas Woman's University, USA

Mahesh S. Raisinghani
Texas Woman's University, USA

ABSTRACT

IT governance or IT outsourcing both have their own unique benefits but the decision to choose one over other is not always so clear. This chapter examines the impact of globalization of software development and localization of service delivery in the offshore software development and outsourcing services sector. A case study is used to illustrate the key ideas that helped contribute to a successful IT project that was outsourced by a US organization to a transnational IT outsourcing services provider based in India. The two key points illustrated by the case study discussed in this chapter are what are the issues facing a North American company that deals with an IT service supplier thousands of miles and many time zones away and what are the lessons learned from a successful outsourcing relationship.

DOI: 10.4018/978-1-5225-7784-3.ch002

INTRODUCTION

The first wave of offshore information technology (IT) outsourcing efforts began approximately 25 years ago as a way to reduce the cost of maintenance for legacy systems. The second wave of offshore IT was focused on resolving the Y2K problem. These two waves of IT offshore outsourcing had mixed results due to telecommunications difficulties, immature systems-development methodologies and cultural differences. In the current, third wave of offshore IT outsourcing, vendors demonstrate project management responsibility, vertical industry experience and/ or business process outsourcing capabilities (Perkins, 2003). Although offshore development has traditionally focused on application development and maintenance, some large financial firms in the U.S. have grouped together in this third wave to outsource some of their real-time IT (i.e., live operations, including production support and other IT infrastructure operations). Outsourced software development is focused on new product development, custom development for the enterprise, and support and maintenance, especially for mainframe and other legacy systems. This chapter also includes a case study discussion that is an application of the transnational management strategy in an IT offshore outsourcing context.

In the ever-changing landscape of the modern business, companies are forced to adopt new means of sustainability in not just the products and services they provide but also in their overall business structure as a whole. Prior to this change, the structure of most businesses were simple. Senior partners at the top sending orders down to middle management that gave instructions to the day-to-day workforce. However, when things go contrary to what is expected with computers and the like, everyone remembers the IT person. In today's world information technology and its' adoption into any and all industries are synonymous with the overall success of any company. That being said, there exist a divide of sorts forcing many organizations to wonder if IT governance or IT out sourcing is the correct means of securing long term profitability but more immediate, meeting the overall IT needs of a business.

The two key questions to reflect upon are as follows: Does adopting IT into the overall structure of a business lead to greater profitability as well as decrease down time associated with internal IT changes or does IT out sourcing provide a cost efficient means to ensure companies ever expanding needs are met without having to directly employee and train those needed to provide such services? This chapter will describe what IT governance and IT out sourcing means; the benefits of each; their respective impact on the business world and finally where each is going.

LITERATURE REVIEW AND SYNTHESIS

The concept of reinforcing your understanding and ability to meet the needs of those around you, to better your position in the market, is not a new concept. It has long been openly embraced as universal truth by those who seek to do business, both domestic and abroad, that furthering current IT infrastructure is an essential element, which leads to long-term profits while simultaneously allowing companies' to remain relevant in a rapidly evolving market place. "IT governance is considered a more broad concept and concentrates on transforming information technology to meet the current and future demands of the business as well as the needs of the business customer" (Dawson, Denford, Williams, Preston, & Desouza, 2016). IT governance refers to "the organizational capacity exercised by the board [of directors], executive management and T management to control the formulation and implementation of IT strategy and in this way ensure the fusion of business and IT" (Dawson et al., 2016).

The majority of IT governance research comes from the private sector. For IT governance to be effective it requires that "both board and executive management involvement as essential to the achievement of alignment, and further asserts that through the involvement of all levels of leadership, the IT organization can better execute the organization's strategies and objectives" (Dawson et al., 2016). This leads to greater consistency in information systems application throughout the organization as well as higher performance metrics overall. It has been reported that companies that embrace a functional system of IT governance yield approximately 40 percent higher returns on IT investments than firms of equal standing whom do not employ such organization wide initiatives (Dawson et al., 2016).

Shao and Smith-David (2007) conclude that "When work sent offshore can be done in a timely fashion with high quality and lower cost, companies facing intensified global competition and trying to maximize their profits have little choice but to outsource some of their IT needs overseas. As global market dynamics keep driving companies to acquire IT services from locations that provide the most cost-effective solutions, offshore outsourcing will remain a viable option on the corporate strategic agenda."

Not to be confused with IT management, IT governance is focused on the development of the IT needs of the company as a whole. Its' approach is focused on the immediate requirements of the company, future demands and the current expanding needs of customers. Planning for expansion and future development is a must. IT management is focused on meeting the day-to-day operational needs of a company. This includes IT supplies and services (Dawson et al., 2016).

In order to tackle IT governance appropriately, organizations must turn their attention to the quality of information systems while establishing adequate control. As the world continues its trend toward heavy use of IT resources, there is a constant need to integrate these resources with other managerial processes. "Despite considerable research on IT governance here appears to be limited investigation on the effectiveness of IT governance in deriving business value from IT investments" (Zhang et al., 2016). To further investigate this deficit, studies have been conducted to deduce just how effective IT governance is for various organizations and firms. The results were a 20% increase in profits for those organizations that held superior IT governance (Zhang et al., 2016). These organizations tend to also have a stronger ability to nurture organizational learning thus continuing growth through expanding knowledge and understanding, however there is more to explore.

DISCUSSION

"The ideal governance structure is created when there is a correct fit between governance decision-making and location of domain and technical specific knowledge" (Dawson et al., 2016). This means that it is important to have decision makers on the same wavelength as the future direction of the overall IT processes, both in their expectations and understanding of what will be achieved. It is just as crucial to have sufficient controls in place to govern IT management so that the overall benefit is reached and sustained. To ensure this occurs there must be a specific person selected to make key decisions as it relates to IT decisions. "Without a formal and structured IT governance process, organizational leaders handle IT governance decisions on an individualized, ad hoc basis", potentially creating a conflict with solving a specific problem that may cause a direct conflict with achieving the overall goal set previously. Strong systematic controls eliminate potential conflict with individual decisions that may be at odds organizational goals (Dawson et al., 2016).

Hesham Bin-Abbas & Haj Saad (2014) defines five benefits to the successful implementation of IT governance. "The first is saving time and leading to "faster" achievements; the second is saving cost through "cheaper" business activities. The third is providing services with "better" quality, while the fourth is opening new opportunities by introducing "different" capabilities. The fifth is enhancing trust by providing new "security" measures that are not feasible without IT" (Bin-Abbas & Haj, 2014). Rapid achievement allows for organizations to continuously expand and compound upon their success in an effort to push their firms to the next level. Through IT governance, organizations save costs and provide themselves with an added layer of funds as well as protection thus making these growing businesses more successful. Companies are then also given the added support needed to supply customers with high quality services thus opening up new capabilities (Bin-Abbas & Haj, 2014). Finally, through the use of new security channels, IT governance works to continuously build successful companies and organizations with a clear vision of both their current and future needs.

With companies constantly searching for cost efficient means to produce and provide their services to both their current and ever expanding customer base, so too must they strive to reduce the cost of operations. Antonucci and Tucker (1998) define information systems and technology outsourcing as "contracting with outside vendors for the provision of various IT functions, including data entry, data center operations, application maintenance and development, disaster recovery, and network management and operations". Accepting this definition allows one to see the broad application IT outsourcing can be applied to any organization no matter the sizes. These types of companies consist of individual IT professionals, consulting firms, and full-service providers (Antonucci & Tucker, 1998). They vary in size, application and specialty, furthering their broad application and adoption in the modern business era. IT outsourcing is by no means a new phenomenon. In the 1960s, companies utilized "computer services bureaus" to run programs from general ledger, payroll and inventory to name a few. The customers of these were mostly small to medium-size firms, although some large companies used them for specialized needs that included confidential executive payroll (Antonucci & Tucker III, 1998).

Prior to 1990, preexisting staff handled minor day-to-day IT needs internally. The main needs for IT outsourcing were to grant companies' access to specialized computing power or specific capabilities not available in house. This was a cost effective alternative to redeveloping current infrastructure and training of new skills related to completing specific task (Antonucci & Tucker III, 1998). The question still remains why would organizations turn to other companies to further their own respective footprint versus building their own.

Out sourcing in general has been seen by many as an inexpensive alternative to meeting the expanding needs of an organization with limited resources. However, as characterized by those surveyed by Antonucci and Tucker (1998) there are both five short term and five long-term reasons companies chose to outsource current IT needs.

A key benefit of offshoring is strategic flexibility; outsourcing organizations are able to use the best mix of external resources to meet their business needs (Rasmussen, 2007). In addition, outsourcing can give an organization the adaptability required in this quickly changing global economy and also allows an organization to fully focus on its core competencies. Other valuable benefits of offshoring include:

- **Complementary Resources:** Working with global partners gives enterprises access to a deeper and wider range of IT skills
- **Improved Quality of Products and Services at Lower Cost:** Enhanced potential to use tested and proven software modules and processes that vendors have developed
- Ability to capitalize on vendor's strengths in areas such as new system development, implementation, testing, and quality assurance
- Less dependence upon internal resources as offshoring reduces the need to manage larger pools of in-house IT resources
- Reduced ongoing investment in internal infrastructure
- Potential for early implementation of systems/applications compared to end-to-end in-house development
- Ability to benefit from innovations from other enterprises and individuals
- Improved productivity and efficiency

The short-term reasons for IT outsourcing include:

- Reducing and limiting operational expenses, this is achieved by gaining access to lower cost structure that outside vendors typically have, reduces cost in general by 9%. Increase access to capital funds, through outsourcing companies eliminate the need to invest capital in areas that are deemed as non-essential, thus eliminating a need for many to report or show a return on equity from a capital investment. Increased availability of cash, expenses typically held by companies such as equipment, licenses, vehicles and facilities are built into the cost passed on to its' customers, by out sourcing the payments received from customers adds more cash to the bottom line despite the built in cost of using a provider. Lack of available internal resources, as companies continue to expand to new markets, cost associated with operating in those markets increase as well as a greater demand is placed on the resources they currently have. Outsourcing allows them to gain access to needed resources immediately. Functional management of difficult projects and problems, although outsourcing does give companies access to specific IT industry professionals, it does not however, eliminate management from being involved in the process (Antonucci & Tucker III, 1998).

Long-term reasons for IT out sourcing include the following:

- **Improve Business Direction:** Outsourcing allows companies to focus on other key components of their businesses without dedicating management resources as projects related to IT, are devoted to the provider for operational details with input from management versus previous hands on involvement.
- **Access to World-Class Capabilities:** IT outsourcing providers bring specialized industry knowledge, extensive network of resources to meet the needs of customers. Partnering with organizations with such capabilities offers companies' access to new technologies and techniques that companies do not currently possess.
- **Accelerated Reengineering Benefits:** This allows an organization to immediately benefit of a change to standards and advancements, as the outside organization, is designed to assimilate and prioritizes being able to instantaneously utilizes a new standard or change without redeveloping its own systems.
- **Shared Risks:** Outsourcing allows companies greater flexibility and adapt to coming changes, this allows for risk associated with any investment to be shared between both parties leaving the company less exposed to inevitable changes standards and the market place.
- **Free Resources for Other Purposes:** With access to limited resources, outsourcing permits an organization to redirect its resources from non-core activities towards those that grant greater return in serving their customers (Antonucci & Tucker III, 1998).

Benoit et al. (2105) point out that innovation has traditionally been associated with the organization striving to make a change internally by having cross-departmental collaboration to reach the best beneficial solution. This exchange of idea leads to innovation and greater rewards for the company as a whole. As it applies to IT outsourcing a significant change has been made as it relates to innovation requiring organizations to be even more flexible. The exchange of ideas is essential to furthering innovation in the field of information technology. The mass exchange and collaboration of ideas between providers, suppliers and customers alike lead to greater innovation (Benoit et al., 2015). This open flow of information between parties goes against the common mindset, "organizations cannot solely rely on their internal skills" forcing companies to acknowledge the importance of being open to "both internal and external knowledge in order to innovate" (Benoit et al., 2015). Out sourcing allows for access to borders and sections of industry that are typically cut off by the geographic location and internal restraints of a company. Providers grant access to vast networks of skilled professional, processes, new ideas and solutions to problems not yet encountered. This embrace in change has led to a significant increase in the adoption of out sourcing, as it promotes innovation for all to benefit immediate and long-term success, however it is measured, simultaneously (Benoit et al., 2015).

As with any inherent benefit that is achieved through outsourcing, there to will be a loss in some respect. Benoit et al. (2015) argues that the specific knowledge needed to conduct a task, implement it into the daily need of a firm and redesigned for greater use, is in its self the process of innovation. By outsourcing a company loses its ability to innovate in that field, as it is no longer taking steps in the learning and developing process. Innovation requires the ability to gain knowledge over time and application of that knowledge in practice. A co-dependency relationship can form with the manufacturers, vendors and customers involved in the supply chain (Benoit et al., 2015).

Taking outsourcing even further, Wiener and Saunders (2014) introduce the concept of IT multi-sourcing. IT multi-sourcing is "delegation of IT projects and services in a managed way to multiple vendors who must (at least partly) work cooperatively to achieve the client's business objectives" (Wiener & Saunders, 2014). It allows companies to spread risk through multiple outlets at once. Traditionally, when working with another company to provide a specific resource essential to the firms, a great level of risk isolated to a single location, where multi sourcing spread risk between competing vendors. The benefit of multi sourcing include "lower IT service costs due to competition among vendors, reduced opportunistic rent appropriations by any one vendor, improved quality through best-of-breed services, enhanced flexibility in adapting to changing market conditions, and easier access to specialized expertise and capabilities" (Wiener & Saunders, 2014). Along with this change has shifted the need for long-term contracts with one specific vendor. Now contracts can be made shorter and in multiple geographic locations

(Wiener & Saunders, 2014). This in essence allows companies the advantage of forcing completion between suppliers as they will only solicit services in specific geographic foot prints thus eliminating cost associated with managing, shipping and handling in specific regions not typically in one venders specific service area versus another (Wiener & Saunders, 2014). This also forces competing vendors to work with one another to achieve success for the firms they represent. This form of cross collaboration forces all those involved to innovate at rates both faster and with greater efficiency.

Next this chapter focuses on a case study discussion that is an application of the transnational management strategy in an IT offshore outsourcing context.

CASE STUDY DESCRIPTION AND ANALYSIS

The case used in this study is an outsourced IS development project by a leading financial services provider to credit unions and their members worldwide to a transnational outsourcing company headquartered in India. Since the use of varied data sources permits a certain level of triangulation (Benbasat et al., 1987), data acquisition was based on a variety of data sources such as documentation, semi-structured interviews, direct observation and physical artifacts.

Overview of the Fortune 1000 Mutual Insurance Company

Fortune 1000 Mutual Insurance Company (name withheld at the company's request), a leading financial services provider to credit unions and their members worldwide, offers more than 300 insurance, investment and technological solutions through strategic relationships and multiple service channels. In fact, no other company in the world offers so many credit union-specific products. At present there are 10,400 credit unions and the number of credit unions is shrinking, but the number of credit union members is growing. Fortune 1000 Mutual Insurance Company, since its existence, has over 40 million members, and has a relationship with over 5000 credit unions.

Selection of the IT Outsourcing Vendor

The Fortune 1000 Mutual Insurance Company Group engaged Mastek Limited to provide an in-house web-based replacement to its Wynstar Claims Processing Engine. Mastek is a $79.5 million transnational IT applications outsourcing corporation headquartered in India, employing over 1,700 professionals. It is the world's first software company to use SW-CMM Level 5 processes and P-CMM Level 3 teams. In addition, Mastek is an ISO-9001 accredited company since 1994 and has a 93% on-time delivery track record far exceeds the industry average. In October 2002, Mastek was one of the 13 Indian companies to be listed in the Forbes global list of 200 best small companies in the world based on profitability, earnings and sales growth.

A full scope project that included needs analysis, requirement definition, systems analysis, design, & development used the IBM's DB2 database management system as the back-end system and Microsoft's Visual Basic/Active Server Pages as the front-end system. Mastek deputed a team to Fortune 1000 Mutual Insurance Company's facility in Madison, Wisconsin, to understand the existing system and requirements analysis for enhancements. Mastek intends to create the proposed system to be rule-based, and hence, more flexible.

Mastek's three-tier transnational engagement model relieves the client of responsibility for risk management and places accountability for the success of the project with Mastek's team. Mastek's employees therefore become an integral part of the customer's organization. Through processes such as Mastrack, not only are our customers kept fully informed, but all members of the Mastek team, both on- and off-shore, are aware of the exact status of their projects at all times.

Business Issues

There are several business issues that Fortune 1000 Mutual Insurance Company is facing that need to be addressed. At present Fortune 1000 Mutual Insurance Company processes over 4000 claims per day against a customer policy base of over 13 million. Processing of claims usually takes about 45 days and this results in high claims processing costs with low controls. Manual adjudication of all the claims results in poor information on claims experience for decision making. Multiple claims processing systems with inefficient systems integration result in high maintenance costs and it takes approximately 2 to 4 months to incorporate new product requirements for claims processing.

Fortune 1000 Mutual Insurance Company is trying to reduce the claims processing cost and improve claims processing efficiency with Automatic Adjudication of claims. To overcome the problems it needs to build tighter controls and flexibility by reducing the processing time in the new claims system, build efficient management information systems with appropriate technology, build effective partnership with other credit unions, and improve member experience on claims.

Strategic Partnership With Mastek

The strategic partnership between Fortune 1000 Mutual Insurance Company and Mastek enables it to resolve some of the issues mentioned above. It 'maximizes leverage' by generating savings in cost, productivity, time-to-market and enhanced quality. Mastek can offer unified claims engine for all of Fortune 1000 Mutual Insurance Company's products with flexible business rules for end-to-end claims processing. Business rules driven workflow automation forms provide a comprehensive solution from claims notification to claims settlement. This will empower Fortune 1000 Mutual Insurance Company with tighter controls to detect fraudulent claims, efficient integration engine for interfacing with multiple policy administration and satellite systems. Mastek will be able to track the claim processing time between stages to enhance claims processing efficiency and it will build systems for the Fortune 1000 Mutual Insurance Company based on Microsoft's .Net technology with n-tier architecture.

The Fortune 1000 Mutual Insurance Company's IT department, which includes operations, application development and support staff, has only about 600 employees. Hence it decided to outsource this project to Mastek based on important criteria such as size and culture and their mutual understanding to see each other as strategic partners. The Fortune 1000 Mutual Insurance Company was interested in leveraging the better, faster, cheaper theme with the IRA direct as its first pilot. When this business was acquired it was in a very bad condition both from the business and the IT perspective. After the implementation of the project, zero bugs were found since Mastek believes in an environment of continuous improvement. Another important factor is that Mastek provides a cost effective, high quality solution for those real business requirements that need customized solutions.

In keeping with its strategy of being successful by helping the customer succeed, Mastek is very honest and upfront with its customer about this analysis. At present, Fortune 1000 Mutual Insurance Company is planning to move 50 percent of the company's application development and support to offshore locations, mostly in India. It is also trying to determine how to leverage IT infrastructure offshore. The Fortune 1000 Mutual Insurance Company is approaching its business structure in a very consistent manner. New claims systems have been in a process of building and Mastek is involved in approximately 70-80% of the development. Mastek currently has a blended team for maintenance support of that system between India and Madison.

Tangible Measures of Success

After partnering with Mastek, the Fortune 1000 Mutual Insurance Company has significantly improved its time to market since the development time has been reduced 50-70% in building claims system for new products. The claims processing has become more efficient since the time for processing claims has been reduced by 50%. Automated adjudications of claims have been introduced. Fraudulent claims detection system has led to 5% reduction in claims expenses. The departmental efficiency rose by 20% resulting in lower operational costs and there has been an over 50% reduction in reconciliation across systems, thus providing improved service to other credit unions and members.

CONCLUSION

The case study illustrates that a successful offshore project requires clear requirements and client agreements, common configuration management, continuous feedback, ability to cycle resources, a joint project management that respects and leverages the time zone differential, and a dedication of adequate resources for managing the relationship.

In generalizing the findings of the case study, caution is advised since there are several moderating factors that may affect the needed control and coordination from the transnational organization and impact the final outcome. The moderating factors could be the age of partnership, economy, client attributes, vendor attributes, and contextual factors. The influence factors could be project structure, technological uncertainty, functional complexity, criticality of outsourced IT, interdependency, and cultural differences (Kumar and Palvia, 2002). Global IT outsourcing for transnational organizations is both an opportunity and a challenge. Despite the challenges, global IT outsourcing is inevitable due to the cost, quality and speed advantages. Responsibly implemented, offshore outsourcing expands opportunity and can only benefit us all.

Is the gain in efficiency worth the loss in ability to innovate on one's own, this is the question each firm will have to answer for its self. IT governance employees companies to develop eternally by taking the active steps necessary to improve current standards while at the same time planning for future needs. It can be clearly argued that when firms cease putting usable skills in to practice, skills and training that ultimately lead to greater understanding to the benefit of the firm as a whole. Returns from those advancements are no longer accessible. With technological advances on the cusp of creation daily, IT governance will continue to be utilized and implemented across the country as a means of bettering organizations and building relationships with companies worldwide. While studies tend to illustrate mixed conclusions on the success of IT governance, those whom execute it properly remain to be the outliers that set the bar for other companies to follow. As it applies to IT out sourcing, it fundamentally leads to answering problems associated with cost, as a result of forced competition through multi sourcing, greater collaboration across geographic locations and increase ability for firms to benefit from modern standards with out making a large restructuring capital investment. Risk is a necessary undertaking in any industry, however IT outsourcing allows companies to diversify risk across multiple out lets, with each working together in recognition that greater and open collaboration is to the benefit of all. The stage has been set and all options weighed, however the decision will consistently remain as to the correct choice.

REFERENCES

Antonucci, Y. L., & Tucker, J. J. III. (1998). IT outsourcing: Current trends, benefits, and risks. *Information Strategy: The Executive's Journal, 14*(2), 16.

Aubert, A. B., Kishore, R., & Iriyama, A. (2015). Exploring and managing the "innovation through outsourcing" paradox. *The Journal of Strategic Information Systems, 24*(4), 255–269. doi:10.1016/j.jsis.2015.10.003

Bin-Abbas, H., & Haj Bakry, S. (2014). Assessment of IT governance in organizations: A simple integrated approach. *Computers in Human Behavior, 32,* 261-267. Retrieved from http://www.sciencedirect.com/science/article/pii/S074756321300472X

Dawson, G. S., Denford, J. S., Williams, C. K., Preston, D., & Desouza, K. C. (2016). An Examination of Effective IT Governance in the Public Sector Using the Legal View of Agency Theory. *Journal of Management Information Systems, 33*(4), 1180–1208. doi:10.1080/07421222.2016.1267533

Rasmussen, D. N. (2007, March 7). Build an Insourcing Environment for Excellence. *Cutter IT Journal E-Mail Advisor*.

Wiener, M., & Saunders, C. (2014). Forced competition in IT multi-sourcing. *The Journal of Strategic Information Systems, 23*(3), 210–225. doi:10.1016/j.jsis.2014.08.001

Zhang, P., Zhao, K., & Kumar, R. L. (2016). Impact of IT Governance and IT Capability on Firm Performance. *Information Systems Management, 33*(4), 357–373. doi:10.1080/10580530.2016.1220218

KEY TERMS AND DEFINITIONS

Capability Maturity Model (CMM): A description of the stages through which software organizations evolve as they define, implement, measure, control, and improve their software processes.

Credit Union: A non-profit financial institution that is owned and operated entirely by its members. Credit unions provide financial services for their members.

Financial Services: The part of finance concerned with the design and delivery of advice and financial products to individuals, business, and government.

International Standards Organization (ISO): A network of national standards institutes from 148 countries working in partnership with international organizations, governments, industry, and business and consumer representatives. A bridge between public and private sectors.

Outsourcing: The process of subcontracting network operations and support to an organization outside your company.

Requirements Analysis: The process through which you define and evaluate the business needs of your network system.

Transnational Management Strategy: A strategy of multinational corporations under which the overseas components are integrated into the overall corporate structure.

Chapter 3
Project Teamwork Assessment and Success Rate Prediction Through Meta–Heuristic Algorithms

Soumen Mukherjee
RCC Institute of Information Technology, India

Arup Kumar Bhattacharjee
RCC Institute of Information Technology, India

Arpan Deyasi
RCC Institute of Information Technology, India

ABSTRACT

In this chapter, machine learning algorithms along with association rule analysis are applied to measure how the project teamwork success rate depends on various technical and soft skill factors of a software project. A real-life dataset is taken form UCI archive on project teamwork, which comprises of 84 features or attributes with 64 samples. The most effective feature set is therefore selected using meta-heuristic algorithms (i.e., particle swarm optimization [PSO] and simulated annealing [SA]) and then the data are given to support vector machine (SVM) and k-nearest neighbor (KNN) classifier for classification. Association rule mining is also used for rule generation among the different features of software project team to determine support and confidence. This chapter deals with how the project-based learning helps to manifest the students towards professionalism.

DOI: 10.4018/978-1-5225-7784-3.ch003

INTRODUCTION

In present era of technology teaching and learning, Management Information System(MIS) plays a vital role in assessing and implementing the knowledge transition process through different activities implemented beyond the classroom barrier, basically by means of two newly coined pedagogic methodologies, activity learning and flipped learning. Discovery of knowledge about all the stakeholders of the Institute is one of the primary requirements for their successful transition from student to corporate professionals, and thus representation of knowledge in structured forms are essential. This process can be implemented once the concept of teaching and learning will be deviated from the traditional teacher-centric approach to learner-centric approach through incorporation of projects in the curriculum, which is one of the principal requirements of Outcome Based Education (OBE) from the perspective of present engineering teaching and learning; prescribed by Bloom's Taxonomy (Gog, 2016). If the reader can devour h(is/er) mindset from the teacher-centric attitude, then it can be revealed that the MIS will play vital role in shaping the future of the students considering the present radical change in socio-humanitarian categorization based on newly emerging financial classification; which modifies the concept of classroom teaching. In twenty-first century, learning resources are become available truly outside the barriers of the bricks, through the World Wide Web (www) (Antonis *et al*, 2011). While implementation fo activity learning is not totally dependent on the web connection all the time, but more precisely, depends on the skill and thinking capabilities of the young minds; but flipped learning methodology is totally dependent on high-speed web connections in uninterrupted form at the time of preparation beyond class and before class. Teaching is now become a challenging task, where continuously changing academic and industrial requirements generates a new branch of research sector, may be termed as pedagogic principles. Individual assessments are partially replaced by group work's activity, and Think-Pair-Share (TPS) methodology (Pradana *et al*, 2017; Lee *et al*, 2018; Afthina *et al*, 2017) becomes one of the responsive methods of activity learning (McGrath &MacEwan, 2011; Khan *et al*, 2012) or flipped learning (Zainuddin & Halili, 2016; Karabulut-Ilgu *et al*, 2018; Guan, 2016) methodologies. Since both the learning technologies required group-based activities, so communication skill within the group plays the critical role in measuring success of the MIS, and simultaneously, information policy o the organization. In this context, system analysis gives the vital information about assessing the teamwork, formed while solving the project tasks assigned, and several meta-heuristic algorithms are required for feature selection; while machine learning algorithms are used for classification purpose.

Industry always demands the end-user product development, and ability of a person to be hired or to be with the changing dynamics can be better judged by group-activity, and that's why the new pedagogy concepts are becoming arena of strategic teaching (Suriyanti & Yaacob, 2016).Analysis of the data measures the success rate of the pedagogic approaches, and that speaks in favor of system analysis and design, which also ensures the successful accomplishment of MIS. Modernization of curricula in a periodic manner comes into play due to the ever-increasing failure rate of the industrial projects (Khan & Malik, 2017) measured statistically over a considerable period of time, which is correlated with the increased cost and extended schedule (Haron *et al*, 2017; Sarif *et al*, 2018). This leads the concept of project-based learning (Sababha *et al*, 2016), one of the key elements in activity learning process, where along with individual performance; group performance is also equally valued.

If the scope of the present chapter is slightly narrowed down from the general engineering teaching to the field of computer and information science, then it is found out that it should possess one of the most significant dynamic curricula with the emerging and expanding software sector, and in order to become at par with the latest technological trends, new teaching and assessment methods should be incarnated to produce new generation professionals. Conservative and traditional ways of teaching this domain will only increase the failure rates (Arcidiacono, 2017; Emam & Koru, 2008). Therefore, several new teaching concepts are applied precisely in this domain in the last decade (Yadav & Korb, 2012; Fancsali *et al*, 2018) embedded with innovation and productivity for the future technology-rich society. Programming skill mingled with art of communication and presentation(Ruff&Carter,2009) is the demand of present day curriculum, and modified assessment methodologies based on the various learning tools and materials available in web (Saini*et al*, 2014) are invoked for industry-ready. Here the organization will play a crucial part by allowing the industry-based curriculum in the transition phase of the academics, whereby market requirement is the key factor to design and implement the learner-centric syllabi, and project-based activity becomes one key technique of assimilation of knowledge compared to the customary classroom lectures. In this aspect, software engineering becomes the area of research (Capretz & Ahmed, 2018) where importance of soft skill based project development is emphasized; where the role of teamwork(Jia *et al*, 2017), leadership (Capretz*et al*, 2015), interpersonal skill and socio-cultural factors (Fritz *et al*, 2014) are incorporated. The team factor now gains importance looking at the industrial perspective, and analysis is made based on the primary work carried out Hoegl and Gemuenden in 2001. Policy of the organization should be clearly understood by the team members before implementing the project considering all ethical and environmental point-of-view. In the next few paragraphs, the capstone experience through agile methodology is discussed in details with keen focus to assess one individual's performance and contribution to the team's outcome.

Pedagogy is one of the most neglected areas till this date both in primary, secondary and higher education, and that's is reflected through poor outcome at all the levels, as suggested by NASSCOM (www.nasscom.in). Without proper assimilation of pedagogic principle in the syllabi, traditional teaching is driven away from learner-centric attitude; which is impersonated by the Gross Domestic Product (GDP) of the country, as poor quality of human resource are not added the value in either industrial development, or innovative research. This situation needs to be restored, and thus education technology becomes one of the key subjects of research in recent times (Brown, 2016; Galvis, 2018). When focusing the implementation of pedagogy in the area of computer and information science (Jones, 2013), it is found out that software engineering is the subject where scope of experimentation is possibly maximum through both self and peer assessment techniques (Mcgourty *et al*, 1998). Here comes the concept of teamwork, its assessment and teamwork (Petkovic *et al*, 2006) for effectiveness computation. From classroom boundary (Petkovic *et al*, 2008) to product development, effect of Team Work Quality (TWQ) model is evaluated based on the factors prescribed by Hoegl (Hoegl & Gemuenden, 2001). These six factors include coordination, communication, mutual support, effort, balance of member contribution and cohesion. These factors are basically considered in order to remove the ambiguity and uncertainty generated at the implementation phase, and only mutual coupling and collaboration with good communication between team members can drive to attain the intended result. Performance of each team is judged by both academia and industry level where effective application lies in team formation, and also satisfactorily development of software products are estimated. Team formation and solution of real time projects in software engineering are now considered as a major skill (Petkovic *et al*, 2014) where theoretical concept of project management is reflected through measurable learning outcomes. The outcome may not be the exact solution desired by the industry, but a working prototype will be the best choice under consideration with a good percentage of mappings with required performance. Evaluation methodologies are therefore becomes important, and this becomes a very good classification problem, where analysis should be done by machine learning techniques and other statistical tools for association analysis. One key point may be noted in this context that above-mentioned evaluations can only be performed through project-related activities, may be individual or group; and henceforth, importance of activity based pedagogic principle becomes important in al format of engineering education.

BACKGROUND

Activity learning methodology as described in different textbooks of pedagogy finds the way of implementation in software project management (Likun, 2010) where innovation pattern at managerial level gets extreme priority, and that ensures leadership quality in a team by one of the team members. Role of communication here becomes important between the team leader with other group members. This eventually supports the one of the six attributes prescribed by Hogel (Hoegl & Gemuenden, 2001) mentioned as member contribution. The major goal of software engineering research is to develop software in more reliable and efficient manner where new methodologies and tools are continuously invoked (Vijiyan, 2015); thus speaks in favor of uninterrupted growth. Team Work Quality (TWQ), asset information and configuration management together have a major influence in success of the project (Whyte *et al*, 2016), and huge database handling in efficient manner becomes critically important for analysis of the objective. Percentage of success in these cases fundamentally depends on the attributes considered, which simultaneously enhances complexity of the problem. Apart from computation complexity and initial attributes considered, success rate of a project also depends on several other stray factors, which can't directly influence the course of project, but the time management statistics can heavily be affected. In this context, Gantt chart design is extremely crucial. Thus in a course of computer and information science, strategic teaching in software engineering through project related work can be assigned with group activities, and it also enriches the probability of acquaintance, ultimately helps to produce better human resource in terms of knowledge and skill. This requires critical need of effective assessment methods which will generate measurable outcome of student's performance through project work, and those assessment techniques should be validated by globally (industry representatives) and locally (academicians) distributed software teams. Hence setting up of measurable parameters in generalized form for different projects has the equivalent importance of choices of the parameters, by which actual success rate will be measured. Rigorous testing of the output is required in order to consider it s per industry-standard, and that may also be achieved by publication/presentation in front of independent third parties. Here comes the importance of academic perspective, where meaningful outcome is presented globally and documented based on the findings. In the next sub-section, one of the crucial non-technical points is discussed related with software project management; and the term is teamwork skill.

Teamwork Skill

Teamwork skill is an integral part of engineering education as far recommendation of Accreditation Board for Engineering and Technology (ABET) (www.abet.org), which is not a subject of explicit discussion (Lingard, 2010), but can be learned through active participation in group activities.In the context of present chapter, therefore, one can conclude that software project management is one of the excellent opportunities for the young learners to build the skill, which will prove beneficial once they will join the industry.In this context, the crucial factor is generally oversimplified s the team's success is directly proportional to the teamwork, but that basically ignores the individual's contribution in the team. If one can consider a project is failure that does not mean that all the members have not contributed. Similarly success of a project also gives no warranty that all members equally contribute. Here lies the importance of teaching teamwork skill, and the assessment of individual's contribution, irrespective of success or failure of the project.Introspection to the final outcome of any project reveals that many non-technical factors greatly affect the degree of achievable outcome of it (Lingard& Berry, 2002), like, socio-cultural diversity of the team members, their age and gender, previous work experience and degree of distribution of workload. Therefore, irrespective of final outcome, a certain set of attributes are already set by researchers (Lingard, 2010) which are well established to weigh up individual's performance. According to the researchers ((Lingard, 2010; Lingard& Berry, 2002), success of a project requires collaborative effort, and the team members should attain the following important factors:

1. Attend periodical meetings
2. Completion of individual's task within scheduled time
3. Collection of required information to achieve objective
4. Detailed research as per requirement
5. Active participation in think-pair-share activity
6. Expression of understanding in meetings
7. Propose of alternative and effective ideas
8. Adaptation of different suggestions for better outcome
9. Commitment towards predefined objective

There are other factors as enlisted, but the present group of authors considered these is the fundamentals as these are directly related with the first objective of achieving goals. While actual classification purpose, a set of 85 attributes are considered; whereas these 9 key factors sets the team's motivation for accomplishing the desired. Since teamwork is an essential part as far the pedagogy is concerned, so the evaluation is made by three independent methods: [i] by collecting evidences of one's contribution, [ii] through independent observation, [iii] peer-review by industry. However, development of a new scientific teaching approach is also essential in this context, and where role of the teacher will be the facilitator of thick-pair-share activities. This will cover all detailed discussions between the team members, they are free to share their ideas, they can also take suggestions from peers, and ultimately a contentious will be reached after comprehensive discussion for together reaching ultimate outcome.

If this teamwork is measured w.r.t timescale, then several small incremental steps will be identified which sets the tone of the project. These steps should not be static; rather it should be dynamic, so that errors can be corrected whenever detected. In other words, agile methodology is required for successful teamwork, which will be discussed in following sub-section.

Agile Methodology

It is one of the latest software project management method based on incremental sequences in order to solve any unprecedented errors, if any, and thus allows flexibility than the conventional techniques. Since errors are checked at every stage, so backlogs are cleared and sprint goals are always in track. Empirical study on this method is already carried out by Microsoft (Choudhary&Rakesh, 2016) in development, testing and management phases. Comparative study of different agile methods and hybrid agile methods (Al-Zewairi*et al*, 2017) are also conducted, and result clearly suggests that it is possibly the best method among Software Development Life Cycle (SDLC) models. Depending on type of project, employee characteristics, their mutual cohesion and teamwork skills (Rasnacis&Berzisa, 2017); several types of agile methodologies are already proposed which leads to various types of adaptation and implementation processes. EXtreme programming (XP), Scrum, lean software development, feature driven development, dynamic systems development method are a few which are immensely popular as agile methodologies due to improved accuracy of final outcome (Mikulenas&Kapocius, 2011; Qumer& Henderson-Sellers, 2008). It is customarily different than traditional software development models with 4 aspects(Fowler &Highsmith, 2001), which are listed below:

1. Think-Pair-Share activities between self-organizing and cross-functional teams are more valued than SDLC processes and tools
2. Documentation of the project is less valued than the running status of the software
3. Quality management by satisfying the customer's demand is highly prioritized than contract renewal
4. Plans are flexible in order to give space to innovative ideas

Figure 1 shows a brief life-cycle model using eXtreme programming.

Comparative studies are already carried out (Casteren, 2017) with traditional waterfall model, and severe changes are reflected in industry which is reflected through the adaptation of this technique, precisely Scrum (Raunak & Binkley, 2017). Few preliminary results are reported (Ullah *et al*, 2017) after adaptation of agile method in both local and global contexts.

As far the textbooks are concerned, all the software development life cycles have clear technical approaches which do not consider the human aspect i.e., employee's characteristics. Agile methodology is the first one which takes into account different socio-humanitarian aspects such as competency, cohesion, decision-making ability, analytical ability (Capretz & Ahmed, 2018) etc. Thus, this SDLC may alternatively be termed as mindset of a group of people, clustered to achieve common objective. Thus soft skills play an important aspect in development of software product(Ahmed *et al*, 2012), where Team Work Quality (TWQ) ultimately determines the success rate. Here lies the importance of activity learning implementation in the undergraduate curriculum, where teacher will judge the performance of any student through project management, assigned in different groups, peer-reviewed at the end by industry experts. Though this methodology has certain drawbacks for not considering the conflict and relationship management in the workplace, work environment and ethics etc; still it is best suited for software project management in amore versatile manner by incorporating the six factors proposed by Hogeland Gemuenden. Thus a proper blend of activity learning through project related activities in the curriculum of software engineering will help to essentially measure the outcome of learning (Cordes, 2002) in undergraduate course, together creating a world of computing education.

Figure 1. Brief life cycle model using eXtreme programming

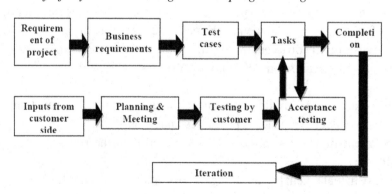

METHODOLOGY

In the present chapter, machine learning based classification problem is described along with statistical measurement for clustering analysis, and ultimately success rate is calculated using various machine learning and meta-heuristic algorithms. Agile methodology is implemented after formation of teams, and henceforth TWQ is calculated for predicting final outcome. The result section is divided of different sub-modules as [i] forming of dataset, [ii] classification and prediction using machine learning techniques, [iii] preprocessing, [iv]authors contribution. Each section is discussed in details with the findings, and based on that, a definite conclusion is reached.

Dataset Used

The dataset is the collection of the team activity of student learning of software engineering teamwork. The data is collected from SETAP Project under San Francisco State University (/archive.ics.uci.edu; Petkovic *et al*, 2016). The data contains information of 74 students teams and more than 100 features are measured for each team and one outcome (class). The details of the dataset is given in Table 1.

The data is collected over a period of time containing software engineering class information of several semesters from students. Student Activity Measures are collected from weekly timecards, instructor observations, and logs containing information about software engineering tool usage. Classes or outcomes are the grade, A (performance at or above expectation) and F (performance below expectation). Data consist of Software engineering process and software engineering product values. Software engineering process represents how well the team applies software engineering practices, and software engineering product measures the quality of the finished product the team produced. Data contains information about software engineering process or software engineering product component of the student team's evaluation for 11 different time interval. Time intervals represent time periods required to achieve different milestone by each team. Various milestones are given in Table 2.

Table 1. Properties of the dataset used

Properties	Values
Number of Instances	64
Number of Attributes	85
Type of value	Real value
Number of Class	2

Table 2. Description of different milestone

Milestone Id	Description
M1	Specification of high level requirements
M2	Specification of more detailed requirements
M3	Release of first prototype
M4	Release of beta version
M5	Final delivery of product

Classification and Prediction

The classification work is done with the UCI dataset of Software Engineering Teamwork Assessment and Prediction (SETAP) process with 85 features or attributes and 64 samples of different software engineering project team. The Table 3 and Table 4 show description of the different features used in the data collection. In Table 3 the description of 40 attributes/features are shown and in Table 4 the description of rest of the 45 attributes/features are shown. In the Table 3 and Table 4, "Avg" means Average and "SD" means Standard Deviation.

In this dataset one of the features is expectation of the completion of the project by the teams which is divided into two classes, above expectations and below expectations. These expectations are used as a class level for the classification task. So for classification rest of the 84 features and 64 samples are used. In this classification task 70% data are used for training and 30% data are used for testing. The classification accuracy with different classifier is shown in the Table 5.

Using decision tree and bagged tree classifier the system is achieving 73.4% accuracy. The Support Vector Machine (SVM) and K-Nearest Neighbor (KNN) give lesser accuracy than Decision tree and Bagged tree when all the 84 attributes are taken together. In respect of the accuracy level this value is not good enough using feature size as much as 84.

RESULT AND DISCUSSION

Two popular Meta-heuristic algorithms namely Particle Swarm Optimization (PSO) (Kennedy &Eberhart, 1995) and Simulated Annealing (SA) (Kirkpatrick *et al*, 1983) is used for optimized feature set selection. PSO is showing far better result with respect to SA when compared with classification accuracy. Using only 2 features the system achieves an accuracy of 78.1% using K-Nearest Neighbor (KNN) (Cover &Hart, 1967) and Support Vector Machine (SVM) (Cristianini&Shawe-Taylor, 2000)

Table 3. Attribute or feature details used in the classification work

Attribute / Feature No	Attribute/ Feature Description
1	Number of Members in the Team
2	Female Team Member Percentage
3	Team Leader Gender
4	Team Distribution
5	Team Member Response Count
6	Number of Meet Hour in Total
7	Number of Meet Hour in an Avg
8	Number of Meet Hour SD
9	In Person Meet Hour in Total
10	In Person Meet Hour in an Avg
11	In Person Meeting Hour SD
12	Non-Code Project Output Hour Total
13	Non-Code Project Output Hour in an Avg
14	Non-Code Project Output Hour SD
15	Code Project Output Hour in Total
16	Code Project Output Hour in an Avg
17	Code Project Output Hour SD
18	Help Hour in Total
19	Help Hour in an Avg
20	Help Hour SD
21	Avg Response in Week
22	SD Response in Week
23	Avg Meet Hour Total in Week
24	SD Meet Hour Total in Week
25	Avg Meet Hour Avg in Week
26	SD Meet Hour Avg in Week
27	Avg in Person Meet Hour Total in Week
28	SD in Person Meet Hour Total in Week
29	Avg in Person Meet Hour Avg in Week
30	SD in Person Meet Hour Avg in Week
31	Avg Non-Code Project Output Hour Total in Week
32	SD Non-Code Project Output Hour Total in Week
33	Avg Non-Code Project Output Hour Avg in Week
34	SD Non-Code Project Output Hour Avg in Week

continued on following page

Table 3. Continued

Attribute / Feature No	Attribute/ Feature Description
35	Avg Code Project Output Hour Total in Week
36	SD Code Project Output Hour Total in Week
37	Avg Code Project Output Hour Avg in Week
38	SD Code Project Output Hour Avg in Week
39	Avg Help Hour Total in Week
40	SD Help Hour Total in Week

Table 4. Attribute or feature details used in the classification work

Attribute / Feature No	Attribute/ Feature Description
41	Avg Help Hour Avg in Week
42	SD Help Hour Avg in Week
43	Avg Response by Student
44	SD Response by Student
45	Avg Meet Hour Total by Student
46	SD Meet Hour Total by Student
47	Avg Meet Hour Avg by Student
48	SD Meet Hour Avg by Student
49	Avg In Person Meet Hour Total by Student
50	SD In Person Meet Hour Total by Student
51	Avg In Person Meet Hour Avg by Student
52	SD In Person Meet Hour Avg by Student
53	Avg Non-Code Project Output Hour Total by Student
54	SD Non-Code Project Output Hour Total by Student
55	Avg Non-Code Project Output Hour Avg by Student
56	SD Non-Code Project Output Hour Avg by Student
57	Avg Code Project Output Hour Total by Student
58	SD Code Project Output Hour Total by Student
59	Avg Code Project Output Hour Avg by Student
60	SD Code Project Output Hour Avg by Student
61	Avg Help Hour Total by Student
62	SD Help Hour Total by Student

continued on following page

Table 4. Continued

Attribute / Feature No	Attribute/ Feature Description
63	Avg Help Hour Avg by Student
64	SD Help Hour Avg by Student
65	Commit Count
66	Unique Commit Message Count
67	Unique Commit Message Percentage
68	Commit Message Length in Total
69	Commit Message Length in an Avg
70	Commit Message Length SD
71	Avg Commit Count in Week
72	SD Commit Count in Week
73	Avg Unique Commit Message Count in Week
74	SD Unique Commit Message Count in Week
75	Avg Unique Commit Message Percentage in Week
76	SD Unique Commit Message Percentage in Week
77	Avg Commit Message Length in Total in Week
78	SD Commit Message Length in Total in Week
79	Avg Commit Count by Student
80	SD Commit Count by Student
81	Avg Unique Commit Message Count by Student
82	Bug Count
83	On Time Bug Count
84	Late Bug Count
85	SE Process Grade (Class Level)

Table 5. Classification with 84 features and 64 samples

Sl No.	Classifier Used	Accuracy (%)
1.	SVM	68.8
2.	Decision Tree	73.4
3.	KNN	71.9
4.	Bagged Tree	73.4

classifier. In Table 6 the accuracy percentage with different number of feature set and the corresponding feature number are shown when the features are selected using Particle Swarm Optimization (PSO) and classification is done using K-Nearest Neighbor (KNN) classifier. In Table 7 the accuracy percentage with different number of feature set and the corresponding feature number are shown when the features are selected using Particle Swarm Optimization (PSO) and classification is done using Support Vector Machine (SVM) classifier. The corresponding description of the feature number given in Table 6, Table 7, Table 8 and Table 9 are given in Table 3 and Table 4. The authors have chosen KNN and SVM for classification with selected features for their stability though their performance with all the features is not good enough. It can be seen that with selected features the accuracy percentage increased around 8-10% in both the cases. Two optimization algorithm used in the work are:

Table 6. Classification with feature selection by PSO using KNN

No of Features	Accuracy (%)	Feature Number
2	78.1	[5, 9]
4	78.1	[15, 28, 67, 59]
10	70.3	[70, 11, 25, 76, 4, 62, 52, 29, 5, 66]
20	68.8	[2, 35, 53, 23, 47, 1, 25, 83, 42, 52, 18, 74, 7, 12, 27, 9, 11, 51, 58, 44]
30	60.9	[44, 62, 68, 39, 4, 1, 73, 36, 37, 65, 18, 82, 67, 48, 66, 50, 6, 83, 60, 34, 21, 13, 15, 32, 19, 46, 57, 35, 9, 8]
40	64.1	[75, 38, 17, 54, 74, 61, 65, 7, 72, 14, 5, 81, 34, 69, 71, 47, 44, 24, 30, 84, 49, 82, 12, 23, 50, 10, 58, 40, 41, 80, 51, 4, 35, 16, 57, 77, 66, 25, 18, 42]
50	68.8	[3, 47, 41, 49, 59, 52, 80, 2, 19, 57, 35, 69, 33, 58, 9, 73, 25, 5, 63, 8, 27, 43, 79, 74, 7, 32, 46, 48, 36, 62, 53, 70, 67, 42, 84, 83, 38, 66, 20, 10, 6, 76, 45, 64, 28, 18, 4, 54, 81, 44]
60	68.8	[50, 38, 15, 66, 17, 16, 78, 4, 34, 65, 33, 21, 52, 57, 42, 46, 49, 63, 80, 25, 39, 11, 26, 28, 59, 82, 2, 79, 35, 64, 31, 61, 62, 12, 18, 32, 75, 19, 56, 84, 20, 5, 29, 54, 36, 51, 6, 40, 53, 45, 24, 27, 69, 10, 73, 70, 76, 72, 41, 83]
70	71.9	[11, 65, 32, 3, 39, 15, 30, 78, 50, 47, 24, 6, 7, 4, 60, 33, 71, 34, 46, 69, 70, 84, 16, 26, 18, 17, 73, 54, 66, 45, 42, 80, 64, 31, 12, 59, 27, 49, 61, 56, 21, 9, 44, 5, 57, 72, 8, 36, 79, 1, 63, 62, 58, 53, 83, 74, 13, 55, 29, 22, 35, 2, 23, 77, 37, 43, 28, 48, 68, 82]
80	71.9	[77, 6, 26, 72, 36, 25, 34, 70, 69, 83, 60, 29, 45, 82, 11, 67, 33, 4, 23, 79, 81, 24, 7, 59, 16, 2, 21, 9, 57, 48, 10, 74, 63, 31, 56, 78, 71, 68, 27, 20, 47, 12, 14, 35, 43, 19, 15, 75, 62, 53, 17, 66, 44, 8, 54, 80, 46, 1, 37, 39, 5, 65, 49, 73, 58, 13, 84, 50, 32, 61, 30, 52, 3, 38, 22, 42, 40, 55, 18, 28]
84	71.9	All 84 Features

Table 7. Classification with feature selection by PSO using SVM

No of Features	Accuracy (%)	Feature Number
2	78.1	[5, 9]
4	75.0	[15, 28, 67, 59]
10	71.9	[70, 11, 25, 76, 4, 62, 52, 29, 5, 66]
20	65.6	[2, 35, 53, 23, 47, 1, 25, 83, 42, 52, 18, 74, 7, 12, 27, 9, 11, 51, 58, 44]
30	59.4	[44, 62, 68, 39, 4, 1, 73, 36, 37, 65, 18, 82, 67, 48, 66, 50, 6, 83, 60, 34, 21, 13, 15, 32, 19, 46, 57, 35, 9, 8]
40	59.4	[75, 38, 17, 54, 74, 61, 65, 7, 72, 14, 5, 81, 34, 69, 71, 47, 44, 24, 30, 84, 49, 82, 12, 23, 50, 10, 58, 40, 41, 80, 51, 4, 35, 16, 57, 77, 66, 25, 18, 42]
50	62.5	[3, 47, 41, 49, 59, 52, 80, 2, 19, 57, 35, 69, 33, 58, 9, 73, 25, 5, 63, 8, 27, 43, 79, 74, 7, 32, 46, 48, 36, 62, 53, 70, 67, 42, 84, 83, 38, 66, 20, 10, 6, 76, 45, 64, 28, 18, 4, 54, 81, 44]
60	62.5	[50, 38, 15, 66, 17, 16, 78, 4, 34, 65, 33, 21, 52, 57, 42, 46, 49, 63, 80, 25, 39, 11, 26, 28, 59, 82, 2, 79, 35, 64, 31, 61, 62, 12, 18, 32, 75, 19, 56, 84, 20, 5, 29, 54, 36, 51, 6, 40, 53, 45, 24, 27, 69, 10, 73, 70, 76, 72, 41, 83]
70	64.1	[11, 65, 32, 3, 39, 15, 30, 78, 50, 47, 24, 6, 7, 4, 60, 33, 71, 34, 46, 69, 70, 84, 16, 26, 18, 17, 73, 54, 66, 45, 42, 80, 64, 31, 12, 59, 27, 49, 61, 56, 21, 9, 44, 5, 57, 72, 8, 36, 79, 1, 63, 62, 58, 53, 83, 74, 13, 55, 29, 22, 35, 2, 23, 77, 37, 43, 28, 48, 68, 82]
80	67.2	[77, 6, 26, 72, 36, 25, 34, 70, 69, 83, 60, 29, 45, 82, 11, 67, 33, 4, 23, 79, 81, 24, 7, 59, 16, 2, 21, 9, 57, 48, 10, 74, 63, 31, 56, 78, 71, 68, 27, 20, 47, 12, 14, 35, 43, 19, 15, 75, 62, 53, 17, 66, 44, 8, 54, 80, 46, 1, 37, 39, 5, 65, 49, 73, 58, 13, 84, 50, 32, 61, 30, 52, 3, 38, 22, 42, 40, 55, 18, 28]
84	68.8	All 84 Features

Particle Swarm Optimization (PSO)

This meta-heuristic optimization algorithm is proposed by Kennedy, Eberhart which is simulated on the social behavior of animals and fish. The search starts from local optima and finds global optima using multiple particles. This PSO is a good optimization algorithm which makes good optimization between local and global optimization.

Simulated Annealing (SA)

This meta-heuristic optimization algorithm simulates the controlled heating and cooling of a metal. This is a single solution meta-heuristic algorithm. SA gives better solution in some cases rather than PSO.

The two classification algorithms used in the work are:

Table 8. Classification with feature selection by SA using KNN

No of Features	Accuracy (%)	Feature Number
2	71.9	[24, 45]
4	70.3	[76, 1, 28, 19]
10	68.8	[56, 75, 9, 3, 73, 54, 57, 51, 60, 29]
20	65.6	[44, 14, 16, 33, 67, 35, 23, 24, 10, 28, 65, 53, 82, 29, 66, 70, 81, 47, 48, 22]
30	68.8	[37, 54, 31, 48, 73, 83, 34, 30, 40, 69, 53, 29, 4, 13, 11, 64, 77, 50, 72, 39, 44, 25, 23, 1, 59, 71, 65, 18, 81, 9]
40	68.8	[11, 54, 15, 25, 3, 63, 55, 75, 59, 50, 69, 39, 32, 74, 78, 20, 57, 14, 18, 36, 6, 49, 4, 16, 62, 10, 83, 48, 56, 33, 24, 60, 82, 17, 65, 47, 19, 67, 68, 5]
50	68.8	[78, 47, 84, 40, 68, 71, 59, 82, 63, 70, 14, 16, 69, 1, 42, 51, 13, 20, 81, 73, 22, 24, 21, 60, 54, 77, 27, 8, 45, 7, 34, 37, 43, 36, 5, 17, 74, 80, 15, 62, 39, 31, 2, 61, 26, 38, 44, 72, 28, 4]
60	68.8	[64, 2, 32, 79, 6, 21, 44, 45, 12, 61, 41, 25, 74, 42, 77, 23, 1, 33, 11, 65, 43, 14, 52, 29, 5, 37, 55, 71, 4, 15, 83, 59, 84, 82, 48, 34, 40, 30, 76, 27, 72, 73, 18, 78, 60, 58, 16, 17, 8, 3, 70, 66, 63, 19, 50, 26, 75, 13, 36, 47]
70	67.2	[51, 34, 70, 43, 40, 82, 48, 47, 3, 84, 75, 52, 73, 25, 15, 68, 21, 32, 57, 45, 41, 65, 71, 17, 7, 36, 81, 37, 35, 23, 20, 22, 60, 67, 55, 33, 80, 72, 76, 58, 13, 5, 24, 77, 2, 50, 42, 64, 10, 1, 12, 14, 28, 27, 8, 31, 49, 53, 9, 74, 16, 39, 30, 19, 78, 69, 11, 79, 4, 38]
80	70.3	[7, 35, 13, 76, 23, 9, 74, 54, 8, 41, 17, 31, 16, 77, 30, 18, 21, 56, 53, 3, 66, 47, 45, 51, 48, 64, 46, 62, 36, 44, 38, 82, 50, 6, 32, 83, 70, 67, 11, 42, 25, 12, 22, 43, 61, 4, 28, 69, 71, 10, 81, 55, 29, 58, 63, 75, 26, 24, 33, 20, 80, 19, 5, 72, 59, 57, 65, 52, 79, 14, 27, 60, 39, 1, 34, 49, 15, 37, 40, 78]
84	71.9	All 84 Features

K-Nearest Neighbor (KNN)

It is a simple machine learning technique, where the input is K number of neighboring training points in the feature space and output is the class membership. It is a fast algorithm with good classification result.

Support Vector Machine (SVM)

It is a supervised classification technique proposed by Siegelmann and Vapnik which constructs a single or multiple hyperplanes in a multi-dimensional space to separate the class. SVM gives better classification result in most of the cases.

Similarly In Table 8 and Table 9 the accuracy percentage with different number of feature set and the corresponding feature number are shown when the features are selected using Simulated Annealing (SA) and classification is done using K-Nearest Neighbor (KNN) and Support Vector Machine (SVM) classifier respectively.

Table 9. Classification with feature selection by SA using SVM

No of Features	Accuracy (%)	Feature Number
2	68.8	[24, 45]
4	68.8	[76, 1, 28, 19]
10	68.8	[56, 75, 9, 3, 73, 54, 57, 51, 60, 29]
20	71.9	[44, 14, 16, 33, 67, 35, 23, 24, 10, 28, 65, 53, 82, 29, 66, 70, 81, 47, 48, 22]
30	68.8	[37, 54, 31, 48, 73, 83, 34, 30, 40, 69, 53, 29, 4, 13, 11, 64, 77, 50, 72, 39, 44, 25, 23, 1, 59, 71, 65, 18, 81, 9]
40	68.8	[11, 54, 15, 25, 3, 63, 55, 75, 59, 50, 69, 39, 32, 74, 78, 20, 57, 14, 18, 36, 6, 49, 4, 16, 62, 10, 83, 48, 56, 33, 24, 60, 82, 17, 65, 47, 19, 67, 68, 5]
50	71.9	[78, 47, 84, 40, 68, 71, 59, 82, 63, 70, 14, 16, 69, 1, 42, 51, 13, 20, 81, 73, 22, 24, 21, 60, 54, 77, 27, 8, 45, 7, 34, 37, 43, 36, 5, 17, 74, 80, 15, 62, 39, 31, 2, 61, 26, 38, 44, 72, 28, 4]
60	71.9	[64, 2, 32, 79, 6, 21, 44, 45, 12, 61, 41, 25, 74, 42, 77, 23, 1, 33, 11, 65, 43, 14, 52, 29, 5, 37, 55, 71, 4, 15, 83, 59, 84, 82, 48, 34, 40, 30, 76, 27, 72, 73, 18, 78, 60, 58, 16, 17, 8, 3, 70, 66, 63, 19, 50, 26, 75, 13, 36, 47]
70	65.6	[51, 34, 70, 43, 40, 82, 48, 47, 3, 84, 75, 52, 73, 25, 15, 68, 21, 32, 57, 45, 41, 65, 71, 17, 7, 36, 81, 37, 35, 23, 20, 22, 60, 67, 55, 33, 80, 72, 76, 58, 13, 5, 24, 77, 2, 50, 42, 64, 10, 1, 12, 14, 28, 27, 8, 31, 49, 53, 9, 74, 16, 39, 30, 19, 78, 69, 11, 79, 4, 38]
80	75.0	[7, 35, 13, 76, 23, 9, 74, 54, 8, 41, 17, 31, 16, 77, 30, 18, 21, 56, 53, 3, 66, 47, 45, 51, 48, 64, 46, 62, 36, 44, 38, 82, 50, 6, 32, 83, 70, 67, 11, 42, 25, 12, 22, 43, 61, 4, 28, 69, 71, 10, 81, 55, 29, 58, 63, 75, 26, 24, 33, 20, 80, 19, 5, 72, 59, 57, 65, 52, 79, 14, 27, 60, 39, 1, 34, 49, 15, 37, 40, 78]
84	68.8	All 84 Features

The Figure 2 and Figure 3 show the variations of accuracy with respect to feature for K-Nearest Neighbor (KNN) and Support Vector Machine (SVM) Classifier when features are selected using Particle Swarm Optimization (PSO) and Simulated Annealing (SA) respectively. It can be seen from the graph that with less number of feature the system produces more accuracy in the class prediction. Also it can be seen that features like Team Member Response Count, In Person Meeting Hours in Total, Standard Deviation Meeting Hours Total by Week, Average Meeting Hours Total by Student, and Standard Deviation in Person Meeting Hours Total by Week are the best features for prediction of class i.e. above expectations and below expectations of the project output.

Figure 2. Number of Feature versus classification accuracy with feature selection by PSO

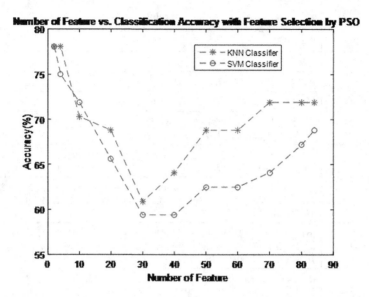

Figure 3. Number of feature versus classification accuracy with feature selection by SA

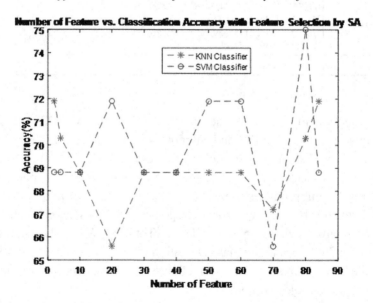

Preprocessing of Dataset for Association Rule Generation

Generally it is found that in a dataset all features do not contributes equally for class determination. Similarly in this work also those top 'n' features are considered which have maximum influence on class. Here top 16 features are considered.

Association Rule Generation

Classification (Agrawal *et al*, 1992; Agrawal *et al*, 1993) is one of the, most popular mechanism of Knowledge Discovery in Databases. Further rule based classifiers are used for determining frequent patterns and correlation between data. In rule based classifier a rule A->B, where A is called antecedent and B is called consequence, represents A can determine B. There are various measures like support, confidence etc. which can be used to determine rules. Popular rule based classifiers are given in Table 10.

These classifiers may generate redundant rules that can be removed by using the concept of closed frequent item sets. In this article authors have used Apriori algorithm for rule generation. Before applying this algorithm, data is preprocessed and converted to binary value.

Apriori Algorithm

Apriori algorithm is one of the most popular rule based classification algorithm in data mining. Data mining or Knowledge discovery is required to predict trends or pattern. Apriori algorithm is used for mining frequent item sets followed by generation of association rules. It is required for databases with lot of transactions. Apriori algorithm is very popular with Market Basket Analysis kind of environment to assist the customers in purchasing items with ease as well as to increases the sales. Apriori algorithm can be represented by following steps-

Table 10. Description of rule based classifier used

Rule Based Classifier	Description
Apriori	Bottom up approach where frequent subsets are extended one item at a time.
FP-Growth	FP tree constructed followed by frequent item sets extraction.
Eclat	Uses vertical dataset for generating frequent item sets

Step 1: Create itemsets containing one item.

Step 2: Calculate support for each itemset.

Step 3: Consider itemsets that have support more than minimum support threshold and remove other itemsets.

Step 4: Use itemsets of step 3 to combine and generate all possible itemsets.

Step 5: Repeat Steps 2 & 4 until there are no more new itemsets.

Apriori uses the above mentioned bottom up approach to generate association rules. In this work as discussed in the preprocessing section, 16 most influential attributes are considered for applying rules given in Table 11 for determining class. In the Table 11, "Avg" means Average and "SD" means Standard Deviation. Values of different parameters are given in Table 12.

Rules generated are in the form antecedent ->consequent. This algorithm has generated many rules, but authors have considered only those rules which have class as consequence. Top 10 such rules with their support and confidence are given in Table 13.

Table 11. Number of attributes used for rule mining

Attribute No	Attribute
1	Number of Members in the Team
2	Female Team Member Percentage
3	Team Leader Gender
4	Number of Meet Hour in Total
5	Number of Meet Hour in an Avg
6	In Person MeetHour in Total
7	Non-Code Project Output Hour Total
8	Code Project Output Hour in Total
9	Help Hour in Total
10	Avg Responses in Week
11	SD Meet Hour Total in Week
12	Avg in Person Meet Hour Total in Week
13	SD in Person Meet Hour Avg in Week
14	Commit Count
15	Bug Count
16	In Time Bug Count

Table 12. Parameters for Apriori algorithm

Parameters	Values
Minimum Support	0.1
Minimum Confidence	0.7
Number of rules generated	2000

Table 13. Top 10 rules generated by Apriori algorithm with class as consequence

Sl. No.	Rules	Support	Confidence
1	SE2 -> SE17	51.5625	75
2	SE10 -> SE17	48.4375	81.5789
3	SE11 -> SE17	35.9375	79.3103
4	SE7 -> SE17	32.8125	77.7778
5	SE13 -> SE17	32.8125	80.7692
6	SE1 -> SE17	31.25	71.4286
7	SE9 -> SE17	31.25	76.9231
8	SE6 -> SE17	29.6875	79.1667
9	SE4 -> SE17	28.125	78.2609
10	SE8 -> SE17	28.125	81.8182

This list is prepared based on decreasing order of support. Here SE17 represents the class and SE1 to SE16 represents the attribute with serial number mentioned in the Table 11 i.e. SE1 means attribute named Number of Members in the Team. Hence a rule, say, SE2 ->SE17 means attribute Female Team Member Percentage determines class with 51.5625% support and 75% confidence. Conversion of each feature to binary value before applying the Apriori rule requires different logic, for example the feature SE1 i.e. Number of Members in the Team is converted to binary based on following logic-

Since mean of Number of Members in the Team is 5.17 so if number of Members in the Team is greater than 5, then the feature is converted to 1 else (number of Members in the Team is less than 5) then it is assigned 0.

Whereas the feature SE2 i.e. Female Team Member Percentage is converted to binary based on following logic-

If number of female member is greater than 0(non- zero), then the feature is converted to 1 else (when number of female member is 0) it is assigned 0.

Similarly for all features different approach is taken for converting them to binary value. Rules generated can be interpreted as (for example) -

Rule 1: SE2 ->SE17 (Support – 51.5625% and Confidence – 75%) means SE2 with value 1 occurs in 51.5625% of transactions (instances/ rows) and out of these many number of transactions, 75% have SE17 also as 1. Hence from the Table 13, one can find which attribute have more occurrence among these transactions as well as which feature have association with class and by what percentage. So these rules can determine the influence of variation of feature value on class and which feature should be given more emphasis for class determination.

CONCLUSION

A methodological approach in system analysis and design for knowledge discovery in Management Information System (MIS) shows the effectiveness of project task assigned in the curriculum of software engineering, and pedagogic approach in this context plays a crucial role for implementation of it in the curriculum. Role of agile methodology becomes decisive as it shows the incorporation of soft skills as attributes while measuring the outcome enhances the success rate of project. Meta-heuristic and machine learning algorithms are applied for computation of classification; and support and confidences are determined by association rule. Maximum accuracy is obtained when two features (Team Member Response Count & In Person Meet Hour in Total) are selected by PSO, and classification is done using KNN and SVM classifiers to obtain the class Software Engineering Process Grade. Maximum confidence is obtained by association rule SE8(Code Deliverable/Project Output Hour in Total)->SE17, whereas it gives minimum support. But maximum support is obtained for SE2(Female Team Member Percentage)->SE17.Nevertheless to mention, SE17 is Software Engineering Process Grade. Thus, a close inspection revealed that formation of team is extremely important as number of female members in a team governs the success of the project, which is also increased by response of the team members in periodical meetings, and time spent by the members in the meeting. These observations also partially support the findings of Hogel where quality of teamwork is prioritized for accomplishment of the project. Thus our research is in accordance with previously predicted observations; whereas novelty lies here in this work, claimed are scientifically justified by meta-heuristic approaches and association analysis. In conclusion, one can say that this finding support the effective implementation of activity learning through project-oriented evaluation, and thus, justifies the title of the chapter.

REFERENCES

Accreditation Board for Engineering and Technology, Inc. (2009). Criteria for Accrediting Engineering Programs. *ABET*. Retrieved from http://www.nasscom. in/sites/default/files/NASSCOM_BPM_Summit_Press_Release_Oct_2017_Final

Afthina, H., Mardiyana, & Pramudya, I. (2017). Think Pair Share Using Realistic Mathematics Education Approach in Geometry Learning. *Journal of Physics: Conference Series, 895*, 012025. doi:10.1088/1742-6596/895/1/012025

Agrawal, R., Ghosh, S. P., Imielinski, T., Iyer, B. R., & Swami, A. N. (1992). An Interval Classifier for Database Mining Applications. *Proceedings of the 18th International Conference on Very Large Data Bases*, 560-573.

Agrawal, R., Imielinski, T., & Swami, A. (1993). Database Mining: A Performance Perspective. *IEEE Transactions on Knowledge and Data Engineering, 5*(6), 914–925. doi:10.1109/69.250074

Ahmed, F., Capretz, L. F., Bouktif, S., & Campbell, P. (2012). Soft skills requirements in software development jobs: A cross-cultural empirical study. *Journal of Systems and Information Technology, 14*(1), 58–81. doi:10.1108/13287261211221137

Al-Zewairi, M., Biltawi, M., Etaiwi, W., & Shaout, A. (2017). Agile Software Development Methodologies:Survey of Surveys. *Journal of Computer and Communications, 5*(05), 74–97. doi:10.4236/jcc.2017.55007

Antonis, K., Daradoumis, T., Papadakis, S., & Simos, C. (2011). Evaluation of the Effectiveness of a Web-Based Learning Design for Adult Computer Science Courses. *IEEE Transactions on Education, 54*(3), 374–380. doi:10.1109/TE.2010.2060263

Arcidiacono, G. (2017). Comparative research about high failure rate of IT projects and opportunities to improve. *PM World Journal, 6*(2), 1–10.

Brown, M. G. (2016). Blended instructional practice: A review of empirical literature on instructors´ adoption and use of online tools in face-to-face. *The Internet and Higher Education, 31*, 1–10. doi:10.1016/j.iheduc.2016.05.001

Capretz, L. F., & Ahmed, F. (2018). A Call to Promote Soft Skills in Software Engineering. *Psychology and Cognitive Sciences, 4*(1), e1–e3. doi:10.17140/PCSOJ-4-e011

Capretz, L. F., Varona, D., & Raza, A. (2015). Influence of personality types in software tasks choices. *Computers in Human Behavior, 52*, 373–378. doi:10.1016/j. chb.2015.05.050

Casteren, W. V. (2017). *The Waterfall Model and the Agile Methodologies: A comparison by project characteristics*. White paper.

Choudhary, B., & Rakesh, S. K. (2016). *An approach using agile method for software development*. Paper presented at the meeting of the International Conference on Innovation and Challenges in Cyber Security. 10.1109/ICICCS.2016.7542304

Cordes, D. (2002). Active learning in computer science: Impacting student behavior. *Frontiers in Education Conference, 1*, T2A/1-T2A/5.

Cover, T. M., & Hart, P. E. (1967). Nearest neighbor pattern classification. *IEEE Transactions on Information Theory, 13*(1), 21–27. doi:10.1109/TIT.1967.1053964

Cristianini, N., & Shawe-Taylor, J. (2000). *An Introduction to Support Vector Machines and other kernel-based learning methods*. Cambridge University Press. doi:10.1017/CBO9780511801389

Emam, K. E., & Koru, A. G. (2008). A Replicated Survey of IT Software Project Failures. *IEEE Software, 25*(5), 84–90. doi:10.1109/MS.2008.107

Fancsali, C., Tigani, L., Isaza, P. T., & Cole, R. (2018). A Landscape Study of Computer Science Education in NYC: Early Findings and Implications for Policy and Practice. *Proceedings of the meeting of the 49th ACM Technical Symposium on Computer Science Education*, 44-49.

Fowler, M., & Highsmith, J. (n.d.). The agile manifesto. *Software Development, 9*(8), 28-35.

Fritz, T., Begel, A., Müller, S. C., Yigit-Elliott, S., & Züger, M. (n.d.). *Using psycho-physiological measures to assess task difficulty in software development*. Paper presented at the meeting of the 36th IEEE International Conference on Software Engineering. 10.1145/2568225.2568266

Galvis, Á. H. (n.d.). Supporting decision-making processes on blended learning in higher education: literature and good practices review. *International Journal of Educational Technology in Higher Education, 15*, 25.

Gog, S. (2016). Competitiveness and Research-Oriented Teaching in Romanian Universities: The Neo-Liberal Transformation of the Higher Education System. *Studia Universitatis Babes-Bolyai Sociologia, 6*(1), 23–62. doi:10.1515ubbs-2015-0002

Guan, X. (2016). The Design and Evaluation of "Flipped Classroom" English Teaching Model Supported by Micro Teaching. *International Conference on Smart City and Systems Engineering.* 10.1109/ICSCSE.2016.0073

Haron, N. A., Devi, P., Hassim, S., Alias, A. H., Tahir, M. M., & Harun, A. N. (2017). Project management practice and its effects on project success in Malaysian construction industry. *Materials Science and Engineering, 291,* ●●●. Retrieved from http://www.abet.org/

Hoegl, M., & Gemuenden, H. G. (2001). Teamwork quality and the success of innovative projects: A theoretical concept and empirical evidence. *Organization Science, 12*(4), 435–449. doi:10.1287/orsc.12.4.435.10635

Jia, J., Mo, H., Capretz, L. F., & Zupeng, C. (2017). Grouping environmental factors influencing individual decision-making behavior in software projects: A cluster analysis. *Journal of Software: Evolution and Process, 29*(10), 1–23.

Jones, D. K. (2013). *Assessment of Communication and Teamwork Skills in Engineering Technology Programs.* Paper presented at the meeting of the 120th ASEE Annual conference & Exposition.

Karabulut-Ilgu, A., Cherrez, N. J., & Jahren, C. T. (2018). A systematic review of research on the flipped learning method in engineering education. *British Journal of Educational Technology, 49*(3), 398–411. doi:10.1111/bjet.12548

Kennedy, J., & Eberhart, R. (1995). Particle Swarm Optimization. *Proceedings of IEEE International Conference on Neural Networks, 4,* 1942–1948. 10.1109/ICNN.1995.488968

Khan, H. H., & Malik, M. N. (2017). Software Standards and Software Failures: A Review With the Perspective of Varying Situational Contexts. *IEEE Access: Practical Innovations, Open Solutions, 5,* 17501–17513. doi:10.1109/ACCESS.2017.2738622

Khan, M., Muhammad, N., Ahmed, M., Saeed, F., & Khan, S. A. (2012). Impact of Activity-Based Teaching on Students' Academic Achievements in Physics at Secondary Level. *Academic Research International, 3*(1), 146–156.

Kirkpatrick, S., Gelatt, C. D. Jr, & Vecchi, M. P. (1983). Optimization by Simulated Annealing. *Science*, *220*(4598), 671–680. doi:10.1126cience.220.4598.671 PMID:17813860

Lee, C., Li, H. C., & Shahrill, M. (2018). Utilizing the Think-Pair-Share Technique in the Learning of Probability. *International Journal on Emerging Mathematics Education*, *2*(1), 49–64. doi:10.12928/ijeme.v2i1.8218

Likun, Z. (2010). *Research on Software Project Management Pattern What Based on Model-Driven.* Paper presented at the meeting of the International Conference of Information Science and Management Engineering. 10.1109/ISME.2010.43

Lingard, R., & Berry, E. (2002). *Teaching Teamwork Skills in Software Engineering based on an understanding of Factors Affecting Group Performance.* Paper presented at the meeting of the 32nd ASEE/IEEE Frontiers in Education Conference. 10.1109/FIE.2002.1158709

Lingard, R. W. (2010). Improving the Teaching of Teamwork Skills in Engineering and Computer Science. Systemics. *Cybernetics and Informatics*, *8*(6), 20–23.

Mcgourty, J., Dominick, P., & Reilly, R. (1998). Incorporating Student Peer Review and Feedback into the Assessment Process. *Proceedings of Frontiers in Education Conference*, 14-18. 10.1109/FIE.1998.736790

McGrath, J. R., & MacEwan, G. (2011). Linking pedagogical practices of activity-based teaching. *The International Journal of Interdisciplinary Social Sciences: Annual Review*, *6*(3), 261–274. doi:10.18848/1833-1882/CGP/v06i03/51803

Mikulenas, G., & Kapocius, K. (2011). *A Framework for Decomposition and Analysis of Agile Methodologies During Their Adaptation. In Information Systems Development* (pp. 547–560). Springer New York.

Petkovic, D., Pérez, M. S., Huang, S., Todtenhoefer, R., Okada, K., Arora, S., . . . Dubey, S. (2014). SETAP: Software Engineering Teamwork Assessment and Prediction Using Machine Learning. *IEEE Frontiers in Education Conference*, 1299-1306.

Petkovic, D., Sosnick-Perez, M., Okada, K., Todtenhoefer, R., Huang, S., Miglani, N., &Vigil, A. (2016). Using the Random Forest Classifier to Assess and Predict Student Learning of Software Engineering Teamwork. *Frontiers in Education FIE 2016.*

Petkovic, D., Thompson, G., & Todtenhöfer, R. (2008). Assessment and comparison of local and global SW engineering practices in a classroom setting. *13th Annual Conference on Innovation and Technology in Computer Science Education*, 78-82. 10.1145/1384271.1384294

Petkovic, E., Todtenhöfer, R., & Thompson, G. (2006). Teaching practical software engineering and global software engineering: case study and recommendations. *36th ASEE/IEEE Frontiers in Education Conference*, 19-24.

Pradana, O. R. Y., Sujadi, I., & Pramudya, I. (2017). Think Pair Share with Formative Assessment for Junior High School Student. *IOP Conf. Series: Journal of Physics*, *895*, 012032. 10.1088/1742-6596/895/1/012032

Qumer, A., & Henderson-Sellers, B. (2008). A framework to support the evaluation, adoption and improvement of agile methods in practice. *Journal of Systems and Software*, *81*(11), 1899–1919. doi:10.1016/j.jss.2007.12.806

Rasnacis, A., & Berzisa, S. (2017). Method for Adaptation and Implementation of Agile Project Management Methodology. *Procedia Computer Science*, *104*, 43–50. doi:10.1016/j.procs.2017.01.055

Raunak, M. S., & Binkley, D. (2017). Agile and other trends in software engineering. *28th Annual Software Technology Conference*. 10.1109/STC.2017.8234457

Ruff, S., & Carter, M. (2009). Communication Learning Outcomes from Software Engineering Professionals: A Basis for Teaching Communication in the Engineering Curriculum. *39th ASEE/IEEE Frontiers in Education Conference*.

Sababha, B. H., Alqudah, Y. A., Abualbasal, A., & AlQaralleh, E. A. (2016). Project-Based Learning to Enhance Teaching Embedded Systems. *Eurasia Journal of Mathematics. Science & Technology Education*, *12*(9), 2575–2585.

Saini, K., Wahid, A., & Purohit, G. N. (2014). Traditional Learning versus Web Based Learning: Performance Analysis. *International Journal of Computer Science and Information Technologies*, *5*(4), 5182–5184.

Sarif, S. M., Ramly, S., Yusof, R., & Fadzillah, N. A. A., & bin-Sulaiman, N. Y. (2018). Investigation of Success and Failure Factors in IT Project Management. *7th International Conference on Kansei Engineering and Emotion Research*, 671-682. 10.1007/978-981-10-8612-0_70

Suriyanti, S., & Yaacob, A. (2016). Exploring Teacher Strategies in Teaching Descriptive Writing in Indonesia. *Malaysian Journal of Learning and Instruction, 13*(2), 71–95.

Ullah, I., Shah, I. A., Ghafoor, F., & Khan, R. U. (2017). Success Factors of Adapting Agile Methods in Global and Local Software Development: A Systematic Literature Review Protocol with Preliminary Results. *International Journal of Computers and Applications, 171*(5), 38–42. doi:10.5120/ijca2017915048

Vijiyan, G. (2015). Current Trends in Software Engineering Research. *Review of Computer Engineering Research, 2*(3), 65–70. doi:10.18488/journal.76/2015.2.3/76.3.65.70

Whyte, J., Stasis, A., & Lindkvist, C. (2016). Managing change in the delivery of complex projects: Configuration management, asset information and 'big data'. *International Journal of Project Management, 34*(2), 339–351. doi:10.1016/j.ijproman.2015.02.006

Yadav, A., & Korb, J. T. (2012). Learning to Teach Computer Science: The Need for a Methods Course. *Communications of the ACM, 55*(11), 31–33. doi:10.1145/2366316.2366327

Zainuddin, Z., & Halili, S. H. (2016). Flipped Classroom Research and Trends from Different Fields of Study. *International Review of Research in Open and Distributed Learning, 17*(3), 313–340. doi:10.19173/irrodl.v17i3.2274

KEY TERMS AND DEFINITIONS

Agile Methodology: It is a continuous iterative procedure of development and testing phases in software development lifecycle in order to enhance the quality of the product, and has been quite significant while incorporating in project teamwork performance evaluation.

Management Information System: It is a computerized database which keeps the track of entire knowledge transmission system in any Institution by means of various activities and also stores the effective outcome by calculating the weight factors of each courses and methods.

Meta-Heuristic Algorithm: It is the algorithm applied to any higher-level procedure (knowledge transition process in this case) to measure the optimized yet efficient outcome from learner-centric point of view where all the input information are not complete enough.

Outcome-Based Education: It is a globally accepted educational model where outcome of the learner is evaluated through project solving based approach by focusing on knowledge gained, skill acquired, and attitude developed.

Project Teamwork Assessment: It is the outcome measurement procedure of knowledge transition through group project activity where application of learning is judged through providing solutions of different industry-oriented real problems.

Success Rate Prediction: It is the final measurement of the percentage of achievement by the group while making the prototype solution of the industry-relevant problem.

Teamwork Quality: It is the parameter which determines the success rate of the project by measuring contributions, problem-solving attitude, focus on the task, working with others; so, it is basically a peer-evaluation rubric.

Chapter 4
Systematic Model for Decision Support System

Ramgopal Kashyap
Amity University Chhattisgarh, India

ABSTRACT

Decision makers require a versatile framework that responds and adjusts to the always changing business conditions. The personal information handling arrangement of an organization can offer the least help since it identified with exchanges. For this situation, the decision support system (DSS) joins human abilities with the abilities of PCs to give productive administration of information, announcing, investigation, displaying, and arranging issues. DSS provides a refinement between organized, semi-organized, and unstructured data. Specifically, a DSS lessens the amount of data to a ridiculous organized sum; because of this, choices are made to help the assembling procedure. The objective of these frameworks is to prevent issues inside the generation procedure. This chapter gives an outline of the state-of-the-art craftsmanship writing on DSS and portrays current methods of DSS-related applications inside assembling situations.

INTRODUCTION

The Decision Support System has three sorts of subsystems which are information administration subsystem, display administration subsystem, and discourse administration subsystem. The DSS manages information and also insight. Information or data which bolster for central leadership could be from inside, outside or individual source except if the information obtained from the sources are appropriately sorted out and recovered, choices won't be right. The model administration will hold the

DOI: 10.4018/978-1-5225-7784-3.ch004

essential models that utilized for investigation. The exchange administration will go about as the UI to the DSS. The leaders speak with the DSS through this subsystem (Renigier-Biłozor, 2013). The theoretical investigation settles on clear that DSS is there in pretty much every one of the associations; anyway, the sort of the frameworks used varies from association to association in light of its degree, development and additionally center capability. The perusing illuminates that choice emotionally supportive network is a need for each association since it truly settles on things less demanding in the primary leadership process through guiding supervisors and also customers to plan choices underneath uncertain conditions — methods for customer server engineering work most of the DSS. It has perceived that present associations make utilization of different sorts of DSS like correspondence driven DSS, information-driven DSS, archive driven DSS, learning driven DSS and model-driven DSS (Chan, Song, Sarker & Plumlee, 2017). Still anyway there is no correct clarification of how a DSS must function; a productive DSS is that offers bolster for chiefs in halfway organized alongside undefined circumstances. In conclusion, an efficient DSS can build by following an orderly approach which comprises of five stages: necessity gathering, plan, prototyping, execution, and also testing and assessment. Moreover, the theoretical investigation clarifies the uniqueness to be controlled by an effective choice emotionally supportive network consequent by the means embroiled in building a productive choice emotionally supportive network.

Decision Support Systems

The principal target of this proposition is proposing a choice emotionally supportive network which can encourage analyzers, progressively organize and select experiments for execution at reconciliation testing. Decision support system is a class of electronic data framework that helps basic leadership exercises. Choice help frameworks planned antiques that have particular usefulness. Also, an appropriately composed DSS is an intelligent programming based structure designed to help leaders assemble valuable data from crude information, archives, individual learning, as well as plans of action to distinguish and take care of issues and settle on choices (Selten, Pittnauer & Hohnisch, 2011). Further, a dynamic basic leadership approach contains the accompanying advances reflected in Figure 1.

As Figure 1 speaks to, to have a dynamic procedure in central leadership, we have to screen, assess and convey our choices ceaselessly. Furthermore, the decisions must be speedy, basic and proficient. By applying this model in our examination, requesting experiments for execution has been changed over to multi-criteria experiment choice and prioritization issue. Through the way toward social event

Figure 1. Dynamic decision-making process

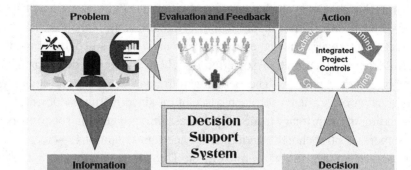

data and directing exploration, we proposed an arrangement of multi-criteria basic leadership strategies for choosing and organizing experiments. Decision support system characterizes "DSS as an intuitive PC based that described DSS as the scholarly assets of an individual with the abilities of the PC to enhance the nature of choices. It is a PC based emotionally supportive network for administration leaders who manage semi-structure issues. The primary goal for which decision emotionally supportive network manufactured today are

- To offer help to Decision producers.
- Discover potential act to determine topics.
- Rank alongside the arrangement distinguished; give a rundown of variable choice and those which can execute.

Subsystems in DSS

A Decision emotionally supportive network has following subsystems.

The Data Management Subsystem

The information which utilized as a part of central leadership originates from database administration framework. The information or data in a primary direction is imperative. The information is of two kinds one is inside the association, i.e., inner source and the other is outside the association, i.e., is an external source. Choices will be legitimate except if the information we gained from these sources is accurately recovered and sorted out. The data can be put away, sorted out and questioned in database administration framework (Bakhrankova, 2010). DBMS programming gives distinctive offices to:

- Database creation can be Modified and erased,
- The information display in the database can control,
- The information in the database can question, and
- Enforce standard and guarantee consistent quality

The Model Management Subsystem

Relationships between various parameters of the framework are possible by demonstrating; models can be planned by examining the activities in an association. A model administration subsystem of decision emotionally supportive network gives offices to viable execution, administration, and production of models. General administration science models arranged into measurable, scientific and operational research models. The model administration subsystem gives the accompanying.

- Creation of models and upkeep of the models should be possible by show administration subsystem.
- Unless interface information from the database can't get in an interface to the database now and again the client may make a particular client model and endeavor to execute the same from the information accessible from the database.

Exchange Management Subsystem

For the client to speak with the DSS, Dialog Management Subsystem goes about as a passage. The significant exercises of Dialog Management Subsystem are

- For the client to discuss effectively with the framework, it gives symbols and menus
- Necessary on-line setting touchy help to various types of clients
- Queries given by the clients are changed over into frames which the other subsystem can perceive and execute and activities performed are followed (Tanure, Nabinger & Becker, 2014).

Decision Making

Decision making as the intellectual procedure bringing the decision of a strategy among the situations, each basic leadership process delivers the last decision. Decisions making is of three kinds:

Structured Decision

The decision accounts of assurance a choice which legitimately arranged known as a Structured Decision. It is anything but difficult to assemble and outline a PC program for organized choice. The choice taken under sureness is dependably the best one (Kang, Lo & Liu, 2014). Anyway, there is a component of hazard appended to future occasions in a few administrative choices because the wild factors are not known totally or with sureness.

Semi-Organized Decision

The decision went out on a limb on account of hazard a choice, in which a few stages organized, and some are an unstructured decision under hazard can have more than one result. It accepted that leaders would know the likelihood of occasions happening, i.e., chiefs will have some learning of how matters will turn out. By considering the probabilities related to the wild info, leaders attempt to take a decent choice which will bring about the great result. Recreation is a model building instrument which is utilized to dissect issues containing wild factors spoke to by likelihood conveyance (Güntzer, Müller, Müller & Schimkat, 2007). The benefit of reenactment demonstrates is that by utilizing arbitrary numbers vulnerabilities can be dealt with factual systems, including probabilities and likelihood appropriation, are the primary devices utilized as a part of tackling issues which have a component of hazard appended to them.

Unstructured Decision

The decision was taken under the instance of vulnerability a choice, in which none of the means organized that is called an unstructured choice. To offer help for structure researcher and specialists are endeavoring to receive human-made brainpower. Basic leadership under vulnerability is only a mystery. Given the levels of vulnerability, probabilities allocated to wild sources of info. Basic leadership in benefit frameworks and their work frameworks can be upheld through different advances also, various means. Choice help inside associations and their different work frameworks regularly connected with DSS. The ordinarily distinguished as having the accompanying three qualities to start with, they are intended to encourage basic leadership forms; second, they should bolster as opposed to robotize central leadership, and; third, they ought to be ready to react to the changing needs of leaders rapidly. The diverse kinds of frameworks and characterizations of DSS are discussed in the chapter. There is no all-around acknowledged definition for the idea of DSS. However, DSSs might be seen all the more barely as original PC based frameworks that are planned to help chiefs tackle specific sorts of choice issues. All the more comprehensively as an umbrella term to depict any data framework that backings central leadership inside an association and its different work frameworks. A case of a tight definition, DSSs as intuitive PC based frameworks, which help leaders in using information and models to take care of unstructured choice issues (Farhadloo, Patterson & Rolland, 2016). DSSs all the more extensively saw as original PC based frameworks, which help individuals utilize PC correspondences, information, records, learning and models to tackle issues and decide. It seen by more specific definition is important to completely catch the idea of necessary leadership and the necessities for choice help inside associations.

Decision Support System Framework

Decision help isn't simply an issue of data frameworks, yet in addition a matter of supporting the advancement of leaders' judgment and understanding, and along these lines a DSS should address as much about demonstrating and understanding the viewpoints, sees, inclinations, qualities and vulnerabilities of the choice producers as helping them use information and models (Kashyap, R., & Gautam, P., 2016). In light of this view DSSs can be characterized as data frameworks that help the basic leadership process, by assisting the chiefs with understanding the issue and investigate the ramifications of their judgment, and henceforth make a choice given comprehension of a specific choice circumstance inside a specific setting. It is likewise seen that choice help inside administration frameworks and their work frameworks ought not to be seen similarly as an issue of data frameworks. as indicated by the current perspective of DSS as a mechanical relic and one of the work framework advancements, yet a more broad perspective of choice help as an issue of utilizing any methods for supporting and encouraging settling on better choices inside administration frameworks and their work frameworks ought to be received. In this way, choice help in benefit frameworks and their work frameworks can improve utilization of any conceivable modernized or no computerized implies for enhancing sense-making and central leadership in a specific dull or non-tedious choice circumstance inside a specific setting. Besides, center around choice bolsters instead of receiving the current perspective of DSS grows the scene to incorporate choice change mediations and systems that may or won't include an ancient mechanical rarity called a DSS (Shibl, Lawley & Debuse, 2013). Given the work framework structure, choice help can originate from a wide range of parts of a working framework through varieties and alterations in any of the nine work framework components. The coming about enhancements estimated regarding choice quality, proficiency and viability of the esteem making work framework procedures and exercises, the mental prosperity of the work framework members. The fulfillment of the clients or other conceivable execution measures a synopsis of potential wellsprings in work frameworks given in Table 1.

Given the coordinated model, it recommended that intricate administration frameworks can see from numerous correlative viewpoints, including the administration biological community, creation framework and work framework points of view. The individual segments and subsystems of the structure through multiple ideas and offering various ramifications for the administration of administration tasks, essential leadership and choice help inside different settings of significant worth creation inside the frame. Inside complex administration frameworks, there are diverse sorts of work frameworks that are related with diverse kinds of generation frameworks' procedures, sanction esteem making exercises vital for benefit arrangement and settle on choices about the activation of administration framework assets, inside various settings of esteem creation at multiple levels of conglomeration inside the biological administration system. Contingent upon the qualities of a workable framework, its related procedures and exercises and its setting of significant worth creation, there

Table 1. Potential wellsprings of choice help in work frameworks

S.N.	Work Framework Element	Potential Choice Helps Sources
1.	Customers	Better approaches to include clients in the primary leadership process and to get a better understanding of their needs
2.	Items and services	Better approaches to assess potential choices and their effects
3.	Procedures and activities	Variations in the methods and exercises, their arrangement of steps, and techniques utilized for performing specific advances
4.	Participants	Better preparing, better ability, and skills information and aptitudes, more elevated amount of responsibility, also, better continuous or deferred criticism
5.	Information	Better data quality, data accessibility, also, data introduction
6.	Technology	Better information stockpiling and recovery, models, calculations, measurable or graphical capacities, and better PC communication
7.	Strategy	A fundamental level different operating system for work framework.
8.	Infrastructure	More viable utilization of a shared foundation
9.	Environment	Better strategies for consolidating worries from the encompassing condition

are contrasts in the idea of necessary leadership procedures and prerequisites for choice help between various sorts of work frameworks (Comes, Hiete, Wijngaards & Schultmann, 2011). It suggested that distinct types of work frameworks, related with multiple kinds of procedures and exercises and working in various settings of significant worth creation inside administration frameworks associated with basic leadership settings where distinctive types of necessary leadership forms overwhelm and diverse sorts of choice help are required, contingent upon the attributes of the primary leadership setting.

Authoritative choices can speak to as a choice chain of importance that mirrors the connection between various levels of hierarchical objectives and destinations that guide the regular exercises and central leadership at multiple levels of an association. Choices relating to the most elevated three levels of the chain of command generally recognized as vital, strategic and operational choices, and necessary leadership forms at these levels usually connected with the hierarchical basic leadership models. The fourth level of options comparing with the operational execution and hands-on exercises is any way additionally critical for the performance of functional activities that convey the work essential to meet the authoritative objectives and goals and execute the procedure (Kashyap, R., Gautam P., & Tiwari, V., 2018). The first leadership forms at this level can frequently connect with naturalistic basic leadership models, and the relating choices are named natural options — the relationship between various kinds of hierarchical exercises and comparing classes given in Figure 2.

Figure 2. An authoritative choice pecking order

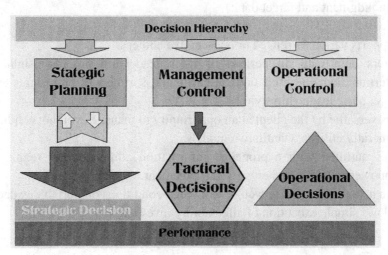

Inside the regular choice pecking order, key level choices characterize general hierarchical objectives also, goals and set the course for an association, they portray an expansive system, in which more nitty-gritty choices can take. Strategic, operational and intuitive options fill in the fundamental points of interest for meeting the authoritative objectives and targets.

Function and Highlights

The DSS's are beneficial devices in Business Intelligence; enable the examination of various factors to help business necessary leadership procedure of administrators:

- It can remove and control data in a flexible way.
- Help unstructured choices.
- Allows the client to characterize data needs and how to join intelligently.
- It, as a rule, incorporates reenactment devices, demonstrating, and so forth.
- It can consolidate data from value-based frameworks inside the organization with another remote organization.

Its primary component is the ability of the multidimensional examination that permits top to bottom data to achieve an abnormal state of detail, examining information from alternate points of view, influence projections of data keeping in mind the end goal to foresee what should occurring later on, incline examination, planned investigation, and so forth (Ursavas, 2014). A DSS bolsters individuals who need to settle on choices at any level of administration, regardless of whether people or gatherings, semi-organized circumstances and in casual, through the mix of human judgment and target data:

- Supports variously related or consecutive choices.
- Offers help with all periods of basic leadership process-insight, plan, determination, and execution, and also an assortment of procedures that are more, basic leadership styles.
- It is versatile by the client at an opportunity to manage evolving conditions.
- Generally utilizes quantitative models.
- DSS outfitted with a propelled information administration segment that empowers a viable and effective arrangement of complex issues.
- Can actualize for use in web or work area conditions on portable gadgets.
- Allows simple execution of affectability investigation.

Architectures

Once more, extraordinary creators distinguish distinctive parts of a DSS identify three essential segments which clarified in more detail:

- The administration arrangement of the information base: Stores data from different sources, may originate from information vaults of a common association, from external sources, for example, Internet or staff of thoughts furthermore, encounters of individual clients.
- The model administration framework: It manages portrayals of occasions, certainties or circumstances by utilizing different kinds of models two illustrations are models of inquiry streamlining and target models (Cheung & Babin, 2006).
- The administration framework and the discoursed generator: It comprises on a client interface; is, apparently, the segment that permits a client to associate with the frame.

   A DSS has four fundamental parts:

- The UI's.
- The information base.
- The logical and demonstrating instruments.
- The DSS's engineering and net.

   Five parts in a DSS:

- **Users:** With various parts or capacities in the basic leadership process leader, specialists, area specialists, framework specialists, information gatherers.
- **Decision Setting:** Must be particular and perceptible.
- **Target Framework:** This portrays a large portion of the inclinations.
- **Knowledge Premise:** Composed of outside information sources, learning databases, working databases, information distribution centers and meta-databases, numerical models and techniques, methodology, deduction and inquiry motors, managerial projects, and frameworks reports.
- **Work Condition:** For the arrangement, investigation, and documentation of choice choices a general design comprising of five particular parts:
- The administration information framework.
- The administration models framework.
- The motor of learning.
- The UI.

- The clients.

Development Conditions

The DSS frameworks are not entirely unexpected from different frameworks and require an organized approach. It gave a situation of three fundamental levels:

Technology Levels

Is the equipment and programming level for DSSs:

1. **Particular DSS:** A Real application that will be utilized by the client. It is the piece of the application that permits the choices making in a fixed issue. The client will have the capacity to act over this fixed issue.
2. **DSS Generator:** This level contains ecological equipment and programming that permits people to have the capacity to grow effortlessly DSS particular applications. This level uses case devices. Likewise incorporates extraordinary programming dialects, capacities libraries, and connected plans.
3. **DSS's Apparatuses:** Contains low-level equipment and programming.

People Required

For the DSS's advancement cycle, five kinds of clients recommended:

1. Last client
2. Middle person
3. Designer
4. Specialized help
5. Frameworks master

The Advancement Approach

The approach given the improvement of a DSS ought to be exceptionally iterative. That will enable the application to be changed and overhauled at various interims. The underlying issue is used to outline the framework, and afterward, it is tried and modified to guarantee that it accomplishes the coveted outcome. There are some ideal models to portray the basic human leadership. Among them, the worldview proposed by Simon is generally tried and utilized. It comprises of three stages, insight, outline and decision. The procedure starts with the Intelligence stage. In this stage, a leader builds up comprehension of the related openings and the issue area by watching the truth a. In the design stage, utilizing a particular model the choice criteria and choices are produced, with the important wild occasions distinguished. The connections between the choices, occasions, and choices must be unmistakably determined and estimated (Szymaniec-Mlicka, 2017). It empowers the choice occasions and other option to be assessed intelligently in the following stage, i.e., Decision stage. In the Implementation stage, the leaders need to reexamine the choice assessment and investigations, and in addition to measuring the outcomes of the proposal.

Types of Decision Support System

Decision Support frameworks are more extraordinary and more typical today than when alter completed his examination and assessed his system, so present DSS requires a most recent more extensive typology of development. A couple of sorts of DSS can be regularly specialists, and also, intelligent people have contended building choice emotionally supportive network as far as four fundamental parts:

- The UI,
- The database,
- The models and investigative instruments and

The DSS design and system these four parts are significant because it can assist troughs and additionally examiner develops a crisp choice emotionally supportive network by discovering the sorts of choice emotionally supportive network or similitudes and dissimilarities between classes. At the point when frameworks are in truth made the accompanying broadened DSS system is at first based on different accentuations situated on DSS parts. This quality, the hugeness of components of a DSS perceived as a principle separating variable. At first from one central component, a few DSS seem to get their usefulness. To keep up the numeral classes in a mostly new structure advantageous. They are Data Driven, Model Driven, and Knowledge-Driven. The expanded structures center on single key measurement by methods for five kinds alongside three auxiliary measurements. The principle qualities in the structure are the first advances that drive or else give choice help usefulness. Five essential composes relying on the common components are contended beneath. They are Communication Driven, Data-driven, Document-driven, Knowledge-driven, and Model-driven choice emotionally supportive networks. A couple of DSS are half breed driven by extra than one key DSS component. The consequent stretched out DSS structure encourages to order the larger part of usually utilized DSS today.

Communication Driven Decision Support System

The correspondence driven DSS comprises of structures developed by choice help aptitude and correspondence partnership. These structures worked, and they distinctively contrasted with DSS writes perceived. That highlights on Shared central leadership bolster, collaboration and also collision. A correspondence driven DSS energizes cooperative choice errands, allow connection between gatherings of individuals, and backings administration and organization together among individuals and comforts sharing of data. An uncomplicated strung or report electronic board mail is the, for the most part, crucial phase of usefulness by methods for differing programming devices and arrangement of individuals works aggregately. Electronic sends, intelligent recordings Video conferencing, sound conferencing, document sharing and report sheets are ideal models of gathering bolster devices. Guides, vendors, buyers and also scientists allude to them as groupware. It permits the gathering partners to think about, mastermind and delivers data controlled. For the advancement of robust groupware frameworks, web foundation assumes a huge part. The newsgroup is great at enabling individuals to deliver information however they can't organize the information. Newsgroup enables the gathering to gather, sort out, rework and eradicate data that is easy to analyze and can change step by step as most recent updates included. This kind of groupware used in additional common gathering rooms, and to enable gatherings to collect from particular geographic spots. It states that the virtual working environment is one more segment of shared processing surroundings proposed to keep up topographically and quickly disconnected workgroups. It is a structure for joining the shifted communitarian capacities (Papathanasiou & Kenward, 2014). To empower correspondence driven choice backings frameworks Stack of programming bundles are existing. The product created to energize the exertion of master bunches for the activity of troublesome ventures is online. An enormous significance is given to look into individuals to communication driven choice emotionally supportive networks. The real examination comprises of the effect of gathering method and gathering cognizance, multi-client limit, simultaneousness administration, association and synchronization inside the gathering. A correspondence driven choice emotionally supportive network is more than once grouped in light of time or area framework by the methods for the distinction between the approximate time and similar place or unique time and different place.

Data-Driven DSS

The information-driven DSS involves spatial decision support system (SDSS) and official data frameworks, administration revealing frameworks and document cabinet, examination frameworks and information warehousing. A portion of the case of information-driven DSS is Business knowledge frameworks related to the information distribution center. Information-driven DSS highlight reach to and administration of enormous records of arranged information and especially a period succession of incoming business information. Most of the fundamental level usefulness provided from Easy and logical record frameworks entered by recuperation and inquiry apparatuses. Information distribution center frameworks that allow the administration of information via electronic apparatuses tweaked for a specific activity and foundation or by new basic devices and administrators offer additional usefulness (Kashyap, R., 2018). Information-driven DSS what's more with online expository preparing gives the first phase of usefulness and addition choice help which is related to the investigation of the large arrangement of prior information. The unordinary information-driven DSS is the Executive Information System (EIS) and the Geographic Information Systems (GIS). An information administration part achieves the data and offers a decision to DSS to pick data given various measures: information-driven DSSare troubled by past information than value-based information (Deng, Hu, Cheung & Luk, 2017). An information-driven choice emotionally supportive network may make utilization of a database intended for the structure, however, for the most part; it is related to new databases.

Document-Driven DSS

The report driven DSS is broadly utilized and pointed at the full help of customer gatherings. Such kinds of DSS are utilized to investigate the web and given the unmistakable arrangement of watchwords and investigate articulations get papers. The standard aptitudes used to partner such DSSs are through customer server framework or web. To offer aggregate record recuperation and concentrate the archive driven DSS set up together a mix of handling and capacity advances. A hunt device to encourage content unique and additionally surveys report bearing offers choice help usefulness, other than the fundamental component is archive base. Cases of records which might include in the database involve rules, and in additional activities, result conditions, pamphlets and past business information including procedures of social event, organization account noteworthy communications likewise. An essential choice bolstered instrument associated with a record driven DSS is investigating motor (Chan, Song, Sarker & Plumlee, 2017). These structures as content situated DSS. Content and archive administration emerged as a critical and widely used robotized route planned for introducing and creating parts of content. The World Wide Web innovation impressively enhanced the convenience of certifications and also, helped the development of Document-driven DSS.

Knowledge-Driven DSS

The learning driven DSS are the comparable Suggestion DSS, which can advise or ask measures to chiefs. There is specific critical thinking expertise for these sorts of choice emotionally supportive networks. The capability comprises of data in regards to a particular field understanding the challenges encompassed inside the area and ability to settle a couple of issues. These frameworks portrayed as proposal DSS and information based DSS. These structures upheld digital reasoning innovation. Human-made brainpower frameworks are developed to find the trick and accelerate monetary exchanges. A great deal of included therapeutic indicative frameworks based on AI and master frameworks; they utilized for setting up a created activity and system based consultative frameworks (Baumeister & Striffler, 2015). As of late learning drive DSS are extensively utilized in light of the interfacing master frameworks innovations to social databases with electronic front closures.

Model Driven DSS

The model-driven DSS are extreme frameworks that help look at choices or select among different choices. These frameworks are utilized by, director, workers of industry or specialists who speak within the association for some; reasons depend upon how the shape is gather planning, choice investigation, and so forth. The model-driven DSS comprises of frameworks that use money related alongside bookkeeping models, advancement models and showing models. A plain deliberate and arithmetical instrument gives the greater part essential usefulness level. In demonstrating driven DSS, the decision producers offer fractional imperative and data to help the chiefs to explore the current conditions anyway in like manner enormous databases isn't for display driven DSS. The essential business device utilized for developing model-driven DSS by the quantitative and budgetary model was called IFPS, a short frame for intuitive monetary arranging framework. Another DSS made for the development of clear frameworks in light of the analytic hierarchy process called expert choice. Individual and cooperative choice settling on is energized by Expert Choice as mechanized portrayal grew liberally; explore enhanced model administration and additionally building up special fluctuated kind of outlines to use in DSS (Logvinov & Tarasov, 2017). Information-driven spatial DSS are additionally normal. Information-driven, record driven and learning driven DSS require specific database components. The model-driven module offers the main usefulness in a model-driven DSS. Ultimately the correspondence and systems administration module is the principal driver of interchanges driven DSS.

BACKGROUND

The levelheaded decision show, together with the idea of limited levelheadedness, gives a premise to some endorsed models of authoritative basic leadership in the administration and choice help writing. The reality setting of authoritative basic leadership and limited judiciousness of human leaders together require following an organized approach and organized process in authoritative basic leadership. The endorsed model of authoritative basic leadership process can partition in three primary stages:

1. Knowledge stage; which includes looking nature for conditions requiring a choice.
2. Configuration stage; which includes designing, creating and breaking down conceivable courses or activity.
3. Decision stage; which includes choosing a specific game-plan from those accessible.

In spite of the fact that the periods of primary leadership process, for the most part, continue in a direct manner, the insight stage by and large going before the plan stage, and the outline stage for the most part going before the decision stage, the general procedure can be more intricate than this succession proposes. Each step in a specific choice circumstance would itself be able to be a problematic primary leadership process, and the general primary leadership process can or may view as a progression of associated and settled sub-forms. For instance, the planning stage may require new knowledge exercises and issues at any given level can produce sub-issues that, thus, have their insight, outline and decision stages (Chen, 2016). The three principle stages can all things considered usually be recognized as the official primary leadership process unfurls. The recommended reliable basic leadership process models, for the most part, expand on the insight; plan Furthermore, decision stages; however much of the time additionally the fourth period of usage is included the models (Ramey, 2013). The usage stage depicts the way toward actualizing an excellent game-plan in the authoritative setting. A case of an endorsed hierarchical primary leadership process shows that expands on this model—the central leadership process display spoke to in Figure 3.

Knowledge Stage

The fundamental knowledge stage exercises incorporate issue distinguishing proof, issue arrangement, and issue disintegration. Issue recognizable proof spotlights on distinguishing a potential issue of concern and characterizing its connection to

Figure 3. Decision-Making process

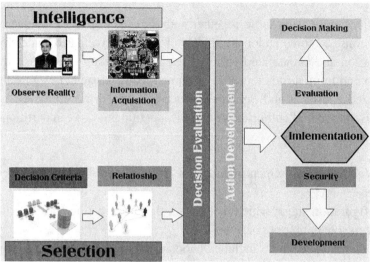

authoritative objectives and targets. Issue circumstances happen due to disappointment with the seen current circumstance in connection to hierarchical objectives and destinations. Disappointment is the consequence of a distinction between what is normal and what is seen to happen truly. In this stage, choice producers endeavor to decide if an issue requiring a choice exists, distinguish its indications and decide its extent, and expressly characterize the issue. Issue characterization includes conceptualizing the choice issue trying to put it in a perceptible class, potentially prompting a standard arrangement approach for natural choice issues. Decision issues can be for the most part sorted agreeing to their level of structured, running from completely organized to absolutely unstructured issue deterioration includes partitioning complex issues into singular sub-issues (Nam, Mi-Jung & Seonhwa Kwag, 2011). Unstructured choice issues may as often as possible made out of numerous interrelated and organized sub-issues. Fruitful decay may conceivably permit concentrating on fathoming an interrelated arrangement of related subproblems, may help to infuse both quantitative and subjective components into choice models and may encourage simpler correspondence between singular chiefs.

Configuration Stage

Amid the outline stage, the first exercises incorporate model plan, decision criteria definition and choice elective age. Show detailing has the reason for conceptualizing the choice issue and abstracting it to a suitable quantitative or subjective shape or a blend of these. The display depicts the relevant piece of the framework and the choice issue in light of the apparent rearranged reality. For some standard issues, there are standard classes of models accessible that give the reason to demonstrating detailing. Decision criteria definition builds up the guideline of decision among choice choices given their attractive quality. Choosing the guideline of decision isn't a piece of the decision stage yet is a piece of characterizing choice targets and consolidating those goals in the detailed choice model (Ramey, 2013). Choice elective age has the motivation behind creating conceivable approaches. Producing choice choices can be a huge and tedious piece of the outline stage that includes looking and inventiveness, is vigorously subject to the accessibility and cost of data and requires mastery in the issue space.

Decision Stage

The decision stage is the one in which the genuine choice and the promise to take after a specific course of action made. Decision stage exercises incorporate the scan for, assessment of any suggestion of a fitting answer for the model. Tackling the model, in any case, isn't the same as illuminating the choice issue that the model speaks. The answer for the model gives a suggested arrangement different option to the choice issue, yet the choice issue can view as illuminated just if the prescribed arrangement elective effectively executed.

Usage Stage

The usage stage exercises rely on the qualities of the choice issue and the chosen arrangement elective, making the exercises hard to characterize. The stage may conceivably incorporate numerous exercises and may include numerous individuals from association partners, making it a mind-boggling process with obscure limits. A shortsighted definition for these exercises can be applying the chose arrangement elective.

Characteristics Controlled by Productive Decision

There is no specific perspective of what a choice emotionally supportive network is. Alongside the regulatory specialist, even the clients offer particular perspectives concerning a DSS. The rundown underneath gives the standard plan of attributes to be controlled by productive choice emotionally supportive networks. It must offer support for central leadership featuring on semi-organized and unstructured position by passing on together individual choice and robotized data chiefs are energized basically in semi-organized and unstructured condition. Such inconveniences can't be replied through mechanized frameworks or throughout standard quantitative techniques or mechanical assembly. Typically these issues include development because the DSS developed. DSS has been able to take care of a couple of related issues. It must offer basic leadership consolation to the executive in every single stage beginning from highest directors to chiefs in addition to must help in joining distinctive levels of administration. It must convey every last period of decision making strategy and additionally ought not totally to lie on the singular model but rather empower a scope of decision-making models (Alfredson & Ohlander, 2016). It must empower both free and related strategies, and additionally, it must not be to a great degree troublesome and befuddling. It ought to energize swarms and additionally people. There might be a situation when the potential client might be specific. In this position, the client's primary concern must determine as hoisted weight age. The above primary uniqueness enables the leaders to make enhanced, more solid choices sensibly and the most vital DSS components give them.

Constructing a Productive Decision Support System

The following section discusses in detail; the stages attracted gathering necessities, outlining, building notwithstanding testing a proficient authoritative choice emotionally supportive network. Purchase a DSS business off the rack bundle and utilize it as may be, purchase a COTS bundle and change it or assemble the DSS to one's desires. For customers wishing a typically arranged Decision Support Systems, the COTS bundles won't be accessible. The necessities planned for the DSS can be perceived and created by relating the customer or authoritative clients (Alfredson & Ohlander, 2016). After the originator has acceptably perceived the client necessities and changes these into framework capabilities, the Decision Support System demonstrating procedure can start. In developing a decision support system, a framework which at all with another PC framework in an official system anyway which perhaps will be connected to the web or else advance database administrations. This framework will comprise the following five things:

- A Computer and USB drive;
- A screen, console, and mouse;
- A printer;
- A modem; and
- Appropriate programming says that the first framework allows a client to acknowledge an outline or sound-related introduction from the PC and to enter from whichever the mouse generally console to PC. A portion of the most recent PCs additionally consent to voice enters, yet these frameworks are by and large limited in their phrasing and furthermore perhaps will

experience issues understanding a couple of the customer's verbiage. The PC may likewise get contributions through a conservative circle or else a floppy plate anyway these won't be moment contributions from the chief which/what are of fixation here. The modem allows the customer to pick up information from assets like web or other electronic records. The product must contain a working framework, web availability, an RDBMS, a spreadsheet, a word processor, a compiler notwithstanding a prototyping dialect. These are fundamental apparatuses one wants to run a PC framework, to develop a Decision Support Systems that can utilize for particular basic leadership activities. As examined before the development of a Decision Support System outline should view as that the Decision Support System will potentially be reached out to contain additional means as time passes.

Designing the DSS in Building a Decision Support System

Decision support system experiences a couple of changes toward achieving the dynamic necessities of the customer. Examination rules circumstance characterized as a case of how a model can arrange to it be able to do effectively unmitigated a while later. Examination rules are four sorts: "correlation against a standard, correlation crosswise over qualities, examination inside traits and judgmental correlation." These standards can a performance screen has appeared in order to the architect may develop a one of a kind outline which has only one dynamic administer with the point of correlation close by a standard by the by the framework ought to make arrangements for whichever of the four choices; the client wants to expand the capacity later. The extensible model through the creator tolerating the imminent of the aggregate arrangement of examination controls other than the planner requires not executing everything.

PROTOTYPING THE DECISION SUPPORT SYSTEM

The change of a model of the decision support system will begin promptly after the decision support system necessities are perceived and assembled. The model must be an execution of a simple release of the plan so the client can test the screens of the decision support systems. Think about an illustration; an architect can assemble a HyperCard model by methods for different screen plans to achieve the customer necessities even though build the screens alluring to keep the client's fixation on the choice system. Instantly after a model has begun the product ought to be a remedy. The strategy utilized in this example was to fabricate an uncomplicated contextual analysis in the organization of perceived outcomes. The architect can check if the model is noting appropriately by applying the required subtle elements (Tiwari S., Gupta R.K., & Kashyap R., 2019). Generally, the framework must be examined to perceive the emergency and repair the model when the mishap has perceived. It is an unmistakable methodology to encourage the developers towards redressing the product.

Implementing the DSS

To shoppers have the capacity to in truth use model like an operational framework if they are eager to. At a few circumstances, it may connote stacking model translator for running the framework albeit prototyping programming licenses the customer to accumulate a run-time framework without the need of the product. e.g., Tool Book. Subsequently prototyped programming can use as an operational framework. Then again, the dominant part customers want an ingeniously arranged programming bundle planned for the decision support systems figure 4 is showing the DSS process.

Figure 4. Decision making process model

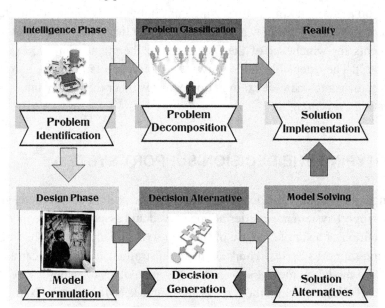

Testing and Evaluating the DSS

Testing and assessment strategy reason for existing is toward allowing the authoritative buyer to explore on the decision support systems to watch whether it fills in as they are willing it to and see the way to improve the decision support system screens. If there should arise an occurrence of any mistakes, the purchaser must note down the blunders and clarify the necessities they wish to have.

Process to Be Attempted for Productive Decision Support System

The accompanying is a few rearrangements about outline and advancement of choice emotionally supportive networks. First, once an errand design foresaw, the focal point of consideration must be on clarification and distinguishing proof of central leadership alongside an examination of choice and the activities embroiled. This technique is known as decision oriented determination. Second, ensuring to distinguishing proof, the designers should do plausibility consider and, in a few conditions, put a possibility report altogether. Third, gave if the errand seems doable, in this manner creator and IS workforce must settle on a choice to buy or build up the foreseen decision emotionally supportive network. In a few conditions, an answer will exist customizing for the decision emotionally supportive network. Fourth, originators must remember that, in like manner, information-driven DSS and model-driven DSS developed by methods for quick prototyping. The correspondence driven DSS are for the most part acquired by purchasing and afterward are introduced in business PC frameworks and end up acquainted with the reasonable strategies (Shukla R., Gupta R.K., & Kashyap R., 2019).

Finally, engineers require broadening deep learning on planning and creating various types of choice emotionally supportive network. The outline drafters are responsible for ensuring that DSS bolstered organization goals and gave being gainful to business. Therefore they need to make sure to go for appropriate arranging and improvement strategies joined with activities to instruct shoppers during the time spent the most recent Decision emotionally supportive network to guarantee it to achieve the business targets and benefit the client. This approach when taken after can help each association to design, execute and pass on efficient and client-responsive DSS to their customers.

Implications for Informatics

The examination of the decision support systems has extraordinary ramifications for informatics. The informatics procedures give an extraordinary help to DSS and enhance basic leadership forms. A DSS can offer the scope of data you require for the central leadership. The administrations gave by such innovation will incorporate the main effect on people and also associations. At display data is circled to the right individual on fitting time, therefore, giving a chief a chance to procure a learned choice. Previously, owed to the low capability of associations to assemble the total data, a leader used to obtain choices considering prior outcomes notwithstanding self-encounters (Xiao & Benbasat, 2018). DSS offers the capacity to complete examinations and judge your choice even before they made and checked what impacts it might cause on your association. Development in data framework grows the points of confinement for decision support systems in compelling and efficient basic leadership. DSS make conceivable the business directors with the choices to choose, design, make, advertise and convey inventive and very much oversaw items and administrations utilizing data.

METHOD EVALUATION

In this part, keeping in mind the end goal to supply possible help and orderly condition for exact research content examination has been set up before interviews. Finding if close by there is a particular example for developing DSS in the present day. The proposing approach for building a client conscious choice emotionally supportive network by investigating the present writing associated with DSS. These designs when customized will assist any establishment with devising, put without hesitation and pass on effective and user responsive DSS to end-customers. The exploration methods we have chosen are related to the DSS give speculations beneficial results and research inquiries; this is built up consequent to the open investigation, information examination, and exact discoveries. In this examination, the significant trouble is about the majority of the decision support system designers must exercise choice situated technique and after that applies either prototyping or software design life cycle (SDLC) strategy. End-user decision emotionally supportive network can be worthy and sparing, and MIS staff must cooperate to keep up such change by one means or another than baffling it when it seems appropriate. Quick prototyping is profitable in developing different sorts of decision emotionally supportive network. However, SDLC has an obligation in developing complex, arrange, venture wide, data-driven Decision emotionally supportive network. DSS examiners and chiefs require being outstanding with every one of the practices for building Decision emotionally supportive network. It makes us out of hermeneutic essentialness to this examination. The reason for the open investigation in our examination is for perceiving the basic attributes of choice emotionally supportive network. The kind of choice emotionally supportive network utilized as a part of the present association, finding if there is a particular standard for building DSS. The recommending approaches for developing a client conscious choice emotionally supportive network by analyzing the introduced writing associated with DSS. Then again exact examination finds answers for the inquiries by social event perceptions of individuals who are extremely worried about developing DSS and passing on them to the customers.

Result Evaluation

In this section, result assessment will take after these criteria: Creditability, Transferability, Dependability, and Conformability.

Creditability

In this part, respectability evaluates from the personal research. While translating the truth specialist's perspective is difficult to escape. Specialists own perspective can acclimate by going completely through the analyst's particular systems and experience practiced in the exploration. In this writing, Credibility assumes an indispensable part in evaluating the outcome. Respectability is the technique for finding out that the results of the personal research are persuading (Kashyap, R., & Gautam, P.,2015). It portrayed that the sort of research methodology utilized as a part of our examination is hermeneutics. The observational examination includes personal research in which exact investigation gives a general thought of cognitive difficulties engaged with developing DSS that is client responsive (Lourenço, Morton & Bana e Costa, 2012). Exact research, for the most part, makes utilization of essential information and the information accumulation strategy. We start with a brief presentation of choice emotionally supportive network took after by how to build a proficient DSS.

Transferability

Transferability is likewise essential in surveying an exploration result can likewise be evaluated from Structure perspective. On the off chance that it is magnificent structure it is simple and evident for the individual who peruses to know the point. We isolated our postulation into experimental and hypothetical outcome to speak to the high caliber and simple structure. The theoretical investigation clarifies that DSS is there in about each organization; anyway, the sort of the framework used changes from organization to organization in light of its volume, arrangement and focus competency. The perusing clarifies that choice emotionally supportive network is a need for any organization since it, by and large, settles on simple the basic leadership process by coordinating the supervisors and additionally customers to get choices in farfetched conditions. In spite of the way that there is no official clarification of how a DSS need to function, an efficient DSS is one that offers to bolster for chiefs in for all intents and purposes organized and also amorphous conditions.

Dependability

Dependability is similar to the possibility of consistent quality in quantitative research. Steadfastness is concerned for the most part with when if the examination rehashed it will give similar outcomes when exploration for the first time. As subjective investigation grants adaptability and singularity of the respondents, it is difficult to figure the condition of trustworthiness (Lourenço, Morton & Bana e Costa, 2012). Notwithstanding, the specialists have tried to set up trustworthiness by keeping up the records and other data assembling in an information stockpiling framework. In the open investigation, data accumulated from a system called as content examination. It is a procedure for looking at printed or oral correspondence in an orderly and perfect form.

Conformability

In this examination, the analysts give the foul data gathered from the audit respondents to ensure similarity. Auxiliary information is foul information that has been beforehand assembled by some others for some official data reason like government review or other approved information or a positive research improvement. In both of these basics the fundamental reason in a social event, such data may be disparate as of the optional client for the most part in the circumstance of a past research venture. The utilization of auxiliary information is every now and again to an optional examination. It is at display conventional for information position to be filed and made available for examination by new specialists.

Possibilities to Sum Up

It is significantly content and meeting based, the respondents are the general population who are working with multinational organizations that are had some expertise in developing and conveying choice emotionally supportive networks. It makes our examination desultory. It is useful for the analysts and individuals contemplating informatics.

Decision Circumstance System

In this part, the non-exclusive decision circumstance structure is a relevant entire of related viewpoints that concerns a chief. The proposed system gives an all-encompassing perspective of the choice circumstance, and it can, for instance, be utilized as a guide while examining a choice circumstance within reach amid early periods of choice help advancement. In the accompanying, the structure introduced completely.

Description of the Choice Circumstance Structure

The structure in Figure 4 is the aftereffect of an intensive examination of basic leadership writing. It portrays critical perspectives identified with a leader and shows the unpredictability of central leadership. Choices can be settled on by various classes of leaders: a) a person leader, b) a group or c) a gathering. Regardless of whether the leader is a person, he or she is additionally frequently a piece of a gathering or an association. It is a piece of the setting in which the chef demonstrations and the choices of intrigue regularly related to an association. The chief manages a choice issue to rearrangement of an organization, another advertising effort or another venture. Such choices issues are not only a decision between options but rather a few more ventures inside a choice procedure are required (Kachwala, Parmar & Vhora, 2012). The choice procedure partitioned into two sections, a "pre-decision" part, and a "post choice" part. The pre-decision stage incorporates, for instance, understanding the issue, creating options, assessing options, and this procedure closes when the leader settles on a decision, i.e., brings about a choice. This choice sees as a result of the choice procedure. The choice is then actualized and maybe later on likewise followed up. As a supplement to the choice circumstance system, we propose the choice procedure display delineated in Figure 5.

A choice procedure comprises of a few basic leadership exercises which can be depicted by choice hypotheses. There are two kinds of distinct speculations of person central leadership, the "customary" predictions that depend on research facility consider, i.e., Judgment and Decision-Making (JDM) and speculations in light of concentrates made in common habitats, i.e., Naturalistic Decision-Making (NDM). JDM speculations center on how individuals settle on decisions from an arrangement of choices, for instance, how decision makers utilize heuristics in complex circumstances and which predispositions, i.e., examples of blunders, they can prompt. Concentrates inside NDM, which expect to depict how choices made in the normal condition. The train of gathering decision making (GDM) addresses questions concerning what describes central leadership with numerous members, what sort of issues they face and how to amass decision making can be enhanced.

Figure 5. Organizational decision-making process

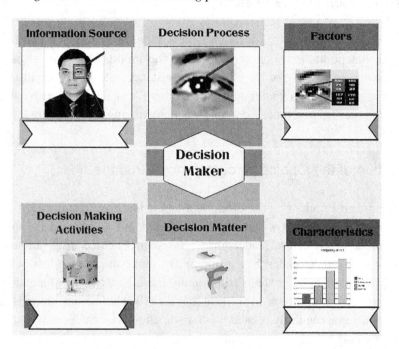

The authoritative basic command considered from various methodologies, e.g., a procedure arranged view, robust strategies see, and a political perspective. The process-oriented viewpoint of ODM depicts how central leadership in associations completed and what objectives utilized. The hierarchical methods see concerns the formal and casual structures of the association, authoritative parts, strategies, and correspondence channels. From the political approach, the bartering procedure is essential, and it likewise centers around control also, its effect on the choice.

Three perspectives influence the chief's conduct while completing basic leadership exercises. These contain a) the qualities of the decision maker, b) elements, and c) data. The leader has attributes, for example, learning, background, identity, and individual capacities, which influence how the chief completes the basic leadership exercises. While a few characteristics, for example, mental composes, and choose styles are unique, different attributes, for example, level of skill, can be recognized for a specific gathering of leaders. The chief's conduct in basic leadership exercises is additionally influenced by factors that start from the unique circumstance (Zhou & Zhao, 2010). There is uncertainty which might be caused by not well-organized issues; general, powerful situations; moving, poorly characterized, or contending objectives or qualities; uncertainty of data; and understanding of the history of choices. Rehashed options and a longitudinal setting that calls for activity and input circles likewise exist. Lastly, there can be hierarchical objectives and standards, time pressure, and high stakes.

The leader gets input, e.g., data from a database or thoughts from an associate that he or she can utilize. This info has attributes, e.g., information quality by including every one of these perspectives, we can portray a relevant entire of related viewpoints that worries a leader, i.e., we can give a photo of the choice circumstances of leaders. The proposed applied model of central leadership and choice help in benefit frameworks gives another point of view on the idea of central command and necessities for choice help in complex administration frameworks. The conventional models of authoritative essential guidance recognize the critical notion of primary direction and choice help in associations and are seen to be appropriate in complex administration frameworks. However, their basic suspicions are perceived to be to a great extent in light of the assembling rationale see on associations and are not saw to be entirely substantial in complex administration frameworks. The qualities of various sorts of basic leadership settings and the types and attributes of their run of the mill choice circumstances are seen to be related to following levels of authoritative exercises. However, it is understood that the conventional portrayal neglects to consider the impacts that the diverse sorts of significant worth making forms, their assignments, and exercises, and the qualities of the standard set of significant worth creation have on the merits of basic leadership settings and their average choice circumstances inside work frameworks at various levels inside complex administration frameworks. Rather than the general see, and suggested that different work frameworks, related with several types of generation frameworks' forms and authorizing esteem making assignments and exercises inside various sorts of shared settings of significant worth creation inside the administration environment (Kashyap, R., & Tiwari, V., 2018). These are with multiple kinds of basic leadership settings whose qualities are not controlled by their level inside complex administration frameworks, yet by the conditions of their esteem making forms, their undertakings and exercises, and the attributes of their shared set of significant worth creation inside the administration biological community. A portrayal of various kinds of basic leadership settings inside complex administration frameworks recommended that locations the run of the mill qualities of different sorts of basic leadership settings inside complex administration frameworks and the sequence of the mill center regions of choice help inside various kinds of basic leadership settings. Customarily, levelheaded necessary leadership forms are seen to rule central leadership in associations. Rather than the customary view, it suggests that the idea of the required leadership forms in complex administration frameworks is double, both levelheaded necessary leadership forms and naturalistic necessary leadership forms existing in complex administration frameworks, and having a vital and integral part in central leadership.

Rundown and Reflections

In this part the bland choice circumstance structure the decision circumstance system is a hypothetically based structure that adopts an all-encompassing strategy of the choice circumstance from the perspective of a chief. The system encourages personal investigation of exact information when contemplating central leadership in a specific setting. It might likewise be active in a quantitative explore setting, for instance, organizing the exploration plan. Be that as it may, in this explore venture, it has utilized as a part of a personal research setting. In this manner, we can claim convenience for individual examination. The system underpins the subjective test in three principles a) it empowers a more total portrayal of the choice circumstance; b) it allows the social event of broad data inside each piece of the choice circumstance; and c) it drives us to distinguish genuine choice exercises and in addition finding the actual issues and challenges confronting the chiefs.

In a broad sense, the system empowers an entire portrayal of the choice circumstance and gives predefined classifications, where every classification is spoken to by a "case" in the structure. These predefined classes make it conceivable, in an organized route, to stroll through the information, level by classification, which diminishes the danger of missing vital parts of the choice circumstance. If the expert finds that there isn't sufficient data concerning a specific role, e.g., choice result, it is conceivable to gather corresponding information on this part. The exemplified for the situation think about while missing data concerning the choice result found amid the information examination (Kashyap, R. and Tiwari, V., 2017). Following the contextual investigation examination, it wound up clear there was insufficient data concerning choice result (Zhou & Zhao, 2010). While ten choice matters and two distinctive choice procedures were found for the situation considerably, it was most certainly not conceivable to state how each of these communicated. For instance, the choice matter 'In what manner should the specific prerequisites change overseen?

Moreover, questions raised, for example, are these choices reported and has data concerning the decision disperse to others? The interviewees had depicted how the principle options communicated. By fundamental choice we mean the last choice settled on in every choice process. The first decisions can likewise view as characterizing what the leaders' work "is about." Nonetheless, the results of all sub-choices, which went before the primary choice, were not in the information. We needed to make reciprocal meetings to "fill in the holes." (Waoo, N., Kashyap, R., & Jaiswal, A., 2010). On the off chance that we had not examined our information regarding both choice issue also, choice result, which is recommended by the structure, we question that we had watched the error. Accordingly, a total picture was picked up.

The system empowers the social occasion of large data inside each piece of the choice circumstance, by guiding our thoughtfulness regarding perspectives found in the information that we accept are all the more barely noticeable without the structure. It exemplified at the point when choice issues that as choices by the interviewees were distinguished. Amid the examination, we found that there were more real choice matters than unequivocally enunciated by the interviewees. The choices that they guaranteed they made were of a 'last' sort. A portion of these sub-choices, for instance, 'Which framework prerequisites should have a place with which subsystem?', were "covered up" in the information as exercises

The interviewee talked about them as "things they do." The given case was a critical strategic choice consulted between a few leaders. Along these lines, this data was not discovered specifically given the inquiries asked amid the talk with the session, but since the information was dissected as far as choice issues, as endorsed by the structure. This way, more intensive data concerning the classification was picked up. The system compels us to distinguish good choice exercises and in addition to locating the genuine issues and challenges confronting the chiefs, rather than distinguishing, e.g., sound methodology and data streams. Hierarchical methodology and data streams are, obviously, vital. However, they are insufficient. The decision maker point of view of the structure influences us to center around the necessities and prerequisites of individuals who will utilize the DSS. Utilizing the choice circumstance system we can depict a specific choice circumstance of a specific chief in a human-focused and all-encompassing way. In this postulation, the choice circumstance of chiefs is in the center.

DISCUSSION

DSS differ from various perspectives from working frameworks with the point of passing out business dealings. A few current DSS have anticipated the reason that multi-member frameworks will have the capacity to be used in scattered and compelling circumstances. Such undertaking basic DSS require meeting a few necessities like empowering decentralized and also scattered auxiliary plans, running with no blame even though when arrange is deceitful, empowering versatility among various customer frameworks notwithstanding offering help to a few extra low levels and additionally abnormal state capacities. Such DSS comprises of fluctuated subsystems which create it conclusive for originators to blend them into a single valuable framework. These complexities in joining them into a single powerful framework befuddle the execution of light choice emotionally supportive network. Regardless of whether methods for an assortment of devices manage every one of these difficulties, their occasion of improvement will be exceedingly more if they built from the beginning stage. Hence, to diminish the time and use attracted planning an effective choice emotionally supportive network, they should be accurately created to achieve the whole necessities of customers. It is basic to construct choice emotionally supportive network appropriately by methods for RAD and prototyping systems through the guide of devices like UML (Unified Modeling Language) and advancements like Unified Process (UP) procedure to create them facilitate adaptably and client responsive. The Decision emotionally supportive network design and also advancement technique to develop DSS implied for the present associations must depend laying on the amount of information required its premise additionally, the figure of put customers, whichever portrayal and symptomatic apparatuses used, alongside the amount of anticipated utilize. A great deal of little devoted DSS is built quickly by methods for end-client extension or fast prototyping. Vast endeavor wide DSS are outlined utilizing refined devices and also sorted out and arranged framework examination and change techniques. Producing endeavor wide Decision emotionally supportive network environment remains a compound moreover developmental errand. Regardless of the important development assorted variety formed by the degree and also goal of a Decision emotionally supportive network, each Decision emotionally supportive network contains similar logical system besides adding to a general utility, empowering central leadership. The choice emotionally supportive network must enhance the system of central leadership and additionally diminish the unhelpful punishment of individual data preparing limits. This outcome is achievable from another refined learning of basic leadership hypotheses. A few chairmen involve to a great degree authentic stress concerning computerized choice help which they envision to be handled by choice help creators. To handle the comparative, choice emotionally supportive network examiners require making utilization of their data of authoritative basic leadership while conspiring and evaluating choice emotionally supportive network. Moreover, choice emotionally supportive network examiners require being precautious in their DSS configuration undertakings, and they require avoiding reinforcing the limits of decision producers in a choice emotionally supportive network plan.

CONCLUSION

Making "high-quality" choices isn't an easy activity for people or a gathering of supervisors. DSS plan choice process easy. Individuals have significant confinements which hamper their accomplishment as leaders. Regardless of those limitations, a ton of supervisors takes and have taken successful choices of chief worth and weight by utilizing a choice emotionally supportive network. Subsequently, the reason for a choice emotionally supportive network must be to build up the consistency of successful choices in business. Basic leadership depends on seeing and understanding the consolidated data yield by the framework. An accurately managed choice emotionally supportive network is an intuitive programming based framework expected to help the chiefs to initiate valuable data through the archives, plans of action, crude information and additionally singular comprehension to find and repair the issues and additionally make choices. Superb DSS must help the chiefs to make noteworthy judgments notwithstanding refinement in the information advertised. A DSS must guide supervisor settlement with vulnerability. A DSS should encourage a director to complete the appropriate examination; anyway, it must not support pointless examination. A DSS should enhance a leader's confidence. Confident chiefs contract all the more effectively with chances and also dangers. Administrators require using their basic leadership mastery to make the right choice and after that apply to persuade the ability to exchange the choice. A DSS must not be planned to settle on chiefs cut back on choices, any way to take all the more intentionally adjusted choices. Assessing targets and guidelines is an imperative component of central leadership. Additionally, DSS must not decrease the centrality of norms and the criticalness of expecting errand implied for the decision that is made.DSS must help inventiveness. DSS must not constrain too much a ton game plan in conditions that are indistinct or dubious and must support outline of tradition come. Also, they should be amazingly open and additionally client responsive. Low esteemed or pointless data in a choice emotionally supportive network may bring about data surplus or slanted basic leadership. The choice maker can pick up from improved, all around planned, data given properly, adjusted way. Intelligible examination and graphical shows are typically better than multiple displays and long, composite tablets of records. Current programming dialects offer the basic capacities to build a choice emotionally supportive network to complete an assortment of activities like announcing, the practical introduction of directions, arithmetical and efficient tasks, and information demonstrating and information association. In the present day, hierarchical DSS are basic to process information inside and transversely authoritative points of confinement. Correspondence innovation had upgraded enormously even though a great deal required to be made keeping in mind the end goal to influence sure with the aim of choice to emotionally supportive networks be available when wanted and additionally follow up on fine, the vital capacity and fuse among different frameworks. Technology is creating new choice help capacities; even though a great deal of concentrate moreover faces off regarding the need to happen to utilize the innovative potential profitably.

REFERENCES

Alfredson, J., & Ohlander, U. (2016). System Characteristics and Contextual Constraints for Future Fighter Decision Support. *International Journal of Information System Modeling and Design, 7*(1), 1–17. doi:10.4018/IJISMD.2016010101

Bakhrankova, K. (2010). Decision support system for continuous production. *Industrial Management & Data Systems, 110*(4), 591–610. doi:10.1108/02635571011039043

Baumeister, J., & Striffler, A. (2015). Knowledge-driven systems for episodic decision support. *Knowledge-Based Systems, 88*, 45–56. doi:10.1016/j.knosys.2015.08.008

Chan, S., Song, Q., Sarker, S., & Plumlee, R. (2017). Decision support system (DSS) use and decision performance: DSS motivation and its antecedents. *Information & Management, 54*(7), 934–947. doi:10.1016/j.im.2017.01.006

Chan, S., Song, Q., Sarker, S., & Plumlee, R. (2017). Decision support system (DSS) use and decision performance: DSS motivation and its antecedents. *Information & Management, 54*(7), 934–947. doi:10.1016/j.im.2017.01.006

Chen, X. (2016). Celebrating fifty years of organizational behavior and decision doing research (1966–2016). *Organizational Behavior and Human Decision Processes, 136*, 1–2. doi:10.1016/j.obhdp.2016.09.002

Cheung, W., & Babin, G. (2006). A metadatabase-enabled executive information system (Part A): A flexible and adaptable architecture. *Decision Support Systems, 42*(3), 1589–1598. doi:10.1016/j.dss.2006.01.005

Comes, T., Hiete, M., Wijngaards, N., & Schultmann, F. (2011). Decision maps: A framework for multi-criteria decision support under severe uncertainty. *Decision Support Systems, 52*(1), 108–118. doi:10.1016/j.dss.2011.05.008

Deng, L., Hu, Y., Cheung, J., & Luk, K. (2017). A Data-Driven Decision Support System for Scoliosis Prognosis. *IEEE Access: Practical Innovations, Open Solutions, 5*, 7874–7884. doi:10.1109/ACCESS.2017.2696704

Farhadloo, M., Patterson, R., & Rolland, E. (2016). Modeling customer satisfaction from unstructured data using a Bayesian approach. *Decision Support Systems, 90*, 1–11. doi:10.1016/j.dss.2016.06.010

Güntzer, U., Müller, R., Müller, S., & Schimkat, R. (2007). Retrieval for decision support resources by structured models. *Decision Support Systems, 43*(4), 1117–1132. doi:10.1016/j.dss.2005.07.004

Kachwala, T., Parmar, S., & Vhora, S. (2012). Improve Decision Support System in an Uncertain Situation by Custom-made Framework for Data Mining Technique. *International Journal Of Scientific Research*, *2*(4), 55–56. doi:10.15373/22778179/APR2013/21

Kang, L., Lo, Y., & Liu, C. (2014). A Medical Decision Support System Based on Structured Injection Orders. *Advanced Materials Research*, *998-999*, 1527-1531. Retrieved from www.scientific.net/amr.998-999.1527

Kashyap, R. (2018). Object boundary detection through robust active contour based method with global information. *International Journal of Image Mining*, *3*(1), 22. doi:10.1504/IJIM.2018.093008

Kashyap, R., & Gautam, P. (2015). Modified region based segmentation of medical images. In *Proceedings of International Conference on Communication Networks (ICCN)* (pp. 209–216). IEEE. 10.1109/ICCN.2015.41

Kashyap, R., & Gautam, P. (2016). Fast level set method for segmentation of medical images. In *Proceedings of the International Conference on Informatics and Analytics (ICIA-16)*. ACM. 10.1145/2980258.2980302

Kashyap, R., Gautam, P., & Tiwari, V. (2018). Management and monitoring patterns and future scope. In Handbook of Research on Pattern Engineering System Development for Big Data Analytics (pp. 230–251). Hersey, PA: IGI Global.

Kashyap, R., & Tiwari, V. (2017). Energy-based active contour method for image segmentation. *International Journal of Electronic Healthcare*, *9*(2–3), 210–225. doi:10.1504/IJEH.2017.083165

Kashyap, R., & Tiwari, V. (2018). Active contours using global models for medical image segmentation. *International Journal of Computational Systems Engineering*, *4*(2/3), 195. doi:10.1504/IJCSYSE.2018.091404

Logvinov, I., & Tarasov, V. (2017). Geoelectric model of the crust and upper mantle along DSS profile Novoazovsk—Titovka. *Geofizicheskiy Zhurnal*, *37*(3), 139–152. doi:10.24028/gzh.0203-3100.v37i3.2015.111115

Lourenço, J., Morton, A., & Bana e Costa, C. (2012). PROBE—A multicriteria decision support system for portfolio robustness evaluation. *Decision Support Systems*, *54*(1), 534–550. doi:10.1016/j.dss.2012.08.001

Nam, M.-J., & Kwag, S. (2011). The Effect of Individual-Organizational variable on Ethical Decision-making Process in the Organizational Context. *Management & Information Systems Review*, *30*(1), 39–69. doi:10.29214/damis.2011.30.1.002

Papathanasiou, J., & Kenward, R. (2014). Design of a data-driven environmental decision support system and testing of stakeholder data-collection. *Environmental Modelling & Software*, *55*, 92–106. doi:10.1016/j.envsoft.2014.01.025

Ramey, H. (2013). Organizational outcomes of youth involvement in organizational decision making: A synthesis of qualitative research. *Journal of Community Psychology*, *41*(4), 488–504. doi:10.1002/jcop.21553

Renigier-Biłozor, M. (2013). Structure of a decision support subsystem in real estate management. *Folia Oeconomica Stetinensia*, *13*(1), 56–75. doi:10.2478/foli-2013-0007

Selten, R., Pittnauer, S., & Hohnisch, M. (2011). Dealing with Dynamic Decision Problems when Knowledge of the Environment Is Limited: An Approach Based on Goal Systems. *Journal of Behavioral Decision Making*, *25*(5), 443–457. doi:10.1002/bdm.738

Shibl, R., Lawley, M., & Debuse, J. (2013). Factors influencing decision support system acceptance. *Decision Support Systems*, *54*(2), 953–961. doi:10.1016/j.dss.2012.09.018

Shukla, R., Gupta, R. K., & Kashyap, R. (2019). A multiphase pre-copy strategy for the virtual machine migration in cloud. In S. Satapathy, V. Bhateja, & S. Das (Eds.), *Smart Intelligent Computing and Applications. Smart Innovation, Systems and Technologies* (Vol. 104). Singapore: Springer. doi:10.1007/978-981-13-1921-1_43

Szymaniec-Mlicka, K. (2017). The decision-making process in public healthcare entities – identification of the decision-making process type. *Management*, *21*(1), 191–204. doi:10.1515/manment-2015-0088

Tanure, S., Nabinger, C., & Becker, J. (2014). Bioeconomic Model of Decision Support System for Farm Management: Proposal of a Mathematical Model. *Systems Research and Behavioral Science*, *32*(6), 658–671. doi:10.1002res.2252

Tiwari, S., Gupta, R. K., & Kashyap, R. (2019). To enhance web response time using agglomerative clustering technique for web navigation recommendation. In H. Behera, J. Nayak, B. Naik, & A. Abraham (Eds.), *Computational Intelligence in Data Mining. Advances in Intelligent Systems and Computing* (Vol. 711). Singapore: Springer. doi:10.1007/978-981-10-8055-5_59

Ursavas, E. (2014). A decision support system for quayside operations in a container terminal. *Decision Support Systems*, *59*, 312–324. doi:10.1016/j.dss.2014.01.003

Waoo, N., Kashyap, R., & Jaiswal, A. (2010). DNA nano array analysis using hierarchical quality threshold clustering. In *Proceedings of 2010 2nd IEEE International Conference on Information Management and Engineering* (pp. 81-85). IEEE. 10.1109/ICIME.2010.5477579

Xiao, B., & Benbasat, I. (2018). An empirical examination of the influence of biased personalized product recommendations on consumers' decision making outcomes. *Decision Support Systems*, *110*, 46–57. doi:10.1016/j.dss.2018.03.005

Zhou, Y., & Zhao, W. (2010). A study on new product development using a decision circumstance model. *International Journal Of Value Chain Management*, *4*(4), 380. doi:10.1504/IJVCM.2010.036994

ADDITIONAL READING

Juneja, P., & Kashyap, R. (2016). Energy based methods for medical image segmentation. *International Journal of Computers and Applications*, *146*(6), 22–27. doi:10.5120/ijca2016910808

Juneja, P., & Kashyap, R. (2016). Optimal approach for CT image segmentation using improved energy based method. *International Journal of Control Theory and Applications*, *9*(41), 599–608.

Kashyap, R. (2019). Geospatial Big Data, Analytics and IoT: Challenges, Applications and Potential. In H. Das, R. Barik, H. Dubey & D. Sinha Roy, Cloud Computing for Geospatial Big Data Analytics (1st ed., pp. 191-213). Switzerland AG: Springer International Publishing. doi:10.1007/978-3-030-03359-0_9

Kashyap, R., & Gautam, P. (2017). Fast medical image segmentation using energy-based method. *Biometrics: Concepts, Methodologies, Tools, and Applications*, *3*(1), 1017–1042. doi:10.4018/978-1-5225-0983-7.ch040

Kashyap, R., & Gautam, P. (2017). *Fast medical image segmentation using energy-based method* (pp. 35–60). Pattern and Data Analysis in Healthcare Settings, Medical Information Science Reference.

Kashyap, R., & Piersson, A. (2018). *Impact of big data on security. Handbook of Research on Network Forensics and Analysis Techniques* (pp. 283–299). IGI Global. doi:10.4018/978-1-5225-4100-4.ch015

Kashyap, R., & Piersson, A. (2018). Big data challenges and solutions in the medical industries. In Shrivastava, G., Kumar, P., Gupta, B.B., Bala, S., & Dey, N. (Eds.), Handbook of Research on Pattern Engineering System Development for Big Data Analytics (pp. 1-24). Hersey, P.A.: IGI Global. doi:10.4018/978-1-5225-3870-7.ch001

KEY TERMS AND DEFINITIONS

Data Base Management System (DBMS): A DBMS makes it feasible for end clients to create, read, refresh and erase information in a database. The DBMS fills in as an interface between the database and end clients or application programs, guaranteeing that information is reliably sorted out and remains effectively open.

Geographic Information System (GIS): It is a structure for the social affair, overseeing, and examining information. Established in the art of topography, GIS coordinates numerous sorts of information. It explores the spatial area and varieties out layers of data into perceptions utilizing maps and 3D scenes.

Software Development Life Cycle (SDLC): It is a procedure pursued a product venture, inside a product association. It comprises a point by point plan portraying how to create, keep up, supplant and modify or improve explicit programming. The existence cycle characterizes a philosophy for enhancing the nature of programming and the general advancement process.

Chapter 5
Identification of Tectonic Activity and Fault Mechanism From Morphological Signatures

Arunima Nandy
North Eastern Hill University, India

ABSTRACT

Agartala, the capital of Tripura, is one of the most important and populated cities of North-East India. From the aspect of geomorphology, the whole area is characterized by highlands (tilla) and lowlands (lunga). Tectonically, Tripura falls under very active zone (Zone V). Assessment of tectonic activities of this region is very significant. For identification of tectonic activity, morphological or geomorphic signatures play very important role. The chapter identifies the presence of tectonic activity from morphological signatures in and around Agartala city. Landsat 8 OLI, maps from Geological Survey of India, Google Earth imageries have been used in this study. The presence of some lineaments and sag ponds has been identified on the basis of which fault mechanism of Agartala and Baramura hills has been delineated. This study contains a brief note on the conceptual demonstration of application of GIS and RS technologies and how morphological signatures and satellite images can help us to recognize tectonic activities over a region.

DOI: 10.4018/978-1-5225-7784-3.ch005

INTRODUCTION

Geomorphology: Definition and Scope

The word 'Geomorphology' derives from three Greek words: 'Ge' means *earth*, 'morphe' means *form* and 'logos' meaning *discourse* (Huggett, 2007). Geomorphology is the branch of science, that deals with study of landforms and the processes that form those landforms (Addy, 2013). It investigates the development of landforms and the processes which are acting on them at present. Geological structures and processes control the evolution of landform on a large scale as well as on a small scale basis (Hugget, 2007). According to Thornbury, 1969, there are ten important fundamental concepts of Geomorphology, which are elementary pillar for interpretation of landscapes which are as follows:

Concept 1: "The same physical processes and laws that operate today operated throughout geologic time, although not necessarily always with the same intensity as now"

Concept 2: "Geologic structure is a dominant control factor in the evolution of land forms and is reflected in them".

Concept 3: "To a large degree the earth's surface processes relief because the geomorphic processes operate at different rates".

Concept 4: "Geomorphic processes leave their distinctive imprint upon land forms, and each geomorphic process develops its own characteristic assemblage of land forms".

Concept 5: "As the different erosional agents act upon the earth's surface there is produced an orderly sequence of land forms".

Concept 6: "Complexity of geomorphic evolution is more common than simplicity".

Concept 7: "Little of the earth's topography is older than Tertiary and most of it no older than Pleistocene".

Concept 8: "Proper interpretation of present day landscapes is impossible without a full appreciation of the manifold influences of the geologic and climatic changes during the Pleistocene".

Concept 9: "An appreciation of world climates is necessary to a proper understanding of the varying importance of the different geomorphic processes".

Concept 10: "Geomorphology, although concerned primarily with present day landscapes, attains its maximum usefulness by historical extension".

'Geomorphic processes' refers to all those physical and chemical transforms which effect a modification of the earth's surface feature's form and shape. A 'geomorphic agent or agency' means any kind of natural medium which is capable of removing, transporting and depositing earth's material. Some great geomorphic agents include wind, glaciers, running water (including both concentrated and unconcentrated runoff both), groundwater, waves, current tides and tsunami (Thornbury, 1969). Geomorphic processes which shape and reform the earth's surface has been described in Figure 1.

Mathematical analysis and measurement of the configuration of the earth surface, extent and shape of its landforms is known as morphometry (Sedrette et. al, 2016). Geomorphometry or landform morphometry is a branch of geomorphology that deals with quantitative studies of the form of the land surface (Huggett, 2007).

From the concept of Geomorphology, Morphometry and Geomorphometry, the conception of Geomorphic Signatures can be inferred. These signatures are mainly formed and shaped by geomorphic processes that are operating on them from the past and today. Geomorphic signatures are those signatures on the earth surface which help to identify the footprints of tectonic activity and its impact on the formation

Figure 1. Types of geomorphic processes
(Thornbury, 1969)

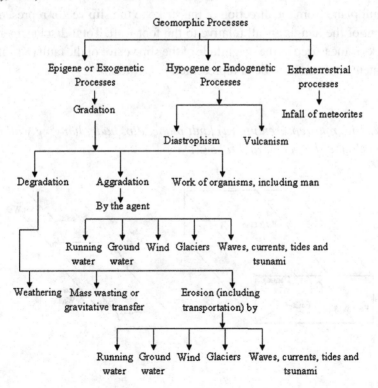

of landforms and on the evolution of earth surface features. These signatures play very important role in assessment of tectonic evolution of the landforms of the earth surface.

Fault: Definition, Elements and Types

Faults are discontinuation or breaks in the continuity of strata associated with a rupture. Displacement of the beds occurs along the plane of rupture. The plane of the discontinuation or fracture, along which relative displacement of rock bed or strata occurs, is called a fault (Vasiliev et. al, 1981).

There are some basic elements of a fault which are fault plane, hanging wall, foot wall, dip, hade, and rake. Fault plane is along which the fault occurs. The blocks above and below of the fault plane is called 'hanging wall' and 'foot wall' respectively. The angle between the fault plane and horizontal surface of the fault is known as 'dip'. The compliment of the dip is known as 'hade'. Another very important element of the fault is the 'angle of slip' or 'rake' (λ). In the concept of movement of blocks along the fault plane 'slip vector' plays a major role. A 'slip vector', that can be characterized by any orientation on the fault plane, is the actual movement of the two wall or blocks on both side of the fault plane. The direction of this slip vector is expressed as the angle of slip or rake (λ). The rake is measured in the fault plane from the direction of the strike to the slip vector representing the movement of the hanging wall relative to the foot wall. Total displacement of the two blocks is measured as the magnitude of the slip vector of the fault (Kayal, 2008). The elements of fault have been represented in figure 2.

Figure 2. Diagram representing (a) fault plane, dip, hade, hanging wall and foot wall; and (b) the slip vector and rake (λ)
(Kayal, 2008)

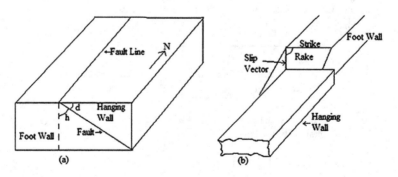

The fault is mainly classified as normal fault, reverse fault, thrust fault and strike slip fault on the basis of the relative movement of the blocks along the fault (Kayal, 2008).

A normal fault refers to that type of fault along which the fault plane dips toward the hanging wall (downthrhrown block) and the downthrown block (hanging wall) is displaced downward in relation to the upthrown block (foot wall). In normal fault, the angle of the fault and the horizontal plane (hade) is 40° to 60°. The fault is referred to as vertical fault when the fault plane is vertical (Vasiliev et. al, 1981).

Another major type of fault is Reverse Fault, where the fault plane dips toward the upthrown block (hanging wall) and this upthrown block is moved upward in relation to the downthrown block (foot wall). The type of fault is characterized by a steeply dipping fault plane that is more than 60° (Vasiliev et. al, 1981).

Tear or wrench fault or strike fault are another important type of fault in which blocks are mostly moved horizontally parallel to the strike of the fault plane. These types of faults are often combinations of normal fault, reverse fault and thrust fault. Complex faults are generally formed when fractures occur in group. Step fault, graben and horst are major example for this complex type of fault. Step fault are actually a system of normal fault where each succeeding block is downthrown in relation to the former one (Vasiliev et. al, 1981).

A system of step faults is a graben. The central part of a graben is downthrown in relation to elevated marginal blocks. A horst is one type of reverse faults. In this type of fault, the peripheral downthrown blocks which are of low elevation in relation to the central part, which is elevated than the surrounding downthrown blocks (Vasiliev et. al, 2008). Different types of fault have been represented in figure 3.

Strike-slip fault is a very unique type of fault along which displacement is basically parallel to the strike of the fault. In this type of fault 'dip-slip component' is less or insignificant which means $\lambda = 0$ or 180°. When $\lambda = 0$, the hanging wall moves to the right and the opposite wall that actually faced by an observer, shift relatively to the left. This type of strike-slip fault is known as left lateral strike slip fault or sinistral fault. When λ is equal to 180°, the hanging wall shifts to the left and in this case the opposite wall that essentially faced by an observer, shifts relatively to the right. This type of strike-slip fault is called as right lateral strike-slip or dextral fault. Generally, λ has a value which is different from special cases of the λ values of dextral and sinistral strike-slip fault. This type of motion is called oblique fault (Kayal, 2008). Different types of slip in faulting have been represented in figure 4.

All these types of faults have some kind of orientation of movement. The dynamic process of seismic wave generation, fault displacement, orientation, and the patterns

Figure 3. Diagram showing the different major types of fault

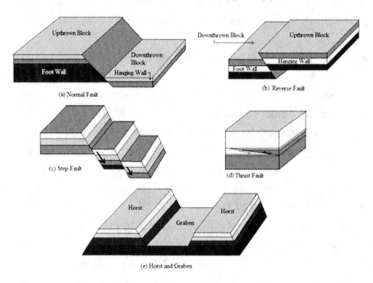

Figure 4. Diagram representing the slip in different faulting: (a) Normal Strike-slip fault, (b) reverse dip-slip fault, (c) strike-slip faulting: Sinistral Fault (dip=90°,λ=0°) and Dextral Fault (dip=90°,λ=180°)
(Kayal, 2008)

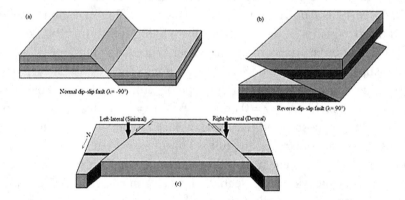

of stress release are referred to as 'Fault-plane solution' or 'focal mechanism'. According to the elastic rebound theory of Reid (1910), the faulting occurs in rock or any rock breaks when the accumulated strain (a change in the size or shape due to any applied forces on any object) in the rock exceeds the strength of the rock (Kayal, 2008). On the basis of elastic rebound theory, the focal mechanism of Strike-slip faulting has been represented in figure 5.

Figure 5. Diagram representing simplistic model of elastic rebound for a focal mechanism (a) dextral fault, (b) sinistral fault and (c) double fault (Llibourty, 2004)

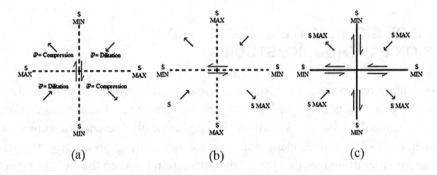

SIGNIFICANCE OF MORPHOLOGICAL SIGNATURES IN TECTONIC STUDY

Tectonic activity and morphological processes and their signatures are interrelated in such a way that identification and examination of morphological signatures can reveal many truths about geomorphological formation and can solve many geological enigmas from the past. Assessments of different morphological signatures that have formed before, during or after any tectonical movement, faulting or earthquake, can expose many facts of tectonic activity of any region. Each morphological processes and tectonic activity have specific surface effects and signatures that are resulted from those processes. These signatures are key factors to identify those specific tectonic activities and their characteristics. For example, surface expressions of folding (result of tectonic movement and compressive force of masses) are folded mountains, valleys, synclinal valley, anticlinal ridge, synclinal ridge, anticlinal valley, homoclinal valley and homoclinal ridge etc. Major resulted landforms from faulting are rift valley (form due to compression and tensional forces), block mountains (form due to raising up of masses during faulting), fault steps (form due to step faults or parallel faults), basins and plateaus (form due to wrapping of earth crust). For strike-slip faulting sag pond is one of the most important surface morphological signatures that give evidence of strike-slip faulting. Sag pond is referred to those ponds or natural lakes or wetlands which are formed between two sides or blocks of an active strike-slip fault or within transtensional or normal fault zone due to tensional movement of the blocks.

Throughout the geological period of tertiary-quaternary, tectonically Tripura remained very active. The geoscientists identified that the evolution of hilly terrain of this region is related with the movement of Indian plate during the past geological period (Dey et. al, 2009). Hence, assessment of tectonic setting of this area is very important from disaster management point of view.

ROLE OF GIS, REMOTE SENSING AND GPS ON EARTHQUAKE STUDIES

Geographical Information System (GIS) is an integrated system of computer hardware, software, spatial and non-spatial data with user interface that captures, stores, retrieves, updates, manipulates, analyzes and displays geographically referenced information or geospatial data. "Remote Sensing is the science of acquiring, processing, analyzing and interpreting of images that record the interaction between the electromagnetic energy and any object" (Sabins, 2013). With the help of these two technologies, researchers, planners and engineers can meet different kind of purposes. Major applications of GIS and RS are: natural resource management, disaster management, geographical and geomorphological studies, urban planning etc.

With the advancement of technology, remote sensing is becoming more important for analyzing, preparedness, forecasting and damage assessment related to various natural hazards example earthquakes, landslides, volcanic eruptions, floods, drought, fires and pollution (soil, water, air).

Among all these major natural and anthropogenic hazards, earthquake is very much devastating hazard which cause a huge damage and loss of habitat and property if it occurs within a populated area. Earthquakes are caused by the sudden "release of strain that has built up in the earth's crust". Maximum zones of high frequency and intensity of earthquake originate at the boundaries between the moving plates that are mainly responsible for the formation of the earth's crust (Sabins, 2013).

An intimate relationship has been established by previous studies (Allen, 1975; Sabins, 2013) that almost all large earthquakes which are generally having magnitudes of greater than 6.0 have originated from ruptures along faults. Some important application of remote sensing and space borne data in earthquake studies are seismic risk analysis, recognition of active faults and mapping of earthquake prone areas with historic earthquakes (Sabins, 2013). Thematic Mapper (TM) and radar data are useful to identify and map actively growing folds, topographic relief and fault scarps. Moderate resolution visible and infrared imageries are used for mapping lineaments. Presence of fresh and active faulting zones is identifiable by the digital image processing of Radar imagery. Presence and extension of discontinuity of contours along the fault zone is identifiable using TM and SAR-DTM data (Dalati, 2018). Some important and basic studies on earthquake, tectonic activities and crustal movement using GPS, Remote Sensing and GIS are:

Mapping of Earthquake Prone Areas

One important method of earthquake studies using remote sensing application is to keep a continuous monitoring of active earthquake zones and also to maintain a historical record of previous earthquakes of those areas. These types of historical records of earthquakes are recorded using seismographs (Sabins, 2013). GIS helps in mapping of these active earthquake zones using the record of historic earthquake with details of magnitude and frequency of earthquakes. Earthquake inventory map can be developed for an earthquake prone region with the help of GIS and RS, which will be helpful for preparing disaster management strategies.

Seismic Risk Analysis

Seismic risk analysis is an established discipline that measures the frequency, intensity of seismicity and its geographical distribution. With the help of GIS and remote sensing, this type of analysis become more accurate as satellite data help to locate accurate location of earthquake in mapping. To find out active earthquake prone zone, GPS data also helps in association with the satellite data. Seismic risk analysis is necessary for planning, locating and designing of power plants, damps, industrial plants, bridges and many more important projects. In those areas which are seismically active (Sabins, 2013). Seismic activities are related with thermal anomalies. Previous studies have find out specific observation on thermal anomalies before strong earthquakes. Thermal anomaly is referred to the unusual increase in the Land Surface Temperature (LST). It occurs few days before an earthquake and the temperature increases between $3°$ to $12°C$ or more and generally it disappears few days after the earthquake. Measurement of the radiation coming from the Earth can be done using the thermal bands. These measurements are used in studies of thermal anomalies for identification of pre-seismic events. Different remote sensing satellites are used for the measurement of thermal anomalies such as Landsat-5, Landsat-7, Landsat-8, Meteosat-5, Terra-MODIS, Aqua-MODIS and NOAA-AVHRR etc. (Kaplan and Avdan, 2017).

Investigation of Crustal Deformation and Active Tectonics

The research fields of crustal deformation, active tectonics and space geodesy evolved with new dimensions with the recent development of Interferometric Synthetic Aperture Radar (InSAR). One of the characteristics of InSAR data has made it unique that it can operate at any weather condition and day or night condition and it can produce continuous high resolution maps of earth's surface strain over large extended areas (InSAR Working Group Report, 2006). The geodetic measurement using InSAR data involves in study with two or more Synthetic Aperture Radar (SAR) images to produce topographic maps or Digital Elevation Model (DEM) using phase information within interferograms. Technique of Differential SAR Interferometry (DInSAR) provides quantification of earth's surface deformation for large spatial coverage with an accuracy of a few millimeters to centimeters. DInSAR provides monitoring of interseismic motion for better assessment of the risk of the seismicity of a region (Karimzadeh et. al, 2011). DInSAR technique which is based on radar satellite data has become a valuable tool for detection and monitoring of ground deformation measurement (Parcharidis et. al, 2009). Inter-seismic activities and post-seismic phases can be studied using InSAR data (Tolomei, 2014). Continuous monitoring and detection of changes of the earth's surface due to activities of seismicity, tectonic, volcanic, hydrologic and anthropogenic with forecasting of wide range of natural hazards is possible with InSAR data. This data has prove its capability in the areas of management of hazards and disasters in terms of monitoring of processes, assessment of damages and forecasting of hazards for example including earthquake, fault, volcanoes, land subsidence, landslides, flood, melting of snow, dam failure, coastal hazards (erosion, shifting etc.), oil spill, forest fire and climatic hazards etc. (Karimzadeh et. al, 2011; InSAR Working Group Report, 2006). Rate of ground movement (both horizontal and vertical) can be measured using InSAR data. For obtaining very high accuracy of deformation studies, different aspects related with GPS processing have to take into consideration such as satellite dynamics, orientation of Earth, reference frame definition, ambiguity resolution (on a global scale), phase centre variation of multipath and antenna, tropospheric and ionospheric delay corrections, tidal and other loading effects (Bastos et. al, 2010). Changes of earth surface in millimeter to centimeter can be detected with the help of this interferometric technique. Large scale crustal movement resulted from active plate motion and earthquake can be studied more precisely with ScanSAR interferometric data (Kumar, 2015). Some of the known limitations of repeat-pass interferometry can be overcome with the recent developments in DInSAR since the end of the 90s. For quantification of fine movement of individual ground and structure points over extended areas, Permanent or Persistent Scatterers Interferometry (PSI) is a useful technique. In this kind of analysis, Interferometric phase stability over time is an important criterion. For mapping scatter deformation history, Interferometric Point target Analysis (IPTA) is one of the most significant methods. IPTA is a specific technique of PSI for studying temporal and spatial characteristics of interferometric signatures that is collected from point targets. Different interferometric techniques such as stacking, repeat-pass and PSI have been widely used for monitoring of faults in urban areas and in seismically active areas worldwide (Parcharidis et. al, 2009).

Application of GIS and Remote Sensing on Identification of Active Fault

Assessment and identification of active fault is now becoming more accurate with the application of GIS and RS. Fault zone mapping, quantification of spatial distribution of scarps (DeLong et. al, 2010), identification and mapping of active faults (Sabins, 2013) can be done using GIS and remote sensing. In remote sensing, slope, aspect, shaded relief, filtering of images, all these processes help to identify fault zones (DeLong et. al, 2010).

Detection of active faults is very much important for assessment of seismic risk. Remote sensing technology and different satellite images provide a detail geological explanation of active fault regions with the field studies of those active faults. Analysis of geomorphic evidences like faulting with surface expression during large shallow earthquakes and radiometric age dating of earlier events of earthquake are new analytical tools for earthquake studies which can be done by remote sensing (Sabins, 2013). Traditional geophysical surveys (in situ) for identification of active faults is time consuming and expensive. Remote sensing technologies can complete these negative drawbacks of procedures of traditional geology. Sometimes transfer of underground water occurs through faults. Some surface parameters are influenced by the presence of underground water, which can be partly identifiable by remote sensing. Among these expressions of surface features which are considered as the representations of the presence of fault are: (a) surface temperature (b) orographic alignments (c) soil moisture. These expressions of surface features can be determined by abrupt discontinuity or alignments of vegetation (Favretto et. al, 2013). To understand framework of faults and deep structures of any geological region, lineament or fault analysis is very efficient remote sensing method. This kind of lineament analysis is based on the identification and examination of analytical features of lineament. These lineaments are identified on the basis of their some specific characteristics such as: (i) ledges and escarpments (ii) rectilinear exposed slopes (iii) rectilinear negative forms of relief (iv) areas with isoline bending and thickening (v) series of small streams straight segments crossing (unidirectional) watersheds and valleys (vi) watersheds characterized by straight axial lines. With the identification of lineaments it is very important to find out which lineament is associated with active fault (Petrov et. al, 2017). Remote sensing technology and satellite images are now widely being used for identification, analysis and mapping of active faults and structures in a certain area (Sabins, 2013; Favretto et. al, 2013; Tronin, 2009). Some important applications of satellite data on identification of active fault are (Sabins, 2013):

- SPOT and Landsat images are very much applicable for identification of stability and regional relationships of faults and also several local details of topographic features and their characteristics.
- Thermal Infrared (IR) images provide record of the presence of active fault with less or no expression on surface.
- Detailed information on landforms and topographic features that are resulted from faulting are provided by aerial photographs and stereo viewing SPOT images.
- Topographic scarps that are associated with active faults are identifiable from the highlight and shadows of aerial photographs which are of low sun angle.
- Radar images are also characterised by highlight and shadows effect that enhance its capability to detect the presence of fault also in forested land.
- Surface effects of earthquakes and identification of surface faulting can be done using satellite data. Radar and SPOT images are useful for analysis of surface effects of earthquake.

Role of GPS on Tectonic Studies

Global Positioning System (GPS) is becoming more promising advanced technology for measuring tectonic movement than conventional methods of tectonic studies. Rate and direction of tectonic movement can be measured using GPS. Continuous monitoring of GPS network and Global Navigation Satellite System (GNSS) data are helpful for examining tectonic characteristics and movement of a region (Aung et. al, 2016). A very high accurate measurement of GPS is necessary for identification and estimation of small plate motions. Space-based techniques such as including GPS, Satellite Laser Ranging (SLR) and Very Long Baseline Interferometry (VLBI) provide accurate quantification of small movements or displacements of points over faults and plate boundaries. The economic advantages and mobility of GPS have increased its applicability for investigation of crustal movement. An accuracy of ±2 mm/yr of horizontal movement of specific points can be detected by GPS. In general, the precision of horizontal displacement or movements of the points are 2 to 4 times higher than the accuracy estimated for changes of elevation (Altiner et. al, 2006). Identification of active lineaments (faults) and examination of their kinematics is possible using Digital Elevation Model (DEM) and from analysis of horizontal surface displacements data of GPS observations (Petrov et. al, 2017). The rapid development Global Navigation Satellite System (GNSS), such as GLObal NAvigation Satellite System (GLONASS) and GPS broadly started to be applied for geodynamic studies from the early 1980s. Global and regional geodynamic problems were started to solve from 1990s with the useful information provided by radio satellite like DORIS (Doppler Orbitography and Radiopositioning Integrated by Satellite) (Bastos et. al, 2010). Space based geodetic measurement is one of the technique to measure rate of motion of all the plates of the earth. Geodesy is the branch of the science that deals with the measurement of the shape and size of the Earth. To monitor phenomena of tectonic activities specific method of geodetic measurement of the NAVSTAR GPS has become popularized worldwide. As the GPS measurement provides positional accuracy with millimeter level, hence GPS measurement allows monitoring of the tectonic movements (Aung et. al, 2016). Application of Seismic and geodetic observations are significant for parameterization of seismic source and fault modeling. Advancement of high rate 1 Hz GPS stations has made it possible to investigate early warning system of earthquake in seismic studies in terms of estimation of total length of rupture area, length of the maximum slip area, approximate position of the centroid of the slip distribution and the value of real time magnitude. GPS measurement can provide better accurate estimation than conventional measurement of intensity of shaking using equations of ground motion prediction. Quantification of early magnitude and shaking intensity can be estimated more accurately with the help of the GPS technology. Compare to the conventional seismic methods, GPS measurement can provide estimation of shaking intensity as a function of distance to the fault rupture rather than distance to the hypocenter (Colombelli et. al, 2013). Crustal deformation can also be studied through GPS observations (Diao et. al, 2016). Intra-plate (deformations within a tectonic plate) and inter-plate (deformations between two or more plates) deformations can be monitored and detectable by permanent networks of GPS. The advantages of continuous GPS data from permanent network of GPS is its capability to detect processes of transient deformation extensively associated with seismotectonic activities and other signals of geophysical activities that were not detectable by fields campaigns of episodic GPS data. Rate of average deformation can be estimated more accurately using daily data of permanent GPS stations rather than periodic GPS measurements of deformations. This continuous GPS deformations data from permanent GPS stations provide better understanding of the properties of noise within the GPS time-series than periodic data, from which, estimation of tectonic motion from the time series of GPS position developed since the last decade (Bastos et. al, 2010). Time series of geodetic displacements signify a valuable contribution to high frequency information provided by the data of seismic studies as GPS stations are capable to register the ground displacement directly without requirement of any complex corrections and any risk of saturation (Colombelli et. al, 2013). Plate boundary observations can be studies using InSAR data with GPS (InSAR Working Group Report, 2006). Monitoring of interseismic behavior of active faults in urban areas is very much important, as the risk increases for the local exposure such as population, infrastructure etc. Recently, repeated measurement of GPS can provide interseismic crustal strains and velocities for active fault areas. In some cases, GPS measurements may face difficulty and get interrupted due to frequent blockage of signal, like in the cases of when the terrain is in remote areas and the accessibility is difficult and sometimes in the case of urban environments (Parcharidis et. al, 2009). These drawbacks can be overcome with the application of satellite images with the measurement of GPS data. Sometimes, inside urban areas, it is not possible to visualize and detect ground measurement easily by traditional survey techniques in terms of with high accuracy and detail. The PSI method has proven to be an exceptional tool to detect ground deformation in urban areas. Specifically, this technique provides much more information on the ground displacements by the method of leveling and D-GPS techniques on the basis of local and regional scale. Several impacts of natural and anthropogenic activities that occur throughout different time and scale and incite ground deformation should be taken into consideration for crustal deformation studies (Parcharidis et. al, 2009). On the basis of the literature survey it can be inferred that, a complete multidisciplinary approach can be an appropriate and compact way of monitoring and quantification of crustal deformation including study of active tectonics, seismology, remote sensing data and continuous GPS monitoring.

METHODOLOGY

This research focuses on identification of tectonic activity and fault mechanism with the help of conventional method as well as with the technical method of using space borne data. To study the tectonic structure of the study area, maps of Geological Survey of India (G.S.I.) 1970s, maps prepared by Khar and Ganju 1984 have been consulted. Landsat 8 OLI data has been used in this study. To understand the geological condition of the region band combinations of 7, 6 and 5 have been prepared. From, the image processing, presence of the tectonic lineaments and the geological structure of the area has been examined. The geomorphological characteristics of the area have been assessed from the landsat data. Google Earth imageries have been used for identifying morphological signatures. Later those images have been compared with the map prepared from the existing tectonic map. From the morphological signatures and tectonic lineaments of the area, fault mechanism of Agartala and its surrounding areas has been studied. Instead of the conventional methods of studying tectonic activity, remote sensing data immensely contributes in assessment of mechanism of fault.

DESCRIPTION OF THE STUDY AREA

For the present study Agartala city, the capital of Tripura has been selected. This is the second-largest city in North-east India after Guwahati in terms of population and economic development. The river Haora lies at the South of the city and Bangladesh is located 2 km from this city. The city extends from latitude 23.75°- 23.90° N and the longitude 91.25°- 91.35° E. As per 2011 census, Population of Agartala city has exceeded 5, 12,000. The land area of Agartala city is mainly depositional composition in character. The region can be divided into two geomorphic units namely highland and low flat land. Agartala has a monsoon influenced humid subtropical climate (District Census Handbook, 2011). According to Dey et. al, 2012, total four types of soils are found at and around Agartala city namely dry sandy soil, sandy clay soil on the highlands and wet clay alluvium and wet sandy alluvium in the lowland areas. The location of the study area has been shown in figure 6.

DATABASE

In this present study, Google Earth Imageries, published maps of Geological Survey of India (GSI), Satellite image have been used. Google Earth Imageries have been studied for identification of wetland in the study area. Tectonic map of GSI has been used to identify the tectonic setting of the region. Landsat image has been used for understanding the surface features of the study area. Landsat 8 OLI data of 26th January, 2017 has been used for this work.

APPLICATION OF GEOGRAPHIC INFORMATION SYSTEM AND REMOTE SENSING ON IDENTIFICATION OF FAULT MECHANISM

The advancement of applications of geomorphometry, geomorphology and geotectonic studies flourishes with the development of Remote Sensing (RS) and Geographical Information System (GIS). Surface characteristics of faulting and geomorphic processes and their signatures become more prominent and easily identifiable with the help of remote sensing. Morphological signatures that can be identified from satellite images reveal the characteristics of tectonic activities and tectonic movement. Fault mechanism of any area can be depicted from this fault movement. Satellite image (Landsat 8 OLI) has been used in this study to assess the tectonic features of the study area. To identify the mechanism of fault, morphological

Figure 6. Location map of the study area

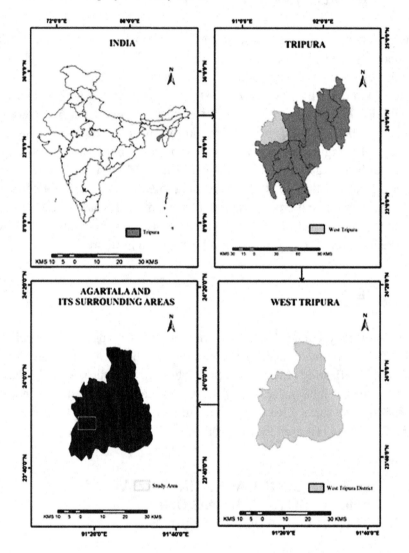

signatures of tectonic activity has been studied of Agartala and its surrounding areas from Google Earth imageries and landsat 8 data.

Morphological Signatures of Tectonic Activity

Morphological signatures are the expression of tectonic activities of any area. In this work, detail study of morphological signatures has been done to identify the tectonic characteristics of Agartala and its surrounding areas. As tectonically this study area fall within very active earthquake prone zone, some prominent fault lines are observed within 75 km of radius from this area. From the evidences of early maps prepared by Geological Survey of India (G.S.I.) 1970s (unpublished), maps prepared by Khar and Ganju 1984, and observation of recent Landsat images (band 7, band 6 and band 5) by the present candidate. Some closer North-South strike-slip faults are detected in Baramura hill (anticlinal part). In the western part of Baramura Hill some South-West to North-East tectonic lineaments are detected. In Agartala city area this tectonic lineament is observed in the low lands of Haora river basin which is presently characterized by thick alluvium deposition. Haora and its tributary river Katakhal developed the elongated valley, most of which are marked by 12-15m elevation. The elevation of the eastern part of this basin in the city is recorded lowest below 6m. Towards the West elevation increases and it rises upto 18-22m. Highlands of this area are mainly observed in Northern and Southern part (more than 22m). Maximum elevation is recorded at North Eastern part. Apart from those highlands a dissected tilla has been measured more than 22m in elevation (College Tilla).

Natural Lakes in the City and Their Tectonic Significances

Agartala and its surrounding areas are marked by many natural lakes. 5 prominent lakes or lake systems are identified towards the Southern part of the detected tectonic lineaments. These lakes are almost parallel and extended from East-West. In the Eastern part of Agartala most prominent natural lakes are founded around Shivnagar, Dhaleswar, and College Tilla. The College Tilla Lake is actually consisting of few lakes surrounding the main College Tilla Lake. Better this College Tilla Lake should be written as College Tilla lake system. Apart from that in the middle part of the basin area another lake has been observed. South to Haora river near Battala very prominent natural lakes are found which are located towards the South of the lineament.

As the city is growing very rapidly, many constructional works are done by capturing wet land areas. The satellite evidences (high resolution image from Google Earth view) shows many parts of the central Agartala where wet lands and evidences of many natural lakes or wet lands are still found. From morphological point of view it can be assessed that Southern part of the detected lineament is characterized by several natural wetlands (lakes which were parallel arranged from South-West direction). Morphological evidences of tectonic activities at and around Agartala and its surrounding areas have been represented in figure 7.

Figure 7. Showing morphological evidences of tectonic activity at and around Agartala City and its surrounding areas

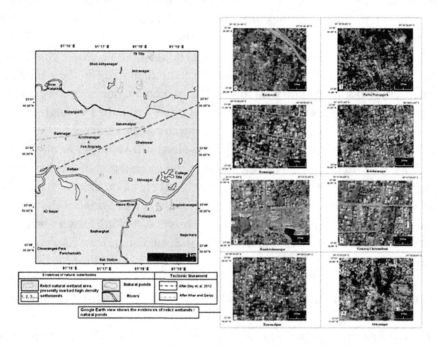

Assessment of Tectonic Features From Satellite Image

Evidences of tectonic activities reveal the tectonic setting of any area. Tectonic structures and landforms revealed by the space borne satellite imagery data has helped in solving many of the geological unsolved questions of the world. In this study, a conceptual theory has been represented that how GIS and Remote Sensing are helpful for studying tectonic characteristics of a region. In Landsat 8 OLI data the Agartala and its surrounding region displays the tectonic setting of the area. From the conventional method of explanation of morphometric signatures, fault mechanism of the study area also has been understood.

To identify the geomorphological characteristics and the morphological signatures bands 7, 6 and 5 of Landsat data have been selected. From the composed image (figure 8.), the river valleys of Agartala region and the ridges are identified. From the West Tripura, only the Agartala city and its surrounding area have been extracted for detail study. From the figure 9, the present natural ponds, wetlands and the relict natural wetlands have been identified. In the center of the city, within Ujjayanta Palace, there are two prominent lakes (known as Rajbari Lake) but as those lakes are man-made, hence those lakes have not been considered as morphological signatures. The relicts

Figure 8. Representation of West Tripura (Bands 7, 6, 5 of Landsat 8 OLI)

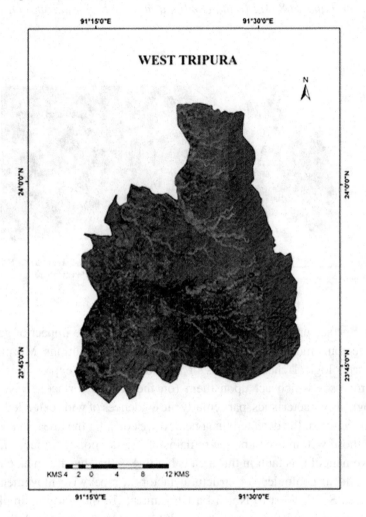

wetlands are now have been covered by settlements and vegetation. According to the explanation in the section b under section no. 7, these evidences of relict wetlands and the present natural wetlands are following the parallel arrangement of South-West direction. The observed natural ponds and relict natural wetlands have been mapped in figure 9.

Identification of Fault Mechanism of Agartala

Evolution of complex and undulating tilla lunga topography can be a resulted landform of a combination of processes of geology, tectonic, climate and surface

Figure 9. Identification of natural ponds and relict natural wetlands in and around Agartala from Landsat 8 OLI (band combination 7, 6, 5 of Landsat 8 OLI)

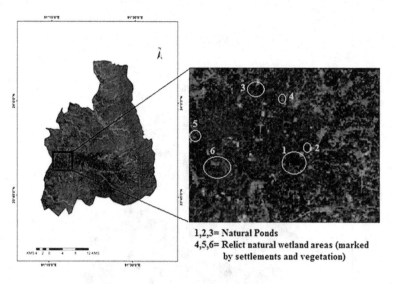

1,2,3= Natural Ponds
4,5,6= Relict natural wetland areas (marked
by settlements and vegetation)

processes. Surface processes make their footprints under the impact of geological structure, tectonic movement, climatic phenomena and conditions. Morphological or geo-morphological characteristics or signatures are the expressions of those surface processes which act upon them (on the earth's surface). Based on the morphological characteristics, particularly the evidences of wide extended wetlands towards the South of the detected lineament, if we consider the lineament as dextral fault then those wetlands can be the remains of the sag ponds. In fact the general strike movement of this fault in this area is North-South. Thus it can be considered that due to local geological or structural factors a clockwise movement started which caused South-West to North-East lineament. In the study a simple model based on Mackenji and Jackson (1983; 1986) has been prepared and plotted with the environmental condition of Agartala. The fault mechanism of Agartala and its surrounding areas has been represented in figure 10. This clearly support that the present existing wetlands are the evidence of early tectonic movements. Between Battala (West) to College Tilla (East) several wetlands were there which are now captured for settlement development (soil filling). In those areas water level detected 2-3m depth which strongly support that before the development of dense settlements, those areas were completely under wetlands environmental condition.

Very sound evidence of early existence of sag ponds is the high level of leaning of houses. Between Battala to College Tilla area high leaning of houses has been observed. The main reason of this leaning is unplanned soil filling in the wetlands.

Figure 10. Showing strike-slip fault mechanism
(Mackenzie and Jackson (1983; 1986))

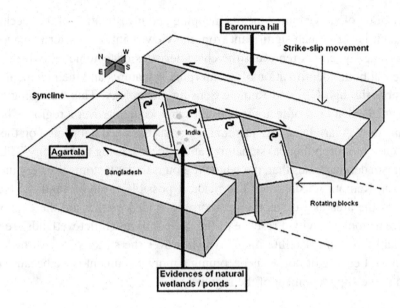

FUTURE SCOPE OF THE STUDY

The application of remote sensing and GIS on identification of geomorphic signatures has been discussed in detail in this study. This work contains a detail description of how satellite image helps to detect the presence and distribution of morphometric signatures which explain the tectonic activities and characteristics of fault movement of a region. Strike slip fault mechanism of Agartala and its surrounding areas has been identified with the help of GIS and remote sensing. The presence of sag ponds and relict wetlands, which have been identified from satellite images and Google earth imageries, reveal the movement of fault of the study area. But only the fault mechanism does not properly represent the sub-surface structural characteristics of Agartala and its surrounding areas. The structural stability of the region can be studied thoroughly through sub-surface geo-electrical investigation. Electrical resistivity represents sub-surface characteristics and stability of earth. For this purpose, research studies are welcome in future in the areas of remote sensing and geo-electrical studies to identify the interrelationship between fault mechanism and sub-surface characteristics of earth surface. With the help of the detail study of sub-surface characteristics and fault mechanism, structural risk assessment can be done accurately for any area. It will be very much applicable and helpful from the point of view of urban planning and disaster management.

CONCLUSION

Identification of active fault zone, its mapping and investigation of the mechanism of the fault is very much significant from the view point of disaster management. Geomorphic signatures represent the characteristics of tectonic activities of past and present both. Identification of geomorphic signatures and their characteristics is possible through GIS and Remote Sensing technology. This technology helps to recognize what kind of tectonic activities are occurring over a region. The fault mechanism of Agartala and its surrounding areas has been delineated on the basis of presence of morphological signatures and remote sensing technology. This fault mechanism demonstrates that, the whole region is under tectonically very unstable condition. Remote sensing data has made it possible to understand the tectonic setting of the area as well as the geomorphic evidences that are the expressions of active tectonic activity. Presence of the sag ponds and relict wetlands are easily identifiable from the satellite image which proves the strike slip fault movement of the area. Leaning of houses is becoming a more prominent issue because of the dextral strike slip movement of the region.

ACKNOWLEDGMENT

The author is grateful to all the faculty members of Tripura University, West Tripura especially late Dr. Sudip Dey for their continuous assistance and support. Lastly but not the least, the author is thankful to North Eastern Hill University, Shillong to provide necessary amenities for the fulfillment of this work.

REFERENCES

Addy, S. (2013). *Geomorphology, river hydrology and natural processes. In SNH Sharing Good Practice Event: Identifying and planning river restoration projects.* The James Hutton Institute.

Aung, P. S., Satirapod, C., & Andrei, C. (2016). Sagaing Fault slip and deformation in Myanmar observed by continuous GPS measurements. *Geodesy and Geodynamics*, *7*(1), 56–63. doi:10.1016/j.geog.2016.03.007

Bastos, L., Bos, M., & Fernandes, R. M. (2010). Deformation and tectonics: Contribution of GPS measurements to plate tectonics – Overview and recent developments. *Sciences of Geodesy, I*, 155–184. doi:10.1007/978-3-642-11741-1_5

Census of India. (2011). District Census Handbook, West Tripura. Directorate of census Operations, Tripura.

Colombelli, S., Allen, R. M., & Zollo, A. (2013). Application of real-time GPS to earthquake early warning in subduction and strike-slip environments. *Journal of Geophysical Research. Solid Earth, 118*(7), 3448–3461. doi:10.1002/jgrb.50242

Dalati, M. (2018). The role of remote sensing in detecting active and fresh faulting zones case study: Northwest of Syria, Al-Ghab Graben Complex. International Society for Photogrammetry and Remote Sensing, 394.

DeLong, S. B., Hilley, G. E., Rymer, M. J., & Prentice, C. (2010). Fault zone structure from topography: Signatures of an echelon fault slip at Mustang Ridge on the San Andreas Fault, Monterey County, California. *Tectonics, 29*.

Dey, S., Mukherjee, G., & Paul, S. (2013). Imaging and visualizing the spectral signatures from Landsat TM and 'τ' value-based surface soil microzonation mapping at and around Agartala (India). *Geocarto International, 28*(2), 144–158. doi:10.1 080/10106049.2012.662528

Dey, S., Sarkar, P., & Debbarma, C. (2009). Morphological signatures of fault lines in an earthquake prone zone of southern Baromura hill, north-east India: A multi sources approach for spatial data analysis. *Environmental Earth Sciences, 59*(2), 353–361. doi:10.100712665-009-0033-5

Diao, F., Walter, T. R., Minati, F., Wang, R., Costantini, M., Ergintav, S., ... Prats-Iraola, P. (2016). Secondary fault activity of the North Anatolian Fault near Avcilar, Southwest of Istanbul: Evidence from SAR interferometry observations. *Remote Sensing, 8*(846), 1–17.

Favretto, A., Geletti, R., & Civile, D. (2013). Remote Sensing as a preliminary analysis for the detection of active tectonic structures: An application to the albanian orogenic system. *Geoadria, 18*(2), 97–111. doi:10.15291/geoadria.165

GeoEarthScope. (2006). *InSAR working group report*. Report of planning meeting.

Huggett R. J. (2007). *Fundamentals of Geomorphology*. Routledge, Taylor and Francis Group.

Kaplan, G., & Avdan, U. (2017). *Thermal remote sensing techniques for studying earthquake anomalies in 2013 Balochistan earthquakes*. Paper presented at the 4th International Conference on Earthquake Engineering and Seismology, Anadolu University, Eskisehir, Turkey.

Karimzadeh, S., Mansouri, B., Osmanoglu, B., & Djamour, Y. (2011). *Application of differential sar interferometry (dinsar) for interseismic assessment of North Tabriz Fault, Iran*. Paper presented at the 1st International Conference on Urban Construction in the Vicinity of Active Faults, Tabrize, Iran.

Kayal, J. R. (2008). *Microearthquake seismology and seismotectonics of South Asia*. New Delhi: Capital Publishing Company.

Kumar, R. (2015). Identification and characterization of active fault by space bornescan sar interferometry and ground based gpr techniques in NW Himalayan foot hill region, India. Andhra University, Visakhapatnam.

Llibourtry, L. (2000). *Quantitative geophysics and geology*. Chichester, UK: Praxis Publishing Ltd.

MacKenzie, D. P., & Jackson, J. A. (1983). The relationship between strain rates, crustal thickening, paleomagnetism, finite stain and fault movements within a deforming zone. *Earth and Planetary Science Letters*, *65*(1), 182–202. doi:10.1016/0012-821X(83)90198-X

MacKenzie, D. P., & Jackson, J. A. (1986). A block model of distributed deformation by faulting. *Journal of the Geological Society*, *143*(2), 349–353. doi:10.1144/gsjgs.143.2.0349

Parcharidis, I., Kokkalas, S., Fountoulis, I., & Foumelis, M. (2009). Detection and monitoring of active faults in urban environments: Time series interferometry on the cities of Patras and Pyrgos (Peloponnese, Greece). *Remote Sensing*, *1*(4), 676–696. doi:10.3390/rs1040676

Petrov, V. A., Lespinasse, M., Ustinov, S. A., & Cialec, C. (2017). GIS-based identification of active lineaments within the Krasnokamensk Area, Transbaikalia, Russia. In *Proceedings 5*[th] *International Conference New Achievements in Materials and Environmental Science* (*Vol. 879*). Nancy, France: Academic Press. 10.1088/1742-6596/879/1/012017

Sabins, F. F. (2013). *Remote Sensing Principles and Interpretation*. Kolkata: Levant Books.

Sedrette, S., Rebaï, N., & Mastere, M. (2016). Evaluation of neotectonic signature using morphometric indicators: Case study in Nefza, North-West of Tunisia. *Journal of Geographic Information System*, *8*(03), 338–350. doi:10.4236/jgis.2016.83029

Thronbury, W. D. (1969). *Principles of Geomorphology*. New Delhi: New Age International Publishers.

Tolomei, C., Salvi, S., Merryman Boncori, J. P., & Pezzo, G. (2014). InSAR measurement of crustal deformation transients during the earthquake preparation processes: A review. *Bollettino di Geofisica Teorica ed Applicata*, *56*(2), 151–166.

Tronin, A. A. (2010). Satellite Remote Sensing in Seismology. A Review. *Remote Sensing*, *2*(1), 124–150. doi:10.3390/rs2010124

Vasiliev, Y. M., Milnichuk, V. S., & Arabaji, M. S. (1981). *General and Historical Geology*. Moscow: MIR Publishers.

Chapter 6

Natural Hazard:
Tropical Cyclone – Evaluation of HE and IMSRA Over CS KYANT

Amit Kumar
India Meteorological Department, India

Anil Kumar Singh
India Meteorological Department, India

Nitesh Awasthi
India Meteorological Department, India

Virendra Singh
India Meteorological Department, India

ABSTRACT

Tropical cyclones are also known as typhoons or hurricanes. Also, special emphasis is given on the various aspects associated with cyclogenesis, like the six essential parameters required for cyclogenesis as given by W. M. Grey, and Dvorak technique is discussed in this chapter. INSAT-3D is an indigenous advanced dedicated meteorological satellite in geostationary orbit, which was launched on 26th July 2013. INSAT-3D was declared operational by IMD on 15th January 2014. INSAT-3D has four payloads, namely. IMAGER, SOUNDER, data relay transponder (DRT), and satellite aided search, aid and rescue (SAR). Three rainfall estimates are being generated from INSAT-3D, namely, hydro-estimator (HE), INSAT multispectral rainfall algorithm (IMSRA), and QPE (quantitative precipitation estimate). It has been found in this study that IMSRA performs better during initial stages of cyclogenesis (i.e., during T1.0, T1.5, and T2.0); during mature stages T2.5 to T3.0, HE performs better. During weakening stages IMSRA gives better results.

DOI: 10.4018/978-1-5225-7784-3.ch006

INTRODUCTION

The intensification of the tropical cyclone (TC) is dependent on the sea surface temperature (SST) which also an indicator for its track movement (Emanuel, 2005). The assimilation of amount of precipitation occurred at the vertex is useful for the prediction of intensity of the cyclone (Huang et al., 2006; Karyampudi et al., 1998; Zou and Kuo, 1996). There are some other studies which suggest the occurrence of the spiral cloud bands of convections is also intensity the TC (Guinn and Schubert, 1993; Willoughby et al., 1984). The necessity of accurate cyclone track prediction, intensity estimation and precipitation estimation plays a major role in the wide range of applications like risk assessment, agricultural sector, and disaster in the coastal regions. Now a days, the numerical weather prediction models and its ensemble prediction techniques given a new approach to the risk assessment to the disaster management and other sectors. But the real time approach will helpful for the changes in the systems can be identified by the satellite observations. In many studies various authors have stressed upon the role of sea surface temperature and ocean thermal energy during cyclone genesis (Riehl, 1954; Fisher, 1958; Malkus andRiehl, 1960; Miller, 1964; Leipper, 1967; Perlroth, 1967, 1969; Leipperand Volgenau, 1972).

In 1975 William M. Gray, from Colorado State University, USA summarized the primary cyclone genesis parameters which are essential for the formation of a Tropical cyclone. These parameters are:

1. Low-level relative vorticity
2. Coriolis Parameter
3. The inverse of the vertical shear of the horizontal wind between the lower and upper troposphere
4. A Sea Temperature Factor of the sea temperature above 26.11°C between the surface and 200 feet ocean depth
5. Vertical gradient of Equivalent Potential temperature between surface and 500hPa
6. Middle troposphere relative humidity

The development of Dvorak Technique (1984), is considered as the single most significant development towards understanding of Tropical cyclones and this technique is being used operationally worldwide for estimating intensity and pattern of the tropical cyclones. The intensity of the low-pressure system in Dvorak Technique is defined with a number from 1-8 in an interval of 0.5 and is known as T number. For assigning these T numbers, maximum sustained surface wind speed is taken as the main criteria. In Table 1, the T numbers assigned to various low-pressure systems and the maximum sustained surface wind speeds associated with these low-pressure systems is shown. A low-pressure system having the maximum sustained surface wind speed (MSW) of less than 17 knots, it is termed as Low Presser Area (LOPAR) and assigned T1.0.When the MSW becomes 17 knots or more but remain less than 27 knots, it is termed as Depression (D) and T number assigned is T1.5. On further intensification, with MSW between 28 knots to 33 knots, the system is termed as Deep Depression (DD) with T2.0. Cyclonic Storm is declared only when, MSW becomes 34 knots but does not exceed 47 knots with T2.5 to T3.0. For Severe Cyclonic storm, the T number assigned is T3.5, with MSW between 48 knots to 63 knots. For Very Severe Cyclonic storm the T number assigned is T4.0 to T4.5, with MSW between 64 knots to 89 knots. For Extremely Severe Cyclonic storm the T number assigned is between T5.0 to T6.0, with MSW between 90 knots to 119 knots. For Super Cyclonic storm, the T number assigned is between T6.5 to T8.0, with MSW of 120 knots or more.

The high temporal, spatial availability of remote sensing data has given a new way to forecaster to assess the current weather system (Yu et al., 2011). It is also possible to assess the track of the TC along with its intensity using the remote sensing approach (Krishna and Rao, 2009). The Geostationary satellites playing a major role in the measuring of IR and VIS with 30 minutes of interval are utilized in the various methods. The recent stages of Geostationary satellites and retrieval methods using visible, infra-red, active and passive microwave methods and its improvement are a confidence to use the data to data assimilation in the real time basis(Kidd and Levizzani, 2011). The fine temporal and spatial resolution of geostationary satellites has also a given a chance to flood monitoring on real time which is more useful to flood assessment and landslides (Hong et al., 2007).

Table 1. Dvorak technique

Category of Low Pressure System	Maximum T No. associated With Low Pressure System	Maximum Sustained Surface Wind Speed
Low Pressure Area (LOPAR)	T1.0	<17 knots
Depression (D)	T1.5	17 – 27 knots
Deep Depression (DD)	T2.0	28-33 knots
Cyclonic Storm (CS)	T2.5-T3.0	34-47 knots
Severe Cyclonic Storm (SCS)	T3.5	48-63 knots
Very Severe Cyclonic Storm (VSCS)	T4.0-T4.5	64-89 knots
Extremely Severe Cyclonic Storm (ESCS)	T5.0-T6.0	90-119 knots
Super Cyclonic Storm (SuCS)	T6.5 or more	>=120 knots

DATA USED AND STUDY AREA

In this case study, we have used satellite derived rainfall estimates from INSAT-3D and GPM (IMERGE) missions. INSAT-3D is an indigenous advanced dedicated meteorological satellite in geostationary orbit, which was launched on 26th July 2013. INSAT-3D was declared operational by IMD on 15th January 2014. INSAT-3D has four payloads namely: IMAGER, SOUNDER, Data Relay Transponder (DRT) and Satellite Aided Search, Aid and Rescue (SAR). (INSAT-3D Algorithm Theoretical Basis Document).

IMAGER is an advanced six spectral channels Very High-Resolution Radiometer (VHRR) in, Visible (VIS), Shortwave Infrared (SWIR), Mid Infrared (MIR), Thermal Infrared 1 (TIR1), Thermal Infrared 2 (TIR2) and Water vapour (WV) part of spectrum covering following bands: VIS (0.55 µm -0.75 µm), SWIR (1.55 µm -1.70 µm), MIR (3.8 µm -4.0 µm), WV (6.5 µm -7.1 µm), TIR1 (10.2 µm -11.3 µm) and TIR2 (11.5 µm -12.5 µm). Resolution and brief purpose of each channel of IMAGER is mentioned in Table 2.

1. Visible Channel Images from INSAT-3D satellite are available in Full Disk (81N/5E-81S/162E), Asia Mercator sector (45°N-10°S to 45°E-105°E), North-West (NW) sector (50°N-20°S to 15°E-85°E), North East (NE) sector (0°N-35°N to 75°E-105°E), High Resolution images with District Boundaries (NW (15°N-35°N to 65°E-85°E), NE (15°N-40°N to 80°E-100°E), SW (0°N-30°N to 40°E-75°E), SE (0°N-30°N to 75°E-105°E) sectors). In Visible

Table 2. INSAT-3D IMAGER specifications

Channel Number	Channel ID	Channel Name	Spectral range (µm)	Resolution (Km)	Purpose
1.	VIS	Visible	0.55 – 0.75	1.0	Clouds, Surface features
2.	SWIR	Short Wave Infrared	1.55 – 1.70	1.0	Snow, Ice and water phase in clouds
3.	MIR	Medium Infrared	3.8 – 4.0	4.0	Clouds, Fog, Fire
4.	WV	Water Vapour	6.5 – 7.1	8.0	Upper-Troposphere Moisture
5.	TIR1	Thermal Infrared 1	10.2 – 11.3	4.0	Cloud top and surface temperature
6.	TIR2	Thermal Infrared 2	11.5 - 12.5	4.0	Lower-Troposphere Moisture

imagery albedo, i.e. the ration of reflected portion to incident sun's energy is measured. These Images are used for monitoring mesoscale weather features such as cloud cover, air mass boundaries, convergence zones, thunderstorms, cloud structure, cloud height (using cloud shadow), sun glint, volcanic ash, Dust Strom, Fog and local snow cover. The only drawback with this imagery is that Visible channel image is only available during daytime.

2. SWIR Channel Images are used for monitoring local snow cover, day time Fog, Convective rainfall estimation, Cloud radiative properties, NDSI. Incident radiation in SWIR, strongly absorbed by water, ice, snow and reflected by cloud While for visible spectrum these objects essentially transparent. Therefore, melting snow patches or lake, ice is seen bright in the visible image while these appears dark in SWIR images and therefore SWIR images are used to differentiate the cloud, rain given cloud and snow. The SWIR band is sensitive to the moisture content soils recently irrigated field therefore appears in darker tones. The only drawback with this imagery is that it is only available during daytime.

3. MIR Channel Interpretation of 3.9 µm data differs from that of the longer wavelength infrared bands, since it contains both reflected solar, and emitted terrestrial, radiation. The 3.9 µm spectral band, energy measured by the satellite can be a mixture of solar radiation that is reflected by the earth's surface or clouds and radiation that is emitted by the earth's surface or clouds. Characteristics of reflected and emitted radiation in this band are different from either the visible or the 10.7 µm bands, thereby promoting enhanced capabilities of INSAT-3D IMAGER multispectral imagery. It isuseful for fog and other liquid water cloud identification, cloud phase changes, distinction of cloud cover over snow fields, and fire detection.

4. This broad water vapor band senses radiation emitted from high clouds and upper level water vapor. This imagery is used to define upper level flow patterns, upper level circulations, and shortwaves moving through the flow.

5. TIR1 around the 10.7 µm region, most of the energy radiated from the surface reach's the sensor, thus the term "atmospheric window" since the temperature measured is close to scene temperature. Used for monitoring cloud top and surface temperature, cloud cover, air mass boundaries, convergence zones, surface lows and thunderstorms both day and night.

6. TIR2 is another window region around 12 µm, is contaminated by low level water vapor, and thus is called the "dirty window" and used to achieve higher accuracy SST and noise correction in RT model.

SOUNDER has 18 infrared channels and 1 visible channel. The 18 infrared channels can be broadly divided into three groups based on their spectral bands i.e. Longwave Infrared (LWIR), Midwave Infrared (MWIR) and Shortwave Infrared (SWIR). Resolution, Spectral band and brief purpose of each channel of SOUNDER is mentioned in Table 3.

Table 3. INSAT-3D SOUNDER specifications

Detector	Ch. No.	l_c (mm)	n_c (cm^{-1})	NEΔT @300K	Principal absorbing gas	Purpose
Long wave	1	14.67	682	0.17	CO_2	Stratosphere temperature
	2	14.32	699	0.16	CO_2	Tropopause temperature
	3	14.04	712	0.15	CO_2	Upper-level temperature
	4	13.64	733	0.12	CO_2	Mid-level temperature
	5	13.32	751	0.12	CO_2	Low-level temperature
	6	12.62	793	0.07	water vapor	Total precipitable water
	7	11.99	834	0.05	water vapor	Surface temp., moisture
Mid wave	8	11.04	906	0.05	window	Surface temperature
	9	9.72	1029	0.10	ozone	Total ozone
	10	7.44	1344	0.05	water vapor	Low-level moisture
	11	7.03	1422	0.05	water vapor	Mid-level moisture
	12	6.53	1531	0.10	water vapor	Upper-level moisture
Short wave	13	4.58	2184	0.05	N_2O	Low-level temperature
	14	4.53	2209	0.05	N_2O	Mid-level temperature
	15	4.46	2241	0.05	CO_2	Upper-level temperature
	16	4.13	2420	0.05	CO_2	Boundary-level temp.
	17	3.98	2510	0.05	window	Surface temperature
	18	3.76	2658	0.05	window	Surface temp., moisture
Visible	19	0.695	14367	-	visible	Cloud Detection

INSAT-3D RAINFALL ESTIMATES

In Operational Chain of INSAT Meteorological Data Processing System (IMDPS), New Delhi, three rainfall estimates are being generated from INSAT-3D namely: Hydro-Estimator (HE), INSAT Multispectral Rainfall Algorithm (IMSRA) and QPE (Quantitative Precipitation Estimate). In this study, we have validated performance/ quality of HE and IMSRA against GPM (IMERG).

HYDRO-ESTIMATOR (HE)

Hydro-estimator provides pixel-scale, half-hourly precipitation rate measurements over land and oceans. INSAT-3D Imager observations in TIR1, TIR2 and WV channels combined with Numerical Weather Prediction (NWP) forecasts are used to estimate high spatial-temporal resolution rainfall estimates. The H-E uses an algorithm based on IR cloud top temperatures, temperature changes and gradients to produce rainfall rate estimates along with NCEP/GFS parameters and earth elevation model on half hourly basis. The various corrections and adjustments are applied to the estimates product such as parallax correction (satellite viewing angle), available moisture (derived from the model) and orographic correction. Thermodynamic model is used for calculating EL / LNB correction for warm rain. Orographic correction is carried out using wind and elevation model. Dry atmospheric correction is carried out using RH. Rain is determined at each pixel using different relationships for convective/ strati form type of cloud and relationship dynamically calculated for each pixel. The spatial resolution of product is Pixel level (4 km at nadir) and temporal resolution is half-hourly. The product dimension is 81° S - 81° N and 3° - 163° E, but for this study daily accumulated rainfall estimate over study area is taken. The description of HE algorithm can also found else wherein (Kumar and Varma, 2017). The algorithm had undergone major revision in 2015 in order to improve the orographic precipitation and modified algorithm was made operational from mid-August, 2015 (Varma et al., 2015).

IMSRA - INSAT Multispectral Rainfall Algorithm

IMSRA combines variety of techniques (IR and MW) in a single and comprehensive rainfall algorithm. The QPE products are derived using TIR1 and WV channels brightness temperature from INSAT-3D imager. The observations in IR and WV bands are utilized to classify clouds into several categories, such as low-level clouds, thin cirrus, convective and deep convective clouds, etc. (Roca et al., 2002). The most important aspect of this scheme is that it allows delineation of cirrus clouds, which is one of the major sources of error (Barret and Martin, 1981) in IR-based rain algorithms and helps identify convective and deep convective rain clouds. The product spatial resolution is $0.1° \times 0.1°$ and temporal resolution is half-hourly. The product dimension is 30° E to 120° E and 40° S to 40° N, but for this study daily accumulated rainfall estimate over study area is taken.

Mission Overview of GPM

Global Precipitation Measurement (GPM) constellation satellites are an international mission to provide next generation observations of rain and snow. NASA and the Japanese Aerospace Exploration Agency (JAXA) launched the GPM Core Observatory satellite on 27 February 2014, carrying advanced instruments that will set a new standard for precipitation measurements from space. GPM constellation satellites provided by the American National Aeronautics and Space Administration (NASA), the Japanese Aerospace Exploration Agency (JAXA), Eumetsat'sMetOp-B and planned MetOp-C, the NASA-NOAA (American National Oceanic and Atmospheric Administration) Suomi National Polar-orbiting, France and India's Megha-Tropiques, NOAA's Polar-orbiting Operational Environmental Satellites, Japan's first Global Change Observation Mission-Water, U.S. Defence Department meteorological satellites and NOAA's Joint Polar Satellite System. The data they deliver will be used to combine precipitation measurements made by an international network of partner satellites to compute when, where, and how much it rains or snows around the world. The GPM Core Observatory satellite flies at a height of 407 km in non-sun-synchronous orbit and proceeds with the TRMM examining methodology and will stretch out the perceptions to higher scopes, covering the globe from the Antarctic Circle to the Arctic Circle (Huffman et al., 2015c). However, as you see in Table 3, at present, this version covers a latitude from 60"N to 60"S.

The expanded affectability of the Dual-frequency Precipitation Radar (DPR) and the high-frequency channels on the GPM Microwave Imager (GMI) will empower GPM to enhance determining by assessing light rain and falling snow outside the tropics, even in the winter seasons, which different satellites can't gauge (Huffman et al., 2015b; 2015c). Researchers and scientists use models for analysis and forecasts of the atmospheric state. The models may have diverse spatial and temporal resolution. Outstanding amongst other models, which is utilized around the world, has been developed by the European Centre for Medium Range Weather Forecasts (ECMWF). They have produced a global reanalysis for the last decades of ERA-40 and ERA-Interim, 12-hourly and daily precipitation fields (Dee et al., 2011). Moreover, ERA-Interim is the latest global atmospheric reanalysis created by ECMWF. The ERA-Interim scheme was conducted in part to prepare a new atmospheric reanalysis to replace ERA-40, which will extend the data to the early part of the twentieth century. Another tool to regulate precipitation at comparatively fine temporal and spatial scale is satellite observation. During the last decade, many researchers have calculated and used satellite data sets and some have found that the TMPA-3B42 post real-time product performed better than other products compared with the rain-gauges (Javanmard et al., 2010; Tobin et al., 2010; Bao et al., 2013; Ashouri et al., 2015; Yong et al., 2015). One of the disadvantages of TMPA-3B42 was the partial area of observation; it covered only the tropical and subtropical belts. Additional disadvantage was the capability to estimate heavy rainfall while light rainfall and snowfall were not identified properly (Javanmard et al., 2010; Huffman et al., 2015b).

As seen in Table 4, IMERG is currently available from mid-March 2014 to the present (with access delay in the order of about three months for the final run version). Based on the initial analysis during beta analysis by Huffman et al. (2015), IMERG is smoother than 3B43 over oceans and at higher latitudes. This was a goal for IMERG, which delivers estimates every half hour, versus the 3-hourly interval for the satellite data contributing to 3B43. Usually, satellite assessment in regions subject to convective precipitation could be challenging whereas they expect that IMERG data sets will be more precise (Huffman et al., 2015a). Contrary to other satellites, such as TRMM, that could not measure light rain and snowfall, GPM-IMERG utilizes diverse sensors from various satellites to identify both light and substantial rain and snowfall. Three basic enhancements in GPM are that (1) the orbital tendency has been expanded from 35" to 65", bearing scope of critical extra atmosphere zones; (2) the radar has been moved up to two frequencies, adding affectability to light precipitation; and (3) high-frequency channels (165.5 and 183.3 GHz) have been added to the passive microwave (PMW) imager, which is required to encourage detecting of light and solid precipitation. In brief, the input precipitation evaluations calculated from the various satellite passive microwave sensors are inter-calibrated to the GPM Combined Instrument (GCI, using GMI and DPR), because it is supposed to be the best snapshot GPM estimate, then transformed and united with microwave precipitation-calibrated geosynchronous earth orbit (geo) infrared (IR) fields, and adjusted with monthly surface precipitation gauge analysis data (where available) to deliver half-hourly and monthly precipitation estimates. Precipitation stage is identified using studies of surface temperature, humidity, and pressure. On the other hand, the TMPA combines microwave data from various satellites, each inter-calibrated to the TRMM Combined Instrument (TCI), using TRMM Microwave Imager (TMI) and TRMM Precipitation Radar (PR). Coverage gaps in space and time are filled in with calibrated infrared (IR) data (which are generally available with near-global coverage every 3 h); coefficients are derived from co-located IR brightness temperatures and the microwave-based precipitation estimates. The final data products reflect scaling the multi-satellite estimates to rain gauge data on a monthly basis, and confirming that the 3-hourly averages in 3B42 sum to the monthly totals in 3B43 (Huffman et al., 2015c). Other advantages for using satellite precipitation data in places such as Ocean include generally lacking of spatial coverage of in-situ data, long delay in data processing and transfer until they become available for the public and scientific use, and absence of data sharing in many trans-boundary basins. As a result, this study aims to assess the accuracy of the new generation of satellite precipitation products.

GPM (IMERG)

The Global Precipitation Measurement (GPM) mission core satellite was launched in February 2014 with the goal of providing the next-generation, state-of-the-art global quantitative precipitation estimates (QPE). Taking advantage of an international constellation of satellites of opportunity, the Integrated Multi-Satellite Retrievals for GPM (IMERG) produces precipitation estimates in the range 60° N-S every half hour at 0.1° resolution. The IMERG precipitation is calibrated to the GPM Microwave Imager/Dual-frequency Precipitation Radar combined product to provide the best possible estimates. IMERG products are produced at three different latencies to accommodate the unique requirements of the various user bases. The "Early" run has a 6-hour latency (for flash flood monitoring, etc.), the "Late" run has a 16-hour latency (for drought monitoring, crop forecasting, etc.) and the "Final" run has a 3-month latency (for research). The "Early" and "Late" data begin in March, 2015 and the "Final" data begin in March 2014. In this study "Final" run dataset has been used, the data is downloaded via https://pmm.nasa.gov/data-access/downloads/gpm.

METHODOLOGY

In IMDPS, New Delhi operational chain HE and IMSRA are generated over four temporal scales- Half Hourly product with gives the rain rate in mm/hr, Daily product which gives the total rain accumulation in mm from 0330UTC of today to

Table 4. Characteristics of satellite/model precipitation products

Products	Temporal Resolution	Spatial Resolution	Regions	Availability Period
IMERG	half-hourly March	0.1 degree	60″N–60″S	2014–present
3B42	3-hourly	0.25 degree	50″N–50″S	1997–April 2015
ERA-INTERIM	daily	0.125 degree	90″N–90″S	1979-present

0300UTC of tomorrow, Weekly and Monthly. In this study, the comparison of HE and IMSRA with GPM(IMERG) is done on daily scale only. As mentioned above the daily accumulated HE and IMSRA daily products are available with binning from 0330UTC of today till 0300UTC of tomorrow, whereas the accumulated GPM(IMERG) daily product is available with binning from 0000UTC till 2330UTC of today. Therefore, the daily accumulated product for GPM(IMERG) available from GPM website was not used. Half Hourly GPM(IMERG) dataset were downloaded and they were used to create the daily accumulated GPM(IMERG) dataset having the same temporal footprint as that of INSAT-3D derived HE and IMSRA daily products. It can be seen from above that, the spatial resolution of HE differs from that of GPM (IMERG) and in case of IMSRA the spatial resolution is same but the starting indexes are different. Therefore, HE and IMSRA dataset are resampled using GPM (IMERG) as reference (Singh *et. al.* 2018). Only those Collocated points which lies within the study area were taken into consideration. The validation algorithm is shown in figure 1.

RESULT AND DISCUSSION

Cyclonic Storm "KYANT"

The summary of Special Tropical Weather Outlooks generated and disseminated by Regional Specialized Meteorological Centre- Tropical Cyclones, New Delhi, IMD for Cyclonic Storm KYANT is mentioned below:

The Well-Marked Low-Pressure Area (WML) over eastcentral and adjoining southeast Bay of Bengal (BoB) concentrated into a Depression (D) with centre near 13.5N/ 88.5E at 0000UTC of 21.10.2016, about 500KM west-northwest of Port Blair. The intensity of the system was T1.5 associated with Broken Low and Medium clouds embedded with intense to very intense convection. During this period both lower level convergence and upper level divergence showed increasing trend. Also, the Madden-Julian Oscillation (MJO) was in Phase-7, but the amplitude was very low. The system intensified into a Deep depression (DD) with T2.0 at 0300UTC of 23.10.2016 near 15.5N/ 93.0E about 420KM north of Port Blair. The convective clouds exhibited shear pattern during this stage. As before both lower level convergence and upper level divergence showed increasing trend and vertical wind shear exhibited decreasing trend which were indicative of further intensification of this system.

The system intensified into Cyclonic Storm "KYANT" with intensity of T2.5 near 17.0N/91.2E at 0300UTC of 25.10.2016, about 620KM north-northwest of Port Blair. Along with all favourable conditions the vertical wind shear of horizontal wind was also moderate around the system centre. The cyclonic storm KYANT showed west-southwest ward movement and weakened into a DD at 0100UTC of 27.10.2016, about 340KM southeast of Vishakhapatnam. The weakening was associated with reduction in ocean thermal energy. The low-level convergence had also reduced. Also, the presence of an anticyclonic circulation to the northwest of the system in middle and upper tropospheric levels had helped in dry air incursion from the Indian landmass. It dry air incursion was responsible for further weakening of the DD into a D and further into a WML over west central BoB off Andhra Pradesh coast.Track of Cyclonic Storm KYANT is shown in figure2.

Statistical Analysis of Rainfall Estimates

The statistical analysis of Cyclonic Storm KYANT is shown in Table5. It can be seen that during initial cyclogenesis stage IMSRA was exhibiting better correlation with GPM(IMERG). Even the Root Mean Square Error (RMSE) and Mean Absolute Error (MAE) were also least for IMSRA during this period. When the D intensified into a DD on 23rd October 2016, HE started to exhibit better correlation and least RMSE and MAE with GPM(IMERG). Similar results can also be seen on 24th and 25th October when the DD further intensified into CS and was on its peak intensity. These results are in line with the results which suggest that IMSRA gives better results up to 75mm/day daily accumulation of rainfall, after this HE exhibits better results (Singh et al. 2018). ON 26th October 2016, the system started to weaken and the same can be verified by the degradation in performance of HE and improvement in the results of IMSRA with GPM(IMERG). Therefore, from statistical analysis, it is demonstrated that, IMSRA gives better results during initial cyclogenesis stages and during weakening stages. During intensification, mature and peak intensity stages HE exhibits better results. Figure 3 shows daily rainfall estimates from GPM(IMERG), HE and IMSRA in row1, 2, 3 from 21st October to 27th October 2016.

Skill Score Analysis of Rainfall Estimates

The skill score analysis of Cyclonic Storm KYANT is shown in Table 6. In this study, we have evaluated the performance of HE and IMSRA using following skill scores: Critical Success Index (CSI), Probability of Detection (POD), Missed Events (M), False Alarm Ration (FAR), (HSS), Bias. CSI is also known as Threat Score (TS). The range of CSI is from 0 to 1 with zero indicating no skill and 1 as perfect score. Bias is also known as Frequency Bias. It can be seen from the table4 that the CSI of HE is better than that of IMSRA during initial cyclogenesis, intensification and mature stages. However, IMSRA exhibited better CSI during weakening stages. POD, M and FAR suggest that both the rainfall estimates are able to capture rainfall during all stages of cyclone genesis, intensification, maturing and weakening. The overall Bias is also near about 1mm during all stages which supplements the information deduced by all other skill scores.

Table 5. Statistical analysis of INSAT-3D rainfall estimates with GPM(MERGE)

GPM(IMERG) Vs HE							
Statistics	21 Oct	22Oct	23Oct	24Oct	25Oct	26Oct	27Oct
CC (R)	0.74	0.63	0.73	0.68	0.69	0.43	0.39
RMSE(mm)	31.56	37.88	19.46	29.25	21.27	14.99	14.39
MAE(mm)	8.75	9.05	5.25	5.58	4.36	4.95	5.09
GPM(IMERG) Vs IMSRA							
CC (R)	0.85	0.58	0.54	0.31	0.43	0.7	0.57
RMSE (mm)	22.71	39.6	29.36	40.91	29.04	12.61	12.03
MAE(mm)	8.66	11.42	11.23	10.68	7.67	4.9	4.44

Table 6. Skill score analysis of INSAT-3D rainfall estimates with GPM(MERGE)

GPM(IMERG) Vs HE							
Skill Score	21 Oct	22Oct	23Oct	24Oct	25Oct	26Oct	27Oct
CSI	0.788	0.732	0.728	0.581	0.579	0.645	0.672
POD	0.934	0.930	0.902	0.744	0.736	0.788	0.857
M	0.065	0.069	0.097	0.255	0.263	0.211	0.142
FAR	0.165	0.224	0.209	0.274	0.268	0.218	0.242
HSS	0.725	0.667	0.648	0.502	0.603	0.613	0.665
BIAS	1.119	1.200	1.141	1.026	1.007	1.008	1.132
GPM(IMERG) Vs IMSRA							
CSI	0.779	0.641	0.658	0.430	0.382	0.681	0.710
POD	0.949	0.904	0.871	0.560	0.819	0.889	0.912
M	0.051	0.096	0.129	0.440	0.181	0.111	0.088
FAR	0.187	0.312	0.271	0.350	0.583	0.256	0.238
HSS	0.703	0.504	0.524	0.304	0.209	0.634	0.705
BIAS	1.168	1.315	1.195	0.862	1.963	1.196	1.196

CONCLUSION AND FUTURE SCOPE OF WORK

In this study, the performance of INSAT-3D derived rainfall estimates: HE and IMSRA which are being generated operationally at IMDPS, New Delhi during Cyclonic storm "KYANT" were compared with GPM (IMERG) dataset. The main aim of performing this study was to validate the INSAT-3D rainfall estimates, as these estimates are available at every half hour. This study will increase the confidence of modelers for using these INSAT-3D rainfall estimates operationally for providing rainfall, flooding and storm-surge forecasts. HE and IMSRA have shown good skill with GPM(IMERG) during different stages of cyclogenesis, intensification, mature and weakening. It can be concluded from this study that IMSRA gives better rainfall estimates during initial cyclogenesis stages and later weakening stages. Whereas HE shows better skill during intensification and mature stages. In future studies attempt will be made to analysis the performance of these rainfall estimates over half hourly time scale. Also, it will be attempted to compare these rainfall estimates with GSMaP rainfall products. Present and future studies will help in removing biases and will help in generating a standard satellite derived rainfall product over Indian Subcontinent, which will perform well for both intense convective systems like tropical cyclones and stratiform rainfall systems like Indian Summer Monsoons.

ACKNOWLEDGMENT

The authors wish to thank DGM, IMD for allowing them to use INSAT-3D rainfall estimates dataset. The data used in this study were acquired as part of the mission of NASA's Earth Science Division and archived and distributed by the Goddard Earth Science (GES) Data and Information Services Center (DISC). The GPM satellite estimated rainfall data were provided by the JAXA, JAPAN and NASA, USA. We thankfully acknowledge the use of GPM data in this project.

REFERENCES

Ashouri, H., Hsu, K.-L., Sorooshian, S., Braithwaite, D. K., Knapp, K. R., Cecil, L. D., ... Prat, O. P. (2015). PERSIANN-CDR: Daily Precipitation Climate Data Record from Multisatellite Observations for Hydrological and Climate Studies. *Bulletin of the American Meteorological Society*, *96*(1), 69–83. doi:10.1175/BAMS-D-13-00068.1

Bao, X., Zhang, F., Bao, X., & Zhang, F. (2013). Evaluation of NCEP–CFSR, NCEP–NCAR, ERA-Interim, and ERA-40 Reanalysis Datasets against Independent Sounding Observations over the Tibetan Plateau. *Journal of Climate, 26*(1), 206–214. doi:10.1175/JCLI-D-12-00056.1

Barrett, E. C., & Martin, D. W. (1981). *Use of satellite data in rainfall monitoring.* Academic press.

Dee, D. P., Uppala, S. M., Simmons, A. J., Berrisford, P., Poli, P., Kobayashi, S., ... Vitart, F. (2011). The ERA-Interim reanalysis: Configuration and performance of the data assimilation system. *Quarterly Journal of the Royal Meteorological Society, 137*(656), 553–597. doi:10.1002/qj.828

Dvorak, V. F. (1984). *Tropical cyclone intensity analysis using satellite data* (Vol. 11). US Department of Commerce, National Oceanic and Atmospheric Administration, National Environmental Satellite, Data, and Information Service.

Emanuel, K. (2005). Increasing destructiveness of tropical cyclones over the past 30 years. *Nature, 436*(7051), 686–688. doi:10.1038/nature03906 PMID:16056221

Fisher, E. L. (1958). Hurricanes and the sea-surface temperature field. *Journal of Meteorology, 15*(3), 328–333. doi:10.1175/1520-0469(1958)015<0328:HATSST>2.0.CO;2

Gray, W. M. (1975). *Tropical cyclone genesis.* Atmospheric science paper; no. 234.

Guinn, T. A., & Schubert, W. H. (1993). Hurricane Spiral Bands. *Journal of the Atmospheric Sciences, 50*(20), 3380–3403. doi:10.1175/1520-0469(1993)050<3380:HSB>2.0.CO;2

Hong, Y., Adler, R. F., Negri, A., & Huffman, G. J. (2007). Flood and landslide applications of near real-time satellite rainfall products. *Natural Hazards, 43*(2), 285–294. doi:10.100711069-006-9106-x

Huang, J.-H., Li, J.-N., Wei, X.-L., Fong, S.-K., & Wang, A.-Y. (2006). Assimilation of QuikScat data and its impact on prediction of Typhoon Vongfong (2002). ZhongshanDaxueXuebao/Acta Sci. *Natralium Univ. Sunyatseni, 45*, 116–120.

Huffman, G.J., Bolvin, D.T., Braithwaite, D., Hsu, K., Joyce, R., Kidd, C., Nelkin, E.J., & Xie, P. (2015c). *NASA Global Precipitation Measurement (GPM) Integrated Multi-satellitE Retrievals for GPM (IMERG).* Algorithm Theoretical Basis Document (ATBD) Version 4.5 26.

Huffman, G. J., Bolvin, D. T., & Nelkin, E. J. (2015a). *Day 1 IMERG Final Run Release Notes 1–9*. Retrieved from http://pmm.nasa.gov/sites/default/files/document_files/IMERG_FinalRun_Day1_release_notes.pdf

Huffman, G.J., Bolvin, D.T., & Nelkin, E.J. (2015b). *Integrated Multi-satellitE Retrievals for GPM (IMERG) Technical Documentation*. NASA/GSFC Code 612, 47. doi:10.1136/openhrt-2016-000469

Javanmard, S., Yatagai, A., Nodzu, M. I., BodaghJamali, J., & Kawamoto, H. (2010). Comparing high-resolution gridded precipitation data with satellite rainfall estimates of TRMM_3B42 over Iran. *Advances in Geosciences*, *25*, 119–125. doi:10.5194/adgeo-25-119-2010

Karyampudi, V. M., Lai, G. S., & Manobianco, J. (1998). Impact of Initial Conditions, Rainfall Assimilation, and Cumulus Parameterization on Simulations of Hurricane Florence (1988). *Monthly Weather Review*, *126*(12), 3077–3101. doi:10.1175/1520-0493(1998)126<3077:IOICRA>2.0.CO;2

Kidd, C., & Levizzani, V. (2011). Status of satellite precipitation retrievals. *Hydrology and Earth System Sciences*, *15*(4), 1109–1116. doi:10.5194/hess-15-1109-2011

Krishna, K. M., & Rao, S. R. (2009). Study of the intensity of super cyclonic storm GONU using satellite observations. *International Journal of Applied Earth Observation and Geoinformation*, *11*(2), 108–113. doi:10.1016/j.jag.2008.11.001

Kumar, P., & Varma, A. K. (2017). Assimilation of INSAT-3D hydro-estimator method retrieved rainfall for short-range weather prediction. *Journal of the Royal Meteorological Society*, *143*(702), 384–394. doi:10.1002/qj.2929

Leipper, D. F., & Volgenau, D. (1972). Hurricane heat potential of the Gulf of Mexico. *Journal of Physical Oceanography*, *2*(3), 218–224. doi:10.1175/1520-0485(1972)002<0218:HHPOTG>2.0.CO;2

Leipper, D. F. (1967). Obaerved ocean conditions and Hurricane Hilda, 1964. *J. Atmoa. Sci.*, *24*, 182-196.

Malltus, J. S., & Riehl, H. (1960). *On the dynamics and energy tranaformation in steady-state hurricanes*. Academic Press.

Miller, B. I. (1964). A study of the filling of hurricane Donna (1960) over land. *Monthly Weather Review*, *94*(9), 389–406. doi:10.1175/1520-0493(1964)092<0389:ASOTFO>2.3.CO;2

Perlboth, I. (1967). Hurricane behavior as related to oceanographic environmental conditions. *Tellus*, *19*(2), 258–268. doi:10.1111/j.2153-3490.1967.tb01481.x

Perlroth, I. (1969). Effects of oceanographic media on equatorial Atlantic hurricanes. *Tellus*, *21*(2), 231–244. doi:10.3402/tellusa.v21i2.10077

Riehl, H. (1954). *Tropical Meteorology*. New York: McGraw-Hill.

Roca, R., Viollier, M., Picon, L., & Desbois, M. (2002). A multi-satellite analysis of deep convection and its moist environment over the Indian Ocean during the winter monsoon. *Journal of Geophysical Research, D, Atmospheres*, *107*(D19), D19. doi:10.1029/2000JD000040

Singh, A. K., & Singh, V. (2018). A Case Study: Heavy Rainfall Event Comparison Between Daily Satellite Rainfall Estimation Products with IMD Gridded Rainfall Over Peninsular India During 2015 Winter Monsoon. *Photonirvachak (Dehra Dun)*. doi:10.100712524-018-0751-9

Singh, A. K., & Singh, V. (2018, April). Validation of INSAT-3D derived rainfall estimates (HE & IMSRA), GPM (IMERG) and GLDAS 2.1 model rainfall product with IMD gridded rainfall & NMSG data over IMD's meteorological sub-divisions during monsoon. *Mausam (New Delhi)*.

Tobin, K. J., Bennett, M. E., Tobin, K. J., & Bennett, M. E. (2010). Adjusting Satellite Precipitation Data to Facilitate Hydrologic Modeling. *Journal of Hydrometeorology*, *11*(4), 966–978. doi:10.1175/2010JHM1206.1

Tyagi, A., Goel, S., Kumar, N., Division, C.W., The, O.O.F., & Meteorology, G.O.F. (2011). A *Report on the Super Cyclonic Storm "GONU" A Report on the Super Cyclonic Storm*. CYCLONE Warn. Div. Off. Dir. Gen. Meteorol. INDIA Meteorol. Dep. IMD MET. Monogr. No CYCLONE Warn. Div. No. 08/2011.

Varma, A. K., Gairola, R. M., & Goyal, S. (2015). *Hydro-Estimator: Modification and Validation*. SAC/ISRO internal report, SAC/EPSA/AOSG/SR/03/2015.

Willoughby, H. E., Marks, F. D. Jr, & Feinberg, R. J. (1984). Stationary and Moving Convective Bands in Hurricanes. *Journal of the Atmospheric Sciences*, *41*(22), 3189–3211. doi:10.1175/1520-0469(1984)041<3189:SAMCBI>2.0.CO;2

Yong, B., Liu, D., Gourley, J. J., Tian, Y., Huffman, G. J., Ren, L., & Hong, Y. (2015). Global View Of Real-Time TrmmMultisatellite Precipitation Analysis: Implications For Its Successor Global Precipitation Measurement Mission. *Bulletin of the American Meteorological Society*, *96*(2), 283–296. doi:10.1175/BAMS-D-14-00017.1

Yu, F., Zhuge, X.-Y., & Zhang, C.-W. (2011). Rainfall Retrieval and Nowcasting Based on Multispectral Satellite Images. Part II: Retrieval Study on Daytime Half-Hour Rain Rate. *Journal of Hydrometeorology*, *12*(6), 1271–1285. doi:10.1175/2011JHM1374.1

Zou, X., & Kuo, Y. (1996). Rainfall assimilation through an optimal control of initial and boundary conditions in a limited-area mesoscale model. *Monthly Weather Review*, *124*(12), 2859–2882. doi:10.1175/1520-0493(1996)124<2859:RATAOC>2.0.CO;2

Chapter 7
Segmentation of Different Tissues of Brain From MR Image

Ankur Priyadarshi
Birla Institute of Technology, India

ABSTRACT

In the most recent couple of decades, medical image processing stood out within picture preparing research fields because of its nonintrusive nature. Restorative imaging modalities, for example, MRI, CT filter, for the most part, rely upon computer imaging innovation to create or show advanced pictures of the inward organs of the human body, which causes the medicine professionals to envision the internal bits of the body. Here the proposed algorithm is thresholding different tissue type of brain MR image. Modes of the histogram represent different tissue types in brain MR image. So, this algorithm depends on the principle of finding maxima and minima using differentiation of the smoothed histogram. Using discrete differentiation, the author finds the multiple thresholds of brain MR image by selecting proper location of minima. The algorithm can be used as an initial segmentation of different tissue types of brain MR image for further accurate detection of the regions.

DOI: 10.4018/978-1-5225-7784-3.ch007

INTRODUCTION TO MR IMAGES

This chapter provides an overview of MR (magnetic resonance) image and basic principles of it.

Overview

MR (Magnetic Resonance) imaging was developed by Paul C. Lauterbur in September 1971 and distributed the hypothesis behind it in March 1973. Human body comprises of for the most part water. Water atoms (H2O) contain hydrogen cores which are otherwise called protons, it winds up adjusted in the attractive field (Gonzalez et al, 2009).

MRI can detect various brain disorders; it can be either stroke-related disorder, structural brain changes or cysts and tumors and many more.

In stroke-related disorder, MRI can be utilized to analyze stroke, which happens when bloodstream to some district of the cerebrum are hindered because of some deterrent. Two noteworthy sorts of strokes are ischemic, caused by the absence of oxygen achieving cerebrum tissue because of corridor narrowing or blockage and hemorrhagic, caused by a broken vein or course.

In auxiliary brain changes the anomalies, for example, birth deserts, improvement distortions, harm caused by therapeutic systems, or cerebral paralysis and these outputs can uncover either extensive or exact moment cerebrum changes. MRI sweeps can likewise be utilized to analyze the impacts of awful cerebrum damage (TBI) on brain tissue. An MRI would pickup be able to little changes caused by the damage, for example, exceptionally modest zones of harm or death.

Since it is touchier than CT examines, MRI is frequently used to track changes in the brain as the individual with a TBI recoups.

Pimples and tumors are particularly little ones or those that are in regions that other imaging strategies like CT filter can't picture well, MRI can be valuable in this circumstance. MRI can be very valuable in helping to diagnose hormonal disarranges that influence the cerebrum.

Characteristics of MR Image

The MR picture shows certain physical attributes of tissue. It is a show of radio recurrence flags that are radiated by the tissue amid the picture procurement process. The wellspring of the signs is a state of polarization that is delivered into the tissue when the patient is put in the solid attractive field. The tissue charge relies upon the nearness of attractive cores. The method utilizes a ground-breaking magnet to adjust the cores of iotas inside the body and a variable attractive field that makes

Figure 1. MRI Machine

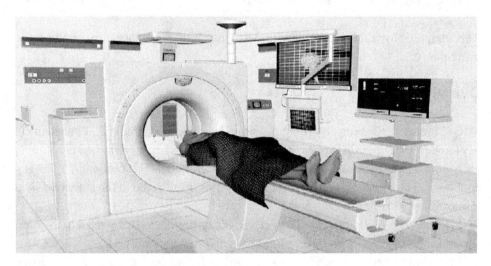

the particle reverberate, a marvel called atomic attractive reverberation. The cores deliver their own particular turning attractive fields that a scanner recognizes and uses to make a picture.

It is also known as nuclear magnetic resonance imaging (NMRI) or Magnetic resonance tomography (MRT).

Visible Tissues Types in a Brain MR Image

Depending on the visible gray sheds found in an MR image of the brain, the tissue present can be classified mainly into three types, namely CSF, Gray-matter, and White-matter.

The CSF (cerebrospinal fluid) is an unmistakable, dull liquid found in the brain and the spinal line shows up as a dim area in an MR picture. It is created in the choroid plexuses of the ventricles of the cerebrum. It goes about as a pad or cradle for the cerebrum, giving fundamental mechanical and immunological insurance to the brain inside the skull.

The outermost part contains skull. Inside the skull lies a connective tissue covering the whole brain and the spinal cord known as meninges. The meningeal covering appears as a whitish-gray envelope about the brain tissue.

The CNS (Central Nervous System) i.e. the brain and the spinal line has two sorts of tissue: dim issue and white issue. The dark issue which has a pinkish-dim shading in the living brain contains the cell bodies, dendrites and axon terminals of neurons, so it is the place all neurotransmitters are. The white issue is made of axons interfacing distinctive parts of dark issue encompassing it.

Figure 2. Classification of MR image

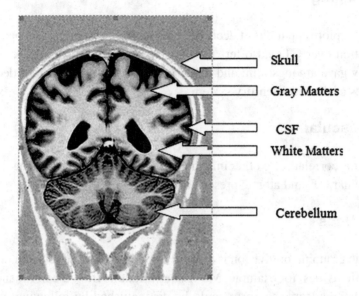

The cerebellum is a structure that is located at the back of the brain, underlying the occipital and temporal lobes of the cerebral cortex

APPLICATION OF MR IMAGE

There are various kinds of applications in real time and medical perspective.

Medical Uses

MRI has an extensive variety of uses in therapeutic conclusion and more than 25,000 scanners are assessed to be in around the world. MRI influences conclusion and treatment in numerous claims to fame despite the fact that the impact on enhanced wellbeing results is questionable.

Since MRI does not utilize any ionizing radiation, its utilization is by and large supported in inclination to CT when either methodology could yield a similar data. MRI is by and large safe strategy, in spite of the fact that wounds can happen because of fizzled security strategies or human blunder.

Neuroimaging

MRI is the explore apparatus of decision for neurological tumors, as it has preferred determination over CT and offers a better representation of the back fossa. The complexity gave amongst dim and white issues settles on it the best decision for some states of the focal sensory system.

Cardiovascular

Heart MRI is correlative to other imaging systems, for example, echocardiography, cardiovascular CT, and atomic prescription.

Clinical Uses

Mind tissue grouping or division is utilized for location and conclusion of ordinary and neurotic tissues, for example, MS tissue variations from the norm and tumors. These variations from the norm could be distinguished by following of changes in volume, shape and local circulation of brain tissue amid follow-up of patients.

Cerebrum picture division assumes an essential part in clinical symptomatic instruments and treatment methods, for example, finding and development and furthermore 3D brain perception for estimating the volume of various tissues in the cerebrum, for example, Gray and White Matter, Thalamus, Amygdala, Hippocampus and so on.

Manual division of brain MRI pictures is a tedious and work utilized for this reason.

Henceforth, the utilization of MR Imaging as an analytic procedure keeps on developing, permitting the investigation of more body parts.

Motivation and Objectives

MR image is the powerful tool for visualizing inside the brain without any surgical intervention. Automatic segmentation of different tissues types can be helpful for finding the pathological changes in the brain.

The main objective is to extract different tissues of the brain from a two-dimensional magnetic resonance brain image.

Proposal Structure

This proposal has been divided into six chapters.

The first chapter consists of a brief overview of Magnetic Resonance Imaging.

The second chapter describes the literature review.

The third chapter describes introduction and brief study about segmentation. It consists of different types of segmentation techniques, its advantages, and disadvantages. It also describes the medical uses and treatments.

The fourth chapter focuses on our proposed approach for segmentation of brain tissue. The proposed method is a modification of conventional histogram based multiple thresholding methods.

The fifth chapter describes the experimental results with detail description of the output images and graphs.

Lastly, we conclude the proposed algorithm by summarizing and discussing the advantages and disadvantages of the proposed method and the future scope.

LITERATURE REVIEW

Annotated Survey

1. This paper introduces the automatic selection of seed points for graph-cut segmentation of MR Images with the tumor. Following are the proposed method s and description (Dogra et al., 2018).
    a. **Centroid Based Seed Selection (CBSS)**: It automatically generates the initial seed point for segmentation. Overall progress starts with an input MR Image which is initially an RGB Image, thus it is converted into a grayscale image. Furthermore, the image is divided into vertical sections and centroid points are calculated. It can be calculated in two steps: Initially, most extreme power distinction between the two vertical parts of the cerebrum ascertained and then centroid focuses from the range above and beneath the most astounding contrast an incentive for foundation and protest district chooses.
    b. **k-Mean Seed Selection (KMSS)**: KMSS system is utilized to enhance the exactness of determination of the seed focuses in lesser time. It is utilized to acquire powerful centroid focuses for the division. Here the number of the cluster must be $k>2$. The increment in the estimation of k brings about increment in bunches which thusly helps in the consideration of miniaturized scale centroid focuses.
2. This paper an automatic brain tumor diagnosis system is presented using a new threshold-based segmentation method. The proposed segmentation method is based on the collaboration of beta mixture model and learning automata (LA). (Edalati-Rad et al., 2018). The proposed method and the results are discussed below:

a. **Preprocessing**: A standout amongst the most critical issues requiring thought is the commotion engaged with the procedure and the way in which to diminish them in restorative images. In light of the current situation of noteworthy contortions in the image, the framework would not adequately distinguish sickness or a few structures in the image. At last, so as to enhance images, disintegration morphological activity is connected.

b. **Segmentation**: The motivation behind image segmentation is to arrange a gathering of pixels in noteworthy locales. This area digs top to bottom also, expansiveness with the components of the proposed technique pointed wat division of MR images in light of edge approach.

c. **Extracting Features**: All things considered, 280 highlights have been extricated from the two arrangements of images histogram and co-event matrix. Correlation, contrast, divergence, vitality, entropy, greatest likelihood, fluctuation and entropy distinction are the absolute most vital of the removed highlights.

d. **Training Process and Classification**: In this paper, SVM classifier is utilized for order purposes. Utilizing SVM in order issues is a legitimate approach that has pulled into the consideration of different scientists. SVM is a managed classifier and claims learning strategy that develops by utilization of a measurable theory originally begat by Vapnik in 1982

3. In this paper, they proposed another; completely computerized T1-w/FLAIR tissue segmentation approach intended to manage images within the sight of WM sores. This approach coordinates a vigorous incomplete volume tissue division with WM exception dismissal and filling, consolidating power and probabilistic and morphological earlier maps. it assesses the execution of this strategy on the MRBrainS13 tissue division challenge database, which contains images with vascular WM injuries, and furthermore on an arrangement of Multiple Sclerosis (MS) understanding images. On the two databases, it approves the execution of there strategy with other best in class strategies. (Valverde et al, 2017).

The Results show that When joining T1-w and FLAIR modalities, their technique has demonstrated extremely focused outcomes with the MRBrainS13 database, positioned at the season of accommodation in the seventh position out of 31 member procedures and being the best non-directed power display approach up until now. With MS information, contrasts in the tissue volume were lower or like the best accessible pipeline made out of the FAST and a best in class technique for injury division and filling. In every one of the analyses, the consideration of the FLAIR methodology into the proposed technique decreased the impact of WM sores on the tissue division, which recommends that this methodology ought to be utilized when accessible. Taking everything into account, their outcomes demonstrate that, in any event with the displayed information, the MSSEG enhances the estimation of cerebrum tissue volume in images containing WM sore.

4. This paper presents a fully automatic brain tumor segmentation method based on Deep Neural Networks (DNNs). The proposed systems are custom fitted to glioblastomas (both low and high review) imagined in MR images (Havaei et al, 2017).

By their exceptional nature, these tumors can show up anyplace in the brain and have any sort of shape, size, and difference. These reasons inspire their an investigation of a machine learning arrangement that endeavors an adaptable, high limit DNN while being to a great degree effective.

5. In this paper a simple three-step algorithm is proposed (Gupta et al., 2017);
    a. Identification of patients that present with tumors
    b. Automatic selection of abnormal slices of the patients, and
    c. Segmentation and detection of the tumor.

Features were extracted by using discrete wavelet transform on the normalized images and classified by support vector machine (for step (1)) and random forest (for step (2)). The 400 subjects were divided into a 3:1 ratio between training and test with no overlap. This study is novel in terms of use of data, as it employed the entire T2 weighted slices as a single image for classification and a unique combination of contralateral approach with patch thresholding for segmentation, which does not require a training set or a template as is used by most segmentation studies.

Using the proposed method, the tumors were segmented accurately with a classification accuracy of 95% with 100% specificity and 90% sensitivity.

6. This paper displays a technique for the programmed division of MR brain images into various tissue classes utilizing a convolutional neural system. (Moeskops et al., 2016).

The outcomes exhibit that the strategy acquires precise divisions in every one of the five sets and subsequently shows its heartiness to contrasts in age and procurement convention.

7.   This paper tells about MSmetrix, an exact and solid programmed strategy for the sore division in light of MRI, free of the scanner or obtaining convention and without requiring any preparation information (Jain et al, 2015).

In MSmetrix, 3D T1-weighted and FLAIR MR images are utilized as a part of a probabilistic model to recognize white issue (WM) sores as an exception to the ordinary brain while fragmenting the cerebrum tissue into the dark issue, WM and cerebrospinal liquid. The real sore division is performed in light of earlier information about the area (inside WM) and the appearance (hyperintense on FLAIR) of sores.

8.   This paper displays a novel strategy of two-phase division. In the principal arrange, it applies Gabor channel banks created utilizing diverse frequencies and introductions. In the sifted image Region Of Interest (ROI) is distinguished and iterative shape discovery strategy is connected to the separated image, which recognizes diverse protests in the image. The division is accomplished by utilizing discrete dim level sets (Havaei et al, 2017).

Tumor area is extricated utilizing edge division and it is broke down for shape and size. The recreation comes about acquired are exceptionally encouraging for the location and investigation of the brain tumor.

9.   In this paper, a PC based technique for characterizing tumor district in the brain utilizing MRI images is exhibited. A characterization of the brain into solid cerebrum or a brain having a tumor is first done which is then trailed by assist order into the benign or harmful tumor. The calculation fuses ventures for preprocessing, image division, highlight extraction and image grouping utilizing neural system procedures.

At long last, the tumor territory is determined by locale of intrigue procedure as affirmation step. An easy to understand Matlab GUI program has been developed to test the proposed calculation (Badran et al, 2010).

10.   This paper represents a review of methods used in brain segmentation. The survey covers imaging modalities, attractive reverberation imaging and strategies for commotion decrease, inhomogeneity remedy, and segmentation. It finishes up with an exchange on the pattern of future research in brain division. The general conclusion of this review paper is, there exist an assortment of the condition of workmanship techniques and great earlier learning for cerebrum MRI division. Yet at the same time, cerebrum MRI division is a testing assignment and there

is a requirement for future research to enhance the exactness, accuracy, and speed of division strategies (Balafar et al, 2010).

11. This paper portrays a programmed tissue division strategy for infant's brains from attractive reverberation images (MRI). The investigation and investigation of infant cerebrum MRI is of awesome enthusiasm because of its potential to concentrate early development designs and morphological changes in neurodevelopmental scatters. Programmed division of infant MRI is a testing assignment chiefly because of the low power differentiates and the development procedure of the white issue tissue. Infant white issue tissue experiences a quick myelination process, where the nerves are canvassed in myelin sheaths. It is important to recognize the white issue tissue as myelinated or non-myelinated locales (Prastawa et al, 2005).

12. The paper display a novel skull-stripping algorithm in view of a mixed approach that joins watershed calculations and deformable surface models.

This technique exploits the strength of the previous and the surface data accessible to the last mentioned. The calculation initially confines a solitary white issue voxel in a T1-weighted MRI image and uses it to make a worldwide least in the white issue before applying a watershed calculation with a flooding stature.

The watershed calculation assembles an underlying assessment of the brain volume in view of the three-dimensional availability of the white issue.

This initial step is powerful and performs well within the sight of force nonuniformities and clamor, however, may disintegrate parts of the cortex that adjoin splendid nonbrain structures, for example, the eye attachments, or may expel parts of the cerebellum. To rectify these mistakes, a surface misshapening process fits a smooth surface to the veiled volume, permitting the joining of geometric requirements into the skull-stripping methodology (Segonne et al, 2004).

13. This paper displays an incorporated strategy for the versatile upgrade for an unsupervised worldwide to-neighborhood division of cerebrum tissues in three-dimensional (3-D) MRI (Magnetic Resonance Imaging) images. Three cerebrum tissues are of intrigue: CSF (CerebroSpinal Fluid), GM (Gray Matter), WM (White Matter).

This coordinated methodology yields a vigorous and precise division, especially in uproarious images. The execution of the proposed strategy is approved by four records on MRI cerebrum ghost images and on genuine MRI images (Xue et al, 2003).

151

14. This paper introduces a basic examination of the present status of semi automated and computerized strategies for the division of anatomical therapeutic images.

Phrasing and critical issues in image division are first exhibited. Current division approaches are then audited with an accentuation on the focal points and hindrances of these strategies for therapeutic imaging applications.

It finishes up with a dialog on the fate of image division strategies in biomedical research (Szilagyi et al, 2003).

15. This paper exhibits an effective and exact, completely programmed 3-D division method for brain MR filters. It has a few striking highlights; to be specific, the accompanying (Marroquin et al, 2002).

    a. Instead of a solitary multiplicative inclination field that influences all tissue powers, isolate parametric smooth models are utilized for the force of each class.

    b. A brain map book is utilized as a part of conjunction with a powerful enrollment technique to locate a nonrigid change that maps the standard cerebrum to the example to be sectioned. This change is then used to section the brain from the nonbrain tissue; figure earlier probabilities for each class at each voxel area and locate a suitably programmed introduction.

    c. Finally, a novel calculation is introduced which is a variation of the desired boost system, that joins a quick and precise approach to discover ideal divisions, given the power models alongside the spatial soundness supposition.

    d. The test comes about with both manufactured and genuine information are incorporated, and also examinations of the execution of this calculation with that of other distributed techniques

SEGMENTATION

Image segmentation is the process of dividing an image into multiple parts. This is typically used to identify objects or other relevant information in digital images. The division of a picture into important structures, picture division, is regularly a basic advance in picture examination, question portrayal, perception, and numerous other picture handling assignments.

An awesome assortment of division strategies has been proposed in the previous decades, and some order is important to show the techniques legitimately here..

Types of Segmentation

The following categories are used:

Threshold Based Segmentation

Histogram thresholding and cutting systems are utilized to section the picture. They might be connected straightforwardly to a picture, yet can likewise be joined with pre-and post-handling methods. Thresholding is presumably the most regularly utilized method to fragment a picture. The thresholding activity is a dim esteem remapping task g characterized by:

$$g(v) = \begin{cases} 0 & if\ v < t \\ 1 & if\ v \geq t \end{cases}$$

where v represents grey value and t is a threshold value.

Thresholding maps a dark esteemed picture to a parallel picture. After the thresholding activity, the picture has been sectioned into two portions, recognized by the pixel esteems 0 and 1 individually.

Numerous strategies exist to choose an appropriate limit an incentive for a division errand. Maybe the most widely recognized technique is to set the edge esteem intelligently; the client controlling the esteem and evaluating the thresholding result until the point that a fantastic division has been acquired. The histogram is frequently a significant device in setting up reasonable edge esteem. At the point when a few wanted sections in a picture can be recognized by their dark qualities, edge division can be reached out to utilize various edges to portion a picture into in excess of two fragments: all pixels with an esteem littler than the main limit are doled out to portion 0, all pixels with values between the first and second edge are relegated to fragment 1, all pixels with values between the second and third edge are doled out to portion 2, and so on.

Edge-Based Segmentation

Since a (paired) protest is completely spoken to by its edges, the division of a picture into discrete articles can be accomplished by finding the edges of those items. An average way to deal with division utilizing edges is (1) figure an edge picture, containing every (conceivable) edge of a unique picture, (2) process the edge picture so just shut protest limits remain, and (3) change the outcome to a common divided picture by filling in the question limits.

Figure 3. Examples of multispectral thresholding, using two channels X and Y. (a)
(x t_1 AND y t_2) (b) (t3 x < t_4 AND t_5 y < t_6)

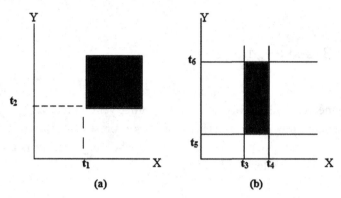

(a)   (b)

Edge Linking

Edge location only here and there gives you the ideal unambiguous and shut limits your requirement for an immediate division.

Region-Based Segmentation

Where an edge based system may endeavor to discover the protest limits and afterward find the question itself by filling them in, an area based procedure adopts the contrary strategy, by (e.g.) beginning amidst a protest and afterward "developing" outward until the point that it meets the question limits.

Locale based division strategies have just two fundamental tasks: part and consolidating, and numerous techniques even component just a single of these. The fundamental way to deal with picture division utilizing consolidating is:

1. Get an underlying (over)segmentation of the picture,
2. Union those nearby fragments that are comparable in some regard to frame single portions,
3. Go to stage 2 until no fragments that ought to be consolidated remain.

Division of pictures is essential to our comprehension of them. Thusly much exertion has been dedicated to conceiving calculations for this reason. Since the sixties, an assortment of methods have been proposed and striven for portioning pictures by distinguishing districts of some normal property. These can be characterized into two principal classes:

Optimum Global Thresholding Using Otsu's Method

One way to choose a threshold is by visual inspection of the image histogram (N. Otsu et al, 1979).

The clearly has two distinct modes; therefore, it is anything but difficult to pick an edge T that isolates them. Another strategy for picking T is by experimentation, picking diverse edges until the point when one is discovered that creates a decent outcome as judged by the eyewitness (Chang et al, 2002).

For the picking the limit consequently, Gonzalez and Woods [2002] depict the accompanying iterative method:

1. Select an underlying evaluation for T. (A proposed introductory gauge is the center point between the base and most extreme power esteems in the picture.)
2. Segment the picture utilizing T. This will create two gatherings of pixels: G1, comprising of all pixels with force esteems $\geq$ T, and G2, comprising of pixels with values < T.
3. Compute the normal force esteems $\mu 1$ and $\mu 2$ for the pixels in the areas G1 and G2.
4. Compute another edge esteem: $T = \frac{1}{2}(\mu 1 + \mu 2)$
5. Repeat stages 2 through 4 until the point that the distinction in T in progressive emphasis is littler than a predefined parameter T_o.

Clustering Techniques

Despite the fact that grouping is here and there utilized as an equivalent word for (agglomerative) division systems, it utilizes it here to mean methods that are principally utilized as a part of exploratory information investigation of high-dimensional estimation designs. In this specific circumstance, bunching techniques endeavor to gather together examples that are comparable in some sense. This objective is fundamentally the same as what it is endeavoring to do when it section a picture, and without a doubt, some grouping procedures can promptly be connected for picture division.

Example

The binary image shown in Table 1 can be represented as a set of data points by listing the coordinates of the 'one' pixels: $\{(1, 0), (1, 1), (2, 1), (2, 2)\}$

While applying to cluster to a double picture, it along these lines utilize a comparative portrayal: every pixel with esteem one is incorporated into an information rundown of organizing sets. For dark esteemed pictures, there may not

Table 1.

0	1	0
0	1	1
0	0	1

be a characteristic change to a rundown of information focuses. For a few sorts of dark esteemed pictures, it is conceivable to consider the dim an incentive as the quantity of information focuses estimated at a specific area.

Application of Segmentation

- Segmentation is, for the most part, the main stage in any endeavor to break down or translate a picture naturally.
- Segmentation crosses over any barrier between low-level picture preparing and abnormal state picture handling.
- Some sorts of division procedure will be found in any application including the discovery, acknowledgment, and estimation of articles in pictures.
- The part of the division is vital in many assignments requiring picture investigation. The achievement or disappointment of the assignment is frequently an immediate outcome of the achievement or disappointment of division.
- However, a solid and precise division of a picture is, by and large exceptionally hard to accomplish by simply programmed implies.
- Industrial examination.
- Optical character acknowledgment (OCR).
- Tracking of items in a succession of pictures Classification of landscapes noticeable in satellite pictures.
- Detection and estimation of bone, tissue, and so on., in medicinal pictures
- Brain MRI segmentation is an essential task in many clinical applications because it influences the outcome of the entire analysis.
- Image segmentation is an imperative advance in numerous medicinal applications including 3-D representation, Computer-aided analysis, estimations, and enrollment (Jain et al., 2015; Joseph et al, 2014).

Proposed Approach to Segmentation

In this section, it will discuss the segmentation approach used here to extract different tissue types from Brain MR Image using the histogram. The initial approach is to disassociate the brain from the skull by using Otsu's algorithm and generate a smooth histogram. As it knows that between every two minima there must be maxima. It will find the minima from the histogram by using differentiation. The smooth histogram will be differentiated twice in order to find the first and second order derivative. it need to segment the MR Image with the help of histogram by giving threshold.

Summary

Image Segmentation is a fundamental starter advance in most programmed pictorial example acknowledgment and scene examination applications. The decision of one division system over another is directed for the most part by the impossible to miss attributes of the issue being considered. The strategies talked about in this section, albeit a long way from comprehensive, are illustrative of systems usually utilized as a part of training. The following are used as the basis for further study of this topic (Bandyopadhyay, 2011; Jana et al, 2014; Sujji et al, 2013).

RESEARCH METHODOLOGY

This chapter discusses proposed algorithm for dissociating brain from the skull and segmenting other tissue types i.e. Cerebro-spinal fluid (CSF), White matter, Gray matter, in high-resolution brain MR images.

The theoretical concept behind segmentation is to use discrete differentiation of the histogram of the smoothed brain image for finding the Multi-level threshold. The local modes of the histogram represent different tissue types of the brain image. Using discrete differentiation the local minima and maxima are computed to extract the regions of the brain.

Introduction

This chapter will discuss methodology behind segmentation and how Fourier descriptor can play an important role in smoothing the histogram. Theoretical aspects of Numerical differentiation are also elaborated in this chapter for a proper description of the proposed algorithm.

The concept of finding local maxima and minima in the histogram is an important measure to decide the different distribution of pixels in an image. Between two local minima, there lies a local maximum that decides the highest concentration of distribution of pixels for a certain gray-level in a region i.e. each hump in the histogram represents some objects in the image. The segmentation operations are performed by searching for these local minima in the histogram by utilizing discrete differentiation as a tool.

The multi-level threshold is preferable as because it is a very fast method for initial segmentation and the representation of different tissue types are more precise and clear with the respect to the original brain MR Image. Segmentation is the vital step to further image analysis and recognition to automate recognition of a pattern in an image. There are different criteria on the basis of which segmentation can be done for e.g. discontinuity, similarity etc.

The multilevel threshold can be a very quick and initial step for helping to extract the desired region from MR Image. By the help histogram representation of the image, it can decide the multi-level threshold and can visualize that specific objects present in an image. Multi-threshold can be divided into a series of the single global threshold.

So, an initial smoothing is required for getting actual distributions of different objects present in an image. Fourier descriptor can be a very good tool in this direction. It has a lot of applications in Image processing in different dimensional. The main objective is to smooth the histogram using the technique of Fourier descriptor.

In next section, there will be a brief discussion about Fourier and inverse Fourier descriptor.

Fourier and Inverse Fourier Descriptor

An image histogram is a graphical representation of the number of pixels in an image as a function of their intensity. In statistics, it shows a visual impression of the distribution of data.

Figure 4. (A) Examples of Brain MR Image and its Histogram

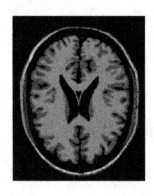
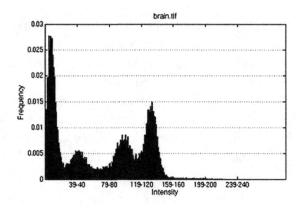

Figure 4 (A) shows Brain MR Image and its histogram, where x-axis denotes the intensity levels and the y-axis denotes frequency.

The histogram peak shows different tissue types like White-matter, Gray-matter, and CSF. The histogram consist lot of fluctuations.

Jean Batiste Joseph Fourier (1768-1830) a renowned mathematician of nineteenth-century introduced the concept of Fourier analysis. To smooth the histogram the concept of Fourier descriptor and inverse Fourier descriptor is used. If the histogram is considered as a curve then forward Fourier transform of the histogram gives a representation it in the frequency domain. By attenuating the higher frequency terms (a low pass filter) the fluctuations in the histogram can be removed. After removing the higher frequencies the resultant curve is returned to the spatial domain. This is the theory of Fourier descriptor which is a way of encoding the shape of an object by taking the Fourier transform of the boundary. Value of Fourier descriptor can be changed according to the desired amount of fluctuations.

Figure 5 shows different histograms of segmented Brain MR Image using different descriptors

Figure 5 (B) shows the histogram representation at different Fourier descriptors.

The inverse Fourier descriptor defines that for different types of functions it is possible to recover a function from its Fourier descriptor. I=IFRDESCP (Z, ND) computes the inverse Fourier descriptors of Z, which is a sequence of Fourier descriptor obtained. Here, ND is the number of descriptors used for computing the inverse and ND must be an even integer no greater than the length (Z).

NUMERICAL DIFFERENTIATION

It is the process of finding the numerical value of a derivative of a given function at a given point. The derivative function f '(x) is defined as:

$$f'(x) = \frac{df(x)}{dx} = \lim_{\Delta x \to 0} \frac{f(x + \Delta x) - f(x)}{(x + \Delta x) - x}$$

The derivative and the slope is here shown by drawing a curve of the histogram and defining the key terms used in differentiation (Wickert et al, 1997).

The derivative of f(x) at "*a*" is the slope of the line tangent to f(x) at "*a*". It can be represented as shown in Figure 6.

In figure 6 (A) points where the derivatives of f (x) are equal to zero are known as Critical points.

Figure 5. (B) An Example of (i) Original segmented MR Image, (ii) Fourier descriptor at 12, (iii) Fourier descriptor at 8, (iv) Fourier descriptor at 3

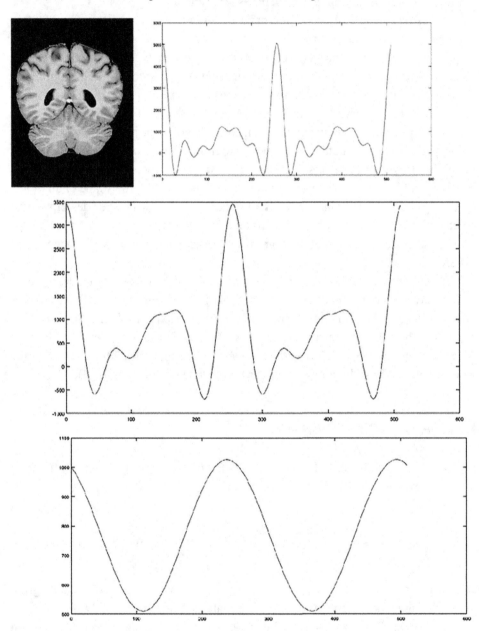

Figure 6. (A) Derivative and the slope

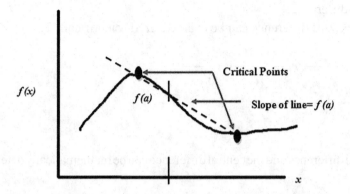

The function might be horizontal in this region or may have achieved a purported extraordinary point, a point where f (x) is at a neighborhood (worldwide) most extreme or nearby (worldwide) least. The second derivative can be utilized to decide whether an outrageous is a most extreme or least.

If the second derivative of f (x) is positive the extreme is a minimum and if it is positive then the extreme is a maximum. Here the concept of Numerical differentiation is used by using two times derivative on the resultant smooth histogram and then inverse the negative values.

Now, will see the concept of local minimum, global and local maximum. It can be shown as in Figure 7.

Figure 7 (B) shows the function f (x) in the histogram which has global maximum, local maximum and local minimum.

Numerical calculations for processing the subordinate of a capacity require the gauge of the slant of the capacity requires the gauge of the slant of the capacity for some specific scope of x esteems.

Figure 7. (B) Maxima and minima in function

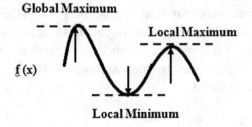

Three basic methodologies are the backward difference, forward difference and the central difference.

The backward difference can be characterized scientifically as

$$f'(x_k) \approx \frac{f(x_k) - f(x_k - 1)}{x_k - x_{k-1}}$$

Forward difference and the central difference can be mathematically determined as:

$$f'(x_k) \approx \frac{f(x_{k+1}) - f(x_k)}{x_{k+1} - x_k}$$

$$f'(x_k) \approx \frac{f(x_{k+1}) - f(x_{k-1})}{x_{k+1} - x_{k-1}}$$

Approach in Numerical Differentiation

Our approach in numerical differentiation initially is to smooth the histogram and find the derivatives of it. After performing Fourier transform higher frequency levels are discarded. In derivative,

- If f `(x) is rising at f `(x) = 0, there is local minima in f (x)
- If f `(x) is falling at f `(x) = 0, there is local maxima in f (x)
- If f ``(x) is rising at f ``(x) = 0, there is local minima in f ` (x) and f (x) is falling
- If f ``(x) is falling at f ``(x) = 0, there is local maxima in f ` (x) and f (x) is rising.

Figure 9(B) numerical differentiation the smoothed histogram has been shown. Here, the red one represents the first order derivative whereas the blue one represents second order derivative. The resultant histogram has some negative integers which need to discard. Say, if the histogram named as f (x), then f (x)> 0. The x-axis denotes the number of grayscales and the y-axis denotes the frequency of grayscales or number of grayscale found.

Figure 8. (A) (i) Original Brain MR Image and (ii) Smooth Histogram

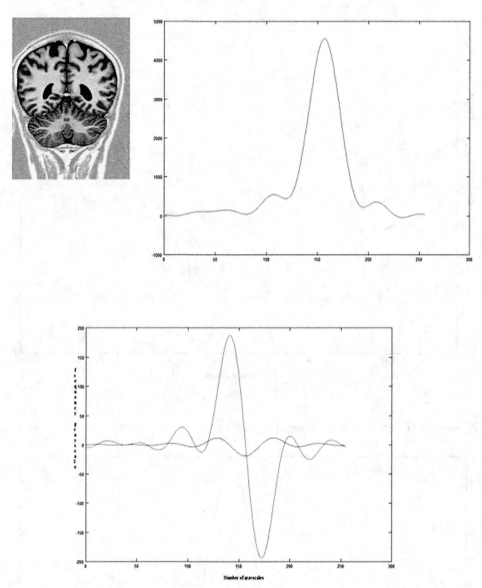

The humps showed in the next histograms shows the non-zero value. It can also be derived as the inverse is taken from the last obtained histogram and the new histogram is obtained:

Figures 9 and 10 (B), (C) shows the non –zero values. The blue ones represent the non- zero value defining different tissue types and frequency of grayscale found in the acquired MR Image. The tallest hump shows the Gray-matter, left side humps

Figure 9. (B) Differentiated histogram of Brain MR Image

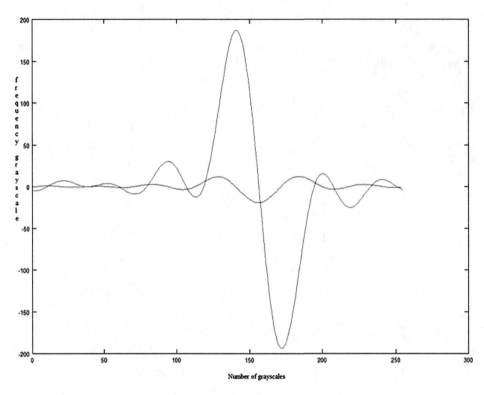

Figure 10. (C) Resultant Histogram

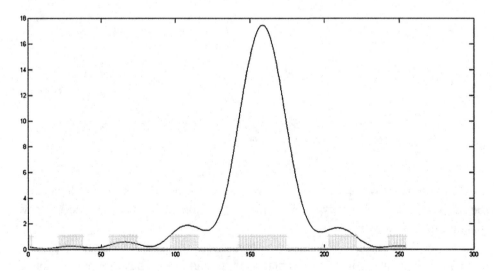

are CSF and right to the tallest hump is White-matter. Numerical differentiation helps us to visualize the intensity of tissue effortlessly.

Multilevel Threshold

Multilevel thresholding is a procedure that portions a dark level image into a few particular locales. This strategy decides in excess of one edge for the given image and sections the image into certain brilliance areas, which compare to one foundation and a few articles. The limit is iteratively re-evaluated as the mean of two class implies. The most troublesome assignment is to decide the suitable number of edges naturally.

Multilevel thresholding uses a number of thresholds $\{T_1, T_2, T_3...., TL\}$ in the histogram of the image f (x, y) to isolate the pixels of the items in the image. By utilizing the got edges, the first image is edge and the divided image T (f (x, y)) is made. The histogram beneath demonstrates the accompanying philosophy and execution.

Figure 11 shows six modes with threshold T_1, T_2, T_3, T_4, T_5 and T_6. It helps to extract the region of the MR Image desired. While giving threshold T_1 and T_2 or T_2 and T_3, it will show the CSF distribution in MR Image. Whereas T_4 and T_5 are Gray-matter and T_5 and T_6 consists of White-matter.

The optimal thresholds are often found by maximizing or minimizing a standard

Figure 11. Five distinctive distributed histogram having Five threshold value T_1, T_2, T_3, T_4, T_5 separates histogram into five nonoverlapping distribution

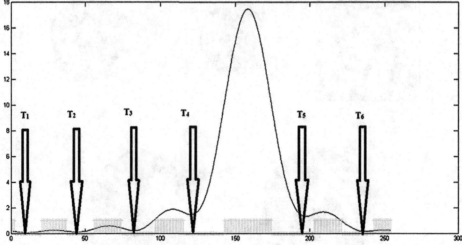

DATA SETS

Here we have used the original brain MR Images retrieved from the medical center. The images used or shown here are the MRI scan of a patient taken during the treatment. The images are protected by copyright.

The images are two dimensional with axial and front views.

The prosposed algorithm was tested over more than 80 MR Images and different tissue types were extracted.

The dataset used here is standard and certified by the medical expertise. Dissociation of the skull is the preliminary step of the proposed algorithm. These MR images of the brain are helpful to detect abnormalities in tissue types. A brain tumor is one of the common problems which is found in most of the test.

Figure 12. Few MR Images of Brain (Data Sets) with different views

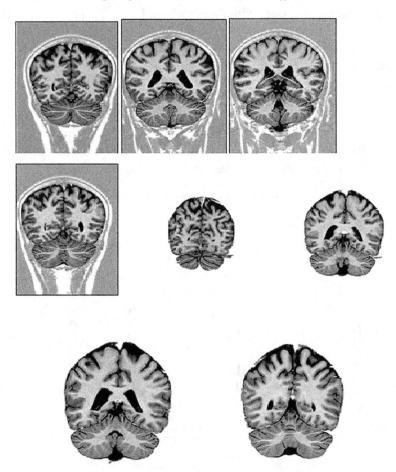

There are few resources available where the authentic and standard data sets are provided by the medical expertise, these images should not be shared to maintain the privacy of the patient report.

SUMMARY

This chapter discusses theatrical approach towards segmentation of Brain MR Image using Numerical differentiation and multilevel threshold technique. Here, it will show the overall distribution with intensity levels.

Figure 13 shows the Axial MR Image and tissue types with proper distribution over histogram. The x-axis denotes the intensity where a total number of points in grayscale and the y-axis denotes frequency occurrence of grayscale. It shows different tissue types where WM (White-matter), GM (Gray-matter) and CSF (cerebrospinal fluid).

RESULTS AND DISCUSSION

This chapter will describe the steps and show the results obtained after performing various operations using the algorithm discussed in the last chapter.

Figure 13. An overview explanation of brain MR Image

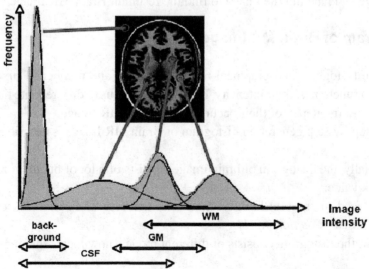

Procedure

This section exhibits the results of our thresholding algorithm after extraction of different tissue types by performing various operations on brain MR Image. As though the whole process, it will examine different modes of the histogram.

Segmentation of Brain from the Skull

In the initial step remove the skull by using Otsu's algorithm, and filling the holes in the resulting image, this gives us a mask for extraction of the brain from the given image (Somasundaram et al, 2010).

The step-by-step segmentation of skull is described below:

- Read an MR Image on which segmentation will be performed.
- An optimal threshold is determined using Otsu's method, and all the pixels above this threshold will is considered as pixels from the skull, so they are eliminated.
- The last step creates some holes in the region of brain tissue because the intensity of the white matter region is near to gray-values of the pixels from the skull. These holes are filled by Mathematical morphology operations. The resultant image is the mask to extract the brain from the original image.

The mask created in the last step is multiplied with the original image to get the image of the brain without background and skull.

Figure 14 shows the process of removal of background (skull) from the original MR image and labeling the image to find the resultant Brain MR Image

Histogram of Brain MR Image

An image histogram is a graphical representation of the number of pixels in an image as a function of their intensity. Histogram helps us to differentiate tissue type intensity and frequency of their occurrence in brain MR Image.

The step-by-step generation histogram of Brain MR Image is described below:

- Initially, the histogram of brain image consists of a lot of fluctuation at every peak value.
- We need to smooth the histogram with the help of Fourier descriptor *[as discussed in section 4.2.1]*.
- Now, the histogram consists of different modes, now locate the minima.

Figure 14. Experimental results after segmentation of brain from the skull, (i) original brain MR Image, (ii) segmented mask, (iii) holes and (iv) Multiplied brain MR image

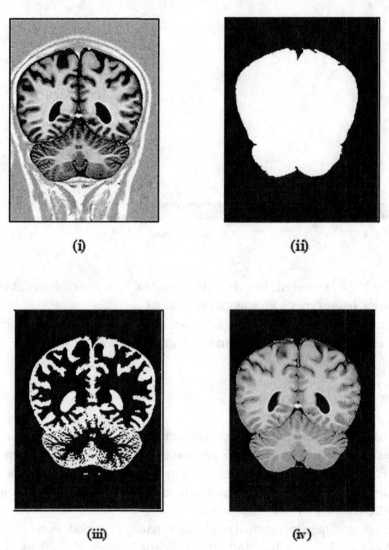

(i)   (ii)

(iii)   (iv)

- The smooth histogram of Brain MR Image helps us to differentiate the different tissue types

Here, histogram representation each mode maps an object in the image. In this case, it shows the three distinctive modes of Brain MR Image. The distinctive modes have local minima and in a continuous histogram between every two minima there exist maxima.

Figure 15. (A) Histogram of Brain MR Image

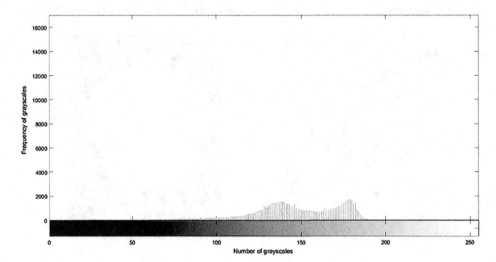

Figure 15 (A) shows the histogram of brain MR Image, the blue peaks denote the different tissue types with a lot of fluctuations.

Figure 16 (B) shows the smooth histogram where humps denote the tissue type. The tallest hump shows the Gray-matter, right to it shows White-matter and left side hump shows the CSF.

Modes of the Histogram

The modes of the histogram are pixels that occur most often in the histogram. Here, in context of Brain MR Image pixels are in the form of Gray-matter, White matter and CSF. They are overall distributed in the histogram. The different modes of the histogram contain different tissue types and can be extracted while giving threshold to the different modes of the histogram.

In this section, the experimental results focus on different modes which are shown in the diagram where it will examine the brain MR Image with skull and the other one which is segmented. The hump in each histogram shows various disposure. Modes in histogram depend on Fourier descriptor. Further with the help of these modes, find the local minima and threshold the histogram of brain MR Image on the basis of different tissue types present.

Here, in next figure, the different brain MR Images shows various modes.

Figure 17 shows the histogram of different tissue types of Brain MR Image where the tissues are marked as of the presence in brain MR Image. Figure 5.1.3 (iii) histogram of MR Image with a skull which contains a lot of fluctuations.

Figure 16. (B) Smooth histogram of brain MR Image

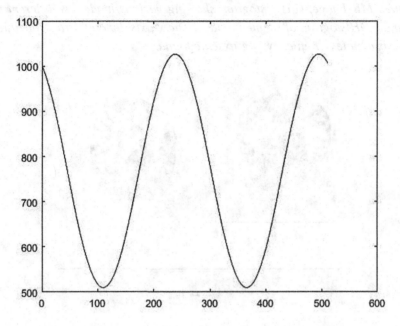

Figure 18 shows different modes of tissue types. In this diagram, there are two local minima. The x-axis denotes the intensity of grayscale and y-axis denotes the frequency of grayscale found. The value of local minima will be less than both the previous value and next value.

Threshold of the Histogram to Acquire Different Tissue Types

It is a non-linear operation that converts a gray-scale image into a binary image where the two levels are assigned to pixels that are below or above the specified threshold value. This section will see different thresholds say $\{T_1, T_2, \ldots, Tn\}$ in the histogram to obtain tissue types. Otsu's method selects the threshold by minimizing the within a class variance of the two groups of pixels separated by the thresholding operator. Assuming that it has set the threshold at T, the normalizedfraction of pixels that will be classified as background and object will be

$$Q_b(T) = \sum_{i=1}^{T} P(i) \, ,$$

For each gray-level value i, P(i) is the normalized frequency of i

Figure 17. Different modes of brain MR Image, (i) Original MR Image and (ii) segmented MR Image, (iii) histogram showing various modes as different tissue types and (iv)Histogram of segment image. The x-axis denotes Grayscale intensity and Y-axis denotes Frequency of grayscale found.

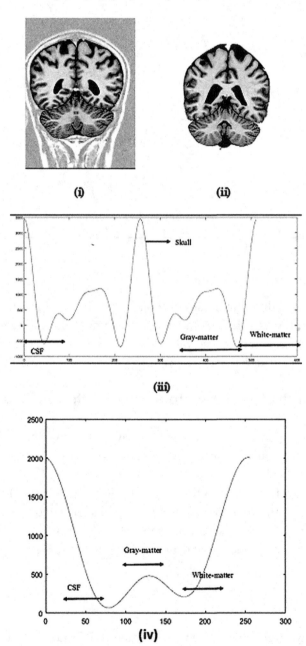

Figure 18. Local minima for brain MR image

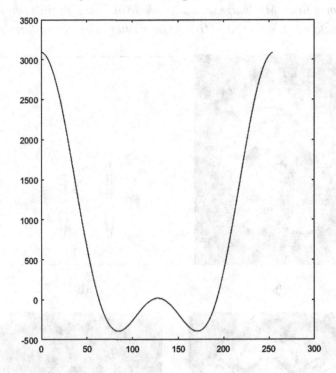

Figure 19 shows the histogram of brain MR Image with threshold locations as T_1 and T_2. Here, when we threshold T_1 and T_2 is given to the histogram, the Gray-matter tissue is extracted and after T_2 White matter is found whereas before T_1 CSF is found.

In next section, we can clearly observe each tissue type with the threshold given at an instance.

RESULTS

In this section, we will see the results of different Brain MR Image. We will discuss the modes, local minima and about tissue types.

Figure 20 (A) shows the process of segmentation of different tissues of Brain from MR Image. Initially Figure 20 (A) (i), it shows the original brain MR image with the skull. Our first step will be to segment the brain from skull so that to get a smooth histogram with different tissue types. We will create a mask and multiply the mask with the MR Image. Figure 20 (A) (ii), shows the dissociation of the skull. The

Figure 19. Threshold to extract different tissue types (i) segmented brain MR image, (ii) Histogram of Brain MR Image with a threshold as T_1 and T_2 (iii)Gray matter after giving threshold i.e. $T_1 < T < T_2$ and (iv) White-matter after giving threshold $T > T_2$

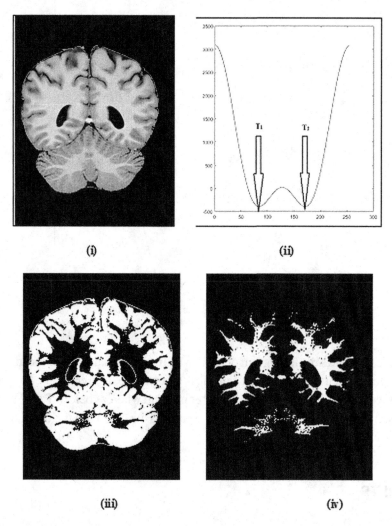

histogram is generated for dissociated skull image. Now we have to find the minima and it will be obtained by differentiating two times the smoothed histogram. Figure 20(A) (iii) shows the local minima obtained. After getting the local minima we need to threshold the brain MR Image by using the histogram. By giving threshold at the minima mode location we will find different tissue types of brain Image. Figure 20(A) (iv), shows the Gray-matter mask. This mask is multiplied with the dissociated brain MR Image. Figure 20(A) (v), shows the resultant image after multiplication. In this way, we can obtain various tissue types from the histogram of brain MR Image.

Figure 20. (A) (i)Original Brain MR Image, (ii)Dissociation of skull, (iii)Local Minima of brain MR Image (iv) Cerebro Spinal Fluid (CSF), (v) Gray-matter mask (vi) Gray-matter, (vii) White-matter mask and (viii) White-matter

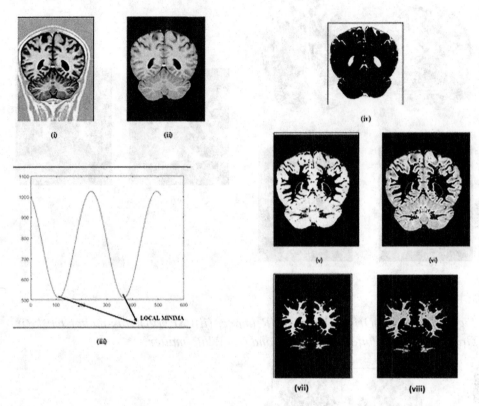

Figure 20(A) (vi), shows the extracted white matter and Figure 20(A) (vii), shows the multiplied resultant. In the end, we got the CSF as shown in Figure 20(A) (viii).

We will use different brain MR Images to study the same results.

The figure 21 (B) is segmented brain MR Image so, we will visualize different tissue types.

TABULAR REPRESENTATION

After experimental analysis with few of the images, the locations of different tissue types are almost same because of uniform brain MR Images.

Figure 21. (B) (i)Original Brain MR Image, (ii) Cerebro Spinal Fluid (CSF), (iii) Gray-matter mask (iv) Gray-matter, (v) White-matter mask and (vi) White-matter

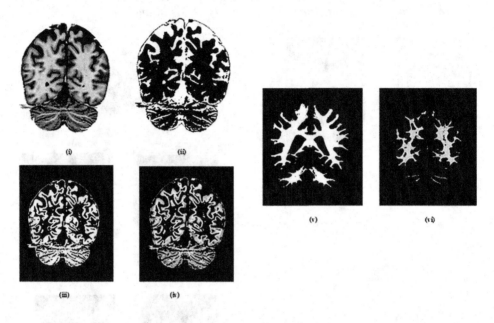

Figure 22. (C) (i)Original Brain MR Image, (ii)CSF, (iii)Gray-matter mask (iv) Gray-matter, (v)White-matter mask and (vi) White-matter

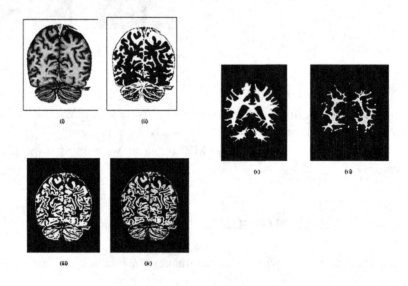

Table 2. Different brain MR Image representing tissue types at their threshold locations

Figure Name	Csf	Gray-Matter	White-Matter
5.2(A)			
5.2(B)	T < 85	85 < T < 172	T > 172
5.2(C)			

CONCLUSION AND FUTURE WORK

Conclusion

Segmentation of brain Image in various tissue parts is indispensable in careful arranging and treatment arranging in the field of medication. The proposed algorithm is the novel technique of segmenting different tissues of the brain from MR Image. The threshold is the quick technique for initial segmentation. The advantage of this technique is that from the local minima we can give multilevel threshold can easily extract different tissue types.

It shows that the various experimental results on various Brain MR Images give a better result. There is a disadvantage of this proposed algorithm is that for few images the results do not show the effective output.

The strength of this chapter is multilevel segmentation which helps discretely to detect various tissue types using the smoothed histogram. It helps in detection of disorder in any particular tissue using derived algorithm. This algorithm works with more objects in single image and retrieves each tissue type.

The weakness of segmentation for particularly MR Image is clarity and removal of noise. It becomes tough task in few cases where the removal of skull is not properly executed and the tissue type's extraction becomes a challenging task. Another big problem with most segmentation algorithms is lack of repeatability in presence of even a slight change in visual content. If you change the scale of the scene while keeping the content roughly the same, we will notice over-segmentation or under-segmentation depending on whether you zoom in or zoom out respectively.

Future Work

Our future work would be on improvisation in segmentation technique to get better results. In brief, when we segment the skull from Brain MR Image we got few results which do not work efficiently. As because after removal of the skull from Brain MR Image there is need to generate smooth histogram which is not possible if the skull is not segmented in a good manner or the threshold do not properly. So, segmentation is an important fundament to extract different Tissue types. We have to implement a better way to segment it.

REFERENCES

Badran, E. F., Mahmoud, E. G., & Hamdy, N. (2010). An algorithm for detecting brain tumors in MRI images. In *Computer Engineering and Systems (ICCES), 2010 International Conference on*. IEEE. 10.1109/ICCES.2010.5674887

Balafar, M. A., Ramli, A. R., Saripan, M. I., & Mashohor, S. (2010). Review of brain MRI image segmentation methods. *Artificial Intelligence Review*, *33*(3), 261–274. doi:10.100710462-010-9155-0

Bandyopadhyay, S. K. (2011). *A survey on Brain Image Segmentation Method. Journal of Global Research in Computer Science, 2.*

Chang, Fan, & Chang. (2002). Multi-Modal Gray-level histogram modeling and decomposition. *Image and Vision Computing, 20*, 203-216.

Dogra, J., Jain, S., & Sood, M. (2018). Segmentation of MR Images using Hybrid kMean-Graph Cut Technique. *Procedia Computer Science*, *132*, 775–784. doi:10.1016/j.procs.2018.05.089

Edalati-rad, A., & Mosleh, M. (2018). Improving Brain Tumor Diagnosis Using MRI Segmentation Based on Collaboration of Beta Mixture Model and Learning Automata. *Arabian Journal for Science and Engineering*, 1–13.

Gonzalez, R. (2009). *Digital Image Processing* (3rd ed.). Addison- Wesley.

Gupta, T. (2017). *Tumor Classification and Segmentation of MR Brain Images.* arXiv preprint arXiv:1710.11309

Havaei, M., Davy, A., Warde-Farley, D., Biard, A., Courville, A., Bengio, Y., ... Larochelle, H. (2017). Brain tumor segmentation with deep neural networks. *Medical Image Analysis*, *35*, 18–31. doi:10.1016/j.media.2016.05.004 PMID:27310171

Jain, S., Sima, D. M., Ribbens, A., Cambron, M., Maertens, A., Van Hecke, W., ... Smeets, D. (2015). Automatic segmentation and volumetry of multiple sclerosis brain lesions from MR images. *NeuroImage. Clinical*, *8*, 367–375. doi:10.1016/j. nicl.2015.05.003 PMID:26106562

Jana & Chatterjee. (2014). *Automatic segmentation of different brain tissue from MR image*. IEEE CALCON.

Jodoin, P.-M., & Lalande, A. (2008). Markovian method for 2D, 3D and 4D segmentation of MRI. *Proceedings International Conference on Image Processing*. 10.1109/ICIP.2008.4712429

Joseph, Singh, & Manikandan. (2014). Brain Tumour MRI Image Segmentation and Detection In Image Processing. *IJRET, 3*.

Joshi, Charan, & Prince. (2015). A novel methodology for brain tumor detection based on two-stage segmentation of MRI images. In *Advanced Computing and Communication Systems, 2015 International Conference on*. IEEE.

Marroquin, J. L., Vemuri, B. C., Botello, S., Calderon, E., & Fernandez-Bouzas, A. (2002). An accurate and efficient Bayesian method for automatic segmentation of brain MRI. *IEEE Transactions on Medical Imaging*, *21*(8), 934–945. doi:10.1109/ TMI.2002.803119 PMID:12472266

Moeskops, P., Viergever, M. A., Mendrik, A. M., de Vries, L. S., Benders, M. J. N. L., & Isgum, I. (2016). Automatic segmentation of MR brain images with a convolutional neural network. *IEEE Transactions on Medical Imaging*, *35*(5), 1252–1261. doi:10.1109/TMI.2016.2548501 PMID:27046893

Otsu, N. (1979). A threshold selection method from gray level histograms. *IEEE Transactions on Systems, Man, and Cybernetics*, *SMC-9*(62-66).

Prastawa, M., Gilmore, J. H., Lin, W., & Gerig, G. (2005). Automatic segmentation of MR images of the developing newborn brain. *Medical Image Analysis*, *9*(5), 457–466. doi:10.1016/j.media.2005.05.007 PMID:16019252

Ségonne, F., Dale, A. M., Busa, E., Glessner, M., Salat, D., Hahn, H. K., & Fischl, B. (2004). A hybrid approach to the skull stripping problem in MRI. *NeuroImage*, *22*(3), 1060–1075. doi:10.1016/j.neuroimage.2004.03.032 PMID:15219578

Somasundaram, K., & Kalaiselvi, T. (2010). A Method for Filling Holes in Objects of Medical Images using Region Labelling and Run Length Encoding Schemes. In *Image processing* (pp. 110–114). NCIMP.

Sujji, Lakshmi, & Jiji. (n.d.). MRI brain Image Segmentation based on Thresholding. *International Journal of Advance Computer Research, 3*, 97-101.

Szilagyi, L. (2003). MR brain image segmentation using an enhanced fuzzy c-means algorithm. In *Engineering in Medicine and Biology Society, 2003. Proceedings of the 25th Annual International Conference of the IEEE* (Vol. 1). IEEE. 10.1109/IEMBS.2003.1279866

Valverde, S., Oliver, A., Roura, E., González-Villà, S., Pareto, D., Vilanova, J. C., ... Lladó, X. (2017). Automated tissue segmentation of MR brain images in the presence of white matter lesions. *Medical Image Analysis, 35*, 446–457. doi:10.1016/j.media.2016.08.014 PMID:27598104

Wickert, M. (1997). *Numerical differentiation (tutorial)*. University of Colorado at Colorado Springs.

Xue. (n.d.). An integrated method of adaptive enhancement for unsupervised segmentation of MRI brain images. *Pattern Recognition Letters, 24*, 15.

Chapter 8
Sentilyser:
Embedding Voice Markers in Homeopathy Treatments

Arunima Mookherjee
Symbiosis International University
(Deemed), India

Pranav Sunil Prajapati
Symbiosis International University
(Deemed), India

Preeti Mulay
Symbiosis International University
(Deemed), India

Sonali Johari
Symbiosis International University
(Deemed), India

Rahul Joshi
Symbiosis International University
(Deemed), India

Swati Sunil Prajapati
Independent Researcher, India

ABSTRACT

Cognitive and somatic health is predominantly congruous. Happiness creates a propitious impact on a person's wellbeing. Likewise, stress can be detrimental to a person's overall health. Nevertheless, it is perplexing to truly understand an emotional state of a patient for an unerring diagnosis. Considering the old adage, necessity is the mother of invention, there is a need for a sentimental and emotional analysis tool for the accurate identification of the mental state of the patient. Thus, Sentilyser was created. It is a clinical decision support system. Using the recorded voice of a person, the mood is analyzed using support vector regression. Arousal and valence of the audio file is calculated, and thus, the corresponding mood is predicted. The objective of this chapter is to propose the use of Sentilyser as a part of a patient's diagnosis, which will not only help the physician reach a better conclusion but will also help them in cases where the patients themselves are unaware about their own psychological state.

DOI: 10.4018/978-1-5225-7784-3.ch008

INTRODUCTION

Homeopathy has the power to treat patients well and is basically it's a preventive approach of healthcare world. Homeopathy works both on physical and psychological levels of an individual. In addition to physical ailments, psychological set up also plays an important role. To utilize this power of homeopathy in this busy world with ever growing patients, technology support for the doctor is must. One of the aspects of providing technical support to homeopathy doctor is considered in this research and that is mood of the patient. It is necessary to collaborate technology with homeopathy treatment, so as to provide helping hand to the doctor, maintain the history of patient in soft form and on cloud for ease of access, and also to learn from the history for effectual treatment of the patient. Such collaboration is also able to find the hidden ailments if any, during the patients visit to the doctor, based on the frequency of the voice using mobile apps. It is necessary to extend this research further to tackle the various other aspects of humans or any other leaving entity for their wellbeing as homeopathy is useful not only for humans.

Vocal biomarkers: the future of diagnostic medicine, a diagnostic tool for your physician to indicate signs of illnesses ranging from stress and depression to cardiovascular diseases (Rath et al, 2019). Technology enabled healthcare (Rath and Pattanyak, 2018; Rath et al, 2018). service is the prospect. Hence in this research proposed a very handy, user-friendly, effectual support system for homeopaths. The sky is the limit for use of biomarkers, voice markers and the available variety these days, in almost all aspects of healthcare. The various applications of Machine Learning with collaboration with biomarkers is possible in allopath as well, to not only diagnose but predict and prevent, with emphasis on historical data of patients, valuable notes by doctor taken time to time and prescriptions suggested etc.

Technology Collaborated homeopath's practice will not only give an edge to the patient but also to the healthcare professionals. Patients details can be easily summarized using such a technology collaborated research, it can be used as the patient consults with doctor or vice versa, in case of emergency also. Machine learning with focus on incremental learning approaches is exercised in this research to achieve the said collaborated homeopath practice.

Discovery of knowledge from patient's data is challenging task. Sentilyser is intended to use techniques that discover hidden patterns and establish linkage between the voice and mood of the patient. If a doctor often records sessions with patients for analyzing their development through different therapy sessions, it generates an incessant flow of data which can be used further for betterment in patient's treatment. It in turn be a tool to harness the innate characteristics of the generated data but can be convenient and beneficial. Sentilyser is an intelligent decision-making tool in the clinical workflow. This tool will not only analyze mood of the patient but also spawn out patients' mood variation graph during his visits to clinic. This in turn generates a brief summary for a patient from his/her reports. On the top of this, Sentilyser can also analyze whether the physician is in a good health condition/ mood to consult the patients or not.

BACKGROUND

Homeopathy treats every disease from psychosomatic point of view and history about psychological and emotional disturbed states is evoked along with appropriate Homeopathic remedy to attend cure.

The emotional state of mind can be influenced through Homeopathic therapies. Homeopathic therapies can quell psychological disturbance such as anxiety, irritability, obsessive-compulsive traits, jealousy, neurosis, fears, depression, etc.

Work stress, lack of physical exercise, unbalanced diet and the dearth of sharing sentiments put strain in everybody's life acting as predisposing factors for psychosomatic and psychological illness. A WHO (World Health Organization) survey shows that psychiatric disorders become the leading causes of diseases all over the world (Sayers, 2001). Few people can handle stress positively treating it as a motivating factor to excel, but in others cases, it can act as a burden almost taking a toll on their health, affecting both physically and emotionally. Affecting the thought process, forcing compensation with feelings and altering behavior also. If overlooked, it may lead to chronic diseases like diabetes, hypertension, hypothyroidism, insomnia or psychiatric illness (Russell et al, 1997; Patel et al, 1967).

The first step Homeopathic physician's does in order to cure the convalescent individual is conducting an elaborate interview, termed as an homeopathic case enlisting his thorough details. It also captures history narrated by the patient and his relatives/friends, leading to an unprejudiced observation, perception made by the physician and record of carried out clinical examinations. This collective data is the key for finding out suitable remedy required for the patient along with Homeopathic Materia Medica, Organon of Medicine, and Repertory (Fontaine et al, 2007; Awad et al, 2015).The psychological symptoms help to differentiate among number of available remedies whose physical symptoms are similar. Thus, detailed cognitive symptoms and peculiar physical symptoms acts as a combo for the physician as a correct remedy to treat patients which in a way assures a holistic cure. Underlying emotions can be interpreted accurately using Voice analysis and provides faster, precise conviction in the selection of remedy.

Across the globe there are different Regulation for the Homeopathy practice. India is the capital of Homeopathic Physicians practicing in hospitals, dispensaries, and clinics. It comes under the umbrella of AYUSH (Ayurveda, Yoga and Naturopathy,

Unani, Siddha, and Homoeopathy), statute of the Indian government. In the United States (US), the FDA (Food and Drug Administration) regulates homeopathic remedies. According to the Federal FD&C Act 1938 and HPUS (Homeopathic Pharmacopoeia Of The United States), there is a practice in USA for making the homeopathic drugs official, they need to be manufactured and labeled as per guidelines of the Act and need to be tested for the intended scope of effect.

Literary Review

Nowadays people are inclined towards holistic approach of treatment which Homoeopathy offers. Homeopathy is a medication system where a detailed history of a patient is created and physical, emotional and intellectual symptoms of the patient are evaluated. These symptoms are then converted to rubrics and it is then further referenced to conclude the correct remedy (a.k.a. *Similimum*). Homeopaths are now using *Repertorisation, a Software* useful in identifying the correct remedy. Repertories are now incorporated into software to ease the patient evaluation. The search engine allows quick rubric selection with various cross-references. The tool then computes and suggests a single or group of probable curative remedy. Picking the right sentimental - emotional symptom is subjected to skill set of the physician.

In Homeopathy, psychological symptoms are at the highest priority while deciding a curative remedy for the patient. If the physician fails in accurately judging the patient's symptoms then he may end up in selecting a remedy which will result in relief or cure to the patient. Thus, appropriate gathering and intermittent interpretation of psychological symptoms are critical. There are multiple factors which influence the incorrect interpretation of such patients – in some cases patients are unable to open up their entire story on the first visit. Language can be barrier due to which the patient may not be able to describe his/her feeling correctly. Some patients have extremely compensated state of mind and they cannot elicit their deeper feelings at all. On the other hand, some patients are impatient and fail to recognize the importance of questioning and hence avoid answering or may end in wrong answers.

The outcome of *"Sentilyser"* is voice analysis tool which can be a significant help to Homeopaths – This tool/application can identify and interpret the complex human emotions. Using this tool the Homeopathic physician can differentiate between joy, happiness, amusement, enthusiasm, anxiety, sadness, anger, fear, and other emotions – and can conclude the right symptoms. This enables them to choose the right remedy or to identify the curative remedy which in turn will give relief to the patient. This in a way makes the case taking process prompt and easy. To achieve expected cure, it needs series of follow-ups and consultation. Emotions are dynamic and symptoms intensity can vary during each follow-up. *Sentilyser* can be useful in picking-up these subtle variances. Hence, it's iterative use will surely accelerate process of healing in Homoeopath therapy.

Sentilyser is developed in Python and so, it is a open source tool, which means there won't be any further hindrance for further develop and upgrade of this tool. *Sentilyser* has ability to correctly identify the mood and current psychological situation of the patient. It can also be able to classify emotional and intellectual state of patient. This tool can be trained as per needs and can evolve over the period, thus the efficiency will automatically increase as the machine learning (Nijeweme-d'Hollosy et al, 2018) algorithms are incorporated into this system. Once the tool is completely trained, doctors can process their dataset using this tool to achieve best results. In most of the cases physicians are unable to provide relief to the patient due to limited understanding about patients' emotion; *Sentilyser* can help them for finding out the exact *Similimum*!

COALESCENCE OF HOMEOPATHY AND MACHINE LEARNING

The Art and Science of Case Taking

Every individual is different and can react differently to similar situations. No two individuals are alike in nature/temperament (Mulav et al, 20017). Every individual has a unique tendency by hereditary, these tendencies have direct relationship with disease symptoms deciding psychophysical disposition of an individual. Dr. Samuel Hahnemann the founder of the Homeopathic system emphasized that sound psychological health can keep individual healthy (Fisher et al, 2007). Dr.George Vithoulks, a well known Homoeopath said that *"When something is created by man, it is first conceived in his mind"* so disease is not an invader from outside but an expression of susceptibility from within. Homeopathy treats the person as a whole and involves in-depth study about patient's physical complaints, medical history and emotional makeup viz., feelings and temperament. A thorough understanding of the psychological, physical and subconscious state of a human is a prerequisite for treating a person holistically (Fisher, 2012).

Case taking is the process of facts gathering about the patient, through narration given by the patient and his/her relatives, clinical examinations, family history, observation and perception of the physician about patient. These facts can then be used to find a remedy to the patient. An elaborated interview is mandatory to record the symptoms and to analyze the person (Patel, 1967).

Hahnemann has highlighted the importance of unprejudiced observation in the sixth aphorism of the book titled Organon of Medicine (Awad et al, 2015). It is of utmost importance that the homeopathic has to observe and to take down notes about patient's symptoms without any preconceived theories, interpretation regarding how, why and what symptoms are expressed by the patient. This is one of the essential skills a physician needs to acquire to become a successful homeopath practitioner. Sometimes preconceived notions are also common to remedies and physician may start questioning to confirm remedy to related symptoms.

A well-recorded case can be a key for assuring cure to the patient. Thus, deeper elicitation of psychological symptoms and peculiar physical symptoms lead the physician to decide the correct remedy for their patient which in turn assures a holistic cure.

Analysis and Evaluation of Case with the Help of Repertory

Homeopathic Materia Medica is a compilation of therapeutic properties of each drug. These properties are determined through process called "Provings" or "Homeopathic Pathogenetic Trials". Unlike modern medicine, the Homeopathic drugs are also proved to effective to humans. Detailed reaction of each drug to the physical and intellectual level are noted. The same drug can be tested on different individuals viz., men, women, and children. There are more than 3000 proven remedies in Homeopathy (Lake et al, 2007). Typically each remedy can have 100 to 500 symptoms ("Information Week", n.d.). This platter of symptoms can often be a hurdles to a physician. Just imagine if there is a need of browsing these many remedies for finding out which are the most suitable symptoms for a particular case.

Compiled indexes of the Homeopathic Materia Medica are termed as 'Repertory '. During past 170 years, more than 110 different repertories have been published as existing Homeopathic literature. Such repertory is a compilation of information gathered from various sources viz. proven remedies, history about sources and patients, physiology of disease, clinical practices, and toxicology.

A physician is required to have sound knowledge of repertory in order to select the symptoms. The physician decides the symptoms from the patient's narrations, his/her unprejudiced observations, physical gestures and lastly confirmation of interpretation by the patient. Repertory use should be absolutely judicious. Every physician must know that each repertory is based on certain philosophy and principle, simply selecting the rubrics and adding the totality will not give a suitable remedy. Repertory can't be used as a mechanical tool available but also comprehensive knowledge about each repertory can optimize the efforts and result of the physician. In most of the scenarios what a patient says upfront may not be his correct feeling, understanding these feelings and aptly converting them to Rubric is a skill. Once that dexterity is achieved, use of repertory will nail the desired remedy.

Each symptom in the repertory is known as a Rubric. Rubrics are graded and drugs each rubric indicate their intensity and relevance.

There are three grades for rubrics ranging from three to one, obviously three is the highest grade.

- Grade 3 remedies are written in Bold letters. They are Proved, Re-Proved and Clinically verified rubrics
- Grade 2 remedies are written in Italics. They are Proved, Re-Proved and occasionally verified
- Grade 1 remedies are written in plain text. These are not been clinically verified. Remedies are graded as per the intensity of involved symptoms and higher the number of provers, the remedy was supposed to be susceptible to undertaken symptoms during proving. For remedies grade one is the highest and grade three is the lowest.
- Grade 1 remedies are written in Bold. The experienced symptoms here were of highest intensity during proving.
- Grade 2 remedies are written in Italics. Symptoms experienced here are relative of low intensity as compared to Grade 1.
- Grade 3 remedies are written in plain text. The involved symptoms have mild intensity.

The gradation of remedies allows the physician to choose the precise remedy from the repertorisation table. In repertorisation, more weight is given for achieving right match among the intensity of symptoms experienced by a patient and symptoms covered under a particular repertory (Polony et al, 2005).

Different repertorisation software are available nowadays to aid and provide ease in the process of referring prescription to the patient after referring to hundreds of thousands of symptoms from multiple remedies. They simplify the process of rubric selection and prepares repertorisation by computation. Mathematical approach is used here, acting as a helping hand in selection of emotional and intellectual symptoms. The foresee value of *Sentilyser* is to analyze voice and assist in interpretation of emotions, to give immediate *sentinalysis*™ of an underlying psychological symptom of the patient (Van Hootegem, 2007) using some s machine learning regression algorithm like support vector regression or convolution neural networks, etc. Incorporating such an important tool can enhance the case understanding. Many cases who fail to extract the exact similimum can be aided by using this tool (Fichefet et al, 1991).

Role of Voice Analysis Tool in Journey Towards Cure

Distance is no longer a barrier. People are now availing online consultation from physician. Long distance treatments are easy to undertake nowadays with the enablement of technology. There is a drastic increase in online consultation via Skype, Google, and Mobile Phones.

Lifestyle illness and illness due to stress are at the peak. Conditions like depression, bipolar diseases, suicidal disposition, anxiety, and phobias are more often nowadays than that before. Such conditions require a detailed understanding about the person. Sometimes physicians are unable to comprehend true feeling of the patient during consultation or unable to recognize the correct pitch and tone of a person over the telephonic conversation or over the internet. Hence, physician may not be able to narrow down the correct symptom and its conversion will lead to an inaccurate rubric. This reduces the success rate of a physician. On the other hand If use of *Sentilyser* is incorporated in such cases, the physician can be able to easily draw the apt emotional symptom of the patient allowing them to inquest further in detail (Xue et al, 2009). More accurate assessment about the patient's condition can be done, which will undoubtedly uplift the success rate statistics of physician.

Psychological symptoms are variegated in nature (Bell et al, 2004). A physician is supposed to examine different mind states of the patient with more precision for e.g. if a patient pretends that he is a very anxious person, anxiety need to be defined in this case like anxiety for what in particular or is it due to fear or panic attack. The tone, pitch of words used by patient to narrates his/her symptoms can help in identifying the deeper emotions, acting as inputs to the voice analysis tool, adding value to the process. In some cases patient is unable to talk due to big pause with deep sigh during narration, such indications can be easily picked up by the voice analyzer in order to judge the underlying emotion.

Physicians understandings, observations, and *sentinalysis* all in conjunction will improvise the process of case taking and analysis. If these preliminary steps are carefully exercised by the physician, more than half of the path of cure can be conquered.

Follow-up consultations are an integral part of homeopathic treatment. In Homeopathy every follow-up is handled like an initial interview in order to examine the patient as a whole. During subsequent visits, post first consultation, the physician revisits the earlier symptoms recorded for the patient. The Homeopaths then evaluates their response against the remedy prescribed by them. The physician is ultimately intends to provide sign of reliefs to the patient. Mere and insignificant frequency relief signs can be reduced, symptoms intensity and decrease in number of disease symptom be either at a physical or cognitive level. Use of *sentinalysis* can play an important role throughout the case lifecycle of the patient till he/she is free from illness and the same can be reflected as an alleviation of his/her physical, emotional symptoms.

Moreover, when a physician is enquiring to the patient's about his/her symptoms during the first consultation or during follow-up consultations the *Sentilyser* can aptly pick signs about physicians emotions. In retrospect, this will also help the physician to analyze his own emotions while noting down the case, will help him to recognize whether he is reacting with emotions to patients answers, asking questions after being influenced by these emotions. This iterative of use of *Sentilyser* can definitely accelerate the process of healing in Homoeopathy.

Usability Survey Carried out in this Research

A brief questionnaire was shared with 4000 Homeopaths. The survey was populated on SurveyMonkey.com and based on captured responses against populated question below mentioned six graphs were prepared. The aim of this survey was to understand challenges involved in clinical practice and role of emotional symptoms in healing the patient, to identify the usage probability of Voice Analysis interface in clinical practice.

Summary for the 4000 responses received can be observed in Figure 1:

1. Would a homeopath like to use a voice analysis tool to help understand/interpret the emotional state of the patient?
2. Do the homeopaths use any system to identify the emotional state of the patient?
3. Are any homeopath using any software/ technology in remedy for a patient?
4. Do correct interpretation identify the right symptoms of mind (emotional state of the patient) and positively impacts the outcome of cases and gives lasting relief to patients?
5. How difficult is it to elicit/interpret symptoms of cognitive state during the initial consultation taking?

Knowledge Discovery by Clinical Decision Support System (CDSS)

Discovery of hidden patterns from an unwearying flow of data is extremely arduous. There is a human tendency to ferret for some significant detail from a huge dataset is abstruse, it is time-consuming and inefficient. After all humans are prone to error! Subtle distinctions might be missed. As a remedial measure, Artificial Intelligence (AI) is integrated into the process of knowledge discovery to prepare the data

Figure 1. Responses of 4000 homeopaths

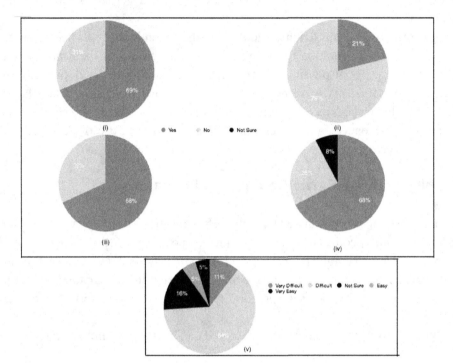

veracious and precise. To make the system decisions acute, there is a profound use of Machine Learning models which makes these systems intelligent and smart.

The first such example of a clinical decision support system was MYCIN (Shortlifffe et al, 1975) created by Edward Shortliffe under the guidance of Bruce G. Buchanan, this can be considered to be an early example of AI, which used the quotidian backward chaining IF-ELSE rule. Nonetheless, it set a precedence for many existing intelligent CDSS systems (Murphy, 2006) like Archimedes IndiGO, DiagnosisOne etc as these are solely based on electronic health record generation.

This knowledge discovery can be used to design and develop the state of art decision support system (Keen, 1980; Wright et al, 2008). Sentilyser, the Clinical Decision Support System (CDSS) is carefully designed to be a non-knowledge-based inference rather than just an assessment system. Generally, there are two types of decision support system, knowledge based and non-knowledge based. Knowledge based DSS are usually built on IF-ELSE rule or switch cases for multiple conditions, non-knowledge base DSS are built on Artificial Intelligence. The Non Knowledge based DSS might use artificial neural network. DSS using ANN are made on multiple layers deep, feed-forward artificial neural networks like Convolution Neural Networks, recurrent neural networks, etc. The DSS based on Genetic algorithms are generally inspired from biology and based on adaptive heuristic algorithms. The third type uses regular machine learning algorithm. In the case of Sentilyser, a regular machine learning algorithm called Support Vector Regression is used.

The decision intelligence consolidates findings on cognitive bias, decision making and conditional perception lead to collaboration and organizational design, with engineering application. This intelligent CDSS will in a way help each and every technologically equipped physician to twirl the trenchant sword of machine learning to prepare his diagnosis scrupulous, therefore extending data science to the fathom of problems categorized as Black Swan Events (Taleb, 2007). Black Swan events are extremely rare, and might surprise people. It might have a positive or a negative effect on the system. These are severe cases of outlier detection.

There are three main components of the support system proposed in this research chapter, which effectually creates the knowledge base of patient's details, treatments given etc. with proper timestamp. These patient and treatment details can be fetched by the doctor as and when required during revisits or in case of emergencies too, with the help of the cloud computing concepts. The knowledge base or the dataset is primarily used to train the model, the Conceptual Model is training the data over Support Vector Machine (SVM) and the user interface is application that can be used by the doctor during the entire diagnostic process. Figure 2 will elucidate the various components of the DSS in Sentilyser. The conventional session at homeopathy clinic involves communication with the patient, taking quantitative and qualitative notes if any, manually, to prescribe medicines. The session is purely driven by the details provided by the patient. To identify whether the patient is carrying fake or true emotions while conversing with the doctor, the time of visit to the doctor, past history & treatment of the patient, time in hand for the doctor etc. plays an important role before giving the treatment. Hence the voice of the patient during communication is recorded and utilized as an additional input by the homeopathy doctor, in this research. From the recorded voice clip, features are extracted; SVM technique is applied to provide additional emotional details to the doctor, which may be skipped during mere communication with the patient.

According to Berner (2016), "Clinical Decision Support Systems (CDSS) are computer based systems designed to impact clinical decision making process about individual patients at the point in time when these decisions are made" (Berner, 2007). Sentilyser is blended with the clinical workflows. It provides decision in time and location about care rather than prior or after the patient encounter any emergency. Hence, Sentilyser intends to generate Electronic Health Records (EHR). It can also spawn a graph manifesting the emotions of a person changed over a series of his/ her visit to the physician. It can analyze if the patient is convalescent or is getting worse or is just in the same condition. Figure 3 shows collaborating Sentilyser in a case taking by homeopath.

Figure 2. Components of Decision Support System in Sentilyser

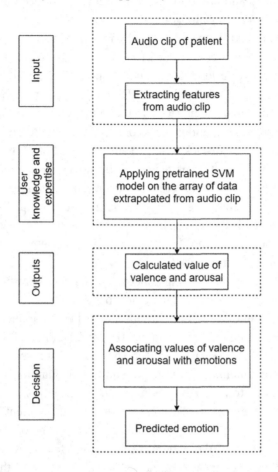

SENTILYSER AND SOFTWARE ENGINEERING

Sentilyser was created with well-defined principles and techniques of software engineering. Model Verification and Validation methods were used to develop Sentilyser.

1. **Requirement Gathering:** Taking into account a brief conversation carried out with a few veteran practitioners of Homeopathy, the following basic requirements were gathered.
   a. The system should be able to determine sentiments
   b. The system must be capable to analyze past history of a patient
   c. The system should be easy to use and easy to comprehend
   d. The all time data should be available with the doctor

Figure 3. System Flow graph of visits

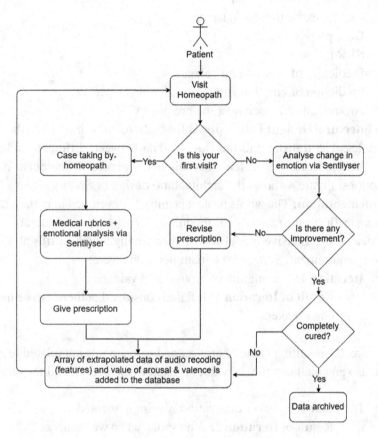

2. **System Analysis:** The use of this software should not necessarily require the knowledge of computers or artificial intelligence. An amateur should be able to saunter through the system. Manoeuvering through this application must not be difficult at all. The homeopaths should be able to use this application easily on their smartphones. Therefore, this application must be compatible with existing and upcoming Android, iOS versions. Therefore, a python based cross-platform application is required.

To meet all these aspects, Kivy an open source Python library is used. It in a way be useful in the development from mobile applications (Rath et al, 2019) point of view making use of ingenious UI, such as multi-touch apps.

3. **Module Design:** This application spans over some basic modules which are:
   a. Taking audio input

  b. Splitting audio into frames

  c. Feature extraction from frames

  d. Data-prepossessing

  e. SVR training

  f. Prediction of arousal and valence

  g. Prediction of emotion from arousal and valence

  h. Arousal and Valence over the previous visits

4. **Architectural Design:** This step establishes the relationship among the different modules. The transfer and the flow of data between different modules that take the input audio and calculate result, hence predict the output as predicted emotions. Figure 4 shows the architectural design of Sentilyser.

5. **Implementation:** The whole project is initially developed in python2.7. After cross verification of individual modules execution. various iterations of the code, a comprehensive model was created finally which fulfills all the boxes of the requirement. Some of the main iterations were:

  a. **Iteration 1:** Calculation of arousal and valence

    i. **Result of Iteration 1:** It failed consider that there can be more than one speakers.

Therefore, the resulting value of arousal and valence was not related to patient's only, but also an amalgamation of values related to the patient and the physician.

  b. **Iteration 2:** Speaker diarization was implemented

    i. **Result of Iteration 2:** Who spoke when was analyzed? It still could not be able to calculate separate values of arousal and valence for the patient and physician both.

  c. **Iteration 3:** All audio frames that corresponded to the voice of the physician should be in a particular, other clips can be discarded and only the arousal and valence of the remaining clips to be calculated. The physician is expected to speak first.

    i. **Result of Iteration 3:** Emotions of the patient to be predicted. Therefore, the result can be conclusive.

  d. **Iteration 4:** Generating past records of the patient

    i. **Result of Iteration 4:** Previous details and specificities to be fetched from the database for the perusal of the doctor.

  e. **Iteration 5:** Graph of the past records to be generated

    i. **Result of Iteration 5:** Previous records of arousal and valence to be graphically demonstrated to physician so that he can analyse the condition of the patient and be able to justify improved or worsened state of the patient over the time. Figure 5 gives an example of the generated graph of arousal and valence by 6 visits of a patient. As the value of valence decreases, the person becomes more pleasant.

    f.   **Iteration 6:** Sentilyser to be integrated with clusters on Amazon Web Services (AWS) cloud platform.

        i.   **Result of Iteration 6:** With the help of MongoDB Atlas, Sentilyser is deployed on a cloud. The values of generated features from the audio clip along with the calculated value of arousal and valence is stored on the cloud. Cluster is created and all the patient related information is stored in it.

6.   **Unit Testing:** All the modules are tested so that they should be error-free. All modules are expected to produce the correct and arrant result that are required to make sure that the next steps will be followed through properly.

7.   **Integration Testing:** This ensures that all the recorded values of arousal and valence are stored so that these values can be used at the doctor's disposal. After integration, all the functionalities need to be tested to make sure all software units are working fine individually, are thus integrated flawlessly.

8.   **System Testing:** This process ensures that software will work with proper functionality, interdependency, and communication between modules.

9.   **User Acceptance Testing:** The product was subjected to Alpha testing wherein, the developed application was given for use to two homeopaths in a development environment and the process of case taking was exercised.

After fixing a few user interface related glitches, Sentilyser was subjected to a Beta testing. This step ensured that the developed product met with the requirement of the homeopaths and hence it was concluded that the product is ready for real-time use.

METHODOLOGY USED FOR PREDICTING MOOD

The concept of Arousal and Valence is given by Mehrabian's and Russel's Pleasure-Arousal-Dominance model (Russell et al., 1977) states that these independent and bipolar dimensions, pleasure-displeasure (also acknowledged as valence), level of arousal which is the behavior or action tendency to be identified as ready or relaxed state and dominance-submissive state which can be associated with the likelihood of taking control or being controlled is necessary and sufficient to adequately define emotional state. Complementing this study, Fontaine's GRID analysis found that emotions can be specified by at least 4 dimensions viz., pleasantness, potency-control, activation-arousal, and uncertainty. Fontaine's model adds a fourth dimension of unpredictability to the P-A-D model. Any two out of these four dimensions to extrapolate the underlying emotions. In the continuing part of chapter, arousal and

Figure 4. Architectural Design of Sentilyser

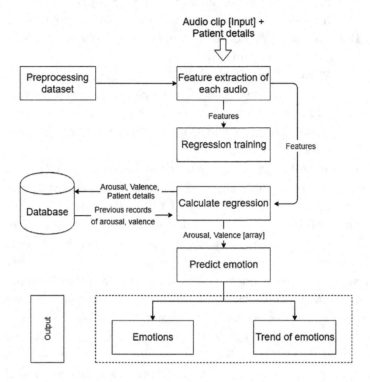

Figure 5. Variation in the value of valence and arousal of a patient in his 6 visits

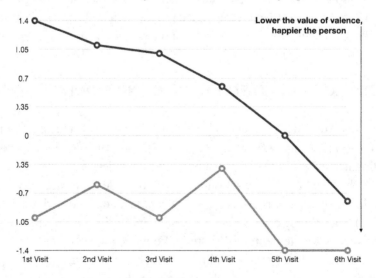

valence, i.e, ready/relaxed state and pleasantness/unpleasantness scrutinized to glean the necessary results. The value of arousal and valence lies between -1.5 to 1.5 respectively.

Conceptual Model of Clinical Decision Support System

Data Collecting and Preprocessing

For training, a dataset of audio files and their corresponding arousal and valence are taken into deliberation. A dataset consisting of 54 audio clips and their associated value of arousal and valence were collected and scrutinized properly. Arousal and valence were recorded in two separate .CSV files. In both .CSVs, column1 corresponds to the name and column 2 corresponds to the value of arousal or valence. In continuation to this data gathering step, data preprocessing is initiated. Deturius data is recognized and discarded. Deturius data like the rows having the value of arousal more than 1.5 or less than -1.5 and rows without the value of arousal and valence. Using libraries like pandas, numpy and matplotlib in python 2.7 are utilized.

Feature Extraction

There are variegated features that can be extrapolated from an audio clip. In this study, 34 features were extracted from the given input audio clips. The audio which is being analyzed is split into small frames and these 34 features are calculated for each frame. These 34 features are Zero Crossing Rate, Energy, Entropy of Energy, Spectral Centroid, Spectral Spread, Spectral Entropy, Spectral Flux, Spectral Rolloff, Mel Frequency Cepstral Coefficients(13 coefficients that forms this cepstral representation, Chroma Vector (12 vectors relating to 12 different pitch classes), Chroma Deviation (Ellis et al., 2011) (deviation of these 12 chroma vectors from each other). These features are computed using Librosa (Fichefet et al, 1991) a python package for music and audio analysis. The results obtained in a series of values for each frame. At the final part of the analysis of small frames, mean of each for the features is calculated and following to that, the standard deviation is obtained.

Support Vector Regression

Emotional state as a conspicuous float-point(real) value can be calculated as valence or arousal. For regression model, the value of valence and arousal are dependent to the value of the 34 calculated features during the process of feature extraction. Here, valence and arousal are functions of the audio features i.e (Awad et al, 2015).

F(features)= α x arousal, and

F(features)= β x valence, where α and β will be the constants.

Therefore, SVR will approximate the function used to generate the training set. Support Vector Regression, a covariance function of the Gaussian process is an excellent method to make use of efficient precomputed details.

The most important parameter here is to focus on the kernel which is to be used. Whether it should be a linear, polynomial or the Gaussian Kernel or also commonly known as the RBF kernel. Here, RBF kernel was selected as it is not a polynomial regression, a mere linear kernel will not give a fitting result. Now, the regression needs to fit with the dataset. The matrixes of features and dependent variable, arousal or valence are trained. Since, after the training, function calculating the value of arousal and valence is approximated and can be used to calculate the same values for any new audio clip to be processed. SVR can be easily implemented in python using scikit-learn module of the python library.

Predicting the Emotion

After the calculation of arousal and valence, these values can be plotted on a two-dimensional graph (Refer figure 6). The X-axis corresponds to Arousal and the Y-axis to Valence. Three nearest neighbors are found on the basis of smallest Euclidian distance. Euclidian distance is the distance between the two points is the square root of the sum of the square coordinates. Always three nearest points lie within the same cluster. For example, if arousal=0.56 and valence=1, and all the 3 nearest falls within the cluster of jealousy, emotion will be calculated as hate. However, if, arousal=0.6 and valence=-1.4, the three nearest neighbors lie in different clusters, the emotions will be categorized as joy, pleasure, happiness.

Speaker Classification

Each and every person has a distinct tonal quality. The audio fingerprint of each voice is different. To make this function work properly the physician must start the conversation and must speak for 15 seconds at the beginning. The first few small frames are selected and their average, standard deviation, the Mel frequency spectral coefficients are calculated. Now, if any other frame that has the mel frequency spectral coefficients within the plausible range are to be taken expunged. Arousal and valence for those particular frames are therefore not calculated, and the resulting values further go into emotion prediction are purely related to the patient only.

Figure 6. Arousal x valence
Source: Fontaine et al, 2007

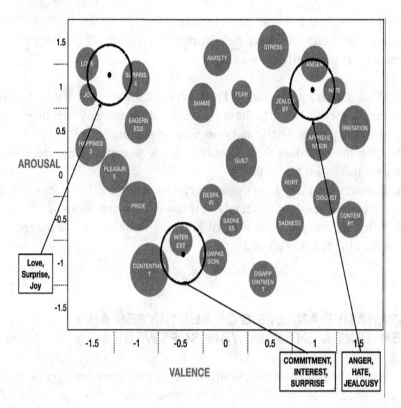

Sentilyser and Database

As these audio files have been analyzed, the recordings are expunged automatically, if it is not explicitly canceled by the doctor. Separate login ID and password are provided to each doctor. The data generated from these audio clips are stored in MongoDB against the details of the patient along with the date of the session during which they were calculated. Database for Sentilyser is integrated into clusters of Amazon Web Services (AWS). It is connected to the application via a Python driver. Data from existing MongoDB deployments are transferred to the cluster by considering features of mongomirror. Replica of already existing MongoDB database is created. Live or current data is also migrated to the cloud. This ensures that all the recorded values of arousal and valence are stored so they can be used at the doctor's disposal and also ensures that even if the doctor's phone has any technical issues, the data is protected and will not lost.

SENTILYSER: HOW IT WORKS?

Disguised to look like a simple voice recorder, Sentilyser can do much more than a voice recorder! Figure 7 shows the systematic blueprint of Sentilyser. This gives a rudimentary flow Sentilyser working.

Step 1: Login screen for the doctor. The doctor can login using his/her credentials.

Step 2: The doctor will be led to the home screen of Sentilyser where he is supposed tp enter the patient details and start voice recording.

Step 3: After the recording the doctor can choose to expunge the recording or to store it locally on his mobile.

Step 4: The detailed analysis of the voice can be observed. The doctor can decide to discard the result of this analysis if it was done erroneously.

Step 5: After the analysis, summary of previous visits will be displayed. Also, a graph of the result is plotted.

COMPARATIVE ANALYSIS OF SENTILYSER AND OTHER SENTIMENT ANALYSIS SOFTWARES

Table 1 shows the final result of Sentilyser and other voice markers on few audio clips. The other voice marker used in this case works on the principle of word tokenization, detecting emotion using the polarity of words. Systems like these fail to take consider sarcastic comments, long deep sigh and yelling at high pitched voice or rate of speech. Other software systems use Neural Network for sentiment analysis. However, SVM is a feasible option in comparison to other options like Neural Network which inadvertently proves to be an expensive option.

As discussed by authors in (Rowe et al., 2018; Mulay et al, 20017) and in many researches, maintaining emotional health of an individual is a mandate. To help achieve this primarily, it is necessary to integrate technology in all possible healthcare practices. With the integration of technology it is feasible to achieve the personalization in healthcare sector with each and every patient. "The touch of personalization heals the patient quickly, increases the will power, etc." is a popular saying accepted and heard for many years.

Figure 7. Wireframe of Sentilyser

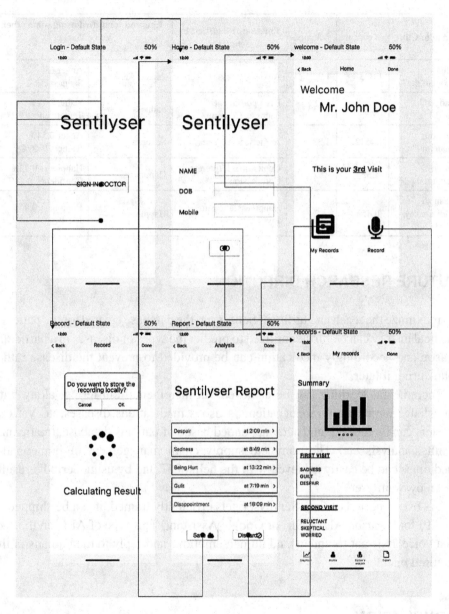

Table 1. Arousal and Valence and the corresponding value of emotions.

Audio Clip	Arousal	Valence	Emotions Identified by *Sentilyser*	Emotion Identified using some other Voice Marker 1 2	
angry_woman.mp3	1.023	1.223	Anxiety, Stress, Anger	Anger, Anxiety	Anger 68% Sadness 32%
sad_child.mp3	-1.321	0.733	Disappointment, Sadness, Contempt	Sadness	Sadness 77% Tentativeness 0.23%
anxious_male.mp3	1.4512	1.3	Anxiety, Fear, Stress	Sadness	Anger 0.54% Sadness 0.46%
professor_lecture.mp3	-1.33	-0.9	Contentment, Interest, Compassion	Happiness	Happiness 0.72% Confidence 0.28%
spanish_radiojockey.mp3	-0.45	-1.2	Happiness, Pleasure, Joy	Happiness	Happiness 0.96% Joy 4%

FUTURE RESEARCH DIRECTION

To maximize the reach and utility of Sentilyser, the database created for the patient's medical history can be further utilized to predict the types of diseases in a particular season and accordingly medication can be provided to prevent the disease rather than curing it later.

Incremental learning can be achieved via incremental clustering, along with knowledge augmentation about patients, seasons, medications, diseases, etc. Various clusters can be formed, updated / appended based of patients database, treatments, results, analysis etc. The complete supply chain management of homeopathy medicines can be easily achieved with the help of IT and by using periodic results given by Sentilyser.

As over a period of time Sentilyser gets efficiently trained, it can be shipped as an API for Amazon Alexa, Siri or Google Assistant. This type of API can thus act as a voice assistant to understand human emotions and reply to the humans in the required manner.

CONCLUSION

This working model demonstrates the necessity of voice markers for improved analysis of emotion during homeopathic case taking. It will be helpful to Homeopaths to analyse the patient's sentiments and maintain their cognitive history. If we are able to incorporate Sentilyser use in such cases, accurate assessment of the patient's condition can be done, which will undeniably uplift the success rate of physician diagnosis.

This research is *"one-of-its-kind" type of* amalgamation of homeopathy and IT. Voice makers are the most beautiful gifts given by technology to analyze the frequency of voice and know can inspect various psychological states of an individual. The integration of valuable inputs from voice markers into homeopathy treatment will bring revolutionary changes in future. Homeopathy is the only "pathy" which works on patients mind, body and soul. Hence the analysis of the patient can be done holistically using doctor's experience, knowledge, history of patient combined with technology. The entire history of patient, treatment / prescription suggested by doctor, symptoms along with voice marker values are stored using Cloud Computing Environment (Abatal et al, 2018; Rath et al, 2019) so as to retrieve the empirical data as and when required by homeopath. Instead of maintaining hard copies of patients records or in memories of doctor, Cloud is the smartest way, for easier access, security, availability, reliability etc.

To ensure privacy and confidentiality of the patient's details no voice recording is stored, only audio frame structures are captured. Though a physician might choose to store the recording locally in his phone, no voice is stored on to the cloud. Since only a panoply of numbers are being stored, and not the variegated audio clips of patients, this makes the application less expensive.

Having a psychological illness is not easy and it's even harder when people assume you can just get over it. Sentiyser is a tool that can positively work towards the betterment of individuals who are suffering from such problems and can also help doctors to increase their efficacy of cure.

REFERENCES

Abatal, A., Khallouki, H., & Bahaj, M. (2018, May). A Smart Interconnected Healthcare System using Cloud Computing. In *Proceedings of the International Conference on Learning and Optimization Algorithms: Theory and Applications* (p. 44). ACM. 10.1145/3230905.3230936

Awad, M., & Khanna, R. (2015). *Efficient learning machines: theories, concepts, and applications for engineers and system designers*. Apress. doi:10.1007/978-1-4302-5990-9

Bell, I. R., Lewis, D. A. II, Schwartz, G. E., Lewis, S. E., Caspi, O., Scott, A., ... Baldwin, C. M. (2004). Electroencephalographic cordance patterns distinguish exceptional clinical responders with fibromyalgia to individualized homeopathic medicines. *Journal of Alternative and Complementary Medicine (New York, N.Y.)*, *10*(2), 285–299. doi:10.1089/107555304323062275 PMID:15165409

Berner, E. S. (2007). *Clinical decision support systems* (Vol. 233). New York: Springer Science Business Media, LLC. doi:10.1007/978-0-387-38319-4

Ellis, D. P., Zeng, X., & McDermott, J. H. (2011, May). Classifying soundtracks with audio texture features. In *Acoustics, Speech and Signal Processing (ICASSP), 2011 IEEE International Conference on* (pp. 5880-5883). IEEE. 10.1109/ICASSP.2011.5947699

Fichefet, J. (1991). Computer-aided homoeopathy. *The British Homoeopathic Journal*, *80*(1), 34–38. doi:10.1016/S0007-0785(05)80421-1

Fisher, P. (2012). 1. Abstract 2. Introduction 2.1. Homeopathy and Allopathy 2.2. Homeopathic Pathogenetic Trials 3. Development of homeopathy 3.1. Homeopathy Worldwide 4. Contemporary Homeopathic Practice 4.1. Individualised Homeopathy. *Frontiers in Bioscience*, *4*, 1669–1682. doi:10.2741/e489

Fisher, P. (2012). What is Homeopathy An Introduction. *Frontiers in Bioscience*, *4*(5), 1669–1682. doi:10.2741/e489

Fontaine, J. R., Scherer, K. R., Roesch, E. B., & Ellsworth, P. C. (2007). The world of emotions is not two-dimensional. *Psychological Science*, *18*(12), 1050–1057. doi:10.1111/j.1467-9280.2007.02024.x PMID:18031411

Fontaine, Scherer, Roesch, & Ellsworth. (2007). The World of Emotions Is Not Two-Dimensional. *Psychological Science, 18*(12), 1050–57.

How Negative Emotions Can Affect Your Health. (2018). Retrieved from https://articles.mercola.com/sites/articles/archive/2018/05/17/effect-of-negative-emotions-on-health.aspx

Informationweek.com. (n.d.). *10 Innovative Clinical Decision programs*. Retrieved from: http://www.informationweek.com

Keen, P. G. (1980). *Decision support systems and managerial productivity analysis*. Google Scholar.

Lake, J. H., & Spiegel, D. (Eds.). (2007). *Complementary and alternative treatments in mental health care*. American Psychiatric Pub.

McFee, B., Raffel, C., Liang, D., Ellis, D. P., McVicar, M., Battenberg, E., & Nieto, O. (2015, July). librosa: Audio and music signal analysis in python. In *Proceedings of the 14th python in science conference* (pp. 18-25). Academic Press. 10.25080/ Majora-7b98e3ed-003

Mulay, Kadlag, & Shirodkar. (2017). Smart Supply-Chain Management Learning System for Homeopathy. *Indian Journal of Public Health Research and Development, 8*(4), 914-922.

Murphy, R. (2006). *Homeopathic clinical repertory. Homeopathy in Practice, 57.*

Nijeweme-d'Hollosy, W. O., van Velsen, L., Poel, M., Groothuis-Oudshoorn, C. G., Soer, R., & Hermens, H. (2018). Evaluation of three machine learning models for self-referral decision support on low back pain in primary care. *International Journal of Medical Informatics, 110*, 31–41. doi:10.1016/j.ijmedinf.2017.11.010 PMID:29331253

Patel, R. P. (1967). *The art of case taking and practical repertorisation in homoeopathy.* Athurasramam Homoeopathic Medical College.

Polony, I. V. (2005). The use of manual and computer aided search methods in the homeopathic repertory. *Aeon Group*, 1-6.

Rath, M., Pati, B., Panigrahi, C. R., & Sarkar, J. L. (2019). QTM: A QoS Task Monitoring System for Mobile Ad hoc Networks. In P. Sa, S. Bakshi, I. Hatzilygeroudis, & M. Sahoo (Eds.), *Recent Findings in Intelligent Computing Techniques. Advances in Intelligent Systems and Computing* (Vol. 707). Singapore: Springer. doi:10.1007/978-981-10-8639-7_57

Rath, M., Pati, B., & Pattanayak, B. K. (2018). Relevance of Soft Computing Techniques in the Significant Management of Wireless Sensor Networks. In Soft Computing in Wireless Sensor Networks (pp. 86-106). New York: Chapman and Hall/CRC, Taylor & Francis Group.

Rath, M., & Pattanayak, B. (2018). Technological improvement in modern health care applications using Internet of Things (IoT) and proposal of novel health care approach. *International Journal of Human Rights in Healthcare.* doi:10.1108/ IJHRH-01-2018-0007

Rowe & Fitness. (2018). Understanding the Role of Negative Emotions in Adult Learning and Achievement: A Social Functional Perspective. *Journal of Behavioral Science*. Retrieved from https://www.mdpi.com/2076-328X/8/2/27/pdf

Rtah, M. (2018). Big Data and IoT-Allied Challenges Associated With Healthcare Applications in Smart and Automated Systems. *International Journal of Strategic Information Technology and Applications*, *9*(2). doi:10.4018/IJSITA.201804010

Russell, J. A., & Mehrabian, A. (1977). Evidence for a three-factor theory of emotions. *Journal of Research in Personality*, *11*(3), 273–294. doi:10.1016/0092-6566(77)90037-X

Sayers, J. (2001). The world health report 2001-Mental health: New understanding, new hope. *Bulletin of the World Health Organization*, *79*, 1085–1085.

Shortliffe, E. H., & Buchanan, B. G. (1975). A model of inexact reasoning in medicine. *Mathematical Biosciences*, *23*(3-4), 351–379. doi:10.1016/0025-5564(75)90047-4

Taleb, N. N. (2007). *The black swan: The impact of the highly improbable* (Vol. 2). Random house.

The Medical Futurist. (2016). *Vocal biomarkers: the future of diagnostic medicine. The Most Exciting Medical Technologies of 2017*. Retrieved from https://medicalfuturist.com/the-most-exciting-medical-technologies-of-2017

Van Hootegem, H. (2007). Can homeopathy learn something from psychoanalysis? *Homeopathy*, *96*(2), 108–112. doi:10.1016/j.homp.2006.11.013 PMID:17437938

Wright, A., & Sittig, D. F. (2008). A framework and model for evaluating clinical decision support architectures. *Journal of Biomedical Informatics*, *41*(6), 982–990. doi:10.1016/j.jbi.2008.03.009 PMID:18462999

Xue, S. A., de Schepper, L., & Hao, G. J. (2009). Treatment of spasmodic dysphonia with homeopathic medicine: A clinical case report. *Homeopathy*, *98*(1), 56–59. doi:10.1016/j.homp.2008.11.009 PMID:19135961

Chapter 9
Intelligent Information System for Academic Institutions:
Using Big Data Analytic Approach

Mamata Rath
C. V. Raman College of Engineering, India

ABSTRACT

Research and publication is considered an authenticated certificate of innovative work done by researchers in various fields. In research, new scientific results may be assessed, corrected, and further built up by the scientific neighborhood only if they are available in published form. Guidelines on accountable research and publication are currently set to encourage and promote high ethical standards in the conduct of research and in biomedical publications. They address various aspects of the research and publishing including duties of editors and authorship determination. The chapter presents research and publication system using big data analytics and research data management techniques with a background of information systems and need of information in research data management.

INTRODUCTION

Research which is an essential section of advanced higher education system is experiencing a transformation. Researchers crosswise over controls are progressively using electronic apparatuses to gather, break down, and sort out data. They are presently delivering, putting away, and spreading advanced data in substantially bigger volumes than the text. Vast amounts of conceived computerized data are being delivered in a wide assortment of structures at a quick rate in colleges and

DOI: 10.4018/978-1-5225-7784-3.ch009

research institutes (Cox AM et.al, 2014).This "data storm" makes a need to create approaches, foundations and administrations in associations, with the target of helping researchers in making, gathering, controlling, breaking down, transporting, putting away and protecting datasets. This blast of conceived computerized research (data that are made in advanced shape) implies that the time of BIG DATA has arrived (Whyte A et.al, 2011). Alongside this computerized over-burden comes the developing requirement for astute and viable Research Data Management (RDM).

The proceeded with presence and access of this data is worry since the data isn't at present efficient and put away in libraries. Research is presently led in the computerized domain, with researchers producing and trading data among themselves (Whyte A et.al, 2011). Sharing research data and grant is of national significance because of the expanded spotlight on augmenting return on the administration's interest in research programs. Research funders are proactive and urge great practices and to accomplish more noteworthy quantifiable profit and incentive for the research supported, and in this manner require or command certain particular measures of data administration and sharing to be trailed by the researchers.

Research data administration (RDM) is about "the association of data, from its entrance to the research push through the spread and chronicling of profitable outcomes" (Whyte and Tedds, 2011).Cox and Pinfield(2014)mentioned that RDM comprises of various diverse exercises and procedures related with the data lifecycle, including the plan and formation of data, stockpiling, security, protection, recovery, sharing, and reuse, all considering specialized abilities, moral contemplations, lawful issues and administration systems. Data created as a feature of research take an extensive variety of structures, from insights and exploratory outcomes to talk with chronicles and transcripts (Borgman, 2012). Data could exist as physical records or documents on a researcher's PC or terabytes of data on shared servers.

INFORMATION IN RESEARCH

All people, organizations and, when all is said in done, all associations are constantly catching data, a considerable lot of which are of no essentialness to them by any means. Nonetheless, other data are accessible that would bear the cost of them their very own superior comprehension condition and of themselves. These data – what we know as data – empower them to settle on more precise choices. Hence, the appropriate measure of data at the ideal time is a key factor for each association. Organization administrators take choices, get ready designs and control their organization's exercises utilizing data that they can get either from formal sources or through casual stations, for example, eye to eye discussions, phone calls, social contacts, and so on. Chiefs are tested by an inexorably mind boggling and indeterminate condition. In these conditions, administrators ought to hypothetically have the capacity to characterize and acquire the sort of data they require. Notwithstanding, this isn't what occurs by and by; rather, the manner in which supervisors play out their work relies upon the accessible data that they approach. Most choices are in this manner made without total learning, either on the grounds that the data isn't accessible or on the grounds that entrance to it would be expensive.

All people, organizations and all associations are constantly communicating information, a significant number of which are of no hugeness to them by any means. Be that as it may, other information are accessible that would bear the cost of them a superior comprehension of their claim condition and of themselves. These information – what we know as information empower them to settle on more exact choices. Hence, the perfect measure of information at the ideal time is a key factor for each association. Organization chiefs take selection, get ready designs and control their organization's exercises utilizing information that they can acquire either from formal sources or through casual stations, for example, up close and personal discussions, phone calls, social contacts, and so forth. Supervisors are tested by an undeniably perplexing and indeterminate condition. In these conditions, supervisors ought to hypothetically be ready to characterize and get the sort of information they require. Be that as it may, this isn't what occurs practically speaking; rather, the manner in which administrators play out their work depends on the accessible information that they approach. Most choices are in this manner made without supreme learning, either on the grounds that the information isn't accessible or on the grounds that entrance to it would be exorbitant (Rath et.al, 2018).

In spite of the troubles in acquiring information, chiefs require applicable information on which to base their arranging, control and basic leadership capacities. In spite of the fact that the terms information and information are some of the time utilized unpredictably, they do have distinctive implications. Information are non-arbitrary images that speak to the estimations of properties or occasions. Subsequently, information are certainties, occasions and exchanges put away as indicated by a concurred code. Information are actualities gotten through perusing, perception, count, estimation, and so forth (Rath et.al, 2019). The sums and different points of interest on an association's solicitations, checks or pay slips, and so forth, are alluded to as information, for instance. Information are acquired consequently, the after effect of a standard methodology, for example, invoicing or estimation forms.

IMPORTANCE OF DATA & INFORMATION IN ORGANISATION

Firstly, we have to study why the data has to be processed. There are certain reasons for which the data is being processed. The data can have the features such as

- **Incomplete:** Lacking attribute values, containing attribute data.
- **Noisy:** Containing errors or outliers,
- **Inconsistent:** Containing discrepancies in code or names. The quality data should be available.

To obtain the required information from huge, incomplete, noisy and inconsistent set of data is the need of data processing.

The way toward contemplative and understanding data is the thing that enables the message to have distinctive implications for various individuals. This procedure likewise suggests that the data examined, outlined or prepared to deliver messages will just move toward becoming data if its beneficiary comprehends its importance. For data to be changed into data, there must be a consciousness of what the individual getting the message will utilize it for, his or her preparation, position in the association and commonality with the dialect and computations utilized in the message.

While all managers require data, they don't all need a similar sort of data. The sort of data required will rely upon a scope of elements: their level in the chain of command, the work they are doing, privacy, earnestness, and so on (Rath et.al, 2016). Without a doubt, the convenience of data is a disputable point, and what for one individual is data, for another is data. In an association, for instance, when data is exchanged starting with one authoritative level then onto the next its importance may change fundamentally, to such an extent that at one progressive level it is viewed as noteworthy data, while at another level it is just data (Menguzzato and Renau, 1991). Data is the beneficiary's information and cognizance of data. Data diminishes vulnerability and manages the beneficiary something he or she didn't know beforehand.

Data is one of many organization assets, nearby capital, crude materials and work, since no organization is reasonable without data. As to as a rare asset obliges us to think about the issue of data financial matters, at the end of the day, how to set up the essential connection between the estimation of data and its expense. The following section summarizes and reviews major and selected articles relating to various aspects of Research Data Management as per the following themes:

1. Need and Basics of Research Date Management
2. Big Data
3. Some existing Tools for Data management and Repositories

It has increasingly become a pressing issue in research organizations as they strive to assist researchers in addressing new public funding requirements surrounding data dissemination and preservation (Rath et.al, 2016). The trend of data-fuelled research has now become a global and across all sectors, creating the need to manage this vast data in a manner which can be used by other researchers and derive benefit.

Research Data Management is defined as the organization and description of data, from its entry to the research cycle through the dissemination and archiving of valuable results.(White, 2011)

Research DataServices (RDS) and Research Data Management (RDM) services are two umbrella phrases authors have used to describe data curation (Jones, Pryor, & Whyte 2013;Tenopir, Sandusky, Allard,&Birch2013).

Charles Bailey's (2012) *Research Data Curation Bibliography* with over 200 citations and growing, is comprehensive bibliography on the subject. However, other distinctive bibliographies include The Westra, et al. (2010) bibliography of *Selected Internet Resources on Digital Research Data Curation which* presents a thematically organized bibliography of the more important Internet based resources. Witt and Giarlo (2012) provide a description of another unique guide, *Databib: An Online Bibliography of Research Data Repositories. Databib* currently provides records on over 500 repositories worldwide and is an example of the growth and geographical breath in digital data repository services. Graham Pryor's *ManagingResearchData* (2012) also compiles important literature on this topic.

Although a variety of research data life cycle models exist, most generally contain variations on several common stages as follows:

- Planning (potentially including creation of a formal data management plan, or DMP, to meet funder
- requirements),
- Data assortment or acquisition,
- Data analysis or interpretation (including data visualization),
- Data maintenance and curation, and
- Data sharing

Many articles used the theme of life cycle management and long--term preservation of research data center as one of the primary reasons to preserve research data: so it may be shared and reused. A broad overview of the reasons for sharing (and not sharing) research data and an agenda for future research is provided by Christine Borgman (2012)

Federer (2016) states that the ways that scientific research are practiced have shifted fundamentally in the last several decades. Researchers of the 21st century often rely on large digital datasets, and sometimes they are using data that they themselves did not gather, but that they obtained from public sources for reuse.

Big Data describes innovative techniques and technologies to capture, store, distribute, manage and analyze datasets that traditional data management methods are unable to handle. The concept of "Big Data" was first defined by Laney in his research note. Laney described the characteristics of big data as which cannot be processed by traditional data management tools. Three Vs were first used to characterize the Big Data. With further study on big data, the "Three V's" have been expanded to "Five V's": volume, velocity, variety, veracity (integrity of data), value (usefulness of data) and complexity (degree of interconnection among data structures)

Gordon-Murname specifically addresses the rise in big data and in her article "Big Data: A Big Opportunity for Librarians." Gordon-Murname points out four key areas: (1) organization, (2) search and access of internal datasets, (3) awareness of external data sources, and (4) to serve as authorities on copyright and intellectual property issues for the management of research data.

Tools

Services specific to data management plans for grant-funded research may include consultations with grant writers, DMP training and workshops, and form-based tools for creating a DMP. Some libraries have begun to review larger sets of DMPs (Parham and Doty2012). Understanding researcher needs, and presenting services with measurable positive impacts on those needs are critical to the success of DMP services. The data curation profile provides a framework for determining data management practices and needs of researchers (Carlson, J., & Stowell-Bracke, M. (2013).

The DMP Online tool developed in the United Kingdom, and its relative, the DMP Tool developed by the California Digital Library and partners in the U.S., are employed by some libraries to walk grant-writers through the process of developing a data management plan for submission with a grant proposal. Sallans and Donnelly (2012) compare and contrast these two forms-based web resources. The DMP Tool links to data plan requirements published by the funding agency units, and local guidance materials can also be incorporated into the web pages.

SOURCES OF INFORMATION FOR RESEARCH

Data is a basic, key asset that can be gotten from various sources. In this segment, we recognize inward data identifying with the earth inside the organization, and data about its outer condition. A considerable lot of the data caught by data frameworks allude to the working of the association and are utilized to deliver inside data. This interior data gives administration information about how the organization is working and regardless of whether it is accomplishing its targets. Most inner data originates from the bookkeeping framework and factual examinations (deals, creation, and so on.). Other inner data sources, for example, studies and meetings with organization individuals give quantitative data on, for example, specialists' inspiration levels or different pointers that are not effectively measured.

Organization chiefs likewise require data on nature: deals volume of their most direct rivals, potential customer sections for the organization's product offerings, topographical conveyance of its investors, and so forth. An organization must be effective on the off chance that it adjusts to the requests of its outside condition. The earth is spoken to by various gatherings that change in their ability to impact the organization's satisfaction of its goals. Beneath, we distinguish these intrigue gatherings and the distinctive kinds of data about them that the organization requires:

- **Customers:** Advertising, deals, levels of fulfillment.
- **Distributors:** Advertising and coordinations (circulation).
- **Competitors:** Advertise infiltration, advancements, item quality.
- **Suppliers:** Exchange conditions.
- **Trade Associations:** Compensations and work soundness.
- **Shareholders:** Organization execution.
- **Financial Establishments:** Money related conditions and venture openings.
- **Government:** legitimate and political advancements.

The organization must be educated always about every one of these outside gatherings and, in the meantime, a portion of these gatherings (e.g., investors and the administration) should likewise get data from the organization.

Data on the earth can be gotten from the accompanying sources:

- Personal data sources, which give data through contact deals staff, clients, providers, wholesalers, investors, and so on.
- Impersonal data sources, which run from general productions (e.g., provides details regarding the momentum circumstance, bank and authority substance reports, particular diaries) to particular examinations (e.g., statistical surveying, sentiment considers, experts' reports).

Google Scholar: As a Case Study

Google Scholar is a freely available web internet searcher that files the full content or metadata of scholarly writing over a variety of distributing arrangements and orders. Discharged in beta in November 2004, the Google Scholar list incorporates most friend audited online scholastic diaries and books, meeting papers, theories and papers, preprints, abstracts, specialized reports, and other scholarly writing, including court feelings and licenses. While Google does not distribute the extent of Google Scholar's database, scientometric specialists assessed it to contain around 389 million records including articles, references and licenses making it the world's biggest scholastic internet searcher in January 2018. Beforehand, the size was evaluated at 160 million records as of May 2014. Prior measurable gauge distributed in PLOS ONE utilizing a Mark and recover strategy assessed around 80– 90% inclusion of all articles distributed in English with a gauge of 100 million.[4] This gauge likewise decided what number of archives were freely accessible on the web.

Google Scholar is comparable in capacity to the freely accessible CiteSeerX and getCITED. It additionally takes after the membership based apparatuses, Elsevier's Scopus and Clarivate Analytics' Web of Science. Google Scholar has been condemned for not checking diaries and incorporating ruthless diaries in its record.

Google Scholar enables clients to look for advanced or physical duplicates of articles, regardless of whether on the web or in libraries. It lists full-content diary articles, specialized reports, preprints, postulations, books, and different records, including chosen Web pages that are esteemed to be 'scholarly. Because a significant number of Google Scholar's list items connect to business diary articles, the vast majority will have the capacity to get to just a dynamic and the reference subtleties of an article, and need to pay a charge to get to the whole article. The most important outcomes for the sought catchphrases will be recorded first, arranged by the creator's positioning, the quantity of references that are connected to it and their pertinence to other scholarly writing, and the positioning of the distribution that the diary shows up in.

Utilizing its "group " characteristic, it demonstrates the accessible connects to diary articles. In the 2005 adaptation, this component gave a connection to both membership get to forms of an article and to free full-content renditions of articles; for a large portion of 2006, it gave connections to just the distributers' variants. Since December 2006, it has given connects to both distributed forms and real open access storehouses, yet at the same time does not cover those posted on individual personnel web pages;[citation needed] access to such self-filed non-membership adaptations is currently given by a connection to Google, where one can discover such open access articles.

Through its "cited by" highlight, Google Scholar gives access to edited compositions of articles that have cited the article being seen. It is this element specifically that gives the reference ordering already just found in CiteSeer, Scopus, and Web of Science. Through its "Related articles" highlight, Google Scholar displays a rundown of firmly related articles, positioned fundamentally by how comparative these articles are to the first outcome, yet additionally considering the pertinence of each paper.

COMPONENTS OF INFORMATION SYSTEM

All frameworks can be separated into subsystems. Since the organization carries on as a framework, its distinctive components can be separated into subsystems. As indicated by the association hypothesis writing, the organization can be isolated into the accompanying frameworks: business, tasks, budgetary, work force, and data. The data framework is identified with the various frameworks and the earth. The reason for the organization's data framework is to accumulate the data it needs and, following fundamental changes, guarantee that it achieves the individuals from the organization who require it, regardless of whether for basic leadership, vital control, or for executing choices received by the organization (Menguzzato and Renau, 1991). A director's execution along these lines relies upon his or her abilities in misusing the data framework's abilities keeping in mind the end goal to get positive business results.

For the motivations behind this chapter we embrace the meaning of a data framework given by Andreu, Ricart and Valor (1991). As per these creators the data framework is a formal arrangement of procedures that, working from an accumulation of data organized depending to the organization's needs, assembles, forms and disperses the data important for the organization's tasks and for its relating administration and control exercises, consequently supporting, at any rate to a limited extent, the basic leadership forms vital for the organization to play out its business capacities in accordance with its technique.

This definition, thusly, just incorporates the formal data framework, which is the piece of the data framework that all the organization's individuals know about and know how to utilize. This does not imply that casual data frameworks are not vital, but rather essentially perceives the restriction that they are, by their extremely nature, more hard to study, plan and oversee, in any event from a strong and all encompassing perspective. Casual data frameworks are not the aftereffect of a planned procedure; rather they give chance data. We should not, notwithstanding, disregard the presence of casual data channels, and the speed and productivity with which they can work, on events spreading bits of gossip through the association more rapidly than data that takes after the standard channels.

The above definition alludes to the capacities and techniques of the organization; by this, we expect to transmit an organization's data framework must serve its business approach. At last, the data framework is just a single of the numerous components that the organization outlines and uses to accomplish its destinations, and all things considered, it must be expressly planned in accordance with these targets.

To finish this meaning of a data framework, we currently endeavor to clear up any disarray between data framework and PC framework. The PC framework comprises of an unpredictable interconnection of various equipment and programming parts, which are basically determinist, formal frameworks in that particular information dependably gives a similar yield. Data frameworks are social frameworks whose conduct is generally impacted by the goals, qualities and convictions of people and gatherings and by the execution of innovation. The manner in which a data framework acts isn't determinist and does not take after the portrayal of any formal algorithmic model.

BIG DATA AND RESEARCH DATA MANAGEMENT

Today it is generally centered around taking care of the data which is audited here as far as the most valuable approaches and classifications of data apparatuses to browse. Each time another capacity medium was invented, the measure of data open detonate in light of the fact that it could be effectively gotten to. They have been discovered in applications that create hundreds or thousands of solicitations in a second. Destinations where deals is done like Amazon or Flipcart; and the product that procedure terabytes or even petabytes of data. Continuous calculations done for deciding Twitter's drifting tweets.

Big data is a wonder that is portrayed by the fast extension of crude data. The test is identified with how an expansive degree of data is being bridled, and the open door is identified with how effectively it is utilized for breaking down the data from it. It is presently regular place to recognize big data solutions from traditional IT arrangements by thinking about the accompanying four measurements.

- **Volume:** Volume depicts the measure of data produced by associations or people. Big data solutions must oversee and process bigger measures of data.
- **Velocity:** Velocity portrays the recurrence at which data is created, caught and shared. Big data arrangements must process all the more quickly arriving data. By Velocity, they mean both the rate at which data arrive and the time in which it must be followed up on
- **Variety:** Big data arrangements must manage more sorts of data, both organized and unstructured in nature. By Variety, they typically mean heterogeneity of data composes, portrayal, and semantic interpretation
- **Veracity:** Big data arrangements must approve the rightness of the huge measure of quickly arriving data.

Today it is generally centered around taking care of this Big Data. The most valuable methodologies and classifications of data apparatuses are inspected to look over data stockroom to Business Intelligence (BI) now, we as a whole are experiencing startling development in organized and unstructured data is exceptionally colossal.

The unstructured data can be from word, exceed expectations, PowerPoint records or PDF, HTML report, telecom data, satellite data etc.

As a matter of fact, in the wake of perusing the material on it, there is one more measurement one can consider, that is Complexity.

- **Complexity:** Organizations catch an assortment of data configurations and search over gigantic data sources in genuine time to examine and recognize designs inside the data. There are a few models, recognizing extortion for credit card clients, monetary patterns for speculation associations, anticipating power utilization for energy companies.

Big Data allows corporate and research organizations to do things not previously possible economically.

It is used for:

- Analysis
- Business Trends

Research Data Management is a piece of the research procedure, and plans to make the research procedure as viable efficient as could be allowed, and meet desires and necessities of the college, research funders, and enactment.

Research data administration (or RDM) is a term which portrays the association, stockpiling, safeguarding, and sharing of data gathered and utilized in a research venture. It includes the administration of research data amid the lifetime of a research venture. It likewise includes choices about how data will be protected and shared after the task is finished. It concerns how a researcher:

- Creates data and plan for its utilization,
- Organizes, structure, and name data,
- Keeps – make it secure, give access, store and back it up,
- Finds data assets, and offer with partners and all the more comprehensively, distribute and get refered to.

Shielding research data from misfortune or incidental changes through great research data administration is especially critical while creating data that are special or arduous to get and reobtain the same.

There are plentiful of reasons why research data administration is critical:

- Data, similar to diary articles and books, is an academic item.
- Data (particularly computerized data) is delicate and effortlessly lost.

- There are developing research data necessities forced by funders and distributers.
- Research data administration spares time and assets over the long haul.
- Good administration forestalls mistakes and expands the nature of your investigations.
- Well-oversaw and available data enables others to approve and duplicate discoveries.
- Research data administration encourages sharing of research data and, when shared, data can prompt important revelations by others outside of the first research group.

In this study, the big data concept is assumed to be extremely large amount of structured, semi structured or unstructured data continuously generated from diversified resources, which inundates business operation in real time and impacts on decision making through mining insightful information from rambling data. For research clarity, what constitutes big data include large structured datasets and unstructured data in the form of text(e.g. documents, natural languages), web data(e.g. web usage, web contents and web structure), social media data(e.g. virtual network), multimedia data(e.g. image, audio, video) and mobile data(viz. sensors. geographical location, application). The research community has developed standards and best practices to induce and improve the quality of data sharing with large data.

ASPECTS IN RESEARCH DATA MANAGEMENT

Emerging from analysis of various Research Data Management developments, a number of key components of an RDM programme have been identified. Following are the components describe the various activities, such as policy development and technology implementation, that together constitute concerted effort in a particular area.

- **Strategies**: defining the overarching vision for research data management within the institution and how it relates to the institutional mission and priorities, and outlining major developmental goals and principles which inform activity.
- **Policies**: specifying how the strategies are to be brought in operation through regular procedures, including not just an RDM policy but also a set of complementary policy frameworks covering issues such as intellectual property rights and openness that may be relevant.

- **Guidelines**: providing detail on how the policies will be implemented often written from the point of view of a particular user group (such as those within a particular disciplinary area) and defining specific activities, and roles and responsibilities.
- **Processes:** specifying and regulating activities within the research data life-cycle including research data management planning for individual projects, data processing, ingesting data into central systems, selecting data for preservation, etc, and involving the use of standards and standardised procedures wherever possible.
- **Technologies:** underpinning processes with technical implementations including data repositories and networking infrastructures allowing for storage and transport of data.
- **Services:** enabling end-user access to systems and providing support for research data life-cycle activities including supporting the creation of data management plans, providing skills training, and delivering helpdesk services. (Pinfield, Stephen, Andrew M. Cox, and Jen Smith,2014)

INSTITUTIONAL INFORMATION SYSTEM

A number of drivers for RDM developments have been identified at an institutional level:

1. **Storage:** There has to be immediate storage facilities for a wide variety of datasets at large scale for the future requirements of researchers which represents value for money and is convenient to use.
2. **Security:** The data must be kept confidential or sensitive, should be held securely with relevant authentication and authorisation mechanisms in place.
3. **Preservation:** The need for medium and long-term archiving of data with associated selection protocols and preservation activities along with a supporting technical infrastructure.
4. **Compliance:** There must be a need to fulfil the requirements and policies of other relevant agencies, and funders, as well as legal obligations, such as data protection, and industry good practice.
5. **Quality:** There is a need to maintain and enhance the quality of research activity in general in order to demonstrate the robustness of findings and enable results verification and reproducibility.
6. **Sharing:** The need to share data amongst targeted users and also to provide mechanisms and systems to enable open access to data where appropriate. There are few 'Influencing Factors' since they are prevailing conditions which may

affect an institutional RDM programme in a variety of complex ways including either facilitating or constraining action. Key Influencing Factors emerging from this research were culture, demand. Incentives. Policies, projects, skills and Governance. It has been observed that there are technical differences in areas such as metadata standards and interoperability protocols, but also in cultures around sharing and reuse. Nevertheless, despite the lack of detailed solutions discussed here, the importance of the issues of disciplinary differences should not be underestimated. In many respects, there is a discussion held on all of the other Influencing Factors.

THE PROPOSED LEARNING BASED SMART ANALYTICAL FRAMEWORK

Figure 1 presents a block diagram of smart methods used in research and publication process. There are multiple framework in smart applications that employ intelligent methods using big data analytics and IoT devices. As shown in the figure the review and selection rubric employs various mechanism starting from similarity checking to searching multiple databases such as DBLP and SCOPUS. DBLP formerly stood for DataBase systems and Logic Programming. As an acronym, it has been taken to arise for Digital Bibliography & Library Project; however, it is now favoured that the acronym be simply a name, hence the new title "The DBLP Computer Science Bibliography (https://en.wikipedia.org/wiki/DBLP). Mechanical advances enable more physical items to interface with the Internet and give their administrations on the Web as assets.

RESEARCH ASSESSMENT USING BIG DATA ANALYTICS

Web search tools are the way to completely use this developing Web of Things, as they connect clients and applications with assets required for their task. Building up these frameworks is a testing and various undertaking because of the decent variety of Web of Things assets that they work with. Every blend of assets in inquiry determination process requires an alternate sort of web search tool with its own particular specialized difficulties and use situations. Fig.2 depicts Factors determining quality of research work . This assorted variety entangles both the improvement of new frameworks and evaluate ment of the cutting edge. DBLP originally stood for DataBase systems and Logic Programming. As acronym, it has been taken to stand for Digital Bibliography & Library Project; however, it is now preferred that

Figure 1. Proposed analytical framework for research paper evaluation

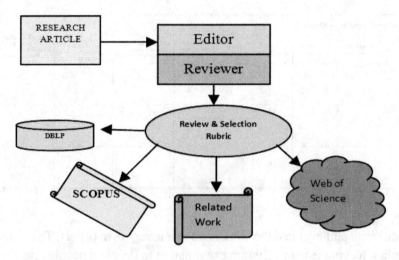

Figure 2. Factors determining quality of research work

Indexing	DOI	Impact Factor	H-index	Authenticity	Copyright	Plagiarism

the acronym be simply a name, hence the new title "The DBLP Computer Science Bibliography (https://en.wikipedia.org/wiki/DBLP)

Figure 2 demonstrates the parameters and important components that certifies good quality research. A digital object identifier (DOI) is a unique alphanumeric string assigned by a registration agency (the International DOI Foundation) to identify content and provide a persistent link to its location on the Internet. The publisher assigns a DOI when your article is published and made available electronically.

Citation Analysis- The procedure whereby the effect or "quality" of an article is evaluated by tallying the occasions different authors notice it in their work. Citation investigation invovles checking the occasions an article is cited by different attempts to gauge the effect of a publicaton or author. The caviat in any case, there is no single citation examination apparatuses that gathers all publications and their cited references. For an exhaustive investigation of the effect of an author or a publication, one needs to look in different databases to locate all conceivable cited references. Various assets are accessible at UIC that distinguish cited works including: Web of Science, Scopus, Google Scholar, and different databases with restricted citation data. To discover how much effect a specific article or author has had, by indicating

Figure 3. Parameters of journal publication and details

Journal Publication Details									
Sl. No.	Year	Depart ment	1st Author	2nd Author	3rd Author	Other Author s	Journal Type (National / Intl. Journal)	Journal Version (Print / E-journal)	Journal Category (Peer Review Journals / Non-Peer Review Journals)

which different authors cited the work inside their very own papers. The H-Index is one explicit technique using citation examination to decide a people affect.

An example of citation in Web of Science is given here. Web of Science gives citation checks to articles recorded inside it. It records more than 10,000 diaries in expressions of the human experience, humanities, sciences, and sociologies.

To discover the citation checks to your own articles - Enter the name of the author in the best inquiry box, Select Author starting from the drop menu on the right. To guarantee exactness for prevalent names, enter Univ Illinois in the center hunt box, at that point select "Address" from the field drop down menu on the right. (You may need to include the second pursuit box by clicking "include another field" before you enter the location) Tap on Search, a rundown of publications by that author name will show up. To one side of every citation, the occasions the article has been cited will show up. Tap the number alongside "times cited" to see the articles that have cited your article

Big data analytics expect to quickly remove learning capable data that aides in making forecasts, recognizing ongoing patterns, finding concealed data, and at last, settling on choices . Fig. 3 shows Parameters of journal publication and details. Data mining procedures are broadly conveyed for both issue particular techniques and summed up data analytics. Likewise, measurable and machine pick up ing techniques are used. The development of big data likewise changes analytics prerequisites. Despite the fact that the prerequisites for productive instruments lie in all parts of big data management, for example, catching, stockpiling, preprocessing, and investigation; for our dialog, big data analytics requires the same or speedier handling speed than conventional data analytics with least cost for high-volume, high-speed, and high-assortment data .

Plagiarism checkers are a compelling method to examine your papers for any warnings that may recommend plagiarism. This particular programming is accessible for the individuals who are not kidding about their scholarly or examine work. Plagiarism checker programming like WriteCheck is accessible on the web. Try not to take the risk of being blamed for plagiarism. There are some motivations to utilize a plagiarism software such as - a few people use Internet web crawlers to search for copied material, plagiarism programming can offer more sources, for example, vast databases that incorporate periodicals and books that may not be accessible on the web. A huge number of periodicals exist. Gigantic databases, for example, EBSCOhost and ProQuest contain such articles. Plagiarism checkers approach these databases.

Different arrangements are accessible for big data analytics, and progressions in creating and enhancing these arrangements are in effect persistently accomplished to make them appropriate for new big data patterns. Data mining assumes a vital part in analytics, and a large portion of the methods are produced utilizing data mining calculations as per a specific situation. Learning on accessible big data analytics alternatives is critical while assessing and picking a proper approach for basic leadership. In this segment, we show a few techniques that can be executed for a few big data contextual analyses. A portion of these analytics techniques are proficient for big IoT data analytics. Different and colossal size data sets contribute more in big data bits of knowledge. Be that as it may, this conviction isn't generally legitimate on the grounds that more data may have more ambiguities and variations from the norm.

Big data analytics techniques have been described here under characterization, grouping, affiliation run mining, and prediction classes. Every classification is a data mining capacity and includes numerous strategies and calculations to satisfy data extraction and investigation necessities. For instance, Bayesian network, support vector machine (SVM), and k-closest neighbor (KNN) offer grouping techniques. Additionally, parceling, various leveled grouping, and co-event are across the board in grouping. Affiliation govern mining and expectation involve noteworthy techniques. Order is a regulated learning approach that utilizations earlier information as preparing data to arrange data objects into groups. A predefined classification is doled out to a protest, and along these lines, the target of foreseeing a gathering or class for a question is accomplished. Discovering obscure or concealed examples is additionally trying for big IoT data. Besides, extricating significant data from extensive data sets to enhance basic leadership is a basic assignment. A Bayesian system is an order strategy that offers show interpretability.

Analysing data designs and making groups are effectively performed utilizing SVM, which is likewise classification approach for big data analytics. SVM uses factual learning hypothesis to break down data designs and make gatherings. A few appli-cations of SVM classification in big data analytics incorporate content classification, design coordinating, wellbeing diagnostics, and trade. Additionally, KNN is normally intended to give effective instruments to finding concealed examples from big data sets, with the end goal that recovered items are like the predefined classification. Utilizing cases hide ther enhance the KNN calculation for application in abnormality identification, high-dimensional data, and logical tests . Classification has different expansions while embracing countless insight and data mining systems. Therefore, classification is one of the across the board data digging systems for big data analytics.

Grouping is another data mining system utilized as a big data analytics strategy. In spite of classification, grouping utilizes an unsupervised learning approach and makes groupes for given articles in view of their unmistakable significant features . Gathering a substantial number of articles as groupes makes data control straightforward. The notable strategies utilized for grouping are progressive grouping and parceling. The progressive grouping approach continues joining little groupes of data articles to shape a various leveled tree and make agglomerative groupes. Disruptive groups are made in the contrary way by separating a solitary group that contains all data objects into littler suitable groupes.

Market investigation and business basic leadership are the most noteworthy utilizations of big data analytics. The procedure of association manage mining includes recognizing intriguing connections among various articles, occasions, or other enti-binds to dissect advertise patterns, purchaser purchasing conduct, and item request predictions. Association control mining centers around recognizing and making rules in light of the recurrence of events for numeric and non-numeric data. Data handling is performed in two behavior under association rules. In the first place, consecutive data handling utilizes priori-based calculations, for example, MSPS and LAPIN-SPAM, to recognize collaboration associations. Another significant data preparing approach under association lead is fleeting succession investigation, which utilizes calculations to examine occasion designs in consistent data.

Perceptive analytics utilize authentic data, which are known as preparing data, to decide the outcomes as patterns or conduct in data. SVM and fluffy rationale calculations are utilized to distinguish connections amongst free and ward factors and to get relapse bends for predictions, for example, for catastrophic events. Moreover, client purchasing predictions online networking patterns are dissected through prescient analytics. On account of big data analytics, preparing necessities are adjusted by the nature and volume of data. Quick data access and digging techniques for organized and unstructured data are real concerns identified with big data analytics. Moreover, data portrayal is a significant prerequisite in big data analytics. Time arrangement analysis lessens high dimensionality related with big data and offers portrayal for enhanced basic leadership.

CONCLUSION

Research and development is the procedure by which an organization attempts to acquire new information that it may use to make new innovation, items, administrations, or frameworks that it will either utilize or move. The objective frequently is to add to the organization's main concern. Various individuals consider pharmaceutical and innovation organizations when they hear "Research and development," yet different firms, including those that create shopper items, put time and assets into R&D also to some extent, the reuse of data as a consequence of data sharing distorts the classic distinction between primary and secondary data. Researchers will likely need assistance in learning how to access and utilize these datasets. It is been observed that, because of digitally archived research objects such as broadcasts and websites, new aspects have been added for data sharing. the amount of freely- and publicly-available research data continues to increase exponentially. This reflects the term "Data Deluge". In conclusion, research data management in context with library data could also be treated as big data without doubt due its property of large volume; high velocity and obvious variety. To sum up it can be said that to make big datasets more useful, visible and accessible. With new and powerful analytics of big data, such as information visualization tools, researchers can look at data in new ways and mine it for information they intend to have.

REFERENCES

Abadi, D., Agrawal, R., & Ailamaki, A. (2014). The Beckman reporton database research. *SIGMOD Record*, *43*(3), 61–70. doi:10.1145/2694428.2694441

Armour, F. (2012). *Introduction to big data*. Presentation at the symposium Big Data and Business Analytics: Defining a Framework, Center for IT and Global Economy, Kogod School of Business, American University, Washington, DC.

Borgman, C. L. (2012). The conundrum of sharing research data. *Journal of the American Society for Information Science and Technology, 63*(6), 1059–1078. doi:10.1002/asi.22634

Borgman, C. L. (2012). The conundrum of sharing research data. *Journal of the American Society for Information Science and Technology, 63*(6), 1059–1078p. doi:10.1002/asi.22634

Carlson, J., & Stowell-Bracke, M. (2013). Data management and sharing from the perspective of graduate students: An examination of the culture and practice at the water quality field station. portal. *Libraries and the Academy, 13*(4), 343–361. doi:10.1353/pla.2013.0034

Charles, W. (2012). *Bailey J. Research Data Curation Bibliography*. Houston, TX: Charles W. Bailey, Jr. Available from http://digital-scholarship.org/rdcb/rdcb.htm

Codd, E. F. (1970). A relational model of data for large shared data banks. *Communications of the ACM, 13*(6), 377–387. doi:10.1145/362384.362685

Cox, A. M., & Pinfield, S. (2014). Research data management and libraries: Current activities and future priorities. *J Librariansh Inf Sci*. Available: http://lis.sagepub.com/cgi/doi/10.1177/0961000613492542

Crosas, M. (n.d.). *Cloud Dataverse: A Data Repository Platform for the Cloud*. Available from https://openstack.cioreview.com/cxoinsight/cloud-dataverse-a-data-repository-platform-for-the-cloud-nid-24199-cid-120.html

Doty, J. (2012). *Survey of faculty practices and perspectives on research data management*. Retrieved from http://guides.main.library.emory.edu/datamgmt/survey

DuraCloud solutions. (n.d.). Retrieved from http://www.duracloud.org/solutions

Farid, M., Roatis, A., & Ilyas, I. F. (2016). CLAMS: bringing quality toData Lakes. In *Proceedings of the 2016 International Conference on Management of Data*. ACM.

Federer, L. (2016). Research data management in the age of big data: Roles and opportunities for librarians. *Information Services & Use, 36*, 35–43. DOI . doi:10.3233/ISU-160797

Godse, M., & Mulik, S. (2009). An approach for selecting Software-as-a-Service (SaaS) product. In *2013 IEEE Sixth International Conference on Cloud Computing* (pp. 155–158). Los Alamitos, CA: IEEE Computer Society. 10.1109/CLOUD.2009.74

Gordon-Murnane, L. (2012). Big Data: A Big Opportunity for Librarians. *Online (Bergheim), 36*(5), 34.

Hai, R., Geisler, S., & Quix, C. (2016). Constance: an intelligent Data Lake system. In *Proceedings of the 2016 International Conference on Management of Data*. ACM.

Halevy, A., Korn, F., & Noy, N. F. (2016). Goods: organizing Google'sdatasets. In *Proceedings of the 2016 International Conference on Management of Data*. ACM.

IBM Big Data & Analytics Hub. (2016). *The four V's of big data*. Available from http://www.ibmbigdatahub.com/infographic/four-vs-big-data-4V

Laney, D. (2001, February 6). 3-*D data management: Controlling data volume, velocity and variety*. META Research Note.

Madduri, R. K., Dave, P., Sulakhe, D., Lacinski, L., Liu, B., & Foster, I. T. (2013). Experiences in building a next-generation sequencing analysis service using Galaxy, Globus Online and Amazon Web Service. In *Proceedings of the Conference on Extreme Science and Engineering Discovery Environment: Gateway to Discovery* (pp. 34:1–34:3). New York: ACM. 10.1145/2484762.2484827

Madera, L. A. (2016). The next information architecture evolution:the data lake wave. In *Proceedings of the 8thInternational Conference on Management of Digital EcoSystems*. ACM.

Parham, S. W., Bodnar, J., & Fuchs, S. (2012). Supporting tomorrow's research: Assessing faculty data curation needs at Georgia Tech. *College & Research Libraries News, 73*(1), 10–13. doi:10.5860/crln.73.1.8686

Parker, Z., Poe, S., & Vrbsky, S. V. (2013). Comparing NoSQL MongoDB to an SQL DB. In *Proceedings of the 51st ACM Southeast Conference*. ACM. 10.1145/2498328.2500047

Pinfield, Cox, & Smith. (2014). Research data management and libraries: relationships, activities, drivers and influences. *PLoS One, 9*(12).

Pryor, G., Jones, S., & Whyte, A. (Eds.). (2013). *Delivering research data management services: Fundamentals of good practice*. London: Facet.

Rath. (2018). Effective Routing in Mobile Ad-hoc Networks With Power and End-to-End Delay Optimization: Well Matched With Modern Digital IoT Technology Attacks and Control in MANET. In *Advances in Data Communications and Networking for Digital Business Transformation*. IGI Global. Doi:10.4018/978-1-5225-5323-6.ch007

Rath, Pati, & Pattanayak. (2018). An Overview on Social Networking: Design, Issues, Emerging Trends, and Security. In *Social Network Analytics: Computational Research Methods and Techniques*. Academic Press.

Rath, M. (2017). Resource provision and QoS support with added security for client side applications in cloud computing. *International Journal of Information Technology, 9*(3), 1–8.

Rath, M. (2018). An Exhaustive Study and Analysis of Assorted Application and Challenges in Fog Computing and Emerging Ubiquitous Computing Technology. *International Journal of Applied Evolutionary Computation, 9*(2), 17-32. Retrieved from www.igi-global.com/ijaec

Rath, M. (2018). A Methodical Analysis of Application of Emerging Ubiquitous Computing Technology With Fog Computing and IoT in Diversified Fields and Challenges of Cloud Computing. *International Journal of Information Communication Technologies and Human Development, 10*(2).

Rath, M. (2018). An Analytical Study of Security and Challenging Issues in Social Networking as an Emerging Connected Technology (April 20, 2018). *Proceedings of 3rd International Conference on Internet of Things and Connected Technologies (ICIoTCT)*. Available at https://ssrn.com/abstract=3166509

Rath, M., & Panda, M. R. (2017). MAQ system development in mobile ad-hoc networks using mobile agents. *IEEE 2nd International Conference on Contemporary Computing and Informatics (IC3I)*, 794-798.

Rath, M., & Pati, B. (2017). *Load balanced routing scheme for MANETs with power and delay optimization. International Journal of Communication Network and Distributed Systems, 19.*

Rath, M., Pati, B., Panigrahi, C. R., & Sarkar, J. L. (2019). QTM: A QoS Task Monitoring System for Mobile Ad hoc Networks. In P. Sa, S. Bakshi, I. Hatzilygeroudis, & M. Sahoo (Eds.), *Recent Findings in Intelligent Computing Techniques. Advances in Intelligent Systems and Computing* (Vol. 707). Singapore: Springer. doi:10.1007/978-981-10-8639-7_57

Rath, M., Pati, B., Panigrahi, C. R., & Sarkar, J. L. (2019). QTM: A QoS Task Monitoring System for Mobile Ad hoc Networks. In P. Sa, S. Bakshi, I. Hatzilygeroudis, & M. Sahoo (Eds.), *Recent Findings in Intelligent Computing Techniques. Advances in Intelligent Systems and Computing* (Vol. 707). Singapore: Springer. doi:10.1007/978-981-10-8639-7_57

Rath, M., Pati, B., & Pattanayak, B. K. (2016). Inter-Layer Communication Based QoS Platform for Real Time Multimedia Applications in MANET. Wireless Communications, Signal Processing and Networking (IEEE WiSPNET), 613-617. doi:10.1109/WiSPNET.2016.7566203

Rath, M., Pati, B., & Pattanayak, B. K. (2017). Cross layer based QoS platform for multimedia transmission in MANET. *11th International Conference on Intelligent Systems and Control (ISCO)*, 402-407. 10.1109/ISCO.2017.7856026

Rath, M., Pati, B., & Pattanayak, B. K. (2019). Relevance of Soft Computing Techniques in the Significant Management of Wireless Sensor Networks. In Soft Computing in Wireless Sensor Networks (pp. 86-106). New York: Chapman and Hall/CRC, Taylor & Francis Group.

Rath, M., & Pattanayak, B. (2017). MAQ:A Mobile Agent Based QoS Platform for MANETs. *International Journal of Business Data Communications and Networking, IGI Global, 13*(1), 1–8. doi:10.4018/IJBDCN.2017010101

Rath, M., & Pattanayak, B. (2018). Technological improvement in modern health care applications using Internet of Things (IoT) and proposal of novel health care approach. *International Journal of Human Rights in Healthcare.*

Rath, M., & Pattanayak, B. (2018). Technological improvement in modern health care applications using Internet of Things (IoT) and proposal of novel health care approach. *International Journal of Human Rights in Healthcare*. doi:10.1108/IJHRH-01-2018-0007

Rath, M., & Pattanayak, B. K. (2014). A methodical survey on real time applications in MANETS: Focussing On Key Issues. *International Conference on, High Performance Computing and Applications (IEEE ICHPCA)*, 22-24. 10.1109/ICHPCA.2014.7045301

Rath, M., & Pattanayak, B. K. (2018). Monitoring of QoS in MANET Based Real Time Applications. Smart Innovation, Systems and Technologies, 84, 579-586. doi:10.1007/978-3-319-63645-0_64

Rath, M., & Pattanayak, B. K. (2018). SCICS: A Soft Computing Based Intelligent Communication System in VANET. Smart Secure Systems – IoT and Analytics Perspective. *Communications in Computer and Information Science*, *808*, 255–261. doi:10.1007/978-981-10-7635-0_19

Rath, M., & Pattanayak, B. K. (2019). Security Protocol with IDS Framework Using Mobile Agent in Robotic MANET. *International Journal of Information Security and Privacy*, *13*(1), 46–58. doi:10.4018/IJISP.2019010104

Rath, M., Pattanayak, B. K., & Pati, B. (2017). *Energetic Routing Protocol Design for Real-time Transmission in Mobile Ad hoc Network. In Computing and Network Sustainability, Lecture Notes in Networks and Systems* (Vol. 12). Singapore: Springer.

Riungu, L. M., Taipale, O., & Smolander, K. (2010). Research issues for software testing in the cloud. In *2010 IEEE Second International Conference on Cloud Computing Technology and Science (CloudCom)* (pp. 557–564). Indianapolis, IN: IEEE. 10.1109/CloudCom.2010.58

Rtah, M. (2018). Big Data and IoT-Allied Challenges Associated With Healthcare Applications in Smart and Automated Systems. *International Journal of Strategic Information Technology and Applications*, *9*(2). doi:10.4018/IJSITA.201804010

Rtah, M. (2018). Big Data and IoT-Allied Challenges Associated With Healthcare Applications in Smart and Automated Systems. *International Journal of Strategic Information Technology and Applications*, 9(2). doi:10.4018/IJSITA.201804010

Sallans, A., & Donnelly, M. (2012). DMP Online and DMPTool: Different Strategies Towards a Shared Goal. *International Journal of Digital Curation*, 7(2), 123–129. doi:10.2218/ijdc.v7i2.235

Sheng, J., Amankwah-Amoah, J., & Wang, X. (2017). A multidisciplinary perspective of big data in management research. *International Journal of Production Economics*, *191*, 97–112. doi:10.1016/j.ijpe.2017.06.006

Son, N. H. (2012). *Module on Data Preprocessing Techniques for Data Mining on Data Cleaning and Data Preprocessing*. Retrieved from http://elitepdf.com/

Tenopir, C., Sandusky, R. J., Allard, S., & Birch, B. (2014). Research data management services in academic research libraries and perceptions of librarians. *Library & Information Science Research*, *36*(2), 84–90. doi:10.1016/j.lisr.2013.11.003

Terrizzano, I., Schwarz, P., & Roth, M. (2015). Data wrangling: the challenging journey from the wild to the lake. *Proceedings of the 7th Biennial Conference on Innovative Data SystemsResearch (CIDR '15)*, 4–7.

UK Data Service. (2016). *Research data lifecycle*. Retrieved from https://www.ukdataservice.ac.uk/manage-data/lifecycle

University of California Digital Library. (2016). *DMPTool*. Available from https://dmptool.org/

University of Virginia Library Research Data Services. (2016). *Steps in the data life cycle*. Available from http://data.library.virginia.edu/data-management/lifecycle/

Vaidya, M. (2016). Handling critical issues of Big Data on cloud. In Managing Big Data in cloud computing environments. IGI Global. doi:10.4018/978-1-4666-9834-5.ch005

Vassiliadis, Simitsis, & Skiadopoulos. (2002). Conceptual modeling for ETL processes. In *Proceedings of the 5th ACM international workshop on Data Warehousing and OLAP*. ACM. 10.1145/583890.583893

Waddington, S. (2012). Kindura: Repository services for researchers based on hybrid clouds. *Journal of Digital Information, 13*(1).

Wang, C. (2016). Exposing library data with big data technology: A review. In *Computer and Information Science (ICIS), 2016 IEEE/ACIS 15th International Conference on.* IEEE. 10.1109/ICIS.2016.7550937

Westra, Ramirez, Parham, & Scaramozzino. (2010). Selected Internet Resources on Digital Research Data Curation. *Issues in Science and Technology Librarianship, 63.*

Whyte, A., & Tedds, J. (2011). *Making the case for research data management.* Edinburgh: Digital Curation Centre. Available http://www.dcc.ac.uk/webfm_send/487

Chapter 10
Developing Logistic Regression Models to Identify Salt–Affected Soils Using Optical Remote Sensing

Nirmal Kumar
National Bureau of Soil Survey and Land Use Planning, India

G. P. Obi Reddy
National Bureau of Soil Survey and Land Use Planning, India

S. K. Singh
National Bureau of Soil Survey and Land Use Planning, India

R. K. Naitam
National Bureau of Soil Survey and Land Use Planning, India

ABSTRACT

A major part of Indo-Gangetic plain is affected with soil salinity/alkalinity. Information on spatial distribution of soil salinity is important for planning management practices for its restoration. Remote sensing has proven to be a powerful tool in quantifying and monitoring the development of soil salinity. The chapter aims to develop logistic regression models, using Landsat 8 data, to identify salt affected soils in Indo-Gangetic plain. Logistic regression models based on Landsat 8 bands and several salinity indices were developed, individually and in combination. The bands capable of differentiating salt affected soils from other features were identified as green, red, and SWIR1. The logistic regression model developed in the study area was found to be 81% accurate in identifying salt-affected soils. A total area of 34558.49 ha accounting to ~10% of the total geographic area of the district was found affected with salinity/alkalinity. The spatial distribution of salt-affected soils in the district showed an association of shallow ground water depth with salinity.

DOI: 10.4018/978-1-5225-7784-3.ch010

INTRODUCTION

Soil salinity/ alkalinity has been identified as a major cause of land degradation after erosion (Oldeman et al., 1991; Bai et al., 2008) and a major threat to agriculture, especially in arid and semi arid areas (Bai et al., 2008; Maji et al., 2010). Current global estimates reveal over one billion ha area affected to various degrees of soil salinity/ alkalinity (Singh 2009). In India, Mandal *et al.* (2009) digitized maps in geographical information system (GIS) depicting salt affected soils (SAS) of the country. An area of 6.73 million hectare of SAS was estimated for the entire country. State wise estimates showed that this extensive area is distributed over the Gangetic plain of Uttar Pradesh; the arid and semiarid regions of Gujarat and the peninsular plains of Maharashtra state. A significant area is also located in the coastal region covering seven states. The SAS are primarily saline in deltaic, coastal and mud flats/mangrove swamps and sodic in alluvial, aeofluvial /aeolian/arid and peninsular plains. Quantifying and monitoring the spatial distribution of SAS is important for increasing productivity and production, apart from increasing area under cultivation. Commonly used method of soil survey is time consuming and hard to reproduce. Remote sensing has proven to be a powerful tool in quantifying and monitoring the development of soil salinity.

A variety of remote sensing data has been used for identifying and monitoring SAS (Kumar and Singh, 2018), including aerial photographs, thermal infrared images, visible and near infrared (NIR) multispectral and microwave images (Metternicht and Zinck, 2003). Different bands of multispectral satellite data have been used individually or in combinations to identify SAS or to differentiate it from other surface features. Alternatively, many image transforms such as, principal components (PC) and Tasseled Cap Transformation (TCT) have been found effective in assessment of SAS. In addition, vegetation indices (VIs) and several salinity indices (SIs) have been used to get better accuracies in identification of SAS. These indices make the required salinity information more prominent while suppressing the effects of other land use/land cover features.

The remote sensing data have been used to identify SAS in two manners: visual interpretation and supervised classification of moderate resolution data such as Landsat. Most attempts to assess and map SAS in India is based on visual interpretation initially of aerial photographs and later of one or more seasons false colour composites (FCC) of moderate resolution satellite data (Sharma and Bhargawa, 1988; Singh and Dwivedi, 1989; Dwivedi, 1992, 1994; Sujatha *et al.*, 2000; Sethi *et al.*, 2006). Visual interpretation of remote sensing data is also time consuming (though, less than survey), subjective, and hard to reproduce. An alternative for visual interpretation techniques is the automatic extraction of the SAS from satellite imagery using different classification techniques based on their spectral responses. This provides a quick and objective tool for identifying and mapping SAS.

SAS have been identified and mapped using both, unsupervised (Khan *et al.*, 2005; Mitchell, 2014) and supervised (Saha *et al.*, 1990; Dwivedi and Sreenivas, 1998a,b; Chen and Rao, 2008; Abbas *et al.*, 2013) classification techniques performed on multispectral bands and/or different indices and PCs. Limited use of unsupervised classifiers in SAS identification have been reported. Khan *et al.*, (2005) applied ISODATA classification on two specifically created composites of IRS-1B LISS-II data: one of Normalized Difference Salinity Index (NDSI), water index, and Normalized Difference Vegetation Index (NDVI) and other of PC1 and 2. Reliable results were obtained in classification of SAS, crop, and lake as compared to SAS maps created based on topographic maps. Mitchell (2014) applied ISODATA method on a composite of Landsat 5 TM/ 8 OLI bands blue, NIR, and TIR along with TC brightness and wetness for three years to identify SAS with an accuracy of 97% to 99.33%.

In supervised classification techniques, Maximum Likelihood Classification (MLC) is the most used method for identifying SAS (Saha *et al.*, 1990; Dwivedi and Sreenivas, 1998a, b; Abbas *et al.*, 2013). Saha, *et al.*, (1990) found MLC effective in identifying salt-affected and water logging areas with an accuracy of about 96 percent. Dwivedi and Sreenivas (1998a) applied MLC on MSS FCC for year 1975 and 1992 to delineate SAS with accuracies of 98.85 and 98.5%, respectively and found shrinkage of 14.55% in area under SAS during the period. Gutierrez (2002) applied MLC on three Landsat TM composites (bands 4, 3, 2; bands 4, 5, 3; bands 4, 5, 7) and the TCT composite 1, 2, and 3. All these FCCs were found similar in their ability to discriminate among SAS and between sandy soils and SAS. Abbas *et al.* (2013) applied MLC on IRS 1B- LISS II data of an irrigated agricultural area in Pakistan to differentiate SAS from bare land, fallow, crop land, urban and waterlogged areas with an overall accuracy of 98.8%. Wu *et al.*, (2008) classified SAS in slightly, moderately, and strongly saline soils and slolonchak with an accuracy of 90.2% by applying MLH on Landsat MSS and TM of three seasons supported by IRS AWiFS and CBERS data when required. However, ML is a parametric classifier which needs the data to be normally distributed and fails in resolving interclass mix-up if the data employed do not have a normal distribution (Rowan *et al.*, 1977; Quinlan, 1993).

Many non parametric classifiers like neural network (ANN) algorithms, decision tree classifiers (DT), and support vector machines (SVM) have been developed and are increasingly being used to cope with non normal distributions and intra-class variation found in a variety of spectral data sets (Hansen *et al.*, 1996; Huang *et al.*, 2002; Venables and Ripley, 1994). Nonparametric classifiers have frequently been found to yield higher classification accuracies than parametric classifiers (Pal and Mather 2003, Rao *et al.* 2006). Rao *et al.* (2005) compared MLC and DTC to identify SAS and found the latter more efficient in differentiating SAS, residential areas, and sand areas. The DT allows using inputs continuous as well as discrete in nature. Elnaggar and Noller (2009) used Landsat TM bands, different indices (NDVI, NDSI, SAVI, and TCT), terrain attributes (elevation, slope, aspect), and discrete attributes like landform, geology, historic vegetation, distance to streams, etc. as DT inputs to classify SAS with an accuracy of 99%. In the same study MLH of the Landsat images could yield only two salinity classes: non-saline soils (EC < 4 dSm⁻¹), prediction accuracy of 97%, and saline soils (EC > 4 dSm⁻¹), prediction accuracy 60%. Ding *et al.* (2011) identified TM band 1, PC3, and NDVI and NDWI as the character variables for slight and moderate saline soils, strongly saline soils, and vegetation and water areas, respectively in a DT analysis. Afrasinei *et al.* (2017) used DT on a composite of several indices derived from Landsat images to identify moderate and strongly saline soils in salt-affected areas of Algeria. Cai *et al.*, (2010) applied SVM classifier on CBERS-02B CCD multi-spectral image to get an accuracy of 82% with the kappa coefficient of 0.79. This accuracy was improved up to 84.7% with the kappa coefficient of 0.82 by using additional inputs of textural feature such as, mean, variance and homogeneity.

In this study, attempt has been made to develop logistic regression models based on individual bands of the Landsat 8 images or different transformations, and indices to identify salt affected soils. Logistic Regression Models are probability classification routines which offer, in most cases, higher degrees of classification accuracy over distance based classifiers such as maximum likelihood.

Logistic Regression

Logistic regression is a variation of ordinary regression which is used when the dependent variable is a dichotomous variable (i. e. it takes only two values, which usually represent the occurrence or non-occurrence of some outcome event, usually coded as 0 or 1) and the independent variables are continuous, categorical, or both. This classification routine incorporates both the mean and variance of the data set into the classification decision rule. The utilization of variance into the classification decision rule provides additional data on which to base the classification, thereby improving overall classification accuracy.

Logistic regression is a useful approach in examining the relationship between a set of independent variables and a dependent variable which takes only two dichotomous values (i. e. it takes only two values, which usually represent the occurrence or non-occurrence of some outcome event as in this case a field comes under conservation tillage or otherwise, usually coded as 0 or 1). The model (Mendenhall and Sincich, 1996) is of the form

$$E(y) = \frac{\exp\left(b_0 + b_1 X_1 + b_2 X_2 + \dots + b_k X_k\right)}{1 + \exp\left(b_o + b_1 X_1 + b_2 X_2 + \dots + b_k X_k\right)}$$

where

$$y = \begin{cases} 1 & if\ category\ A\ occurs \\ 0 & if\ category\ B\ occurs \end{cases}$$

$E(y) = P$ (category A occurs) $= \pi$; i.e., probability that the target is SAS

$X_1, X_2, \dots, X_k$ are qualitative or quantitative independent variables. In this case digital number values of different bands or indices or principal components.

$b_0, b_1, b_2, \dots, b_k$ are the estimated coefficients of the model which are estimated using maximum likelihood method.

A cutoff probability is needed to be fixed to classify the area under SAS or non-degraded lands. In order to be able to structure a logistic regression model, it is necessary to determine certain training areas on a satellite image for which it is known that they belong either to conservation or conventional tillage areas. The sampling areas corresponding to the conservation or conventional tillage should be accurately determined over satellite image which would be done by GPS. The sample areas should represent all the variability occurring on the satellite image.

Many uses of logistic regression have been found in mapping burned areas (Koutsias and Karteris, 1998) and conservation tillage (vanDeventer *et. al.* 1997; Gowda *et. al.*, 2001; Bricklemyer *et al.*, 2002; Vina *et al.*, 2003; Bricklemyer *et. al.* 2006; Kumar et al., 2012). Bricklemyer *et. al.* (2006) compared logistic regression (LR), traditional classification tree analysis (CTA), and boosted classification tree analysis (BCTA) for identifying non-tilled fields in the presence of a crop canopy. Predicting non-tilled and tillage management in the presence of a crop canopy and in a spatially large, management diverse study area proved to be challenging. Logistic regression (94% accurate) outperformed both CTA (87% accurate) and BCTA (89% accurate) for discriminating non-tilled and tilled fields. However, the authors could not found use of logistic regression model in identifying SAS.

MATERIALS AND METHODS

Study Area

The study has been conducted in Kanpur Dehat district of the state Uttar Pradesh, India and lies between 26^0 05 to 26^0 51 North latitudes and 79^0 30 to 80^0 10 East longitudes (figure 1). The district covers an area of 874.65 sq. km. The study area is a part of Indo-Gangetic Plains (IGP). Geologically, the IGP consists of younger and older alluvia brought down by the Ganga and Yamuna rivers and their tributaries during the Pleistocene period. The younger alluvium, locally known as *Khaddar*, developed in the lowlands and is characterized with light colored, non-calcareous materials, which is composed of lenticular beds of sand, gravel and clays. The older alluvial plains known as *Bhangar*, developed on slightly elevated terraces and are characterized with dark colour, calcium carbonate rich concretions and nodules, locally known as *Kankar*.

The area has a continental monsoonal climate with average annual precipitation of 822 mm. Nearly 85% of the total precipitation is received during the monsoon season from June to September. The area is extensively cultivated for rice and wheat. Other crops such as maize, pigeon pea, sugarcane, and lentil substituting either the rice or wheat crop in some years. On the advent of green revolution during sixties, expansion of area and intensification of rice–wheat productions system based on the adoption of Green Revolution (GR) technologies namely high-yielding varieties, fertilizers and irrigation, led to increase production and productivity of both rice and wheat. However, continued intensive use of green revolution technologies in recent years has resulted in lower marginal returns and locational problems of salinization, overexploitation of groundwater, physical and chemical deterioration of the soil. Salinity becomes the major concern at many locations in the district measured in terms of loss of productivity and abandonment of agriculture. The soils of the region are predominantly coarse-textured with patches of silty clay and clay soils. Apart from salinity/sodicity, the region is also affected by erosion and water logging. Gullies and ravines along the rivers Yamuna, Sengar, and Rind are also a concern in the district (Kumar and Singh, 2018).

Data

In this study, open data of Landsat 8 Operational Linear Imager/ Thermal Infrared Sensor (OLI/TIRS) multispectral (30 m) have been used. The characteristics of Landsat-8 data have been given in table1. The data (path 144, row 42, date 26th March, 2018) were downloaded from http://earthexplorer.usgs.gov/ free of cost.

Free to use high resolution Google earth data have also been utilized in the study for verifications.

Method

The overall methodology is shown in the flow chart (figure 2).

Calculation of Salinity Indices

Subsets for the district were clipped from the Landsat bands and different indices reported to be effective in soil salinity assessment (table 2) were calculated. The

Figure 1. Study area location

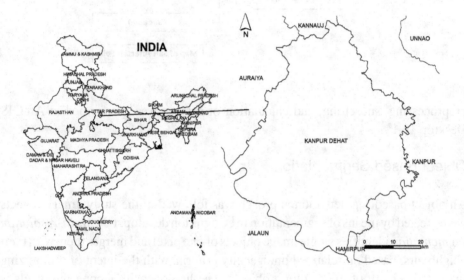

Table 1. Characteristics of Landsat-8 data

Processing	Level 1T - Terrain Corrected
Pixel Size	• Multispectral bands: 30 meters • panchromatic band: 15 meters
Repeativity	• 16 days
Spectral Bands	• 9 bands in visible, NIR, and SWIR wavelengths
Data Characteristics	• GeoTIFF data format • Cubic Convolution (CC) resampling • Universal Transverse Mercator (UTM) map projection • World Geodetic System (WGS) 84 datum • 12 meter circular error, 90% confidence global accuracy • 16-bit pixel values

Figure 2. Methodology flow chart

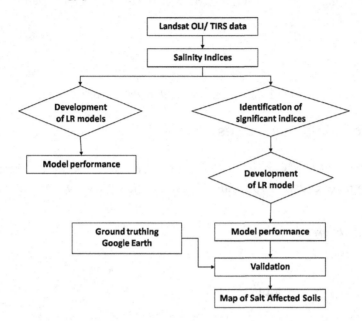

preprocessing, subsetting, and calculation of indices were performed in ArcGIS Desktop 10.1®.

Object Based Segmentation

An object based segmentation approach was followed in the study. Image objects were created by means of segmentation in eCognition developer™. *Multi-resolution segmentation* identifies single image objects of one pixel and merges them with their neighbours, based on relative homogeneity criteria, with the intent of minimizing the heterogeneity of the resulting objects. The homogeneity among the pixels is identified based on both, the spectral and the shape criteria (Benz *et al.*, 2004). The spectral homogeneity is based on the standard deviation of the spectral colours, whereas, the shape homogeneity is based on the deviation of a compact (or smooth) shape. The size of the segments, are decided by the scale parameter. The values of the shape and spectral criteria and the scale parameters were defined empirically based on several trials to get optimum results.

Development of Logistic Regression Models

A total of 3679 segments (1248 SAS and 2431 other features) were selected as training sites and different logistic regression models were developed. Training sites were identified by field observations and using legacy reports available. Separate models were developed with individual bands and indices. Logistic Regression model was also developed with all the bands and indices as inputs and using a backward stepwise logistic regression analysis to get the most significant combination of variables. A cut off probability of 0.5 was selected to classify a particular segment under SAS or under other features. The best identified model was applied to the full image of the study area to generate the SAS map. The classification was validated with field verifications and with high resolution Google Earth™ data.

Table 2. Indices for soil salinity assessment

Index	Formula	References
Normalized Difference Vegetation Index (NDVI)	(NIR-R)/(NIR+R)	Rouse et al., 1974
Normalized Difference Salinity Index (NDSI)	(R−NIR)/(R+NIR)	Major et al., 1990
Salinity Index (SI$_1$)	NIR/SWIR1	Tripathi et al., 1997
Brightness Index	$\sqrt{(R^2 x NIR^2)}$	Khan et al., 2001
Salinity Index (SI$_2$)	$\sqrt{(GxR)}$	
Salinity Index (SI$_3$)	$\sqrt{(G^2 x R^2 x NIR^2)}$	Douaoui et al., 2006
Salinity Index (SI$_4$)	$\sqrt{(G^2 x R^2)}$	
Salinity Index (SI$_5$)	SWIR1/SWIR 2	IDNP, (2002)
Salinity Index (SI$_6$)	(NIR-SWIR1)/(NIR+SWIR1)	
Salinity Index (SI$_7$)	(SWIR1-SWIR2)/(SWIR1+SWIR2)	
Salinity Index (SI$_8$)	B/R	Abbas and Khan, 2007 Abbas et al., 2013
Salinity Index (SI$_9$)	(B-R)/(B+R)	
Salinity Index (SI$_{10}$)	(GxR)/B	
Salinity Index (SI$_{11}$)	$\sqrt{(BxR)}$	
Salinity Index (SI$_{12}$)	(BxR)/G	
Salinity Index (SI$_{13}$)	(RXNIR)/G	
Salinity Index (SI$_{14}$)	$\sqrt{(RxNIR)}$	Dehni and Lounis (2012)
Combined Spectral Response Index (COSRI)	[(B +G)/(R+NIR)]*NDVI	Ferna´ndez-Buces et al., 2006

B- Blue, G- Green, R- Red, NIR- Near Infrared, SWIR1- Landsat TM band5, SWIR2- Landsat TM band 7, L=.0.5.

RESULT AND DISCUSSION

Different bands' DN values and Indices (table 2) were evaluated alone and in combination through logistic regression and were assessed based on accuracy and significance at $p \leq 0.05$.

Performance of Logistic Regression Models Based on Individual Bands/ Indices

It was observed that all the models, developed with single band/ index, were able to identify the areas other than SAS with better accuracy (table 3). However, these were unable to identify SAS with good accuracy. Among the Landsat 8 bands, the accuracy of models developed with green band and NIR band were the maximum and the minimum, respectively. The same trend was observed in identifying SAS. The accuracy of salinity indices in identifying SAS were found ranging from 50 to 70%. Generally, the indices calculated with NIR and SWIR bands showed lower accuracy than the indices calculated with green and red bands. The indices NDVI, NDSI, and COSRI were found very poor in identifying the SAS.

These observations may be justified by looking to the spectra of the major surface features of the study area (figure 3). It can be observed from the spectra that the other features are separable from SAS in blue, green, and red bands of Landsat 8. In NIR region, the spectra of SAS are coinciding with that of vegetation. In SWIR2 band, the spectrum of SAS is coinciding with sands which are restricted near the river banks in the study area. For the same reason, the indices calculated with NIR and SWIR2 bands were found poor in identifying SAS. To get better accuracies in identifying SAS, stepwise backward logistic regression was performed.

Stepwise Logistic Regression

Backward step wise logistic regression was exercised on all the bands/ indices. The backwards-stepwise procedure began by fitting a logistic regression model to the data using all variables. Next, each predictor (i.e., band or index value) was systematically removed, and the residual deviance, at new degrees of freedom, was compared to a Chi-square distribution to determine the significance of that predictor to the model. After each predictor was removed and the significance of each predictor determined, the least significant predictor was removed permanently if it failed to meet the required Chi-square test (*p*-value ≤ 0.05). The process of removing the least significant predictor continued until all remaining predictors were significant, given the other predictors included in the model. The resulting equation contained the most significant variables to predict the occurrence of SAS. The variables with higher standard error were further removed from the final model. The final model is shown in the table 4.

Thus, the equation for probability of falling of a segment into SAS class was of the form:

$$E(y) = \frac{\exp\left[\begin{array}{l}-10.891 + (-24.361COSRI) + (-0.357G) \\ +(0.735SI_{11}) + (-0.379SI_{12}) + (0.002SWIR1)\end{array}\right]}{1 + \exp\left[\begin{array}{l}-10.891 + (-24.361COSRI) + (-0.357G) \\ +(0.735SI_{11}) + (-0.379SI_{12}) + (0.002SWIR1)\end{array}\right]}$$

where

$$y = \begin{cases} 1 & \text{if category is } SAS \\ 0 & \text{if category is not } SAS \end{cases}$$

$$E(y) = P(category\,1\,occurs) = \pi$$

Figure 3. Spectra of different surface features of the study area

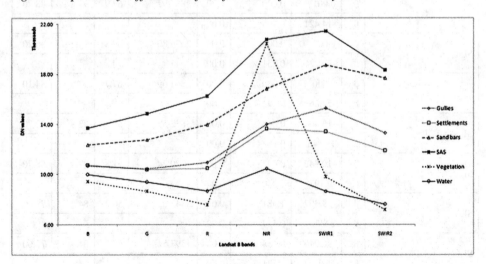

Table 3. Model summary and accuracy of logistic regression models with different bands/ indices

Variables in Equation	Coefficients		Standard Error	Sig.	-2 Log Likelihood	Accuracy		
						SAS	Other	Over all
DN (NIR)	β_1	0.000	0.000	0.00	4173.92	27.7	87.3	67.10
	β_0	-8.995	0.422	0.00				
DN (Red)	β_1	0.001	0.000	0.00	3016.94	67.0	91.0	82.80
	β_0	-11.548	0.374	0.00				
DN (Green)	β_1	0.002	0.000	0.00	2697.16	70.1	94.1	85.90
	β_0	-19.098	0.616	0.00				
DN (SWIR1)	β_1	0.001	0.000	0.00	2970.48	68.7	91.1	83.50
	β_0	-10.219	0.333	0.00				
DN (SWIR2)	β_1	0.001	0.000	0.00	3005.99	67.9	89.8	82.40
	β_0	-8.286	0.266	0.00				
NDSI	β_1	8.516	0.467	0.00	4292.29	8.8	87.7	60.90
	β_0	1.029	0.094	0.00				
NDVI	β_1	8.516	0.467	0.00	4292.29	8.8	87.7	60.90
	β_0	1.029	0.094	0.00				
SI_1	β_1	-4.450	0.215	0.00	3980.73	50.7	77.8	68.90
	β_0	4.292	0.230	0.00				
SI_2	β_1	0.001	0.000	0.00	2881.97	67.9	91.8	83.70
	β_0	-14.421	0.465	0.00				
SI_3	β_1	0.000	0.000	0.00	2536.80	69.8	94.7	86.20
	β_0	-7.922	0.251	0.00				
SI_4	β_1	0.000	0.000	0.00	2842.69	67.7	92.5	84.10
	β_0	-7.686	0.242	0.00				
SI_5	β_1	-16.406	0.662	0.00	3832.52	51.3	83.8	72.70
	β_0	18.946	0.783	0.00				
SI_6	β_1	-10.942	0.497	0.00	3970.24	51.8	77.5	68.70
	β_0	-0.192	0.040	0.00				
SI_7	β_1	-39.397	1.581	0.00	3843.02	50.2	84.7	73.00
	β_0	2.808	0.137	0.00				
SI_8	β_1	-16.046	0.584	0.00	3397.51	63.5	84.9	77.60
	β_0	15.307	0.571	0.00				
SI_9	β_1	-32.525	1.160	0.00	3376.26	62.9	85.5	77.80
	β_0	-0.799	0.045	0.00				

continued on following page

Table 3. Continued

Variables in Equation	Coefficients		Standard Error	Sig.	-2 Log Likelihood	Accuracy		
						SAS	Other	Over all
SI_{10}	β_1	0.001	0.000	0.00	2933.516	67.0	91.2	83.00
	β_0	-9.843	0.314	0.00				
SI_{11}	β_1	0.001	0.000	0.00	2932.21	68.0	91.8	83.70
	β_0	-16.264	0.530	0.00				
SI_{12}	β_1	0.001	0.000	0.00	3156.01	65.1	90.3	81.80
	β_0	-13.872	0.462	0.00				
SI_{13}	β_1	0.001	0.000	0.00	3062.15	62.3	93.5	82.90
	β_0	-20.203	0.726	0.00				
SI_{14}	β_1	0.002	0.000	0.00	2573.41	69.9	94.0	85.80
	β_0	-23.661	0.785	0.00				
Brightness Index	β_1	0.000	0.000	0.00	2557.66	69.6	94.2	85.90
	β_0	-12.148	0.397	0.00				
COSRI	β_1	-13.253	0.687	0.00	4245.70	20.8	85.5	63.60
	β_0	1.369	0.106	0.00				

Table 4. Logistic regression model developed with back ward stepwise method

Band/ Index	B	SE	Sig.	Accuracy		
				SAS	Other	Overall
COSRI	-24.361	3.058	.000	81.1	97.4	91.9
G	-.357	.032	.000			
SI_{11}	.735	.064	.000			
SI_{12}	-.379	.032	.000			
SWIR1	.002	.000	.000			
Constant	-10.891	2.257	.000			

The logistic equation, when solved for y, returned the probability of SAS for each segment in the original image. Applying the equation to the original image produced a map in which each segment had a probability of being SAS, with values ranging from 0 to 1. We reclassified the probability image by classifying segments with probabilities of greater than 0.5 as SAS and probabilities less than or equal to 0.5 as other features. Finally image of SAS and other features was formed (Figure 4.).

Spatial Distribution of SAS in the District

A total area of 34558.49 ha was found to be under SAS in the district constituting ~10% of the total geographic area of the district. SAS were widely spread in north-western and south-eastern part, mostly in the area lying between lower Ganga Canal (Etawah branch) and Pandu river (figure 4). Below the lower Ganga canal, smaller patches of SAS were found. The occurrence of SAS may be associated with the ground water depth (GWD) of the study area. The depth to water level is shallow along canal command area of the north-western and south-eastern part of the district. However, in the canal command area of southern part of the district, the GWD is deeper along the rivers Yamuna and Sengar (Kumar and Singh, 2018).

Validation

The maps were validated with the Google earth images (figure 5) and with geo-tagged field photographs (figure 6) Photo GPS Extractor, a small utility to visualize the GPS coordinates of a JPG photo on a map was used. This allows the users to determine where a certain picture was taken. It was used to extract the GPS locations of the pictures taken during the field survey for verification of the identified degraded lands. A GPS enabled camera was used during the field verification. The GPS information is stored inside the JPG photo. This information is not very useful without a tool to visualize it. PGE extracts the GPS points from the pictures using the Google Maps to show their coordinates. It also allows extracting GPS points in a batch and exporting them in .kml files. The figures (Figure 6) shows the surface conditions and the locations of the salt affected areas surveyed during the ground truthing. The validation with Google earth showed that the areas identified as SAS were matching accurately. However, some of the actual SAS were not captured particularly, near the fringes of salt affected patches. As the accuracy of the model developed in identifying SAS was 81%, these situations were expected.

CONCLUSION

Managing saline soils is highly site specific and needed to be mapped to develop salinity zones which will help to design management plans for sustainable use of soil resources. Remote sensing has been proved to be a promising tool for salinity assessment and mapping. However, the use of remote sensing images in identifying SAS is mostly limited to visual interpretation of satellite imagery. This method has been criticized for being qualitative, subjective, time consuming, and for being hardly reproducible. Isolated efforts to map SAS with digital image processing have also

Figure 4. Spatial distribution of salt affected soils in Kanpur Dehat district

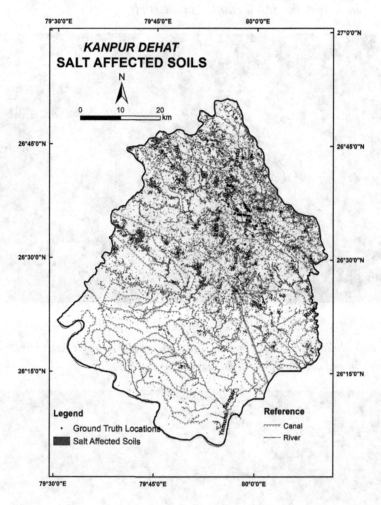

been attempted for specific study areas. However, the uses of advanced statistical procedures are missing. The present study shows the use of logistic regression models for identifying SAS with the help of Landsat -8 data. The study tests the performance of different salinity indices developed for identifying SAS in the Indo-gangetic plains – a major salt affected region of the country.

The study shows that the Landsat 8 OLI bands green, red and SWIR 1 and salinity indices developed by using these bands are suitable for identifying SAS. We understood from the study that logistic regression model, developed using mentioned bands and indices in combination, were able to differentiate SAS and other features accurately.

Figure 5a. Validation of SAS in the study area with Google earth images. The boundaries in red are the SAS identified in the study.

Figure 5b. Validation of SAS in the study area with Google earth images. The boundaries in red are the SAS identified in the study.

Figure 5c. Validation of SAS in the study area with Google earth images. The boundaries in red are the SAS identified in the study.

Figure 5d. Validation of SAS in the study area with Google earth images. The boundaries in red are the SAS identified in the study.

Figure 6a. Filed photographs of SAS in the study area with location on the Google earth

Figure 6b. Filed photographs of SAS in the study area with location on the Google earth

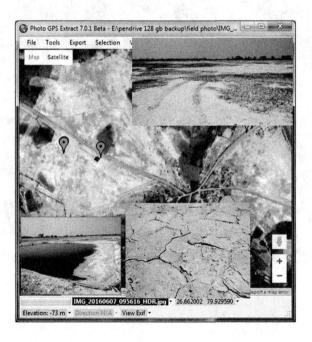

Figure 6c. Filed photographs of SAS in the study area with location on the Google earth

Figure 6d. Filed photographs of SAS in the study area with location on the Google earth

REFERENCES

Abbas, A., & Khan, S. (2007). Using remote sensing techniques for appraisal of irrigated soil salinity. In *Int. Congress on Modelling and Simulation (MODSIM)*. Modelling and Simulation Society of Australia and New Zealand.

Abbas, A., Khan, S., Hussain, N., Hanjra, M. A., & Akbar, S. (2013). Characterizing soil salinity in irrigated agriculture using a remote sensing approach. *Physics and Chemistry of the Earth*, *55-57*, 43–52. doi:10.1016/j.pce.2010.12.004

Afrasinei, G. M., Melis, M. T., Buttau, C., Bradd, J. M., Arras, C., & Ghiglieri, G. (2017). Assessment of remote sensing-based classification methods for change detection of salt-affected areas (Biskra area, Algeria). *Journal of Applied Remote Sensing*, *11*(1), 1–28. doi:10.1117/1.JRS.11.016025

Bai, Z. G., Dent, D. L., Olsson, L., & Schaepman, M. E. (2008). Proxy global assessment of land degradation. *Soil Use and Management*, *24*(3), 223–234. doi:10.1111/j.1475-2743.2008.00169.x

Benz, U. C., Hofmann, P., Willhauck, G., Lingenfelder, I., & Heynen, M. (2004). Multi-resolution, object-oriented fuzzy analysis of remote sensing data for GIS-ready information. *SPRS J. of Photogrammetry & Remote Sensing*, *58*(3-4), 239–258. doi:10.1016/j.isprsjprs.2003.10.002

Bricklemyer, R., Lawrence, R., & Miller, P. (2002). Documenting notill and conventional till practices using Landsat ETM+ imagery and logistic regression. *Journal of Soil and Water Conservation*, *57*, 267–271.

Bricklemyer, R. S., Lawrence, R. L., Miller, P. R., & Battogtokh, N. (2006). Predicting tillage practices and agricultural soil disturbance in north central Montana with Landsat imagery. *Agriculture, Ecosystems & Environment*, *118*, 201–210. doi:10.1016/j.agee.2006.05.017

Cai, S., Zhang, R., Liu, L., & Zhou, D. (2010). A method of salt-affected soil information extraction based on a support vector machine with texture features. *Mathematical and Computer Modelling*, *51*(11-12), 1319–1325. doi:10.1016/j.mcm.2009.10.037

Chen, S., & Rao, P. (2008). Land degradation monitoring using multi-temporal Landsat TM/ETM data in a transition zone between grassland and cropland of northeast China. *International Journal of Remote Sensing*, *29*(7), 2055–2073. doi:10.1080/01431160701355280

Dehni, A., & Lounis, M. (2012). Remote Sensing techniques for salt affected soil mapping: Application to the Oran region of Algeria. *Procedia Engineering, 33*, 188–198. doi:10.1016/j.proeng.2012.01.1193

Ding, J., Wu, M., & Tiyip, T. (2011). Study on soil salinization information in arid region using remote sensing technique. *Agricultural Sciences in China, 10*(3), 404–411. doi:10.1016/S1671-2927(11)60019-9

Douaoui, A. E. K., Nicolas, H., & Walter, C. (2006). Detecting salinity hazards within a semiarid context by means of combining soil and remote-sensing data. *Geoderma, 134*(1-2), 217–230. doi:10.1016/j.geoderma.2005.10.009

Dwivedi, R. S. (1992). Monitoring and the study of the effects of image scale on delineation of salt-affected soils in the Indo-Gangetic plains. *International Journal of Remote Sensing, 13*(8), 1527–1536. doi:10.1080/01431169208904206

Dwivedi, R. S. (1994). Study of salinity and waterlogging in Uttar Pradesh (India) using remote sensing data. *Land Degradation & Rehabilitation, 5*(3), 191–199. doi:10.1002/ldr.3400050303

Dwivedi, R. S., & Sreenivas, K. (1998a). Image transforms as a tool for the study of soil salinity and alkalinity dynamics. *International Journal of Remote Sensing, 19*(4), 605–619. doi:10.1080/014311698215883

Dwivedi, R. S., & Sreenivas, K. (1998b). Delineation of salt-affected soils and waterlogged areas in the Indo-Gangetic plains using IRS-1C LISS-111 data. *International Journal of Remote Sensing, 19*(14), 2739–2751. doi:10.1080/014311698214488

Elnaggar, A. A., & Noller, J. S. (2009). Application of remote- sensing data and decision-tree analysis to mapping salt- affected soils over large areas. *Remote Sensing, 2*(1), 151–165. doi:10.3390/rs2010151

Fernandez-Buces, N., Siebe, C., Cram, S., & Palacio, J. L. (2006). Mapping soil salinity using a combined spectral response index for bare soil and vegetation: A case study in the former lake Texcoco, Mexico. *Journal of Arid Environments, 65*(4), 644–667. doi:10.1016/j.jaridenv.2005.08.005

Gowda, P. H., Dalzell, B. J., Mulla, D. J., & Kollman, F. (2001). Mapping tillage practices with Landstat Thematic Mapper based logistic regression models. *Journal of Soil and Water Conservation, 56*, 91–96.

Gutierrez, C. (2002). *A comparison of false color composites in mapping and discriminating between salt-affected soils in Kings county, California* (Masters thesis). Oregon State University.

Hansen, M., Dubayah, R., & Defries, R. (1996). Decision trees: An alternative to traditional land cover classifiers. *International Journal of Remote Sensing, 17*(5), 1075–1081. doi:10.1080/01431169608949069

Huang, C., Davis, L. S., & Townshend, J. R. G. (2002). An assessment of support vector machines for land cover classification. *International Journal of Remote Sensing, 23*(4), 725–749. doi:10.1080/01431160110040323

IDNP. (2002). *Indo-Dutch Network Project: A methodology for identification of water-logging and soil salinity conditions using remote sensing.* Central Soil Salinity Research Institute.

Khan, N. M., Rastoskuev, V. V., Sato, Y., & Shiozawa, S. (2005). Assessment of hydrosaline land degradation by using a simple approach of remote sensing indicators. *Agricultural Water Management, 77*(1-3), 96–109. doi:10.1016/j.agwat.2004.09.038

Khan, N. M., Rastoskuev, V. V., Shalina, E. V., & Sato, Y. (2001). Mapping salt affected soils using remote sensing indicators- A simple approach with the use of GIS IDRISI. *Proceedings of 22nd Asian conference on Remote Sensing.*

Koutsias, N., & Karteris, M. (1998). Logistic regression modeling of multitemporal thematic mapper data for burned area mapping. *International Journal of Remote Sensing, 19*(18), 3499–3514. doi:10.1080/014311698213777

Kumar, N., & Singh, S. K. (2018). Land degradation assessment using MODIS NDVI time series data. In S. K. Singh, S. Chatterji, S. Chattaraj, P. S. Butte, & R. P. Sharma (Eds.), *ICAR-NBSS&LUP technologies, NBSS Pub. No. 176* (p. 102). Nagpur: ICAR-NBSS&LUP.

Kumar, N., Sinha, N. K., & Sahoo, R. N. (2012). *Discriminating different tillage through remote sensing approach.* LAP Lambert Academic Publishing.

Maji, A. K., Reddy, G. P. O., & Sarkar, D. (2010). *Degraded and wastelands of India, status and spatial distribution.* New Delhi: Indian Council of Agricultural Research and National Academy of Agricultural Science.

Major, D., Baret, F., & Guyot, G. (1990). A Ratio vegetation index adjusted for soil brightness. *International Journal of Remote Sensing, 11*(5), 727–740. doi:10.1080/01431169008955053

Mandal, A. K., Sharma, R. C., & Singh, G. (2009). Assessment of salt affected soils in India using GIS. *Geocarto International, 24*(6), 437–456. doi:10.1080/10106040902781002

Mendenhall, W., & Sincich, T. (1996). *A Second Course in Statistics: Regression Analysis*. Englewood Cliffs, NJ: Prentice-Hall.

Metternicht, G. I., & Zinck, J. A. (2003). Remote sensing of soil salinity: Potentials and constraints. *Remote Sensing of Environment, 85*(1), 1–20. doi:10.1016/S0034-4257(02)00188-8

Mitchell, D. E. (2014). *Dentifying salinization through multispectral band analysis: lake Urmia, Iran* (Masters thesis). Ryerson University, Toronto, Ontario, Canada.

Oldeman, L. R., Hakkeling, R. T. A., & Sombroek, W. G. (1991). *World map of the status of human-induced soil degradation: An explanatory note, second* (revised edition). Wageningen: ISRIC.

Pal, M., & Mather, P. M. (2003). An assessment of the effectiveness of decision tree methods for land cover classification. *Remote Sensing of Environment, 86*(4), 554–565. doi:10.1016/S0034-4257(03)00132-9

Quinlan, J. R. (1993). *C4.5: Programs for machine learning*. San Mateo, CA: Morgan Kauffmann Publishers.

Rao, P., Chen, S., & Sun, K. (2005). Improved classification of soil salinity by decision tree on remotely sensed images. *Proceedings of SPIE-Int. Society for Optical Engineering, 6027, 20th Congress of the Int. Commission for Optics.*

Rouse, J. W., Haas, R. H., Schell, J. A., & Deering, D. W. (1974). Monitoring vegetation systems in the Great Plains with ERTS. In *Third ERTS-1 Symposium*. Washington, DC: NASA.

Rowan, L. C., Goetz, A. F. H., & Ashley, R. P. (1977). Discrimination of hydrothermally altered and unaltered rocks in the visible and near infrared multispectral images. *Geophysics, 42*(3), 522–535. doi:10.1190/1.1440723

Saha, S. K., Kudrat, M., & Bhan, S. K. (1990). Digital processing of Landsat TM data for wasteland mapping in parts of Aligarh District, Uttar Pradesh, India. *International Journal of Remote Sensing, 11*(3), 485–492. doi:10.1080/01431169008955034

Sethi, M., Dasog, G. S., Van Lieshoutc, A., & Salimathd, S. B. (2006). Salinity appraisal using IRS images in Shorapur taluka, Upper Krishna Irrigation Project, Phase I, Gulbarga District, Karnataka, India. *International Journal of Remote Sensing, 27*(14), 2917–2926. doi:10.1080/01431160500472062

Sharma, R. C., & Bhargava, G. P. (1988). Landsat imagery for mapping saline soils and wet lands in north-west India. *International Journal of Remote Sensing, 9*(1), 39–44. doi:10.1080/01431168808954835

Singh, A. N., & Dwivedi, R. S. (1989). Delineation of Salt-affected Soils through Digital Analysis of Landsat MSS Data. *International Journal of Remote Sensing, 10*(1), 83–92. doi:10.1080/01431168908903849

Singh, G. (2009). Salinity-related desertification and management strategies: Indian experience. *Land Degradation & Development, 20*(4), 367–385. doi:10.1002/ldr.933

Sujatha, G., Dwivedi, R. S., Sreenivas, K., & Venkataratnam, L. (2000). Mapping and monitoring of degraded lands in part of Jaunpur district of Uttar Pradesh using temporal spaceborne multispectral data. *International Journal of Remote Sensing, 21*(3), 519–531. doi:10.1080/014311600210722

van Deventer, A. P., Ward, A. D., Gowda, P. H., & Lyon, J. G. (1997). Using Thematic Mapper data to identify contrasting soil plains and tillage practices. *Photogrammetric Engineering and Remote Sensing, 63*, 87–93.

Venables, W. N., & Ripley, B. D. (1994). *Modern Applied Statistics with S-PLUS.* New York: Springer-Verlag. doi:10.1007/978-1-4899-2819-1

Vina Andres, A. J. (2003). Use of Multispectral Ikonos Imagery for Discriminating between Conventional and Conservation Agricultural Tillage Practices. *Photogrammetric Engineering and Remote Sensing, 69*(5), 537–544. doi:10.14358/PERS.69.5.537

Wu, J., Vincent, B., Yang, J., Bouarfa, S., & Vidal, A. (2008). Remote Sensing Monitoring of Changes in Soil Salinity: A Case Study in Inner Mongolia, China. *Sensors (Basel), 8*(11), 7035–7049. doi:10.33908117035 PMID:27873914

Compilation of References

Abadi, D., Agrawal, R., & Ailamaki, A. (2014). The Beckman reporton database research. *SIGMOD Record, 43*(3), 61–70. doi:10.1145/2694428.2694441

Abatal, A., Khallouki, H., & Bahaj, M. (2018, May). A Smart Interconnected Healthcare System using Cloud Computing. In *Proceedings of the International Conference on Learning and Optimization Algorithms: Theory and Applications* (p. 44). ACM. 10.1145/3230905.3230936

Abbas, A., & Khan, S. (2007). Using remote sensing techniques for appraisal of irrigated soil salinity. In *Int. Congress on Modelling and Simulation (MODSIM)*. Modelling and Simulation Society of Australia and New Zealand.

Abbas, A., Khan, S., Hussain, N., Hanjra, M. A., & Akbar, S. (2013). Characterizing soil salinity in irrigated agriculture using a remote sensing approach. *Physics and Chemistry of the Earth, 55-57*, 43–52. doi:10.1016/j.pce.2010.12.004

Accreditation Board for Engineering and Technology, Inc. (2009). Criteria for Accrediting Engineering Programs. *ABET*. Retrieved from http://www.nasscom. in/sites/default/files/NASSCOM_BPM_Summit_Press_Release_Oct_2017_Final

Addy, S. (2013). *Geomorphology, river hydrology and natural processes. In SNH Sharing Good Practice Event: Identifying and planning river restoration projects*. The James Hutton Institute.

Afrasinei, G. M., Melis, M. T., Buttau, C., Bradd, J. M., Arras, C., & Ghiglieri, G. (2017). Assessment of remote sensing-based classification methods for change detection of salt-affected areas (Biskra area, Algeria). *Journal of Applied Remote Sensing, 11*(1), 1–28. doi:10.1117/1.JRS.11.016025

Afthina, H., Mardiyana, & Pramudya, I. (2017). Think Pair Share Using Realistic Mathematics Education Approach in Geometry Learning. *Journal of Physics: Conference Series*, *895*, 012025. doi:10.1088/1742-6596/895/1/012025

Agrawal, R., Ghosh, S. P., Imielinski, T., Iyer, B. R., & Swami, A. N. (1992). An Interval Classifier for Database Mining Applications. *Proceedings of the 18th International Conference on Very Large Data Bases*, 560-573.

Agrawal, R., Imielinski, T., & Swami, A. (1993). Database Mining: A Performance Perspective. *IEEE Transactions on Knowledge and Data Engineering*, *5*(6), 914–925. doi:10.1109/69.250074

Ahmed, F., Capretz, L. F., Bouktif, S., & Campbell, P. (2012). Soft skills requirements in software development jobs: A cross-cultural empirical study. *Journal of Systems and Information Technology*, *14*(1), 58–81. doi:10.1108/13287261211221137

Alfredson, J., & Ohlander, U. (2016). System Characteristics and Contextual Constraints for Future Fighter Decision Support. *International Journal of Information System Modeling and Design*, *7*(1), 1–17. doi:10.4018/IJISMD.2016010101

Al-Zewairi, M., Biltawi, M., Etaiwi, W., & Shaout, A. (2017). Agile Software Development Methodologies:Survey of Surveys. *Journal of Computer and Communications*, *5*(05), 74–97. doi:10.4236/jcc.2017.55007

Andrews, S. S., Flora, C. B., Mitchell, J. P., & Karlen, D. L. (2003). Growers perceptions and acceptance of soil quality indices. *Geoderma*, *114*(3-4), 187–213. doi:10.1016/S0016-7061(03)00041-7

Andrews, S. S., Karlen, D. L., & Cambardella, C. A. (2002). The soil management assessment framework: A quantitative soil quality evaluation method. *Soil Science Society of America Journal*, *68*(6), 1945–1962. doi:10.2136ssaj2004.1945

Antonis, K., Daradoumis, T., Papadakis, S., & Simos, C. (2011). Evaluation of the Effectiveness of a Web-Based Learning Design for Adult Computer Science Courses. *IEEE Transactions on Education*, *54*(3), 374–380. doi:10.1109/TE.2010.2060263

Antonucci, Y. L., & Tucker, J. J. III. (1998). IT outsourcing: Current trends, benefits, and risks. *Information Strategy: The Executive's Journal*, *14*(2), 16.

Arcidiacono, G. (2017). Comparative research about high failure rate of IT projects and opportunities to improve. *PM World Journal*, *6*(2), 1–10.

Armour, F. (2012). *Introduction to big data*. Presentation at the symposium Big Data and Business Analytics: Defining a Framework, Center for IT and Global Economy, Kogod School of Business, American University, Washington, DC.

Ashouri, H., Hsu, K.-L., Sorooshian, S., Braithwaite, D. K., Knapp, K. R., Cecil, L. D., ... Prat, O. P. (2015). PERSIANN-CDR: Daily Precipitation Climate Data Record from Multisatellite Observations for Hydrological and Climate Studies. *Bulletin of the American Meteorological Society*, *96*(1), 69–83. doi:10.1175/BAMS-D-13-00068.1

Aubert, A. B., Kishore, R., & Iriyama, A. (2015). Exploring and managing the "innovation through outsourcing" paradox. *The Journal of Strategic Information Systems*, *24*(4), 255–269. doi:10.1016/j.jsis.2015.10.003

Aung, P. S., Satirapod, C., & Andrei, C. (2016). Sagaing Fault slip and deformation in Myanmar observed by continuous GPS measurements. *Geodesy and Geodynamics*, *7*(1), 56–63. doi:10.1016/j.geog.2016.03.007

Awad, M., & Khanna, R. (2015). *Efficient learning machines: theories, concepts, and applications for engineers and system designers*. Apress. doi:10.1007/978-1-4302-5990-9

Badran, E. F., Mahmoud, E. G., & Hamdy, N. (2010). An algorithm for detecting brain tumors in MRI images. In *Computer Engineering and Systems (ICCES), 2010 International Conference on*. IEEE. 10.1109/ICCES.2010.5674887

Bai, Z. G., Dent, D. L., Olsson, L., & Schaepman, M. E. (2008). Proxy global assessment of land degradation. *Soil Use and Management*, *24*(3), 223–234. doi:10.1111/j.1475-2743.2008.00169.x

Bakhrankova, K. (2010). Decision support system for continuous production. *Industrial Management & Data Systems*, *110*(4), 591–610. doi:10.1108/02635571011039043

Balafar, M. A., Ramli, A. R., Saripan, M. I., & Mashohor, S. (2010). Review of brain MRI image segmentation methods. *Artificial Intelligence Review*, *33*(3), 261–274. doi:10.100710462-010-9155-0

Bandyopadhyay, S. K. (2011). *A survey on Brain Image Segmentation Method*. Journal of Global Research in Computer Science, 2.

Bao, X., Zhang, F., Bao, X., & Zhang, F. (2013). Evaluation of NCEP–CFSR, NCEP–NCAR, ERA-Interim, and ERA-40 Reanalysis Datasets against Independent Sounding Observations over the Tibetan Plateau. *Journal of Climate, 26*(1), 206–214. doi:10.1175/JCLI-D-12-00056.1

Barrett, E. C., & Martin, D. W. (1981). *Use of satellite data in rainfall monitoring.* Academic press.

Bastos, L., Bos, M., & Fernandes, R. M. (2010). Deformation and tectonics: Contribution of GPS measurements to plate tectonics – Overview and recent developments. *Sciences of Geodesy, I*, 155–184. doi:10.1007/978-3-642-11741-1_5

Baumeister, J., & Striffler, A. (2015). Knowledge-driven systems for episodic decision support. *Knowledge-Based Systems, 88*, 45–56. doi:10.1016/j.knosys.2015.08.008

Bell, I. R., Lewis, D. A. II, Schwartz, G. E., Lewis, S. E., Caspi, O., Scott, A., ... Baldwin, C. M. (2004). Electroencephalographic cordance patterns distinguish exceptional clinical responders with fibromyalgia to individualized homeopathic medicines. *Journal of Alternative and Complementary Medicine (New York, N.Y.), 10*(2), 285–299. doi:10.1089/107555304323062275 PMID:15165409

Benz, U. C., Hofmann, P., Willhauck, G., Lingenfelder, I., & Heynen, M. (2004). Multi-resolution, object-oriented fuzzy analysis of remote sensing data for GIS-ready information. *SPRS J. of Photogrammetry & Remote Sensing, 58*(3-4), 239–258. doi:10.1016/j.isprsjprs.2003.10.002

Berner, E. S. (2007). *Clinical decision support systems* (Vol. 233). New York: Springer Science Business Media, LLC. doi:10.1007/978-0-387-38319-4

Bin-Abbas, H., & Haj Bakry, S. (2014). Assessment of IT governance in organizations: A simple integrated approach. *Computers in Human Behavior, 32*, 261-267. Retrieved from http://www.sciencedirect.com/science/article/pii/S074756321300472X

Black, C. A. (1965). Methods of Soil Analysis. American Society of Agronomy, Inc.

Borgman, C. L. (2012). The conundrum of sharing research data. *Journal of the American Society for Information Science and Technology, 63*(6), 1059–1078. doi:10.1002/asi.22634

Bricklemyer, R. S., Lawrence, R. L., Miller, P. R., & Battogtokh, N. (2006). Predicting tillage practices and agricultural soil disturbance in north central Montana with Landsat imagery. *Agriculture, Ecosystems & Environment, 118*, 201–210. doi:10.1016/j.agee.2006.05.017

Bricklemyer, R., Lawrence, R., & Miller, P. (2002). Documenting notill and conventional till practices using Landsat ETM+ imagery and logistic regression. *Journal of Soil and Water Conservation, 57*, 267–271.

Brown, M. G. (2016). Blended instructional practice: A review of empirical literature on instructors´ adoption and use of online tools in face-to-face. *The Internet and Higher Education, 31*, 1–10. doi:10.1016/j.iheduc.2016.05.001

Bruneau, P. M. C., Davidson, D. A., & Grieve, I. C. (2004). An evaluation of image analysis for measuring changes in void space and excremental features on soil thin sections in an upland grassland soil. *Geoderma, 120*(3-4), 165–175. doi:10.1016/j.geoderma.2003.08.012

Cai, S., Zhang, R., Liu, L., & Zhou, D. (2010). A method of salt-affected soil information extraction based on a support vector machine with texture features. *Mathematical and Computer Modelling, 51*(11-12), 1319–1325. doi:10.1016/j.mcm.2009.10.037

Capretz, L. F., & Ahmed, F. (2018). A Call to Promote Soft Skills in Software Engineering. *Psychology and Cognitive Sciences, 4*(1), e1–e3. doi:10.17140/PCSOJ-4-e011

Capretz, L. F., Varona, D., & Raza, A. (2015). Influence of personality types in software tasks choices. *Computers in Human Behavior, 52*, 373–378. doi:10.1016/j.chb.2015.05.050

Carlson, J., & Stowell-Bracke, M. (2013). Data management and sharing from the perspective of graduate students: An examination of the culture and practice at the water quality field station. portal. *Libraries and the Academy, 13*(4), 343–361. doi:10.1353/pla.2013.0034

Casteren, W. V. (2017). *The Waterfall Model and the Agile Methodologies: A comparison by project characteristics*. White paper.

Census of India. (2011). District Census Handbook, West Tripura. Directorate of census Operations, Tripura.

Chang, Fan, & Chang. (2002). Multi-Modal Gray-level histogram modeling and decomposition. *Image and Vision Computing, 20*, 203-216.

Chan, S., Song, Q., Sarker, S., & Plumlee, R. (2017). Decision support system (DSS) use and decision performance: DSS motivation and its antecedents. *Information & Management, 54*(7), 934–947. doi:10.1016/j.im.2017.01.006

Charles, W. (2012). *Bailey J. Research Data Curation Bibliography*. Houston, TX: Charles W. Bailey, Jr. Available from http://digital-scholarship.org/rdcb/rdcb.htm

Chen, S., & Rao, P. (2008). Land degradation monitoring using multi-temporal Landsat TM/ETM data in a transition zone between grassland and cropland of northeast China. *International Journal of Remote Sensing, 29*(7), 2055–2073. doi:10.1080/01431160701355280

Chen, X. (2016). Celebrating fifty years of organizational behavior and decision doing research (1966–2016). *Organizational Behavior and Human Decision Processes, 136*, 1–2. doi:10.1016/j.obhdp.2016.09.002

Cherubin, M. R., Karlen, D. L., Cerri, C. E. P., Franco, A. L. C., Tormena, C. A., Davies, C. A., & Cerri, C. C. (2016). Soil quality indexing strategies for evaluating sugarcane expansion in Brazil. *PLoS One, 11*(3), 1–26. doi:10.1371/journal.pone.0150860 PMID:26938642

Cheung, W., & Babin, G. (2006). A metadatabase-enabled executive information system (Part A): A flexible and adaptable architecture. *Decision Support Systems, 42*(3), 1589–1598. doi:10.1016/j.dss.2006.01.005

Choudhary, B., & Rakesh, S. K. (2016). *An approach using agile method for software development*. Paper presented at the meeting of the International Conference on Innovation and Challenges in Cyber Security. 10.1109/ICICCS.2016.7542304

Codd, E. F. (1970). A relational model of data for large shared data banks. *Communications of the ACM, 13*(6), 377–387. doi:10.1145/362384.362685

Colombelli, S., Allen, R. M., & Zollo, A. (2013). Application of real-time GPS to earthquake early warning in subduction and strike-slip environments. *Journal of Geophysical Research. Solid Earth, 118*(7), 3448–3461. doi:10.1002/jgrb.50242

Comes, T., Hiete, M., Wijngaards, N., & Schultmann, F. (2011). Decision maps: A framework for multi-criteria decision support under severe uncertainty. *Decision Support Systems*, *52*(1), 108–118. doi:10.1016/j.dss.2011.05.008

Cordes, D. (2002). Active learning in computer science: Impacting student behavior. *Frontiers in Education Conference, 1*, T2A/1-T2A/5.

Cover, T. M., & Hart, P. E. (1967). Nearest neighbor pattern classification. *IEEE Transactions on Information Theory*, *13*(1), 21–27. doi:10.1109/TIT.1967.1053964

Cox, A. M., & Pinfield, S. (2014). Research data management and libraries: Current activities and future priorities. *J Librariansh Inf Sci*. Available: http://lis.sagepub.com/cgi/doi/10.1177/0961000613492542

Cristianini, N., & Shawe-Taylor, J. (2000). *An Introduction to Support Vector Machines and other kernel-based learning methods*. Cambridge University Press. doi:10.1017/CBO9780511801389

Crosas, M. (n.d.). *Cloud Dataverse: A Data Repository Platform for the Cloud*. Available from https://openstack.cioreview.com/cxoinsight/cloud-dataverse-a-data-repository-platform-for-the-cloud-nid-24199-cid-120.html

Dalati, M. (2018). The role of remote sensing in detecting active and fresh faulting zones case study: Northwest of Syria, Al-Ghab Graben Complex. International Society for Photogrammetry and Remote Sensing, 394.

Dawson, G. S., Denford, J. S., Williams, C. K., Preston, D., & Desouza, K. C. (2016). An Examination of Effective IT Governance in the Public Sector Using the Legal View of Agency Theory. *Journal of Management Information Systems*, *33*(4), 1180–1208. doi:10.1080/07421222.2016.1267533

Dee, D. P., Uppala, S. M., Simmons, A. J., Berrisford, P., Poli, P., Kobayashi, S., ... Vitart, F. (2011). The ERA-Interim reanalysis: Configuration and performance of the data assimilation system. *Quarterly Journal of the Royal Meteorological Society*, *137*(656), 553–597. doi:10.1002/qj.828

Dehni, A., & Lounis, M. (2012). Remote Sensing techniques for salt affected soil mapping: Application to the Oran region of Algeria. *Procedia Engineering*, *33*, 188–198. doi:10.1016/j.proeng.2012.01.1193

DeLong, S. B., Hilley, G. E., Rymer, M. J., & Prentice, C. (2010). Fault zone structure from topography: Signatures of an echelon fault slip at Mustang Ridge on the San Andreas Fault, Monterey County, California. *Tectonics*, 29.

Deng, L., Hu, Y., Cheung, J., & Luk, K. (2017). A Data-Driven Decision Support System for Scoliosis Prognosis. *IEEE Access: Practical Innovations, Open Solutions*, 5, 7874–7884. doi:10.1109/ACCESS.2017.2696704

Dey, S., Mukherjee, G., & Paul, S. (2013). Imaging and visualizing the spectral signatures from Landsat TM and 'τ' value-based surface soil microzonation mapping at and around Agartala (India). *Geocarto International*, 28(2), 144–158. doi:10.1 080/10106049.2012.662528

Dey, S., Sarkar, P., & Debbarma, C. (2009). Morphological signatures of fault lines in an earthquake prone zone of southern Baromura hill, north-east India: A multi sources approach for spatial data analysis. *Environmental Earth Sciences*, 59(2), 353–361. doi:10.100712665-009-0033-5

Diao, F., Walter, T. R., Minati, F., Wang, R., Costantini, M., Ergintav, S., ... Prats-Iraola, P. (2016). Secondary fault activity of the North Anatolian Fault near Avcilar, Southwest of Istanbul: Evidence from SAR interferometry observations. *Remote Sensing*, 8(846), 1–17.

Ding, J., Wu, M., & Tiyip, T. (2011). Study on soil salinization information in arid region using remote sensing technique. *Agricultural Sciences in China*, 10(3), 404–411. doi:10.1016/S1671-2927(11)60019-9

Dogra, J., Jain, S., & Sood, M. (2018). Segmentation of MR Images using Hybrid kMean-Graph Cut Technique. *Procedia Computer Science*, 132, 775–784. doi:10.1016/j.procs.2018.05.089

Doran, J. W., & Parkin, B. T. (1994). Defying and assessing soil quality. In J. W. Doran, D. C. Coleman, D. F. Bezdicek, & B. A. Stewart (Eds.), *Defying Soil Quality for a Sustainable Environment* (pp. 3–21). Madison, WI: Soil Science Society of America, Inc. doi:10.2136ssaspecpub35.c1

Doty, J. (2012). *Survey of faculty practices and perspectives on research data management*. Retrieved from http://guides.main.library.emory.edu/datamgmt/survey

Douaoui, A. E. K., Nicolas, H., & Walter, C. (2006). Detecting salinity hazards within a semiarid context by means of combining soil and remote-sensing data. *Geoderma*, *134*(1-2), 217–230. doi:10.1016/j.geoderma.2005.10.009

DuraCloud solutions. (n.d.). Retrieved from http://www.duracloud.org/solutions

Dvorak, V. F. (1984). *Tropical cyclone intensity analysis using satellite data* (Vol. 11). US Department of Commerce, National Oceanic and Atmospheric Administration, National Environmental Satellite, Data, and Information Service.

Dwivedi, R. S. (1992). Monitoring and the study of the effects of image scale on delineation of salt-affected soils in the Indo-Gangetic plains. *International Journal of Remote Sensing*, *13*(8), 1527–1536. doi:10.1080/01431169208904206

Dwivedi, R. S. (1994). Study of salinity and waterlogging in Uttar Pradesh (India) using remote sensing data. *Land Degradation & Rehabilitation*, *5*(3), 191–199. doi:10.1002/ldr.3400050303

Dwivedi, R. S., & Sreenivas, K. (1998a). Image transforms as a tool for the study of soil salinity and alkalinity dynamics. *International Journal of Remote Sensing*, *19*(4), 605–619. doi:10.1080/014311698215883

Dwivedi, R. S., & Sreenivas, K. (1998b). Delineation of salt-affected soils and waterlogged areas in the Indo-Gangetic plains using IRS-1C LISS-111 data. *International Journal of Remote Sensing*, *19*(14), 2739–2751. doi:10.1080/014311698214488

Edalati-rad, A., & Mosleh, M. (2018). Improving Brain Tumor Diagnosis Using MRI Segmentation Based on Collaboration of Beta Mixture Model and Learning Automata. *Arabian Journal for Science and Engineering*, 1–13.

Ellis, D. P., Zeng, X., & McDermott, J. H. (2011, May). Classifying soundtracks with audio texture features. In *Acoustics, Speech and Signal Processing (ICASSP), 2011 IEEE International Conference on* (pp. 5880-5883). IEEE. 10.1109/ICASSP.2011.5947699

Elnaggar, A. A., & Noller, J. S. (2009). Application of remote- sensing data and decision-tree analysis to mapping salt- affected soils over large areas. *Remote Sensing*, *2*(1), 151–165. doi:10.3390/rs2010151

Emam, K. E., & Koru, A. G. (2008). A Replicated Survey of IT Software Project Failures. *IEEE Software, 25*(5), 84–90. doi:10.1109/MS.2008.107

Emanuel, K. (2005). Increasing destructiveness of tropical cyclones over the past 30 years. *Nature, 436*(7051), 686–688. doi:10.1038/nature03906 PMID:16056221

Fancsali, C., Tigani, L., Isaza, P. T., & Cole, R. (2018). A Landscape Study of Computer Science Education in NYC: Early Findings and Implications for Policy and Practice. *Proceedings of the meeting of the 49th ACM Technical Symposium on Computer Science Education*, 44-49.

Farhadloo, M., Patterson, R., & Rolland, E. (2016). Modeling customer satisfaction from unstructured data using a Bayesian approach. *Decision Support Systems, 90*, 1–11. doi:10.1016/j.dss.2016.06.010

Farid, M., Roatis, A., & Ilyas, I. F. (2016). CLAMS: bringing quality toData Lakes. In *Proceedings of the 2016 International Conference on Management of Data*. ACM.

Favretto, A., Geletti, R., & Civile, D. (2013). Remote Sensing as a preliminary analysis for the detection of active tectonic structures: An application to the albanian orogenic system. *Geoadria, 18*(2), 97–111. doi:10.15291/geoadria.165

Federer, L. (2016). Research data management in the age of big data: Roles and opportunities for librarians. *Information Services & Use, 36*, 35–43. DOI . doi:10.3233/ISU-160797

Fernandez-Buces, N., Siebe, C., Cram, S., & Palacio, J. L. (2006). Mapping soil salinity using a combined spectral response index for bare soil and vegetation: A case study in the former lake Texcoco, Mexico. *Journal of Arid Environments, 65*(4), 644–667. doi:10.1016/j.jaridenv.2005.08.005

Fichefet, J. (1991). Computer-aided homoeopathy. *The British Homoeopathic Journal, 80*(1), 34–38. doi:10.1016/S0007-0785(05)80421-1

Fisher, E. L. (1958). Hurricanes and the sea-surface temperature field. *Journal of Meteorology, 15*(3), 328–333. doi:10.1175/1520-0469(1958)015<0328:HATSST>2.0.CO;2

Fisher, P. (2012). 1. Abstract 2. Introduction 2.1. Homeopathy and Allopathy 2.2. Homeopathic Pathogenetic Trials 3. Development of homeopathy 3.1. Homeopathy Worldwide 4. Contemporary Homeopathic Practice 4.1. Individualised Homeopathy. *Frontiers in Bioscience, 4*, 1669–1682. doi:10.2741/e489

Fontaine, Scherer, Roesch, & Ellsworth. (2007). The World of Emotions Is Not Two-Dimensional. *Psychological Science, 18*(12), 1050–57.

Fontaine, J. R., Scherer, K. R., Roesch, E. B., & Ellsworth, P. C. (2007). The world of emotions is not two-dimensional. *Psychological Science, 18*(12), 1050–1057. doi:10.1111/j.1467-9280.2007.02024.x PMID:18031411

Fowler, M., & Highsmith, J. (n.d.). The agile manifesto. *Software Development, 9*(8), 28-35.

Fritz, T., Begel, A., Müller, S. C., Yigit-Elliott, S., & Züger, M. (n.d.). *Using psycho-physiological measures to assess task difficulty in software development*. Paper presented at the meeting of the 36th IEEE International Conference on Software Engineering. 10.1145/2568225.2568266

Galvis, Á. H. (n.d.). Supporting decision-making processes on blended learning in higher education: literature and good practices review. *International Journal of Educational Technology in Higher Education, 15*, 25.

GeoEarthScope. (2006). *InSAR working group report*. Report of planning meeting.

Glab, T. (2007). Application of image analysis for soil macropore characterization according to pore diameter. *International Agrophysics, 21*, 61–66.

Godse, M., & Mulik, S. (2009). An approach for selecting Software-as-a-Service (SaaS) product. In *2013 IEEE Sixth International Conference on Cloud Computing* (pp. 155–158). Los Alamitos, CA: IEEE Computer Society. 10.1109/CLOUD.2009.74

Gog, S. (2016). Competitiveness and Research-Oriented Teaching in Romanian Universities: The Neo-Liberal Transformation of the Higher Education System. *StudiaUniversitatisBabes-BolyaiSociologia, 6*(1), 23–62. doi:10.1515ubbs-2015-0002

Gonzalez, R. (2009). *Digital Image Processing* (3rd ed.). Addison-Wesley.

Gordon-Murnane, L. (2012). Big Data: A Big Opportunity for Librarians. *Online (Bergheim), 36*(5), 34.

Govaerts, B., Sayre, K. D., & Deckers, J. (2006). A minimum data set for soil quality assessment of wheat and maize cropping in the highlands of Mexico. *Soil & Tillage Research, 87*(2), 163–174. doi:10.1016/j.still.2005.03.005

Gowda, P. H., Dalzell, B. J., Mulla, D. J., & Kollman, F. (2001). Mapping tillage practices with Landstat Thematic Mapper based logistic regression models. *Journal of Soil and Water Conservation*, *56*, 91–96.

Gray, W. M. (1975). *Tropical cyclone genesis*. Atmospheric science paper; no. 234.

Guan, X. (2016). The Design and Evaluation of "Flipped Classroom" English Teaching Model Supported by Micro Teaching. *International Conference on Smart City and Systems Engineering*. 10.1109/ICSCSE.2016.0073

Guinn, T. A., & Schubert, W. H. (1993). Hurricane Spiral Bands. *Journal of the Atmospheric Sciences*, *50*(20), 3380–3403. doi:10.1175/1520-0469(1993)050<3380:HSB>2.0.CO;2

Güntzer, U., Müller, R., Müller, S., & Schimkat, R. (2007). Retrieval for decision support resources by structured models. *Decision Support Systems*, *43*(4), 1117–1132. doi:10.1016/j.dss.2005.07.004

Gupta, T. (2017). *Tumor Classification and Segmentation of MR Brain Images*. arXiv preprint arXiv:1710.11309

Gutierrez, C. (2002). *A comparison of false color composites in mapping and discriminating between salt-affected soils in Kings county, California* (Masters thesis). Oregon State University.

Hai, R., Geisler, S., & Quix, C. (2016). Constance: an intelligent Data Lake system. In *Proceedings of the 2016 International Conference on Management of Data*. ACM.

Halevy, A., Korn, F., & Noy, N. F. (2016). Goods: organizing Google's datasets. In *Proceedings of the 2016 International Conference on Management of Data*. ACM.

Hansen, M., Dubayah, R., & Defries, R. (1996). Decision trees: An alternative to traditional land cover classifiers. *International Journal of Remote Sensing*, *17*(5), 1075–1081. doi:10.1080/01431169608949069

Haron, N. A., Devi, P., Hassim, S., Alias, A. H., Tahir, M. M., & Harun, A. N. (2017). Project management practice and its effects on project success in Malaysian construction industry. *Materials Science and Engineering*, *291*, •••. Retrieved from http://www.abet.org/

Havaei, M., Davy, A., Warde-Farley, D., Biard, A., Courville, A., Bengio, Y., ... Larochelle, H. (2017). Brain tumor segmentation with deep neural networks. *Medical Image Analysis*, *35*, 18–31. doi:10.1016/j.media.2016.05.004 PMID:27310171

Hoegl, M., & Gemuenden, H. G. (2001). Teamwork quality and the success of innovative projects: A theoretical concept and empirical evidence. *Organization Science*, *12*(4), 435–449. doi:10.1287/orsc.12.4.435.10635

Hong, Y., Adler, R. F., Negri, A., & Huffman, G. J. (2007). Flood and landslide applications of near real-time satellite rainfall products. *Natural Hazards*, *43*(2), 285–294. doi:10.100711069-006-9106-x

How Negative Emotions Can Affect Your Health. (2018). Retrieved from https://articles.mercola.com/sites/articles/archive/2018/05/17/effect-of-negative-emotions-on-health.aspx

Huang, C., Davis, L. S., & Townshend, J. R. G. (2002). An assessment of support vector machines for land cover classification. *International Journal of Remote Sensing*, *23*(4), 725–749. doi:10.1080/01431160110040323

Huang, J.-H., Li, J.-N., Wei, X.-L., Fong, S.-K., & Wang, A.-Y. (2006). Assimilation of QuikScat data and its impact on prediction of Typhoon Vongfong (2002). ZhongshanDaxueXuebao/Acta Sci. *Natralium Univ. Sunyatseni*, *45*, 116–120.

Huffman, G. J., Bolvin, D. T., & Nelkin, E. J. (2015a). *Day 1 IMERG Final Run Release Notes 1–9*. Retrieved from http://pmm.nasa.gov/sites/default/files/document_files/IMERG_FinalRun_Day1_release_notes.pdf

Huffman, G.J., Bolvin, D.T., & Nelkin, E.J. (2015b). *Integrated Multi-satellitE Retrievals for GPM (IMERG) Technical Documentation*. NASA/GSFC Code 612, 47. doi:10.1136/openhrt-2016-000469

Huffman, G.J., Bolvin, D.T., Braithwaite, D., Hsu, K., Joyce, R., Kidd, C., Nelkin, E.J., & Xie, P. (2015c). *NASA Global Precipitation Measurement (GPM) Integrated Multi-satellitE Retrievals for GPM (IMERG)*. Algorithm Theoretical Basis Document (ATBD) Version 4.5 26.

Huggett R. J. (2007). *Fundamentals of Geomorphology*. Routledge, Taylor and Francis Group.

IBM Big Data & Analytics Hub. (2016). *The four V's of big data*. Available from http://www.ibmbigdatahub.com/infographic/four-vs-big-data-4V

IDNP. (2002). *Indo-Dutch Network Project: A methodology for identification of water-logging and soil salinity conditions using remote sensing*. Central Soil Salinity Research Institute.

Informationweek.com. (n.d.). *10 Innovative Clinical Decision programs*. Retrieved from: http://www.informationweek.com

Jackson, M. L. (1950). *Soil Chemical Analysis* (Indian Edition). Delhi: Prentice Hall of India Ltd.

Jain, S., Sima, D. M., Ribbens, A., Cambron, M., Maertens, A., Van Hecke, W., ... Smeets, D. (2015). Automatic segmentation and volumetry of multiple sclerosis brain lesions from MR images. *NeuroImage. Clinical*, *8*, 367–375. doi:10.1016/j.nicl.2015.05.003 PMID:26106562

Jana & Chatterjee. (2014). *Automatic segmentation of different brain tissue from MR image*. IEEE CALCON.

Javanmard, S., Yatagai, A., Nodzu, M. I., BodaghJamali, J., & Kawamoto, H. (2010). Comparing high-resolution gridded precipitation data with satellite rainfall estimates of TRMM_3B42 over Iran. *Advances in Geosciences*, *25*, 119–125. doi:10.5194/adgeo-25-119-2010

Jia, J., Mo, H., Capretz, L. F., & Zupeng, C. (2017). Grouping environmental factors influencing individual decision-making behavior in software projects: A cluster analysis. *Journal of Software: Evolution and Process*, *29*(10), 1–23.

Jodoin, P.-M., & Lalande, A. (2008). Markovian method for 2D, 3D and 4D segmentation of MRI. *Proceedings International Conference on Image Processing*. 10.1109/ICIP.2008.4712429

Jones, D. K. (2013). *Assessment of Communication and Teamwork Skills in Engineering Technology Programs*. Paper presented at the meeting of the 120th ASEE Annual conference & Exposition.

Joseph, Singh, & Manikandan. (2014). Brain Tumour MRI Image Segmentation and Detection In Image Processing. *IJRET, 3*.

Joshi, Charan, & Prince. (2015). A novel methodology for brain tumor detection based on two-stage segmentation of MRI images. In *Advanced Computing and Communication Systems, 2015 International Conference on*. IEEE.

Kachwala, T., Parmar, S., & Vhora, S. (2012). Improve Decision Support System in an Uncertain Situation by Custom-made Framework for Data Mining Technique. *International Journal Of Scientific Research*, *2*(4), 55–56. doi:10.15373/22778179/APR2013/21

Kang, L., Lo, Y., & Liu, C. (2014). A Medical Decision Support System Based on Structured Injection Orders. *Advanced Materials Research, 998-999*, 1527-1531. Retrieved from www.scientific.net/amr.998-999.1527

Kangas, J., Alho, J. M., Kolehmainen, O., & Mononen, A. (1998). Analyzing consistency of experts' judgments- case of assessing forest biodiversity. *Forest Science, 44*, 610–617.

Kaplan, G., & Avdan, U. (2017). *Thermal remote sensing techniques for studying earthquake anomalies in 2013 Balochistan earthquakes.* Paper presented at the 4th International Conference on Earthquake Engineering and Seismology, Anadolu University, Eskisehir, Turkey.

Karabulut-Ilgu, A., Cherrez, N. J., & Jahren, C. T. (2018). A systematic review of research on the flipped learning method in engineering education. *British Journal of Educational Technology, 49*(3), 398–411. doi:10.1111/bjet.12548

Karimzadeh, S., Mansouri, B., Osmanoglu, B., & Djamour, Y. (2011). *Application of differential sar interferometry (dinsar) for interseismic assessment of North Tabriz Fault, Iran.* Paper presented at the 1st International Conference on Urban Construction in the Vicinity of Active Faults, Tabrize, Iran.

Karlen, D. L., & Andrews, S. S. (2004). Soil quality, fertility, and health Historical context, status and perspectives. In P. Schjonning (Ed.), *Managing soil quality: Challenges in modern agriculture* (pp. 17–33). Oxon, UK: CABI International Publication. doi:10.1079/9780851996714.0017

Karlen, D. L., & Stott, D. E. (1994). A framework for evaluating physical and chemical indicators of soil quality. In J. W. Doran, D. C. Coleman, D. F. Bezdicek, & B. A. Stewart (Eds.), *Defining Soil Quality for a Sustainable Environment. SSSA Special Pub. 35* (pp. 53–72). Madison, WI: Soil Science Society of America.

Karlen, D., Mausbach, M., Doran, J., Cline, R., Harris, R., & Schuman, G. (1997). Soil quality: A concept, definition, and framework for evaluation (a guest editorial). *Soil Science Society of America Journal, 61*(1), 4–10. doi:10.2136ssaj1997.03615 995006100010001x

Karthikeyan, K., Kumar, N., Prasad, J., & Srivastava, R. (2015). Soil Quality and Its Assessment: A Review. *Journal of Soil and Water Conservation, 14*(2), 100–108.

Karyampudi, V. M., Lai, G. S., & Manobianco, J. (1998). Impact of Initial Conditions, Rainfall Assimilation, and Cumulus Parameterization on Simulations of Hurricane Florence (1988). *Monthly Weather Review*, *126*(12), 3077–3101. doi:10.1175/1520-0493(1998)126<3077:IOICRA>2.0.CO;2

Kashyap, R., Gautam, P., & Tiwari, V. (2018). Management and monitoring patterns and future scope. In Handbook of Research on Pattern Engineering System Development for Big Data Analytics (pp. 230–251). Hersey, PA: IGI Global.

Kashyap, R. (2018). Object boundary detection through robust active contour based method with global information. *International Journal of Image Mining*, *3*(1), 22. doi:10.1504/IJIM.2018.093008

Kashyap, R., & Gautam, P. (2015). Modified region based segmentation of medical images. In *Proceedings of International Conference on Communication Networks (ICCN)* (pp. 209–216). IEEE. 10.1109/ICCN.2015.41

Kashyap, R., & Gautam, P. (2016). Fast level set method for segmentation of medical images. In *Proceedings of the International Conference on Informatics and Analytics (ICIA-16)*. ACM. 10.1145/2980258.2980302

Kashyap, R., & Tiwari, V. (2017). Energy-based active contour method for image segmentation. *International Journal of Electronic Healthcare*, *9*(2–3), 210–225. doi:10.1504/IJEH.2017.083165

Kashyap, R., & Tiwari, V. (2018). Active contours using global models for medical image segmentation. *International Journal of Computational Systems Engineering*, *4*(2/3), 195. doi:10.1504/IJCSYSE.2018.091404

Kayal, J. R. (2008). *Microearthquake seismology and seismotectonics of South Asia*. New Delhi: Capital Publishing Company.

Keen, P. G. (1980). *Decision support systems and managerial productivity analysis*. Google Scholar.

Kennedy, J., & Eberhart, R. (1995). Particle Swarm Optimization. *Proceedings of IEEE International Conference on Neural Networks, 4*, 1942–1948. 10.1109/ICNN.1995.488968

Khan, H. H., & Malik, M. N. (2017). Software Standards and Software Failures: A Review With the Perspective of Varying Situational Contexts. *IEEE Access: Practical Innovations, Open Solutions*, *5*, 17501–17513. doi:10.1109/ACCESS.2017.2738622

Khan, M., Muhammad, N., Ahmed, M., Saeed, F., & Khan, S. A. (2012). Impact of Activity-Based Teaching on Students' Academic Achievements in Physics at Secondary Level. *Academic Research International, 3*(1), 146–156.

Khan, N. M., Rastoskuev, V. V., Sato, Y., & Shiozawa, S. (2005). Assessment of hydrosaline land degradation by using a simple approach of remote sensing indicators. *Agricultural Water Management, 77*(1-3), 96–109. doi:10.1016/j.agwat.2004.09.038

Khan, N. M., Rastoskuev, V. V., Shalina, E. V., & Sato, Y. (2001). Mapping salt affected soils using remote sensing indicators- A simple approach with the use of GIS IDRISI. *Proceedings of 22nd Asian conference on Remote Sensing*.

Kidd, C., & Levizzani, V. (2011). Status of satellite precipitation retrievals. *Hydrology and Earth System Sciences, 15*(4), 1109–1116. doi:10.5194/hess-15-1109-2011

Kirkpatrick, S., Gelatt, C. D. Jr, & Vecchi, M. P. (1983). Optimization by Simulated Annealing. *Science, 220*(4598), 671–680. doi:10.1126cience.220.4598.671 PMID:17813860

Koutsias, N., & Karteris, M. (1998). Logistic regression modeling of multitemporal thematic mapper data for burned area mapping. *International Journal of Remote Sensing, 19*(18), 3499–3514. doi:10.1080/014311698213777

Krishna, K. M., & Rao, S. R. (2009). Study of the intensity of super cyclonic storm GONU using satellite observations. *International Journal of Applied Earth Observation and Geoinformation, 11*(2), 108–113. doi:10.1016/j.jag.2008.11.001

Kulte, A. (1965). Method of soil analysis part-I. Academic Press.

Kumar, N., Singh, S.K., Mishra, V.N., Obi Reddy, G.P., Bajpai, R.K., & Saxena, R.R. (2018). Soil suitability evaluation for cotton using analytical hierarchic process. *International Journal of Chemical Studies, 6*(4), 1570-1576.

Kumar, R. (2015). Identification and characterization of active fault by space bornescan sar interferometry and ground based gpr techniques in NW Himalayan foot hill region, India. Andhra University, Visakhapatnam.

Kumar, N., & Singh, S. K. (2018). Land degradation assessment using MODIS NDVI time series data. In S. K. Singh, S. Chatterji, S. Chattaraj, P. S. Butte, & R. P. Sharma (Eds.), *ICAR-NBSS&LUP technologies, NBSS Pub. No. 176* (p. 102). Nagpur: ICAR-NBSS&LUP.

Kumar, N., Singh, S. K., Mishra, V. N., Obi Reddy, G. P., & Bajpai, R. K. (2017). Soil quality ranking of a small sample size using AHP. *Journal of Soil and Water Conservation, 16*(4), 339–346. doi:10.5958/2455-7145.2017.00050.9

Kumar, N., Sinha, N. K., & Sahoo, R. N. (2012). *Discriminating different tillage through remote sensing approach.* LAP Lambert Academic Publishing.

Kumar, P., & Varma, A. K. (2017). Assimilation of INSAT-3D hydro-estimator method retrieved rainfall for short-range weather prediction. *Journal of the Royal Meteorological Society, 143*(702), 384–394. doi:10.1002/qj.2929

Kumar, U., Mishra, V. N., Kumar, N., & Rathiya, G. R. (2018). *Methods of Soil Analysis.* Ludhiana: Kalyani Publishers.

Kumpawat, B. S. (2001). Production potential and economics of different crop sequence. *Indian Journal of Agronomy, 46*(3), 421–424.

Lake, J. H., & Spiegel, D. (Eds.). (2007). *Complementary and alternative treatments in mental health care.* American Psychiatric Pub.

Laney, D. (2001, February 6). *3-D data management: Controlling data volume, velocity and variety.* META Research Note.

Lee, C., Li, H. C., & Shahrill, M. (2018). Utilizing the Think-Pair-Share Technique in the Learning of Probability. *International Journal on Emerging Mathematics Education, 2*(1), 49–64. doi:10.12928/ijeme.v2i1.8218

Leipper, D. F. (1967). Obaerved ocean conditions and Hurricane Hilda, 1964. *J. Atmoa. Sci., 24*, 182-196.

Leipper, D. F., & Volgenau, D. (1972). Hurricane heat potential of the Gulf of Mexico. *Journal of Physical Oceanography, 2*(3), 218–224. doi:10.1175/1520-0485(1972)002<0218:HHPOTG>2.0.CO;2

Liebig, M. A., Varvel, G., & Doran, J. W. (2001). A simple performance-based index for assessing multiple agro ecosystem functions. *Agronomy Journal, 93*(2), 313. doi:10.2134/agronj2001.932313x

Likun, Z. (2010). *Research on Software Project Management Pattern What Based on Model-Driven.* Paper presented at the meeting of the International Conference of Information Science and Management Engineering. 10.1109/ISME.2010.43

Lingard, R., & Berry, E. (2002). *Teaching Teamwork Skills in Software Engineering based on an understanding of Factors Affecting Group Performance.* Paper presented at the meeting of the 32nd ASEE/IEEE Frontiers in Education Conference. 10.1109/FIE.2002.1158709

Lingard, R. W. (2010). Improving the Teaching of Teamwork Skills in Engineering and Computer Science. Systemics. *Cybernetics and Informatics*, *8*(6), 20–23.

Li, P., Zhang, T., Wang, X., & Yu, D. (2013). Development of biological soil quality indicator system for subtropical China. *Soil & Tillage Research*, *126*, 112–118. doi:10.1016/j.still.2012.07.011

Llibourtry, L. (2000). *Quantitative geophysics and geology.* Chichester, UK: Praxis Publishing Ltd.

Logvinov, I., & Tarasov, V. (2017). Geoelectric model of the crust and upper mantle along DSS profile Novoazovsk—Titovka. *Geofizicheskiy Zhurnal*, *37*(3), 139–152. doi:10.24028/gzh.0203-3100.v37i3.2015.111115

Lourenço, J., Morton, A., & Bana e Costa, C. (2012). PROBE—A multicriteria decision support system for portfolio robustness evaluation. *Decision Support Systems*, *54*(1), 534–550. doi:10.1016/j.dss.2012.08.001

MacKenzie, D. P., & Jackson, J. A. (1983). The relationship between strain rates, crustal thickening, paleomagnetism, finite stain and fault movements within a deforming zone. *Earth and Planetary Science Letters*, *65*(1), 182–202. doi:10.1016/0012-821X(83)90198-X

MacKenzie, D. P., & Jackson, J. A. (1986). A block model of distributed deformation by faulting. *Journal of the Geological Society*, *143*(2), 349–353. doi:10.1144/gsjgs.143.2.0349

Madduri, R. K., Dave, P., Sulakhe, D., Lacinski, L., Liu, B., & Foster, I. T. (2013). Experiences in building a next-generation sequencing analysis service using Galaxy, Globus Online and Amazon Web Service. In *Proceedings of the Conference on Extreme Science and Engineering Discovery Environment: Gateway to Discovery* (pp. 34:1–34:3). New York: ACM. 10.1145/2484762.2484827

Madera, L. A. (2016). The next information architecture evolution:the data lake wave. In *Proceedings of the 8ᵗʰInternational Conference on Management of Digital EcoSystems*. ACM.

Maji, A. K., Reddy, G. P. O., & Sarkar, D. (2010). *Degraded and wastelands of India, status and spatial distribution*. New Delhi: Indian Council of Agricultural Research and National Academy of Agricultural Science.

Major, D., Baret, F., & Guyot, G. (1990). A Ratio vegetation index adjusted for soil brightness. *International Journal of Remote Sensing*, *11*(5), 727–740. doi:10.1080/01431169008955053

Malltus, J. S., & Riehl, H. (1960). *On the dynamics and energy tranaformation in steady-state hurricanes*. Academic Press.

Mandal, A. K., Sharma, R. C., & Singh, G. (2009). Assessment of salt affected soils in India using GIS. *Geocarto International*, *24*(6), 437–456. doi:10.1080/10106040902781002

Marggraf, R. (2003). Comparative assessment of agrienvironment programmes in the federal state of Germany. *Agriculture, Ecosystems & Environment*, *98*(1-3), 507–516. doi:10.1016/S0167-8809(03)00109-9

Marroquin, J. L., Vemuri, B. C., Botello, S., Calderon, E., & Fernandez-Bouzas, A. (2002). An accurate and efficient Bayesian method for automatic segmentation of brain MRI. *IEEE Transactions on Medical Imaging*, *21*(8), 934–945. doi:10.1109/TMI.2002.803119 PMID:12472266

Masto, R. E., Chhonkar, P. K., Singh, D., & Patra, A. K. (2008). Alternative soil quality indices for evaluating the effect of intensive cropping, fertilisation and manuring for 31 years in the semi-arid soils of India. *Environmental Monitoring and Assessment*, *136*(1-3), 419–435. doi:10.100710661-007-9697-z PMID:17457684

McFee, B., Raffel, C., Liang, D., Ellis, D. P., McVicar, M., Battenberg, E., & Nieto, O. (2015, July). librosa: Audio and music signal analysis in python. In *Proceedings of the 14th python in science conference* (pp. 18-25). Academic Press. 10.25080/Majora-7b98e3ed-003

Mcgourty, J., Dominick, P., & Reilly, R. (1998). Incorporating Student Peer Review and Feedback into the Assessment Process. *Proceedings of Frontiers in Education Conference*, 14-18. 10.1109/FIE.1998.736790

McGrath, J. R., & MacEwan, G. (2011). Linking pedagogical practices of activity-based teaching. *The International Journal of Interdisciplinary Social Sciences: Annual Review, 6*(3), 261–274. doi:10.18848/1833-1882/CGP/v06i03/51803

Mendenhall, W., & Sincich, T. (1996). *A Second Course in Statistics: Regression Analysis.* Englewood Cliffs, NJ: Prentice-Hall.

Metternicht, G. I., & Zinck, J. A. (2003). Remote sensing of soil salinity: Potentials and constraints. *Remote Sensing of Environment, 85*(1), 1–20. doi:10.1016/S0034-4257(02)00188-8

Mikulenas, G., & Kapocius, K. (2011). *A Framework for Decomposition and Analysis of Agile Methodologies During Their Adaptation. In Information Systems Development* (pp. 547–560). Springer New York.

Miller, B. I. (1964). A study of the filling of hurricane Donna (1960) over land. *Monthly Weather Review, 94*(9), 389–406. doi:10.1175/1520-0493(1964)092<0389:ASOTFO>2.3.CO;2

Mitchell, D. E. (2014). *Dentifying salinization through multispectral band analysis: lake Urmia, Iran* (Masters thesis). Ryerson University, Toronto, Ontario, Canada.

Moeskops, P., Viergever, M. A., Mendrik, A. M., de Vries, L. S., Benders, M. J. N. L., & Isgum, I. (2016). Automatic segmentation of MR brain images with a convolutional neural network. *IEEE Transactions on Medical Imaging, 35*(5), 1252–1261. doi:10.1109/TMI.2016.2548501 PMID:27046893

Mukherjee, A., & Lal, R. (2014). Comparison of Soil Quality Index Using Three Methods. *PLoS One, 9*(8). doi:1 0.1371/journal.pone.0105981

Mulay, Kadlag, & Shirodkar. (2017). Smart Supply-Chain Management Learning System for Homeopathy. *Indian Journal of Public Health Research and Development, 8*(4), 914-922.

Murphy, R. (2006). *Homeopathic clinical repertory. Homeopathy in Practice, 57.*

Nam, M.-J., & Kwag, S. (2011). The Effect of Individual-Organizational variable on Ethical Decision-making Process in the Organizational Context. *Management & Information Systems Review, 30*(1), 39–69. doi:10.29214/damis.2011.30.1.002

Nijeweme-d'Hollosy, W. O., van Velsen, L., Poel, M., Groothuis-Oudshoorn, C. G., Soer, R., & Hermens, H. (2018). Evaluation of three machine learning models for self-referral decision support on low back pain in primary care. *International Journal of Medical Informatics*, *110*, 31–41. doi:10.1016/j.ijmedinf.2017.11.010 PMID:29331253

Oldeman, L. R., Hakkeling, R. T. A., & Sombroek, W. G. (1991). *World map of the status of human-induced soil degradation: An explanatory note, second* (revised edition). Wageningen: ISRIC.

Otsu, N. (1979). A threshold selection method from gray level histograms. *IEEE Transactions on Systems, Man, and Cybernetics*, *SMC-9*(62-66).

Pal, M., & Mather, P. M. (2003). An assessment of the effectiveness of decision tree methods for land cover classification. *Remote Sensing of Environment*, *86*(4), 554–565. doi:10.1016/S0034-4257(03)00132-9

Papathanasiou, J., & Kenward, R. (2014). Design of a data-driven environmental decision support system and testing of stakeholder data-collection. *Environmental Modelling & Software*, *55*, 92–106. doi:10.1016/j.envsoft.2014.01.025

Parcharidis, I., Kokkalas, S., Fountoulis, I., & Foumelis, M. (2009). Detection and monitoring of active faults in urban environments: Time series interferometry on the cities of Patras and Pyrgos (Peloponnese, Greece). *Remote Sensing*, *1*(4), 676–696. doi:10.3390/rs1040676

Parham, S. W., Bodnar, J., & Fuchs, S. (2012). Supporting tomorrow's research: Assessing faculty data curation needs at Georgia Tech. *College & Research Libraries News*, *73*(1), 10–13. doi:10.5860/crln.73.1.8686

Parker, Z., Poe, S., & Vrbsky, S. V. (2013). Comparing NoSQL MongoDB to an SQL DB. In *Proceedings of the 51st ACM Southeast Conference*. ACM. 10.1145/2498328.2500047

Patel, R. P. (1967). *The art of case taking and practical repertorisation in homoeopathy*. Athurasramam Homoeopathic Medical College.

Perlboth, I. (1967). Hurricane behavior as related to oceanographic environmental conditions. *Tellus*, *19*(2), 258–268. doi:10.1111/j.2153-3490.1967.tb01481.x

Perlroth, I. (1969). Effects of oceanographic media on equatorial Atlantic hurricanes. *Tellus*, *21*(2), 231–244. doi:10.3402/tellusa.v21i2.10077

Petkovic, D., Pérez, M. S., Huang, S., Todtenhoefer, R., Okada, K., Arora, S., . . . Dubey, S. (2014). SETAP: Software Engineering Teamwork Assessment and Prediction Using Machine Learning. *IEEE Frontiers in Education Conference*, 1299-1306.

Petkovic, D., Sosnick-Perez, M., Okada, K., Todtenhoefer, R., Huang, S., Miglani, N., & Vigil, A. (2016). Using the Random Forest Classifier to Assess and Predict Student Learning of Software Engineering Teamwork. *Frontiers in Education FIE 2016.*

Petkovic, E., Todtenhöfer, R., & Thompson, G. (2006). Teaching practical software engineering and global software engineering: case study and recommendations. *36th ASEE/IEEE Frontiers in Education Conference*, 19-24.

Petkovic, D., Thompson, G., & Todtenhöfer, R. (2008). Assessment and comparison of local and global SW engineering practices in a classroom setting. *13th Annual Conference on Innovation and Technology in Computer Science Education*, 78-82. 10.1145/1384271.1384294

Petrov, V. A., Lespinasse, M., Ustinov, S. A., & Cialec, C. (2017). GIS-based identification of active lineaments within the Krasnokamensk Area, Transbaikalia, Russia. In *Proceedings 5th International Conference New Achievements in Materials and Environmental Science (Vol. 879)*. Nancy, France: Academic Press. 10.1088/1742-6596/879/1/012017

Pinfield, Cox, & Smith. (2014). Research data management and libraries: relationships, activities, drivers and influences. *PLoS One, 9*(12).

Polony, I. V. (2005). The use of manual and computer aided search methods in the homeopathic repertory. *Aeon Group*, 1-6.

Pradana, O. R. Y., Sujadi, I., & Pramudya, I. (2017). Think Pair Share with Formative Assessment for Junior High School Student. *IOP Conf. Series: Journal of Physics*, *895*, 012032. 10.1088/1742-6596/895/1/012032

Prastawa, M., Gilmore, J. H., Lin, W., & Gerig, G. (2005). Automatic segmentation of MR images of the developing newborn brain. *Medical Image Analysis, 9*(5), 457–466. doi:10.1016/j.media.2005.05.007 PMID:16019252

Pryor, G., Jones, S., & Whyte, A. (Eds.). (2013). *Delivering research data management services: Fundamentals of good practice*. London: Facet.

Quinlan, J. R. (1993). *C4.5: Programs for machine learning*. San Mateo, CA: Morgan Kauffmann Publishers.

Qumer, A., & Henderson-Sellers, B. (2008). A framework to support the evaluation, adoption and improvement of agile methods in practice. *Journal of Systems and Software*, *81*(11), 1899–1919. doi:10.1016/j.jss.2007.12.806

Ramanathan, R. (2001). A note on the use of the analytic hierarchy process for environmental impact assessment. *Journal of Environmental Management*, *63*(1), 27–35. doi:10.1006/jema.2001.0455 PMID:11591027

Ramey, H. (2013). Organizational outcomes of youth involvement in organizational decision making: A synthesis of qualitative research. *Journal of Community Psychology*, *41*(4), 488–504. doi:10.1002/jcop.21553

Rao, P., Chen, S., & Sun, K. (2005). Improved classification of soil salinity by decision tree on remotely sensed images. *Proceedings of SPIE-Int. Society for Optical Engineering, 6027, 20th Congress of the Int. Commission for Optics*.

Raskar, B. S., & Bho, P. G. (2001). Producing and economics of winter surghum Sorghwn bicolor summer egetables cropping s stems under irrigated conditions of western Maharastra. *Indian Journal of Agronomy*, *46*(1), 17–22.

Rasmussen, D. N. (2007, March 7). Build an Insourcing Environment for Excellence. *Cutter IT Journal E-Mail Advisor*.

Rasnacis, A., & Berzisa, S. (2017). Method for Adaptation and Implementation of Agile Project Management Methodology. *Procedia Computer Science*, *104*, 43–50. doi:10.1016/j.procs.2017.01.055

Rath, M. (2018). A Methodical Analysis of Application of Emerging Ubiquitous Computing Technology With Fog Computing and IoT in Diversified Fields and Challenges of Cloud Computing. *International Journal of Information Communication Technologies and Human Development, 10*(2).

Rath, M. (2018). An Analytical Study of Security and Challenging Issues in Social Networking as an Emerging Connected Technology (April 20, 2018). *Proceedings of 3rd International Conference on Internet of Things and Connected Technologies (ICIoTCT)*. Available at https://ssrn.com/abstract=3166509

Rath, M. (2018). An Exhaustive Study and Analysis of Assorted Application and Challenges in Fog Computing and Emerging Ubiquitous Computing Technology. *International Journal of Applied Evolutionary Computation, 9*(2), 17-32. Retrieved from www.igi-global.com/ijaec

Rath, M., & Panda, M. R. (2017). MAQ system development in mobile ad-hoc networks using mobile agents. *IEEE 2nd International Conference on Contemporary Computing and Informatics (IC3I)*, 794-798.

Rath, M., & Pattanayak, B. (2018). Technological improvement in modern health care applications using Internet of Things (IoT) and proposal of novel health care approach. *International Journal of Human Rights in Healthcare.*

Rath, M., & Pattanayak, B. (2018). Technological improvement in modern health care applications using Internet of Things (IoT) and proposal of novel health care approach. *International Journal of Human Rights in Healthcare.* doi:10.1108/IJHRH-01-2018-0007

Rath, M., & Pattanayak, B. K. (2014). A methodical survey on real time applications in MANETS: Focussing On Key Issues. *International Conference on, High Performance Computing and Applications (IEEE ICHPCA)*, 22-24. 10.1109/ICHPCA.2014.7045301

Rath, M., & Pattanayak, B. K. (2018). Monitoring of QoS in MANET Based Real Time Applications. Smart Innovation, Systems and Technologies, 84, 579-586. doi:10.1007/978-3-319-63645-0_64

Rath, M., Pati, B., & Pattanayak, B. K. (2016). Inter-Layer Communication Based QoS Platform for Real Time Multimedia Applications in MANET. Wireless Communications, Signal Processing and Networking (IEEE WiSPNET), 613-617. doi:10.1109/WiSPNET.2016.7566203

Rath, M., Pati, B., & Pattanayak, B. K. (2018). Relevance of Soft Computing Techniques in the Significant Management of Wireless Sensor Networks. In Soft Computing in Wireless Sensor Networks (pp. 86-106). New York: Chapman and Hall/CRC, Taylor & Francis Group.

Rath, M., Pati, B., & Pattanayak, B. K. (2019). Relevance of Soft Computing Techniques in the Significant Management of Wireless Sensor Networks. In Soft Computing in Wireless Sensor Networks (pp. 86-106). New York: Chapman and Hall/CRC, Taylor & Francis Group.

Rath, Pati, & Pattanayak. (2018). An Overview on Social Networking: Design, Issues, Emerging Trends, and Security. In *Social Network Analytics: Computational Research Methods and Techniques*. Academic Press.

Rath. (2018). Effective Routing in Mobile Ad-hoc Networks With Power and End-to-End Delay Optimization: Well Matched With Modern Digital IoT Technology Attacks and Control in MANET. In *Advances in Data Communications and Networking for Digital Business Transformation*. IGI Global. Doi:10.4018/978-1-5225-5323-6.ch007

Rath, M. (2017). Resource provision and QoS support with added security for client side applications in cloud computing. *International Journal of Information Technology*, *9*(3), 1–8.

Rath, M., & Pati, B. (2017). *Load balanced routing scheme for MANETs with power and delay optimization. International Journal of Communication Network and Distributed Systems, 19*.

Rath, M., Pati, B., Panigrahi, C. R., & Sarkar, J. L. (2019). QTM: A QoS Task Monitoring System for Mobile Ad hoc Networks. In P. Sa, S. Bakshi, I. Hatzilygeroudis, & M. Sahoo (Eds.), *Recent Findings in Intelligent Computing Techniques. Advances in Intelligent Systems and Computing* (Vol. 707). Singapore: Springer. doi:10.1007/978-981-10-8639-7_57

Rath, M., Pati, B., & Pattanayak, B. K. (2017). Cross layer based QoS platform for multimedia transmission in MANET. *11th International Conference on Intelligent Systems and Control (ISCO)*, 402-407. 10.1109/ISCO.2017.7856026

Rath, M., & Pattanayak, B. (2017). MAQ:A Mobile Agent Based QoS Platform for MANETs. *International Journal of Business Data Communications and Networking, IGI Global, 13*(1), 1–8. doi:10.4018/IJBDCN.2017010101

Rath, M., & Pattanayak, B. K. (2018). SCICS: A Soft Computing Based Intelligent Communication System in VANET. Smart Secure Systems – IoT and Analytics Perspective. *Communications in Computer and Information Science, 808*, 255–261. doi:10.1007/978-981-10-7635-0_19

Rath, M., & Pattanayak, B. K. (2019). Security Protocol with IDS Framework Using Mobile Agent in Robotic MANET. *International Journal of Information Security and Privacy*, *13*(1), 46–58. doi:10.4018/IJISP.2019010104

Rath, M., Pattanayak, B. K., & Pati, B. (2017). *Energetic Routing Protocol Design for Real-time Transmission in Mobile Ad hoc Network. In Computing and Network Sustainability, Lecture Notes in Networks and Systems* (Vol. 12). Singapore: Springer.

Raunak, M. S., & Binkley, D. (2017). Agile and other trends in software engineering. *28th Annual Software Technology Conference*. 10.1109/STC.2017.8234457

Renigier-Biłozor, M. (2013). Structure of a decision support subsystem in real estate management. *Folia Oeconomica Stetinensia*, *13*(1), 56–75. doi:10.2478/foli-2013-0007

Rezaei, S. A., Gilkes, R. J., & Andrews, S. S. (2006). A minimum data set for assessing soil quality in rangelands. *Geoderma*, *136*(1-2), 229–234. doi:10.1016/j.geoderma.2006.03.021

Richards, L. A. (1954). *Diagnosis and improvement of saline-alkali soils. USDA Handbook No. 60*. Washington, DC: U.S. Department of Agriculture.

Richey, J. S., Mar, B. W., & Horth, R. R. (1985). The Delphi technique in environmental assessment. *Technological Forecasting and Social Change*, *23*, 89–94.

Riehl, H. (1954). *Tropical Meteorology*. New York: McGraw-Hill.

Riungu, L. M., Taipale, O., & Smolander, K. (2010). Research issues for software testing in the cloud. In *2010 IEEE Second International Conference on Cloud Computing Technology and Science (CloudCom)* (pp. 557–564). Indianapolis, IN: IEEE. 10.1109/CloudCom.2010.58

Roca, R., Viollier, M., Picon, L., & Desbois, M. (2002). A multi-satellite analysis of deep convection and its moist environment over the Indian Ocean during the winter monsoon. *Journal of Geophysical Research, D, Atmospheres*, *107*(D19), D19. doi:10.1029/2000JD000040

Rouse, J. W., Haas, R. H., Schell, J. A., & Deering, D. W. (1974). Monitoring vegetation systems in the Great Plains with ERTS. In *Third ERTS-1 Symposium*. Washington, DC: NASA.

Rowan, L. C., Goetz, A. F. H., & Ashley, R. P. (1977). Discrimination of hydrothermally altered and unaltered rocks in the visible and near infrared multispectral images. *Geophysics, 42*(3), 522–535. doi:10.1190/1.1440723

Rowe & Fitness. (2018). Understanding the Role of Negative Emotions in Adult Learning and Achievement: A Social Functional Perspective. *Journal of Behavioral Science*. Retrieved from https://www.mdpi.com/2076-328X/8/2/27/pdf

Rtah, M. (2018). Big Data and IoT-Allied Challenges Associated With Healthcare Applications in Smart and Automated Systems. *International Journal of Strategic Information Technology and Applications, 9*(2). doi:10.4018/IJSITA.201804010

Ruff, S., & Carter, M. (2009). Communication Learning Outcomes from Software Engineering Professionals: A Basis for Teaching Communication in the Engineering Curriculum. *39th ASEE/IEEE Frontiers in Education Conference*.

Russell, J. A., & Mehrabian, A. (1977). Evidence for a three-factor theory of emotions. *Journal of Research in Personality, 11*(3), 273–294. doi:10.1016/0092-6566(77)90037-X

Saaty, T. L. (2001). Decision Making for Leaders: The Analytic Hierarchy Process for Decisions in a Complex World, New Edition 2001. Pittsburgh, PA: RWS Publications.

Saaty, T. L. (1980). *The Analytic Hierarchy Process: Planning, Priority Setting and Resource Allocation*. New York: McGraw-Hill.

Saaty, T. L. (1987). Rank generation, preservation and reversal in the analytic hierarchy process. *Decision Sciences, 18*(2), 157–177. doi:10.1111/j.1540-5915.1987.tb01514.x

Saaty, T. L. (2003). Decision-making with the AHP: Why is the principal eigenvector necessary? *European Journal of Operational Research, 145*(1), 85–91. doi:10.1016/S0377-2217(02)00227-8

Sababha, B. H., Alqudah, Y. A., Abualbasal, A., & AlQaralleh, E. A. (2016). Project-Based Learning to Enhance Teaching Embedded Systems. *Eurasia Journal of Mathematics. Science & Technology Education, 12*(9), 2575–2585.

Sabins, F. F. (2013). *Remote Sensing Principles and Interpretation*. Kolkata: Levant Books.

Saha, S. K., Kudrat, M., & Bhan, S. K. (1990). Digital processing of Landsat TM data for wasteland mapping in parts of Aligarh District, Uttar Pradesh, India. *International Journal of Remote Sensing*, *11*(3), 485–492. doi:10.1080/01431169008955034

Saini, K., Wahid, A., & Purohit, G. N. (2014). Traditional Learning versus Web Based Learning: Performance Analysis. *International Journal of Computer Science and Information Technologies*, *5*(4), 5182–5184.

Sallans, A., & Donnelly, M. (2012). DMP Online and DMPTool: Different Strategies Towards a Shared Goal. *International Journal of Digital Curation*, *7*(2), 123–129. doi:10.2218/ijdc.v7i2.235

Sarif, S. M., Ramly, S., Yusof, R., & Fadzillah, N. A. A., & bin-Sulaiman, N. Y. (2018). Investigation of Success and Failure Factors in IT Project Management. *7th International Conference on Kansei Engineering and Emotion Research*, 671-682. 10.1007/978-981-10-8612-0_70

Sayers, J. (2001). The world health report 2001-Mental health: New understanding, new hope. *Bulletin of the World Health Organization*, *79*, 1085–1085.

Sedrette, S., Rebaï, N., & Mastere, M. (2016). Evaluation of neotectonic signature using morphometric indicators: Case study in Nefza, North-West of Tunisia. *Journal of Geographic Information System*, *8*(03), 338–350. doi:10.4236/jgis.2016.83029

Ségonne, F., Dale, A. M., Busa, E., Glessner, M., Salat, D., Hahn, H. K., & Fischl, B. (2004). A hybrid approach to the skull stripping problem in MRI. *NeuroImage*, *22*(3), 1060–1075. doi:10.1016/j.neuroimage.2004.03.032 PMID:15219578

Selten, R., Pittnauer, S., & Hohnisch, M. (2011). Dealing with Dynamic Decision Problems when Knowledge of the Environment Is Limited: An Approach Based on Goal Systems. *Journal of Behavioral Decision Making*, *25*(5), 443–457. doi:10.1002/bdm.738

Sethi, M., Dasog, G. S., Van Lieshoutc, A., & Salimathd, S. B. (2006). Salinity appraisal using IRS images in Shorapur taluka, Upper Krishna Irrigation Project, Phase I, Gulbarga District, Karnataka, India. *International Journal of Remote Sensing*, *27*(14), 2917–2926. doi:10.1080/01431160500472062

Sharma, R. C., & Bhargava, G. P. (1988). Landsat imagery for mapping saline soils and wet lands in north-west India. *International Journal of Remote Sensing*, *9*(1), 39–44. doi:10.1080/01431168808954835

Sheng, J., Amankwah-Amoah, J., & Wang, X. (2017). A multidisciplinary perspective of big data in management research. *International Journal of Production Economics*, *191*, 97–112. doi:10.1016/j.ijpe.2017.06.006

Shibl, R., Lawley, M., & Debuse, J. (2013). Factors influencing decision support system acceptance. *Decision Support Systems*, *54*(2), 953–961. doi:10.1016/j.dss.2012.09.018

Shortliffe, E. H., & Buchanan, B. G. (1975). A model of inexact reasoning in medicine. *Mathematical Biosciences*, *23*(3-4), 351–379. doi:10.1016/0025-5564(75)90047-4

Shukla, R., Gupta, R. K., & Kashyap, R. (2019). A multiphase pre-copy strategy for the virtual machine migration in cloud. In S. Satapathy, V. Bhateja, & S. Das (Eds.), *Smart Intelligent Computing and Applications. Smart Innovation, Systems and Technologies* (Vol. 104). Singapore: Springer. doi:10.1007/978-981-13-1921-1_43

Singh, A. K., & Singh, V. (2018). A Case Study: Heavy Rainfall Event Comparison Between Daily Satellite Rainfall Estimation Products with IMD Gridded Rainfall Over Peninsular India During 2015 Winter Monsoon. *Photonirvachak (Dehra Dun)*. doi:10.100712524-018-0751-9

Singh, A. K., & Singh, V. (2018, April). Validation of INSAT-3D derived rainfall estimates (HE & IMSRA), GPM (IMERG) and GLDAS 2.1 model rainfall product with IMD gridded rainfall & NMSG data over IMD's meteorological sub-divisions during monsoon. *Mausam (New Delhi)*.

Singh, A. N., & Dwivedi, R. S. (1989). Delineation of Salt-affected Soils through Digital Analysis of Landsat MSS Data. *International Journal of Remote Sensing*, *10*(1), 83–92. doi:10.1080/01431168908903849

Singh, G. (2009). Salinity-related desertification and management strategies: Indian experience. *Land Degradation & Development*, *20*(4), 367–385. doi:10.1002/ldr.933

Sinha, N. K., Chopra, U. K., & Singh, A. K. (2013). Cropping system effects on soil quality for three agro-ecosystems in India. *Experimental Agriculture*, *50*(3), 321–342. doi:10.1017/S001447971300046X

Somasundaram, K., & Kalaiselvi, T. (2010). A Method for Filling Holes in Objects of Medical Images using Region Labelling and Run Length Encoding Schemes. In *Image processing* (pp. 110–114). NCIMP.

Son, N. H. (2012). *Module on Data Preprocessing Techniques for Data Mining on Data Cleaning and Data Preprocessing*. Retrieved from http://elitepdf.com/

Subbiah, B. V., & Asija, G. L. (1956). A rapid procedure for the determination of available nitrogen in soils. *Current Science, 25*, 259–260.

Sujatha, G., Dwivedi, R. S., Sreenivas, K., & Venkataratnam, L. (2000). Mapping and monitoring of degraded lands in part of Jaunpur district of Uttar Pradesh using temporal spaceborne multispectral data. *International Journal of Remote Sensing, 21*(3), 519–531. doi:10.1080/014311600210722

Sujji, Lakshmi, & Jiji. (n.d.). MRI brain Image Segmentation based on Thresholding. *International Journal of Advance Computer Research, 3*, 97-101.

Suriyanti, S., & Yaacob, A. (2016). Exploring Teacher Strategies in Teaching Descriptive Writing in Indonesia. *Malaysian Journal of Learning and Instruction, 13*(2), 71–95.

Swarup, A. (2002). Lessions from long –term fertilizer experiments in improving fertilizer use efficiency and crop yield. *Fertilizer News, 47*(12), 59–66.

Szilagyi, L. (2003). MR brain image segmentation using an enhanced fuzzy c-means algorithm. In *Engineering in Medicine and Biology Society, 2003. Proceedings of the 25th Annual International Conference of the IEEE (Vol. 1)*. IEEE. 10.1109/IEMBS.2003.1279866

Szymaniec-Mlicka, K. (2017). The decision-making process in public healthcare entities – identification of the decision-making process type. *Management, 21*(1), 191–204. doi:10.1515/manment-2015-0088

Taleb, N. N. (2007). *The black swan: The impact of the highly improbable* (Vol. 2). Random house.

Tanure, S., Nabinger, C., & Becker, J. (2014). Bioeconomic Model of Decision Support System for Farm Management: Proposal of a Mathematical Model. *Systems Research and Behavioral Science, 32*(6), 658–671. doi:10.1002res.2252

Tenopir, C., Sandusky, R. J., Allard, S., & Birch, B. (2014). Research data management services in academic research libraries and perceptions of librarians. *Library & Information Science Research, 36*(2), 84–90. doi:10.1016/j.lisr.2013.11.003

Terrizzano, I., Schwarz, P., & Roth, M. (2015). Data wrangling: the challenging journey from the wild to the lake. *Proceedings of the 7th Biennial Conference on Innovative Data SystemsResearch (CIDR '15)*, 4–7.

The Medical Futurist. (2016). *Vocal biomarkers: the future of diagnostic medicine. The Most Exciting Medical Technologies of 2017*. Retrieved from https://medicalfuturist.com/the-most-exciting-medical-technologies-of-2017

Thompson, M. L., Singh, P., Corak, S., & Straszheim, W. E. (1992). Cautionary notes for the automated analysis of soil pore-space images. *Geoderma*, *53*(3-4), 399–415. doi:10.1016/0016-7061(92)90067-H

Thronbury, W. D. (1969). *Principles of Geomorphology*. New Delhi: New Age International Publishers.

Tiwari, S., Gupta, R. K., & Kashyap, R. (2019). To enhance web response time using agglomerative clustering technique for web navigation recommendation. In H. Behera, J. Nayak, B. Naik, & A. Abraham (Eds.), *Computational Intelligence in Data Mining. Advances in Intelligent Systems and Computing* (Vol. 711). Singapore: Springer. doi:10.1007/978-981-10-8055-5_59

Tobin, K. J., Bennett, M. E., Tobin, K. J., & Bennett, M. E. (2010). Adjusting Satellite Precipitation Data to Facilitate Hydrologic Modeling. *Journal of Hydrometeorology*, *11*(4), 966–978. doi:10.1175/2010JHM1206.1

Tolomei, C., Salvi, S., Merryman Boncori, J. P., & Pezzo, G. (2014). InSAR measurement of crustal deformation transients during the earthquake preparation processes: A review. *Bollettino di Geofisica Teorica ed Applicata*, *56*(2), 151–166.

Tronin, A. A. (2010). Satellite Remote Sensing in Seismology. A Review. *Remote Sensing*, *2*(1), 124–150. doi:10.3390/rs2010124

Tyagi, A., Goel, S., Kumar, N., Division, C.W., The, O.O.F., & Meteorology, G.O.F. (2011). A *Report on the Super Cyclonic Storm "GONU" A Report on the Super Cyclonic Storm*. CYCLONE Warn. Div. Off. Dir. Gen. Meteorol. INDIA Meteorol. Dep. IMD MET. Monogr. No CYCLONE Warn. Div. No. 08/2011.

UK Data Service. (2016). *Research data lifecycle*. Retrieved from https://www.ukdataservice.ac.uk/manage-data/lifecycle

Ullah, I., Shah, I. A., Ghafoor, F., & Khan, R. U. (2017). Success Factors of Adapting Agile Methods in Global and Local Software Development: A Systematic Literature Review Protocol with Preliminary Results. *International Journal of Computers and Applications*, *171*(5), 38–42. doi:10.5120/ijca2017915048

University of California Digital Library. (2016). *DMPTool*. Available from https://dmptool.org/

University of Virginia Library Research Data Services. (2016). *Steps in the data life cycle*. Available from http://data.library.virginia.edu/data-management/lifecycle/

Ursavas, E. (2014). A decision support system for quayside operations in a container terminal. *Decision Support Systems*, *59*, 312–324. doi:10.1016/j.dss.2014.01.003

Vaidya, M. (2016). Handling critical issues of Big Data on cloud. In Managing Big Data in cloud computing environments. IGI Global. doi:10.4018/978-1-4666-9834-5.ch005

Valverde, S., Oliver, A., Roura, E., González-Villà, S., Pareto, D., Vilanova, J. C., ... Lladó, X. (2017). Automated tissue segmentation of MR brain images in the presence of white matter lesions. *Medical Image Analysis*, *35*, 446–457. doi:10.1016/j.media.2016.08.014 PMID:27598104

van Deventer, A. P., Ward, A. D., Gowda, P. H., & Lyon, J. G. (1997). Using Thematic Mapper data to identify contrasting soil plains and tillage practices. *Photogrammetric Engineering and Remote Sensing*, *63*, 87–93.

Van Hootegem, H. (2007). Can homeopathy learn something from psychoanalysis? *Homeopathy*, *96*(2), 108–112. doi:10.1016/j.homp.2006.11.013 PMID:17437938

Varma, A. K., Gairola, R. M., & Goyal, S. (2015). *Hydro-Estimator: Modification and Validation*. SAC/ISRO internal report, SAC/EPSA/AOSG/SR/03/2015.

Vasiliev, Y. M., Milnichuk, V. S., & Arabaji, M. S. (1981). *General and Historical Geology*. Moscow: MIR Publishers.

Vassiliadis, Simitsis, & Skiadopoulos. (2002). Conceptual modeling for ETL processes. In *Proceedings of the 5th ACM international workshop on Data Warehousing and OLAP*. ACM. 10.1145/583890.583893

Vasu, D., Singh, S. K., Ray, S. K., Duraisami, V. P., Tiwary, P., Chandra, P., ... Anantwar, S. G. (2016). Soil quality index (SQI) as a tool to evaluate crop productivity in semi-arid Deccan plateau, India. *Geoderma*, *282*, 70–79. doi:10.1016/j. geoderma.2016.07.010

Venables, W. N., & Ripley, B. D. (1994). *Modern Applied Statistics with S-PLUS*. New York: Springer-Verlag. doi:10.1007/978-1-4899-2819-1

Vijiyan, G. (2015). Current Trends in Software Engineering Research. *Review of Computer Engineering Research*, *2*(3), 65–70. doi:10.18488/journal.76/2015.2.3/76.3.65.70

Vina Andres, A. J. (2003). Use of Multispectral Ikonos Imagery for Discriminating between Conventional and Conservation Agricultural Tillage Practices. *Photogrammetric Engineering and Remote Sensing*, *69*(5), 537–544. doi:10.14358/PERS.69.5.537

Waddington, S. (2012). Kindura: Repository services for researchers based on hybrid clouds. *Journal of Digital Information*, *13*(1).

Wang, C. (2016). Exposing library data with big data technology: A review. In *Computer and Information Science (ICIS), 2016 IEEE/ACIS 15th International Conference on*. IEEE. 10.1109/ICIS.2016.7550937

Wani, S. P., Rego, T. J., Rajeswari, S., & Lee, K. K. (1995). Effect of legume-based cropping systems on nitrogen mineralization potential of *Vertisol*. *Plant and Soil*, *175*(2), 265–274. doi:10.1007/BF00011363

Waoo, N., Kashyap, R., & Jaiswal, A. (2010). DNA nano array analysis using hierarchical quality threshold clustering. In *Proceedings of 2010 2nd IEEE International Conference on Information Management and Engineering* (pp. 81-85). IEEE. 10.1109/ICIME.2010.5477579

Westra, Ramirez, Parham, & Scaramozzino. (2010). Selected Internet Resources on Digital Research Data Curation. *Issues in Science and Technology Librarianship*, *63*.

Whyte, A., & Tedds, J. (2011). *Making the case for research data management*. Edinburgh: Digital Curation Centre. Available http://www.dcc.ac.uk/webfm_send/487

Whyte, J., Stasis, A., & Lindkvist, C. (2016). Managing change in the delivery of complex projects: Configuration management, asset information and 'big data'. *International Journal of Project Management*, *34*(2), 339–351. doi:10.1016/j. ijproman.2015.02.006

Wickert, M. (1997). *Numerical differentiation (tutorial)*. University of Colorado at Colorado Springs.

Wiener, M., & Saunders, C. (2014). Forced competition in IT multi-sourcing. *The Journal of Strategic Information Systems, 23*(3), 210–225. doi:10.1016/j.jsis.2014.08.001

Willoughby, H. E., Marks, F. D. Jr, & Feinberg, R. J. (1984). Stationary and Moving Convective Bands in Hurricanes. *Journal of the Atmospheric Sciences, 41*(22), 3189–3211. doi:10.1175/1520-0469(1984)041<3189:SAMCBI>2.0.CO;2

Wright, A., & Sittig, D. F. (2008). A framework and model for evaluating clinical decision support architectures. *Journal of Biomedical Informatics, 41*(6), 982–990. doi:10.1016/j.jbi.2008.03.009 PMID:18462999

Wu, J., Vincent, B., Yang, J., Bouarfa, S., & Vidal, A. (2008). Remote Sensing Monitoring of Changes in Soil Salinity: A Case Study in Inner Mongolia, China. *Sensors (Basel), 8*(11), 7035–7049. doi:10.33908117035 PMID:27873914

Xiao, B., & Benbasat, I. (2018). An empirical examination of the influence of biased personalized product recommendations on consumers' decision making outcomes. *Decision Support Systems, 110*, 46–57. doi:10.1016/j.dss.2018.03.005

Xue. (n.d.). An integrated method of adaptive enhancement for unsupervised segmentation of MRI brain images. *Pattern Recognition Letters, 24*, 15.

Xue, S. A., de Schepper, L., & Hao, G. J. (2009). Treatment of spasmodic dysphonia with homeopathic medicine: A clinical case report. *Homeopathy, 98*(1), 56–59. doi:10.1016/j.homp.2008.11.009 PMID:19135961

Yadav, D.S., Singh, R.M., Alok, K., & Ram, A. (2000). Diversification of traditional cropping system for sustainable production. *Indian Journal of Agronomy, 45*(1), 37-40.

Yadav, A., & Korb, J. T. (2012). Learning to Teach Computer Science: The Need for a Methods Course. *Communications of the ACM, 55*(11), 31–33. doi:10.1145/2366316.2366327

Yong, B., Liu, D., Gourley, J. J., Tian, Y., Huffman, G. J., Ren, L., & Hong, Y. (2015). Global View Of Real-Time TrmmMultisatellite Precipitation Analysis: Implications For Its Successor Global Precipitation Measurement Mission. *Bulletin of the American Meteorological Society, 96*(2), 283–296. doi:10.1175/BAMS-D-14-00017.1

Yu, F., Zhuge, X.-Y., & Zhang, C.-W. (2011). Rainfall Retrieval and Nowcasting Based on Multispectral Satellite Images. Part II: Retrieval Study on Daytime Half-Hour Rain Rate. *Journal of Hydrometeorology, 12*(6), 1271–1285. doi:10.1175/2011JHM1374.1

Zainuddin, Z., & Halili, S. H. (2016). Flipped Classroom Research and Trends from Different Fields of Study. *International Review of Research in Open and Distributed Learning, 17*(3), 313–340. doi:10.19173/irrodl.v17i3.2274

Zhang, P., Zhao, K., & Kumar, R. L. (2016). Impact of IT Governance and IT Capability on Firm Performance. *Information Systems Management, 33*(4), 357–373. doi:10.1080/10580530.2016.1220218

Zhou, Y., & Zhao, W. (2010). A study on new product development using a decision circumstance model. *International Journal Of Value Chain Management, 4*(4), 380. doi:10.1504/IJVCM.2010.036994

Zou, X., & Kuo, Y. (1996). Rainfall assimilation through an optimal control of initial and boundary conditions in a limited-area mesoscale model. *Monthly Weather Review, 124*(12), 2859–2882. doi:10.1175/1520-0493(1996)124<2859:RATAOC>2.0.CO;2

About the Contributors

Akhouri Krishna is Professor and Head of the Department of Remote Sensing, Birla Institute of Technology (BIT), Mesra, Ranchi. His specialisation is in Earth Resources Technology comprising Remote Sensing and Environmental Geosciences with extensive research experience and interests in Natural Hazards and Disaster Management, Natural Resources Management, Glacier and Climate Change studies.

* * *

Arup Kumar Bhattacharjee did his Bachelors from University of Calcutta, Master of Computer Application from Kalyani University and MTech from West Bengal University of Technology. He is currently working as an Assistant Professor in RCC Institute of Information Technology, Kolkata, India. He has more than 14 years teaching experience. He has over 10 research publication in different national and international journal and conferences. He has contributed in over 20 internationally acclaimed books. He has edited 2 books. His research areas are software engineering, data mining and machine learning. He is a member of various professional bodies like IETE, Indian Science Congress, Computer Society of India.

Arpan Deyasi is presently working as Assistant Professor in the Department of Electronics and Communication Engineering in RCC Institute of Information Technology, Kolkata, INDIA. He has 12 years of professional experience in academics and industry. He received B.Sc (Hons), B.Tech, M.Tech Degree from University of Calcutta. He is working in the area of semiconductor nanostructure and semiconductor photonics. He has published more than 200 research papers, some of which are in ELSEVIER, IEEE Xplore, SPRINGER, CRC Press, ACEEE, SPIE, IoP, OSA, IET, ASP etc. His major teaching subjects are Solid State Device, Electromagnetics, Photonics; and also conducted projects in these domains. He has already organized One International Conference, One National Conference, a few Faculty Development Programmes, Workshops, Laboratory and industrial visits, seminars and technical events for students under the banner of IE(I) Kolkata section. He is also associated with a few reputed conference as member of programme committee. He is reviewer of a few journals of repute and some prestigious conferences in INDIA and abroad. He has delivered a few talks and conducted hands-on session on Nanolelectronics, Photonics and Electromagnetics in various FDP's, workshops. He is the editor of two conference proceedings, one is published by CRC Press, another is published by Allied Publishers. He is a member of IEEE Electron Device Society, IE(I), Optical Society of India, IETE, ISTE etc. He is working as SPOC of RCCIIT Local Chapter (NPTEL course) and Faculty Adviser of the student chapter of Institution of Engineers (INDIA) in ECE Department.

Michael D. Dorsey is a current MBA candidate in Management at Texas Women's University in Denton, Texas. His time at TWU has been spent excelling in both academic research and student leadership. Michael has expressed an unyielding desire to further his knowledge and practical application in the study of business thus making him the universities only candidate to be selected to participate in a independent study special topics course; Business Analysis and Research Capstone: AT&T along side instructor Dr. John Nugent, LLM. Upon completion of his MBA, Michael will continue his academic journey by attending law school where he will specialize in Business and Technology Law.

Sonali Johari is a graduate student pursuing her MS in Business Intelligence and Analytics. Her passion for Data as well as her background in Computer Science has motivated her to aim for a career in Data Science. She loves to solve real-world problems using a combination of theoretical knowledge and practical applications of Machine Learning, Multivariate Data Analytics, Artificial Intelligence and Deep Learning. She enjoys solving complex tasks using emerging technologies and innovative techniques. Her curiosity in the field of Data and Machine Learning inspires her to research new applications of technologies that challenge the status quo and bring forward solutions that make an impact on the community.

Rahul Joshi is currently working as an assistant professor in CS/IT department of Symbiosis Institute of Technology, Pune. His research interests mainly include incremental clustering, distributed data clustering, IT in healthcare. He has coauthored more than 30 research papers. He is doing PhD at Symbiosis International University, Pune.

Ramgopal Kashyap's areas of interest are image processing, pattern recognition, and machine learning. He has published many research papers, and book chapters in international journals and conferences like Springer, Inderscience, Elsevier, ACM, and IGI-Global indexed by Science Citation Index (SCI) and Scopus (Elsevier).He has Reviewed Research Papers in the Science Citation Index Expanded, Springer Journals and Editorial Board Member and conferences programme committee member of the IEEE, Springer international conferences and journals held in countries: Czech Republic, Switzerland, UAE, Australia, Hungary, Poland, Taiwan, Denmark, India, USA, UK, Austria, and Turkey. He has written many book chapters published by IGI Global, USA.

Amit Kumar is working in Satellite Division with India Meteorological Department, Ministry of Earth Sciences, Government of India in the capacity of Scientist-B. He did his Bachelor of Technology in Electronics and Electronics from Maharshi Dayanand University, Rohtak, Haryana. He has more than five years of experience with India Meteorological Department. He has published three research papers, one article, one user-guide. His research interests are Satellite Remote Sensing, Satellite Derived geophysical products, Inter-Satellite calibration and validation and Satellite Climate Data Record.

Arunima Mookherjee graduated with a B.Tech degree from Symbiosis International University, Pune, India in 2014. She is a software engineer and a fledging data scientist who is skilled at developing complex solutions possessing strong creative thinking skills. Currently, she is working in a startup as a Data Science Engineer. She loves using Python as her tool for developing Machine Learning algorithms. She is deft in data analysis, data visualization, and programming.

Soumen Mukherjee did his B.Sc (Physics Honours) from Calcutta University, M.C.A. from Kalyani University and ME in Information Technology from West Bengal University of Technology. He is the silver medalist for ME examination in the university. He has done his Post-Graduate Diploma in Business Management from Institute of Management Technology, Center of Distance Learning, Ghaziabad. He is now working as an Assistant Professor in RCC Institute of Information Technology, Kolkata. He has 15 years teaching experience in the field of Computer Science and Application. He has over 30 research paper published in different National and International Journal and Conferences. He has contributed in over 20 internationally acclaimed books in the field of Computer Science and Engineering. He has edited 2 books. His research fields are Image Processing and Machine Learning. He is a life member of several institutions like IETE, CSI, ISTE, FOSET, etc.

Preeti Mulay is a full time researcher and associate professor. Her areas of research includes machine learning, incremental learning, knowledge augmentation, data analysis, incremental clustering etc. The specific application areas of research are data analysis, prediction about diabetes, electricity smart meter and combating misinformation in healthcare and political domains. Many international publications are contributed as an outcome of these research areas.

Arunima Nandy received her M.Sc. degree in Geography and Disaster Management from Department of Geography of Tripura University in 2012 and M.Tech. in Geoinformatics from Department of Mining Engineering of Indian Institute of Engineering Science and Technology, Shibpur, Howrah. Currently, she is working as a guest lecturer of Geoinformatics of Department of Geography of North Eastern Hill University, Shillong, Meghalaya. Her research interests are in the area of tectonic geomorphology, disaster management, GIS and Remote Sensing.

Pranav Prajapati is a graduate student currently majoring in Business Intelligence and Analytics with Data science concentration at Stevens Institute of Technology. He is interested in data analysis, data mining, quantitative analysis, data modeling, predictive analysis, machine learning, business issues gathering and recognition. Pranav is fascinated by the stories of customers' activities behind the data, so it leads him to pursue a career as a Data Scientist.

Ankur Priyadarshi is in the first year as a full-time Ph.D. scholar in Computer Science and Engineering at Birla Institute of Technology, Mesra. Working also in SERB (Science and Engineering Research Board) funded a project in Artificial Intelligence. He hold's a Bachelor and Master Degree in Computer Science and Engineering. Interested areas are Machine Learning, Image Processing, and Natural Language Processing.

Mahesh S. Raisinghani is currently a Professor in the Executive MBA program in the at Texas Woman's University (TWU) and a Senior Fellow of the Higher Education Academy, U.K. Dr. Raisinghani was awarded TWU's 2017 Innovation in Academia award, the 2015 Distinction in Distance Education award, the 2008 Excellence in Research & Scholarship award and the 2007 G. Ann Uhlir Endowed Fellowship in Higher Education Administration. He was also awarded the 2017 National Engaged Leader Award by the National Society of Leadership and Success; and the 2017 Volunteer Award at the Model United Nations Conference for his service to the Youth and Government by the Model United Nations Committee. He has edited eight books and published over hundred manuscripts in peer reviewed journals, conferences, and book series and has consulted for a variety of public and private organizations on IT management and applications. Dr. Raisinghani serves as the Editor in Chief of the International Journal of Web based Learning and Teaching Technologies; on the board of Global IT Management Association; and as an advisory board member of the World Affairs Council. He is included in the millennium edition of Who's Who in the World, Who's Who among Professionals, Who's Who among America's Teachers and Who's Who in Information Technology.

Mamata Rath, M.Tech, Ph.D (Comp.Sc), has twelve years of experience in teaching as well as in research and her research interests include Mobile Adhoc Networks, Internet of Things, Ubiquitous Computing, VANET and Computer Security.

G. P. Obi Reddy works as a Principal Scientist and Incharge of GIS & Cartography Sections, Division of Remote Sensing Applications, ICAR-National Bureau of Soil Survey and Land Use Planning (NBSS&LUP), Nagpur. He significantly contributed in application of remote sensing and GIS technologies in applied Geomorphology, Digital Terrain Analysis, Soil-landscape modellings, Land use/land cover studies, Characterization of land use systems, Watershed characterization and development of soil Geoportal. He developed soil information systems on 1:1 m and 1:250,000 of India and 1:50,000 scale for 50 districts in GIS, estimation of soil loss in different of states of India and harmonization of land degradation datasets of India. On ICAR deputation, he visited IWMI, Colombo, Sri Lanka, ITC, The Netherlands and ICIMOD, Kathmandu, Nepal. He published 80 research articles, 30 book chapters, 9 technical reports and edited 3 books. He is a Member, Editorial Board, International Journal of Remote Sensing Applications and reviewer for many international journals. He is the recipient of 'Indian National Geospatial Award'- 2007 and 'National Geospatial Award For Excellence'-2013 from The Indian Society of Remote Sensing, India.

Index

A

active fault 109, 112, 120
agile methodology 35, 39-41, 54, 60
AHP 1-4, 8, 10-11, 14
analysis 2, 5, 8, 10, 27, 29, 32-37, 41, 51, 54, 82, 101, 106-110, 131-132, 135, 137, 158-159, 175, 181, 183-184, 186, 188-189, 195, 197, 200, 202-203, 218, 225, 236-237, 241
application 20-21, 23, 26, 29, 36, 61, 72, 98-99, 106-107, 109, 111-113, 119, 145, 156, 184, 191, 199, 203, 218, 224
Apriori 51-53
arousal 181, 194-199

C

Capability Maturity Model (CMM) 31
characteristics 8, 10, 39-40, 79, 88, 105, 107-110, 112-114, 116, 118-120, 143, 182, 212, 238
Clinical Decision Support System 181, 189-190, 197
Credit Union 27, 31
cyclogenesis 124, 135-137

D

Data Base Management System (DBMS) 98
Data Management Subsystem 64
decision making process 2, 82, 191
Decision Support System 62-64, 67, 73-74, 80-81, 83-84, 181, 189-190, 192, 197

E

EO 2

F

financial services 27, 31
focal mechanism 104-105
Fourier descriptor 157-160, 170

G

Geographical Information System (GIS) 106, 113, 234
GPM(IMERG) 134-135, 137

H

histogram 142, 147, 153, 155-159, 161-165, 167-174, 177-178

I

INSAT Multispectral Rainfall Algorithm 124, 130
INSAT-3D 124, 127, 130, 134, 137
International Standards Organization (ISO) 32

K

K-Nearest Neighbor (KNN) 33, 42, 46, 48-49
knowledge discovery 51, 54, 189-190

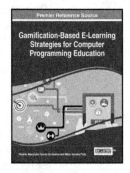
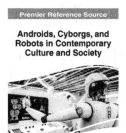

Ensure Quality Research is Introduced to the Academic Community

Become an IGI Global Reviewer for Authored Book Projects

Premier Reference Source

Emerging GIS Applications for Emergency and Disaster Management

Premier Reference Source

Managerial Strategies and Green Solutions for Project Sustainability

Premier Reference Source

Comparative Approaches to Using R and Python for Statistical Data Analysis

Premier Reference Source

Solutions for High-Touch Communications in a High-Tech World

The overall success of an authored book project is dependent on quality and timely reviews.

In this competitive age of scholarly publishing, constructive and timely feedback significantly expedites the turnaround time of manuscripts from submission to acceptance, allowing the publication and discovery of forward-thinking research at a much more expeditious rate. Several IGI Global authored book projects are currently seeking highly qualified experts in the field to fill vacancies on their respective editorial review boards:

Applications may be sent to:
development@igi-global.com

Applicants must have a doctorate (or an equivalent degree) as well as publishing and reviewing experience. Reviewers are asked to write reviews in a timely, collegial, and constructive manner. All reviewers will begin their role on an ad-hoc basis for a period of one year, and upon successful completion of this term can be considered for full editorial review board status, with the potential for a subsequent promotion to Associate Editor.

If you have a colleague that may be interested in this opportunity, we encourage you to share this information with them.

Printed in the United States
By Bookmasters